GUNS OF THE EMPIRE

GEORGE MARKHAM

GUNS OF THE EMPIRE

Firearms of the British Soldier, 1837–1987

ARMS AND ARMOUR PRESS

PREFACE

First published in Great Britain in 1990 by
Arms & Armour Press,
Villiers House,
41/47 Strand,
London WC2N 5JE.

Distributed in the USA by
Sterling Publishing Co., Inc.,
387 Park Avenue South, New York, NY 10016.

Distributed in Australia by
Capricorn Link (Australia) Pty. Ltd,
P.O.Box 665, Lane Cove, New South Wales 2066,
Australia.

© George Markham, 1990

British Library Cataloguing in Publication Data

Markham, George
    Guns of the empire, 1837-1987
    1. Great Britain. Army. Military equipment.
    Weapons, history.
    I. Title
    623.40941

ISBN 1-85409-072-0

Produced by Elex Research Services
Designed and edited by John Walter
Camerawork by Service Twenty Four Ltd
Printed and bound in Great Britain by
Butler & Tanner

The 'British Empire' can be defined, often satisfactorily, in many differing ways; the period accepted here runs from the accession of Queen Victoria in 1837 to the modern era.

Victorian expansionism was helped in no small way by rapid growth in British industrial capacity, which in turn permitted the mass-production of more effectual firearms. It is probably truthful to claim that greater advances in weapons technology were made between 1870 and 1900 than in the preceding five hundred years.

Though the detailed individual coverage begins with the P/53 Enfield rifle-musket, the narrative introduction offers — in a general summary of British ordnance history — additional details of the landmarks between the first regulation musket of 1722 and the perfection of the Minié-pattern expanding ball.

Terminology

Most pre-1870 weapons were known by the year in which the pattern was 'sealed' by the authorities so that specimen guns could be issued to prospective manufacturers. Consequently, the Enfield rifle-musket is generally known as the Pattern 1853 or P/53. This system was not always universal; for example, the P/58 short rifle, the second of its type to appear, was often known simply as 'Pattern No.2'.

After the approval of the Snider, guns were known by their name and a 'Mark' number — e.g., Snider Mk II. Major changes to the gun usually caused the 'Mark number' to advance; minor changes, however, were signified by a additional 'stars' (i.e., Mk I**). By the First World War, the Mark system was occasionally complicated by the addition of a number or letter suffix ('No.1 Mk I', 'Mk IIIA') to distinguish guns with identical actions but differing roles.

The entire system changed in 1926. Essentially, names were dropped and the relationship between marks and numbers was reversed. What had been the 'Rifle, Short, Magazine, Lee-Enfield, ·303-inch, Mark III*' became the 'Rifle No.1 Mk III*'. This system lasted through the Second World War largely intact, though the Roman numerals were changed to Arabic after 1943 ('No.1 Mk 3*') and minor variants were often given distinctive numbers instead of stars — e.g., 'No.4 Mk 1/2'.

Prefixes indicating the service-branch — 'L' for land, 'N' for naval, 'A' for air — were adopted in the late 1950s. In practice, 'L' has come to be used for general issue; thus rifles have been issued as L1A1 or L85A1, though it is important to specify the *type* of store as there may be several differing objects with an 'L1A1' classification. Minor variations are signified by changing the last number. Thus the L2A3 (Sterling) submachine-gun is an improved version of the L2A2, which was itself an upgraded L2A1. Experimental and limited-issue weapons substitute 'X' for 'L', and 'E' for 'A'.

Guns of the Empire has used the designations ruling at the time of introduction. Dimensions are also given in contemporary terms, which may be imperial fractions or the metric system. Fractions serve as an important reminder that the pre-1850 cap-lock was not made to tolerances measurable in thousandths of an inch! Decimal equivalents are given below. Place names are usually rendered in their modern form. Thus Ishapore is 'Ishapur', and the Ashante tribe is 'Asante'.

It is impossible to thank the many people who have contributed to this book individually, and it is hoped that a corporate 'thank you' will suffice. However, I would like to single out Ian Skennerton, whose pioneering work on the British firearms of the cartridge era has advanced the available knowledge so greatly. I am also pleased to acknowledge the assistance of Ian Hogg, Philip Haythornthwaite, De Witt Bailey II, Brian Davis, the Photographic Libraries of the Royal Armouries and the Imperial War Museum, and CSA of Brighton for supplying many of the postcards now credited to Elex archives. Photographs have been credited individually where appropriate.

Thanks are due to the publishers of works from which quotes have taken, for permission to reproduce the extracts noted individually in the text, and to Her Majesty's Stationery Office for allowing reproduction of drawings taken from official textbooks.

Lastly, but by no means least, I must thank Arms & Armour Press for continuing to support my efforts. I sincerely hope that *Guns of the Empire* — somewhat different in approach to its companions — provides the adequate one-volume guide that has been lacking for some years.

GEORGE MARKHAM
Ashby de la Zouch

HALF-TITLE PAGE

'Mounted Infantry in Egypt': an engraving after a painting by W.H. Overend, published in the *Illustrated London News* in September 1882. The Martini-Henry rifle is faithfully recorded — though the back sight leaf is hinged at the wrong end of the sight bed, the cocking indicator has been correctly rotated backward by the opening breech and a necked cartridge case is being ejected. Courtesy of Philip J. Haythornthwaite. **1**

The modern soldier has to come terms with some very strange equipment. Here, a 5·56mm L85A1 (SA-80) rifle fitted with a laser target designator is being used in conjunction with image-intensifying goggles. Author's archives. **2**

TITLE PAGE **3**

Crouching on the fire-step of his trench, his Mark III* SMLE and P/07 bayonet at the ready, a British soldier cautiously surveys No Man's Land on the Western Front. Courtesy of Elex archives.

CONTENTS

PART ONE: INTRODUCTION *7-60*

PART TWO: THE GUNS

NOTES

Figure of Merit
This system was used by the British Army to assess accuracy, being effectively a 'mean radius' – the average distance of the shots from the centre of the target. This will mean very little to many readers, so attempts have been made to equate it to group size. Computer-assisted analysis of a hundred trial groups, obtained from a variety of rifles, revealed a realistic multiplication factor of 4·518: a 'Figure of Merit' of 1ft, therefore, would have been obtained from a group about 4ft 6in in diameter. Of the hundred tests, four out of five lay within ± 20 per cent of the mean. Working on the basis of a 1ft FoM, the smallest group diameter was 3·34ft and the largest 6·98ft.

The major weakness of Figures of Merit was that a miss was allocated a value of half the diagonal measurement of the target, even though it may have flown wide by the proverbial mile.

British monarchs

1702–14: Anne
1714–27: George I
1727–60: George II
1760–1820: George III
1820–30: George IV
1830–37: William IV
1837–1901: Victoria
1901–10: Edward VII
1910–36: George V
1936: Edward VIII
1936–52: George VI
1952 to date: Elizabeth II

FRACTIONS

1/32: ·03125	9/16: ·5625
1/16: ·0625	5/8: ·625
1/8: ·125	11/16: ·6875
3/16: ·1875	3/4: ·75
1/4: ·25	13/16: ·8125
5/16: ·3125	7/8: ·875
3/8: ·375	
7/16: ·4375	**decimal equivalents**
1/2: ·5	

BIBLIOGRAPHY

BIBLIOGRAPHY

This is simply a brief guide to some of the sources consulted during preparation of *Guns of the Empire*. Particularly valuable, in view of the lack of attention paid to the subjects here, are D.W. Bailey's many excellent articles on British military firearms of the flint- and cap-lock periods in *Guns Review*. For the past twenty years, Peter Labbett's 'Cartridge Corner' feature in the same magazine has proffered invaluable information about British military ammunition.

BAILEY, D.W.: *British Military Longarms, 1715–1865*. Arms & Armour Press, London; 1986.
BARTHORP, Michael: *The Anglo-Boer Wars* ('The British and the Afrikaners, 1815–1902'). Blandford Press, Poole, Dorset; 1987.
– *The Zulu War. A Pictorial History*. Blandford Press, Poole, Dorset; 1980.
BAYLY, Dr Christopher ['General Editor']: *Atlas of the British Empire* ('A New Perspective on the British Empire from 1500 to the Present'). The Hamlyn Publishing Group Ltd/Amazon Ltd, London; 1989.
BELFIELD, Eversley: *The Boer War*. Concise Campaigns series. Leo Cooper Ltd, London; 1974.
BLACKMORE, Howard L.: *The British Soldier's Firearm, 1650–1850*. Herbert Jenkins Ltd, London; 1961.
BRITISH OFFICIAL PUBLICATIONS
– *Hand Book for Officers Under Instruction at the School of Musketry, Hythe*. HMSO, London; 1863, 1868, 1877 and 1880 editions.
– *Instructions for Armourers* ("in the care, repair, browning, etc., of small-arms, machine guns, 'parapet' carriages..."). HMSO, London; 1912.
– *Text Book of Small Arms*. HMSO, London; 1894, 1904, 1909 and 1929 editions.
– *Treatise on Military Small Arms and Ammunition* ('With the Theory and Motion of a Rifle Bullet. A Text-book for the Army'). HMSO, London; 1884 and 1888. The 1888 edition was reprinted by Arms & Armour Press, London; 1971.
BRUCE, Gordon, and REINHART, Christian (editors): *Webley Revolvers* ('Revised from W.C. Dowell's *The Webley Story*'). Stocker-Schmidt, Dietikon-Zürich, Switzerland; 1988.
CHICHESTER, Henry Manners, and BURGES-SHORT, George: *The Records and Badges of Every Regiment and Corps in the British Army, 1900*. Second edition. Gale & Polden Ltd, Aldershot and London; 1900. Reprinted by Greenhill Books, London; 1986.
DAVIS, Brian L.: *British Army Uniforms & Insignia of World War Two*. Arms & Armour Press, London; 1983.
DEWAR, [Lieutenant-Colonel] Michael: *The British Army in Northern Ireland*. Arms & Armour Press, London; 1985.
DOWELL, William Chipchase: *The Webley Story* ('A History of Webley Pistols and Revolvers and the Development of the Pistol Cartridge'). The Skyrac Press, Kirkgate, Leeds; 1962.
DUGELBY, Thomas B.: *EM-2 Concept & Design* ('a rifle ahead of its time'). Collector Grade Publications, Toronto, Ontario, Canada; 1980.
– *The Bren Gun Saga*. Collector Grade Publications, Toronto, Ontario, Canada; 1986.
FEATHERSTONE, Donald: *Victoria's Enemies* ('An A–Z of British Colonial Warfare'). Blandford Press, London; 1989.
GARRETT, Richard: *General Gordon*. Arthur Barker Ltd, London; 1974.
GREENER, William Wellington: *The Gun and Its Development*. Ninth edition. London; 1910. Reprinted by Arms & Armour Press, London; 1973.
– *Modern Breech Loaders*. Cassell, Petter & Galpin, London; 1871. Reprinted by Greenhill Books, London; 1985.
HAYTHORNTHWAITE, Philip J.: *The Boer War*. Arms & Armour Press, London; 1987.
– *Victorian Colonial Wars*. Arms & Armour Press, London; 1988.
– *Weapons & Equipment of the Napoleonic Wars*. Blandford Press, Poole, Dorset; 1979.
HOBART, F.W.A.: *Pictorial History of the Machine Gun*. Ian Allan Ltd, Shepperton; 1971.
HOGG, Ian V., and WEEKS, John S.: *Military Small Arms of the 20th Century* ("A comprehensive illustrated encyclopedia of the world's small-calibre firearms"). Arms & Armour Press, London; fifth edition, 1985.
LIDDELL HART, [Captain Sir] Basil H.: *History of the First World War*. Cassell & Co., London; 1970.
– *History of the Second World War*. Cassell & Co., London; 1970.
LLOYD, Alan: *The War in the Trenches*. The British at War series. Granada Publishing, London; 1976.
– *The Zulu War, 1879*. Granada Publishing Ltd, London and Manchester; 1973.
MACDONALD, Lyn: *Somme*. Michael Joseph Ltd, London; 1986.
– *The Roses of No Man's Land*. Michael Joseph Ltd, London; 1984.
– *They Called it Passchendaele* ('The story of the Third Battle of Ypres and of the men who fought in it'). Michael Joseph Ltd, London; 1978.
– *1914*. Michael Joseph Ltd, London; 1987.
MCELWEE, William: *The Art of War: Waterloo to Mons*. Weidenfeld & Nicholson, London; 1974.
MACRORY, Patrick: *Signal Catastrophe* ('The Story of the Disastrous Retreat from Kabul, 1842'). Hodder & Stoughton, London; 1966.
MARLOWE, John: *Mission to Khartum* ('The Apotheosis of General Gordon'). Victor Gollancz, London; 1969.
MIDDLEBROOK, Martin: *The First Day on the Somme*. Allen Lane, The Penguin Press, London; 1971.
– *The Kaiser's Battle* ('21 March 1918: the first day of the German Spring Offensive'). Allen Lane, The Penguin Press, London; 1978.
PAKENHAM, Thomas: *The Boer War*. Weidenfeld & Nicholson, London; 1979.
PITT, Barrie: *1918. The Last Act*. Cassell & Co., London; 1962.
REYNOLDS, Major E.G.B.: *The Lee-Enfield Rifle*. Herbert Jenkins Ltd, London; 1960.
ROADS, C.H., MA PhD: *The British Soldier's Firearm, 1850–1864*. Herbert Jenkins Ltd, London; 1964.
ROGERS, Colonel H.C.B., OBE: *Weapons of the British Soldier*. The Imperial Services Library,

volume V. Seeley Service & Co. Ltd, London; 1960.
SIMMONS, [Major] George: *A British Rifle Man* ('Journals and Correspondence during the Peninsular War and the Campaign of Wellington'). A. & C. Black, Edinburgh; 1899. Reprinted by Greenhill Books, London, in 1986.
SKENNERTON, Ian: *A Treatise on the Snider* ('The British Soldier's Firearm, 1866–c1880'). Published by the author, Margate, Queensland, Australia; 1977.
– *British Small Arms of World War 2*. Published by the author, Margate, Queensland, Australia; 1988.
– *Lists of Changes in British War Material* ('in relation to edged weapons, firearms and associated ammunition and accoutrements'). In three volumes: 1860–86, 1886–1900 and 1900–10. Published by the author, Margate, Queensland, Australia; 1976-9.
– *The British Service Lee* ('Lee-Metford and Lee-Enfield Rifles and Carbines, 1880–1980'). Published by the author, Margate, Queensland, Australia, in association with Arms & Armour Press, London; 1982.
– and RICHARDSON, Robert: *British & Commonwealth Bayonets*. Published by Ian Skennerton, Margate, Queensland, Australia; 1984.
SWINSON, Arthur (editor): *A Register of the Regiments and Corps of the British Army* ('The ancestry of the regiments and corps of the Regular Establishment of the Army'). Archive Military References series. Archive Press, London; 1972.
TAYLERSON, A.W.F.: *The Revolver, 1865–1888*. Herbert Jenkins Ltd, London; 1966.
– *The Revolver, 1888–1914*. Barrie & Jenkins, London; 1970.
– with ANDREWS, R.A.N., and FRITH, J.: *The Revolver, 1818–1865*. Herbert Jenkins Ltd, London; 1968.
TEMPLE, B.A., and SKENNERTON, I.D.: *A Treatise on the British Military Martini* ('The Martini-Henry, 1869– c.1900'). Published privately by B.A. Temple, Burbank, Australia, and in Britain by Arms & Armour Press, London; 1983.
– *A Treatise on the British Military Martini* ('The .40 and .303 Martinis, 1880– c.1920'). Published privately by B.A. Temple, Burbank, Australia, and in Britain by Greenhill Books, London; 1989.
WAHL, Paul, and TOPPEL, Donald R.: *The Gatling Gun*. Arco Publishing Company, New York; 1965.
WALTER, John [editor]: *Arms & Equipment of the British Army, 1866* ('Victorian Military Equipment from the Enfield to the Snider'). Greenhill Books, London; 1986.
– [editor]: *Guns of the First World War* ('Rifles, handguns and ammunition, from the *Text Book of Small Arms*, 1909'). Greenhill Books, London; 1988.
– *The German Rifle* ('A comprehensive illustrated history of the standard bolt-action designs, 1871–1945'). Arms & Armour Press, London; 1979.
YOUNG, Brigadier Peter, DSO MC MA [with Brigadier Michael Calvert]: *A Dictionary of Battles (1816–1976)*. New English Library, London; 1977.
ZIEGLER, Philip: *Omdurman*. William Collins & Sons Co. Ltd, London; 1973.

INTRODUCTION

The history of regulation muskets used by the British Army begins with the "King's Pattern Musket for Land Service", approved in 1722 by George I. However, firearms had been common in the army since the English Civil War; the first attempt at standardization had been made by James II (reigned 1685–8). The battle of Sedgemoor, fought in 1685 between the forces of the Crown and those of the pretender James, Duke of Monmouth, is widely accepted as the last in which matchlocks predominated. It seems likely that matchlocks had all but disappeared from the army by 1700, replaced by the more effectual flintlock.

Marlborough's army had fought successfully through the War of Spanish Succession — at Blenheim, Ramillies, Oudenarde and Malplaquet — with predecessors of the Land Pattern Musket.* Most had dog-catches to retain the cock and had blacked stocks. Typically, they are ungainly — 62in overall with 46in barrels, and weighing 10½–11lb. The bore diameter varies between ·78 and ·80.

Some years elapsed before the Land Pattern musket design stabilized, the earliest period being characterized by variations in stock and furniture. However, salient characteristics remained reasonably constant: an overall length of 62in, and a ·78-calibre barrel measuring 46in. The stock was generally finished with dark brown or russet-colour lacquer, which resulted in the sobriquet 'Brown Bess'.†

The basic (Long) Land Pattern musket was eventually supplemented by a Short Land Pattern with a 42in barrel, introduced as a dragoon carbine in the mid 1740s before receiving the Royal Warrant as an infantry weapon on 11

* Though generally termed 'pre-Land Pattern', these guns are more accurately classified as 'Ordnance Pattern'.

†There has been great debate over the derivation of the name, though the colour has never been in dispute. 'Bess' was presumably corrupted from the German 'Büchse' (gun), which had been assimilated into English in terms such as Arque*bus*.

4 BELOW
Typical British smooth-bore muskets of the Napoleonic Wars. **i** A ·75-calibre India Pattern musket with a swan-neck cock, dating from about 1800. **ii** An improved India Pattern gun with a ring-neck cock, c.1810. **iii** An India Pattern Serjeant's Fusil or carbine, 1797. The gun has a ·65-calibre 37in barrel. **iv** A New Land Pattern Musket, c.1802, **v** A New Land Pattern Light Infantry Musket, one of the few made in 1810-11. Note the back sight in line with the front edge of the lock plate and the scrolled trigger guard. Courtesy of the Board of Trustees of the Royal Armouries, HM Tower of London.

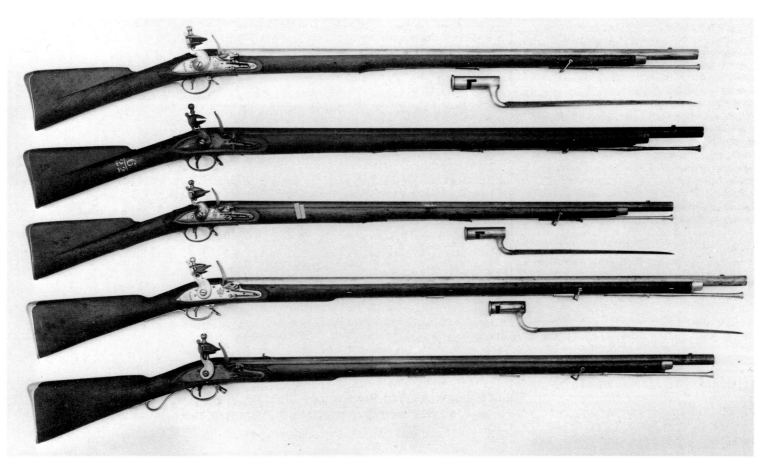

5 RIGHT

'The Line Remained Steady': Sir Charles Belson and the Grenadier Company of the 28th (North Gloucestershire) Regiment of Foot at Quatre Bras, 16 June 1815. A coloured print after an original by Captain G. Jones. Courtesy of Philip J. Haythornthwaite.

Gun performance, 1750–1840

Even the Baker, with an effective range double that of the musket, could not free armies from wars of geometry: the square and the line still ruled the field, just as they had done for centuries. It cannot even be claimed that engagement range had grown appreciably. The firearm remained essentially a close range threat, devastating against massed ranks a hundred yards distant – roughly the length of an association football pitch – but useless against individuals. Lack of range allowed the sabres and lances of the cavalry to retain considerable value, and to allow the cavalry to regain an élite reputation, once weakened by the longbow, that was to last until chanced against the machine-gun.

Judged by a great many standards, the muskets used by the British Army at Waterloo were inferior to the longbows used at Agincourt a half-millenium earlier.*

This was partly due to the lack of rifling in the infantry muskets, but mostly to the loose fit of the projectile. In an emergency, such as the haste and clamour of battle, the ball was simply dropped down the barrel (known as loading 'running ball'), though generally enveloped in a greased wad when time allowed. When the gun was fired, the ball bounced down the bore and out of the muzzle. But who could predict how many times it would bounce, or where along the bore-walls it would strike?

The angle of departure at the muzzle, though constrained to a comparatively narrow band, was a lottery; no wonder that the average musketeer rarely hit his point of aim. Against mass ranks, however, he simply shot the next man along…or the next-but-two. Some balls would plough into the ground short of their target, if the range was long enough; other would whistle harmlessly overhead. Colonel Hanger, in his famous and much quoted *To All Young Sportsmen* (1814), was within his rights to record that a 'soldier's musket, if not exceedingly ill-bored (as many are), will strike the figure of a man at 80 yards; it may be even at a hundred; but a soldier must be very unfortunate indeed who shall be wounded by a common musket at 150 yards, provided his antagonist aims at him; and as to firing at a man at 200 yards with a common musket, you may as well fire at the moon…'

In 1835, trials were undertaken at the Royal Arsenal, Woolwich, to determine the accuracy of a New Land Pattern musket. The results were far from inspiring, maximum range proving to be about 700 yards. Clamping the gun in a rest, raised approximately horizontally, showed that the spent balls struck the ground between 116 and 218 yards away. Accuracy at 100 yards was terrible, the dispersion being 56in vertically and about 72in horizontally; at 200 yards, the vertical dispersion of the shots that could be traced had grown to 112in, but horizontal dispersion was so bad that no acceptable figures could be returned.

*Under favourable conditions, the longbow could attain twelve shots per minute. More than one miss in twelve on a 40in diameter target at eleven-score paces (about 150 yards) was considered a disgrace. At that range, the arrow would penetrate a one-inch wooden plank with ease. Though its 'muzzle velocity' was only $125-150\text{fs}^{-1}$, and the striking energy a mere 25 ft-lb at 100 yards, the piercing arrow wounds were extremely incapacitating.

THE SIMPLIFIED MUSKETS

June 1768. There was also a Militia & Marine Pattern, with a 42in barrel and simplified furniture, perhaps originating as a production expedient during the Seven Years War (1756–63). The flat Militia & Marine side plate was authorized for the Short Land Pattern musket in the mid 1770s, leaving the latter's butt-wrist escutcheon as the primary distinguishing characteristic.

The quality of these muskets was by no means poorer that those of the French, but accuracy was reduced by excessive windage (or gap) allowed between the ball and the bore. Writing in 1860, the Briton Hans Busk damned the Brown Bess as:

The very clumsiest and worst contrived of any firelock in the world. It required the largest charge of powder and the heaviest ball of any; yet owing to the absence of every scientific principle in its construction, its weight and windage were the greatest, its range the shortest, and its accuracy the least; at the same time that it was the most costly of any similar arm in use, either in France, Belgium, Prussia or Austria…

He was being uncharitable; though the India Pattern musket was not particularly well made, the standard patterns were much better. Measurement of surviving French and Austrian muskets suggest that their bore diameters varied as greatly as British equivalents.

Busk also found that 'taking a long series of engagements, only one musket ball out of 460 was found to take effect' – either optimistic or very good, as the French estimated on the basis of several large-scale wars that only one ball in ten thousand found its mark.

Despite continual, if generally minor improvements in the quality of gunpowder by 1815, the performance of the smooth-bore musket had progressed little since the introduction of the Land Pattern musket ninety years previously. Attempts to produce improved infantry weapons began in the 1790s, when the first of the so-called Duke of Richmond's Muskets appeared with Nock screwless locks, but the increasing demands of the French Revolutionary and then the Napoleonic Wars subjugated progress to quantity.

The onset of the French Revolutionary Wars found the Board of Ordnance short of all kinds of firearm; stocks had been depleted by the American War of Independence and the need to arm patriots in Canada, and had never been restored. On 6 February 1794, the governors of the East India Company agreed to cede weapons to the British government; by 31 December, 28,920 muskets, 2,680 carbines and a selection of pistols had been transferred.

Gun performance, 1750–1840

Though little is known about the precise performance of Brown Bess, the French, whose ordnance affairs were the more scientific in the eighteenth century, have left a valuable legacy. The French musket of the Napoleonic Wars was based on a series begun in 1763, when the barrel length had been set at 44·7in. It had a smaller calibre than its British equivalent – ·69, rather than ·78 or ·75. Owing to less windage allowed between the ball and the bore, the French guns shot more accurately; however, the heavier British ball had a much better smashing effect at close range. The disparity was emphasized by the French inclination to fire volleys by the line, comparatively slowly, while the British often fired more rapidly by section. Like Marlborough more than a century earlier, the Duke of Wellington believed that there was nothing more destructive than a volley fired from British muskets. Little could defeat his beliefs in 1815, but such conservatism was to hinder the development of British smallarms for nearly forty years thereafter.

Detailed aiming instructions were issued to enable French musketeers to extract the best from their weapons, which in 1800 were sighted for 120 metres. A typical example reads: 'to strike a man in the centre of his body, up to 100 metres aim at his chest; between 100 and 140 metres, at his throat; from 140 to 180 metres, at the top of his head; from 180 to 200 metres, at the top of his head-dress; and, over 200 metres, above the top of his head-dress... beyond 400 metres the velocity is too low to make wounds, and the effect of fire beyond even 200 metres is uncertain'.

As the maximum point-blank range of British muskets was about 75 yards, so it would be appropriate to reduce the French ranges by a third to get comparable results.

Prior to the Revolution of 1789, the French had also experimented against a target 6ft high and 100ft wide, representing a column of infantrymen. A hundred shots fired from a distance of 100 paces – about 78 metres – gave 67 direct hits and eight ricochets strong enough to pierce a one-inch pine board. At 300 paces, there were sixteen hits and eleven ricochets, two of the latter failing to pierce the board; but at 600 paces, of five hits and two ricochets, only a single ball had the strength to pierce the board.

The probability of hitting a man-size target (2m high, 57cm broad) with the French dragoon musket was subsequently calculated to be 23 per cent at 100 metres; eleven per cent at 150m; seven per cent at 300m; and a mere six per cent at 300m. None of these figures was inspiring.

In addition to the inherent accuracy problems that afflicted the musket, the flintlock, with its priming powder in a less-than-waterproof pan, was prone to misfire. Tests undertaken in Britain in the 1830s reckoned the flintlock to be 6½ times less reliable than an equivalent musket with a cap-lock; experiments elsewhere returned misfire rates as high as one shot in eight.

‡Thus the term 'Black Sea Service Musket' has nothing do with the campaigns in the Crimea, as has occasionally been mistakenly assumed.

Though small quantities of muskets were acquired from the East India Company in 1808–13, the simplest solution was to authorize production of the India Pattern musket as an emergency measure. It was simpler than the Short Land Pattern, much more poorly finished but otherwise comparable. Its ·75-calibre barrel measured a mere 39in, giving an overall length about 55½in; the butt plate tongue was reduced and the wrist escutcheon disappeared, though the stock carving, butt profile and lock-plate design of the Short Land Pattern were perpetuated. In 1797, after proving easier to make and more economical of raw material, the India Pattern was adopted as standard. Production continued until the end of the Napoleonic Wars, guns made after c.1810 substituting a sturdier ring-neck cock for the older swan-neck type.

To accelerate production, standards of view were relaxed. For the first time, sub-contractors were deliberately recruited from outside the traditional gun-making fraternity: cabinet makers, wheelwrights and carpenters, for example, were instructed to make gun stocks. Admittedly, the results were often uninspiring. The most notable feature of the India Pattern guns, particularly those made in the desperate early days, is the poor quality of the wood. There was even an 'extra service' musket, poorer than the poorest India Pattern gun. Demand for extra service guns was sufficiently high for 16,672 stocks to be in store in the Tower of London by 1814.

Total production of Ordnance-type India Pattern muskets in 1804–15 amounted to a remarkable 1,603,711. No fewer than 546,586 were made in 1812–13 alone. The India Pattern musket was supplemented by the New Land Pattern, introduced after the Treaty of Amiens had restored a fragile peace to Europe in 1802. Continuing the process of simplification begun by the India Pattern, the new musket had a plain low-comb stock and an altogether more modern profile. No attempt was made to reinstate the wrist escutcheon, and the carving that surrounded the lock plate and barrel-tang on the Short Land and India Patterns was discarded. The 42in barrel returned, calibre remaining ·75.

Unfortunately, peace proved transitory: only a few thousand New Land Pattern muskets were made before 1815, production being confined to 1802–3 and 1814. A derivative was approved for light infantrymen in 1803, but not made in quantity until 1810. Its features included a standing-block back sight brazed to the barrel, about 3in from the breech, and a distinctively scrolled trigger guard.

Sea Service muskets were also made throughout the period, distinguished by being of the original regulation calibre (·78), but with barrels approximating to 37in. The sturdy locks were plainer than their 'Land' equivalents. The muskets may be stocked in the style of the Land Patterns, though some India Pattern examples were made in the early years of the nineteenth century. Barrels were bright or blacked.‡

A selection of flintlock carbines had also appeared by 1815, the earliest being little more than Short Land Pattern muskets fitted with sling bars; De Witt Bailey, in *British Military Longarms, 1715–1865*, recognizes the introduction of nearly thirty separate patterns dating from 1744–1817. The most distinctive are short barrelled – Elliot's Carbine, c.1760 (·67-calibre, 28¼in barrel); Burgoyne's large-calibre Musketoon of 1781, with an elliptical bore measuring 1in on its vertical axis and a 16⅛in barrel; the Heavy Dragoon or Harcourt's Carbine of 1796 (·73, 28in), originally made with a Nock screwless lock; the India Pattern Serjeant's Carbine or Fusil of 1797 (·65, 37in); and the minuscule Paget Cavalry Carbine of 1812 (·66, 16in).

THE FIRST REGULATION RIFLE

The principal gun makers in England were directed by the Honorable Board of Ordnance to produce a specimen, in order to procure the best rifle possible, for the use of a rifle corps . . . raised by the Government . . . and a committee of field officers was appointed for the purpose of examining, and reporting according to their judgement. There were also many rifles from America and various parts of the Continent produced at the same time. These were all tried at Woolwich; when my barrel, having only one quarter turn in the barrel, was approved by the committee.

Ezekiel Baker, describing the preliminary experiments with his rifle, 1800.

* Renamed the 95th (Rifle) Regiment in 1802, and the Rifle Brigade in 1816.

I was sent out to skirmish against some of those in green – grasshoppers, I call them; you call them Rifle Men. They were behind every bush and stone, and soon made sad havoc amongst my men, killing all the officers of my company, and wounding myself without being able to do them any injury . . .

Lieutenant George Simmons of the 95th, in his posthumous memoir *A British Rifle Man* (1899, reprinted 1986), recording the view of a French officer whose unit had been annihilated at the Battle of Vimiero in 1810.

6 RIGHT

5 January 1808; Rifleman Thomas Plunkett of the 95th (Rifle) Regiment downs French Général Colbert at Villafranca during the retreat to Corunna. Note the Baker Rifle being used in the 'back position', described by A Corporal of Riflemen (Captain H. Beaufroy), in *Scloppeteria*, 1808, as 'not only awkward but painful'. A print after an original by Harry Payne, c.1900. Payne has drawn the flintlock much too far forward in relation to the trigger guard. Courtesy of Philip J. Haythornthwaite.

The most interesting of the Napoleonic muzzle-loaders was the Baker Rifle, the first of its type to be sealed for service in the British Army. Though specialist firearms – Jägerbüchsen – had been widely issued in the Austrian and Prussian armies since the middle of the eighteenth century, no such firearm had ever been considered regulation status in Britain. Riflemen had simply been recruited to fight in the American War of Independence and the French Revolutionary Wars from abroad, generally in Hanover, and were armed with Continental-style rifles. Guns were purchased from Suhl and the Austrian Netherlands, or copied in Birmingham.

By 1800, the utility of specialists had become obvious, and the first attempts were being made to raise the Experimental Corps of Riflemen.*

Its rifling excepted, Baker's rifle contained little that was revolutionary. Indeed, it was very similar to many of the guns that had been bought for the British irregulars from the Austrian Netherlands. Its flintlock was originally based on the India or New Land patterns, suitably reduced in size, although the final post-1806 pattern embodied a raised pan, a safety bolt let into the tail of the lock-plate, and a flat ring-neck cock. Rifles made in 1800–3 may be encountered in musket or carbine bore (·750 and ·625 respectively), after which the latter was preferred.

The butt had a cheek piece on the left and a patch-box, generally brass, let into the right. The original two-compartment box, with a moulded front, was superseded by a smaller rounded pattern with a single compartment. The suggestion of a pistol grip was emphasized by the scroll-type trigger guard. Many post-1806 rifles had a butt-comb sloping upward towards the rear, the opposite of previous practice; this is commonly encountered on modern target rifles developed for shooting while prone and its 'straight line' construction would have minimized the effect of recoil by directing it straight back into the marksman's shoulder.

Pre-1815 Bakers displayed a sturdy bayonet bar on the right side of the muzzle, and the standing-block back sight (unmarked, but set for 200 yards) had a 300-yard leaf folding forward. A typical ·625-calibre rifle measured 46¼in overall, had a 30¼in barrel and weighed about 9lb. The first cavalry rifles were subsequently made with barrels of 20–20½in; later examples, apparently for the 10th Hussars, had conventionally pistol-gripped stocks.

7 ABOVE

A private of the Light Company of the 5th (Northumberland) Regiment of Foot, after an engraving by Genty, Paris, 1815. It is interesting that the engraver should have given the soldier's musket barrel bands; common enough in France, these were not used in British service until the advent of the P/53 rifle-musket. Courtesy of Philip J. Haythornthwaite.

8 ABOVE RIGHT

A rifleman of the North Yorkshire Militia loading his Baker Rifle; an aquatint published in George Walker's *Costume of Yorkshire*, 1814. Courtesy of Philip J. Haythornthwaite.

‡Dispersion on Baker's original specimen targets is markedly vertical, the groups at both 200 and 300 yards being in the region of 3ft high by 18in broad.

The shooting of the new rifle was a revelation to troops accustomed to the common musket. Baker published two specimen targets obtained in the early 1800s at ranges of 200 and 300 yards, showing that it was possible to hit a man with practically every shot. Unfortunately, neither the precise nature of the rifle used in these experiments nor the conditions under which it was fired are known. In the barrel trials at Woolwich in February 1800, all but one of twelve shots hit a 9ft-square target at 300 yards, the twelfth missing entirely. The hits made a group with a diameter of about 54in.

The efficiency of the new rifle was matched by that of the new rifle corps; by 1815, the unit had gained more than twenty battle honours ranging from Copenhagen (1801) through the bloody battles in the Peninsular War (1808–14) to Waterloo (1815). Green-clad riflemen left an indelible impression on the French, whose Voltigeurs were no mean skirmishers.

9 ABOVE

A ·625 or 'Carbine Bore' Baker Rifle, c.1810, with a Second Model (or P/1801) sword bayonet. Note the spurred trigger guard and the butt-trap, and also that the butt-comb is angled upward towards the rear. This helps to direct the recoil straight back into the firer's shoulder. Courtesy of the Board of Trustees of the Royal Armouries, HM Tower of London.

Attempts were made at Woolwich to determine the Baker's capabilities but, as the age of the gun being tried in 1835 was not recorded, the results cannot be compared satisfactorily with Baker's originals. The rifle grouped twenty shots within a three-foot circle at 100 yards; placed fourteen shots out of twenty on a similar target at 200 yards, with a marked horizontal dispersion‡; and hit a twelve-foot square target 21 times out of forty at 300 yards.

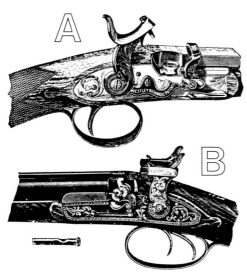

10 ABOVE

Two typical early percussion-ignition systems: Westley Richards' Detonating Gun (A), which used a flanged priming tube, and Joseph Manton's 'Tube Detonating Gun' (B). Tube detonators were fragile and potentially dangerous; within a decade of their appearance, they had been superseded by the cap. From W.W. Greener's *The Gun and its Development* (1910).

* Shaw's cap was not patented until 19 June 1822, and then only in the USA. The relevant papers were lost when fire destroyed the US Patent Office in 1836; consequently, there is now no way of confirming his claim to fame. The first British Patent to be granted on a percussion cap was to John Day, a gunsmith of Barnstaple, Devon, in November 1823.

†Though this sounds insignificant by modern standards, suggesting little more than a clerk, it was an important position in the nineteenth century: 'Controller of Stores' gives a better idea of its status.

11 RIGHT

Advance of infantry at the Battle of Gujarat, 21 February 1849, where British troops commanded by Sir Hugh Gough routed Sikhs under Sher Singh and effectively ended the Second Sikh War. From a contemporary print. Courtesy of Philip J. Haythornthwaite.

12 FAR RIGHT

An example of George Lovell's ·75-calibre Pattern 1838 musket, with the original large back-action lock. Note the back sight and the distinctive 'Hanoverian Spring' bayonet retainer beneath the muzzle. Courtesy of the Board of Trustees of the Royal Armouries, HM Tower of London.

The first major improvement on the flintlock came with the first mechanism in which ignition was accomplished by striking a small portion of mercuric fulminate. Developed by a Scottish clergyman named Alexander Forsyth, early in the nineteenth century, this 'scent bottle' was uncertain, occasionally dangerous and widely distrusted – the Master-General of the Ordnance dismissed Forsyth and 'his rubbish' from the Tower of London in 1807.

That few of the earliest pill- and tube-locks offered much in the way of rivalry was entirely due to the skill with which Forsyth's British Patent 3,032 of 11 April 1807 had been drafted. In common with several other famous Letters Patent, such as Colt's first revolver and Rollin White's bored-through cylinder, its effect was to stifle development for many years. Even Joseph Manton's tube lock was not exempt, Forsyth resorting to litigation against him in 1818.

The French gunsmith Prélat patented a hollow cock containing a fulminate pellet in July 1818, adding a claim for a copper cap two years later. However, Prélat was an incorrigible copyist and it is unlikely that his cap was original. Joshua Shaw is generally credited with perfecting a self-contained percussion cap in 1818.*

Initially capricious, the cap-lock had become sturdy and effectual within a decade. Reliability was reckoned at least six times better than a flintlock, but the message took some time to filter through to the military. Though the Board of Ordnance had entertained submissions during the 1820s, none had commended itself. By 1830, however, experiments had begun in France. Not wishing to be left behind by such an arch-rival, the British authorities turned to George Lovell. Appointed Storekeeper† in the Enfield factory in 1816, Lovell was widely read and conscientious enough to pursue his new goals with enthusiasm. His first experimental musket was made in November 1831, with the ·753-calibre 39in barrel of the contemporary India Pattern. It had a back-action lock with an enclosed hammer, and the way in which its socket bayonet was retained by a small spring catch beneath the muzzle had been adapted from a Hanoverian design. Initial trials were encouraging, an order for two hundred muskets and a hundred pistols for the Royal Navy being followed almost immediately by a request from the Coast Guard for 2,000 pistols.

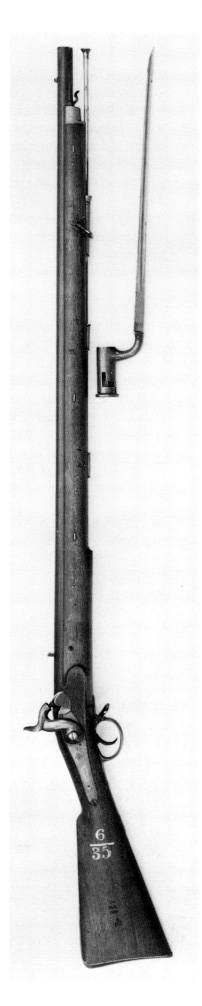

News of the tests spread far and wide, and the Board of Ordnance was soon inundated with percussion-ignition locks of all kinds. By 1834, only four systems remained: Hayward's self-replenishing pellet lock, Lovell's back-action cap-lock, Rivière's cap-lock and Manton's plug lock.

Thirteen muskets had been tested extensively by the end of 1835, Lovell's improved cap-lock, the common cap-lock, Manton's plug lock and Eccles' cap-lock being selected for field trials. Twenty guns of each system were made in the Spring of 1836 for issue to the 52nd Regiment in Gibraltar, the 80th in Chatham, the 85th en route for Canada, and the 12th and 33rd at the Curragh (Dublin). Subsequent reports broadly favoured Lovell's improved cap-lock, though the Royal Marines, to whom the fifth batch of rifles had been issued, regarded the Manton plug as easiest to handle. The Lovell musket was universally approved, except for the enclosed hammer. This had been adjudged difficult to clean and prone to jam if the stock should swell.

The lock was redesigned with an external hammer, whereupon the Navy, traditionally less discerning than the army, immediately adopted the percussion system. Two thousand muskets were ordered in the autumn of 1836.

In February 1837, Lovell suggested standardizing a ball of 14½ to the pound (483 grains) in an effort to simplify issue. This was to be used in the ·753-calibre muskets, new carbines (·733) and the existing rifles (·704), windage allowances reflecting the differing accuracy requirements in each class. Eight hundred converted cap-lock New Land Pattern muskets were issued to the Guards for trials in the Canadian winter, and 700 new carbines were made in the Tower of London armouries. Finally, in March 1838, the Lovell musket and cap-lock were recommended for issue.

The decision was timely, as the Principal Storekeeper reported that stocks of firearms had declined greatly since 1829: almost a half-million had been sent to the colonies, France (88,960 in 1830) and Spain (341,600 in 1834−8). So few replacements had been forthcoming that a growing shortage would soon become critical.

The authorities decided to assemble a last batch of 30,000 India Pattern flintlocks from parts in store. However, two thousand Pattern 1838 (Lovell's) muskets were ordered for the Guards on 25 March 1839 and so the India Pattern arms were completed with cap-locks. Issued to line infantrymen, they were known as the Pattern of 1839.

By 1841, nine longarms had been sanctioned: the P/38 musket for the Foot Guards rank-and-file; the P/39, for line infantry; a musket for the Serjeants of Foot Guards, which was basically a Brunswick Rifle adapted for a socket bayonet; a Serjeant's Fusil for line infantrymen; Lovell's Improved Brunswick Rifle, with a sword bayonet; a carbine for the Royal Sappers & Miners, with a saw-backed socket bayonet; the Victoria Pattern carbine for heavy and light cavalry, fitted with a swivel rammer; a double-barrelled smooth-bore carbine for the Cape Mounted Rifle Corps; the Sea Service Musket; and a heavy naval rifle, adapted from the Brunswick.

The principal ·753-calibre muskets − P/38 (new) and P/39 (converted) − had 39in barrels, were about 55in overall and weighed in the region of 10lb. Their socket bayonets were retained by a Hanoverian-type spring catch beneath the muzzle, moving vertically, or later by the more effectual Lovell's Spring (which moved laterally). Pattern 1838 muskets have back-action locks, later examples measuring 5in instead of 5¾in, while the Pattern 1839 displays a standard side-lock. Many of the latter will show signs of conversion from flintlock, though production began anew c.1846. The P/39 is difficult to distinguish from the succeeding P/42, though it lacks a back sight and usually displays a New

Land-type brass side plate instead of side-nail cups. Barrels were browned, as all post-1815 British service patterns had been.

The three Brunswick-pattern rifles are considered below (see THE BELTED BALL). The Serjeant's Fusil or carbine was either a conversion (P/39) or newly made (P/42), the former lacking the latter's standing-block back sight. These guns measure 49in overall and have ·733-bore 33in barrels. Most Sea Service muskets (calibre ·75–·76) are conversions; though a few of P/42 type were made in the 1850s, all were rifled before issue. They are appreciably shorter than the infantry equivalents, measuring only about 46in with a 30½in barrel.

Approved in March 1841, but not made until the summer of 1842, the Sappers & Miners Carbine had a side-lock and a standing-block back sight. It was similar to the Sea Service musket – 46in overall, 30¼in barrel – but had a bore diameter of ·733. It also accepted a socket bayonet with a saw-back blade and a unique two-bar knuckle guard.‡

The original Victoria Carbine, which reached service status in 1838, the year of Queen Victoria's coronation, had a bolted back-action lock and a trigger-guard scroll adapted from the Manton flintlock carbine of 1833. Heartily disliked by the cavalry, it was replaced in 1843 by a modified gun with a conventional side-lock and a plain iron barrel instead of a twist design. The swivel rammer and scrolled guard were retained. Measuring 41¾in overall, the perfected carbine had a 26in barrel and weighed about 7lb 9oz.

Based on a flintlock approved in 1822, the double-barrelled ·733-calibre Cape Carbine had back-action locks, a swivel rammer mounted in an eccentric, and a scroll guard. It measured 43in overall and had barrels of 26½in.*

‡This was changed after January 1843 to a much simpler pattern with an unadorned socket, a plain blade and a double-edged point. The second-pattern carbine has a longer fore-end, and a Lovell Spring replaces the Hanoverian bayonet catch.

* Calibre and the absence of a sword-bayonet bar distinguishes it from the otherwise similar ·66-calibre Irish Constabulary Carbine of 1839.

13 ABOVE
The Pattern 1839 musket is easily distinguished from the P/1838 (see illustration 12) by its conventional lock. Note the design of Lovell's Spring bayonet retainer, which locks laterally. Courtesy of the Board of Trustees of the Royal Armouries, HM Tower of London.

No sooner had the rearmament programme commenced than the Tower armouries were disastrously burned during the night of 30/31 October 1841 – three days after the approval of a newly-made version of the P/38, with a conventional side-lock. In addition to damage to buildings, fixtures and production machinery, 280,000 longarms were destroyed. Almost all the cap-locks awaiting issue had been lost, as had many flintlocks held in reserve. Super-human reconstruction efforts allowed production of the new muskets—now designated 'Pattern 1842' – to resume early in the new year.

Excepting certainty of ignition, which was undeniably better, the earliest smooth-bore cap-locks offered very little improvement over their flintlock predecessors. Progress in firearms technology was still firmly obstructed by negligible advances in military ammunition design.

One Pattern 1842 musket was tested by the Royal Engineers in 1846, firing out across the River Medway at Chatham in an attempt to gauge maximum range. This proved to be about 650 yards at an elevation of 5°. Accuracy was still very poor, as only five shots out of ten hit a target 5ft 6in high by 11ft 6in broad at 150 yards; at 250 yards, they all missed. It proved necessary to hold the aim 5ft 6in over a man's head at 200 yards to have any chance of a hit…or a staggering 130ft at 600 yards! The Engineers sensibly concluded that shooting should be restricted to ranges shorter than 150 yards.

14 RIGHT

Engraved by J. Harris after a watercolour by Henry Martens, this 1853-vintage picture shows men of the 13th Light Dragoons encamped at Chobham. Note the sketchily observed Second Model (or P/43) Victoria Carbines, which had brass furniture and scrolled trigger guards. Courtesy of Philip J. Haythornthwaite.

THE BELTED BALL

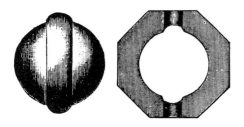

15 ABOVE

The Brunswick rifling, shown here from an engraving in Greener's *The Gun and its Development* (1910), had two grooves of considerable depth. The lead ball had a pronounced rib or belt, which was mated with the grooves before the ball could be rammed down the bore. The system performed well on trial, but was a disaster in the field. Most of the troubles stemmed from damaged or inaccurately cast ribs failing to mesh with the grooves.

A method was urgently required to improve the performance of infantry muskets without drastically changing them. The importance of rifling had been established several hundred years previously, but the first attempts to improve the grip between the projectile and the bore had consisted of simply of wrapping the former in a patch. But this slowed loading appreciably.

During the 1830s, the patched ball was supplemented by the belted ball, raised ribs being inserted in the broad rifling grooves before the bullet was rammed down the barrel. This system is credited to Captain Berners, aide-de-camp to the Duke of Brunswick.

Complaints about the accuracy of the Baker rifles, and their comparatively poor long-range performance, were being voiced by the Rifle Brigade as early as 1828. A rifle with a back-action lock and Delvigne-pattern chambered breech was proffered as a replacement, but trials against a selection of weapons had been uninspiring.

In 1836, with supplies of Baker Rifles dwindling, the Board of Ordnance ordered two thousand new guns of a pattern to be determined by trial. George Lovell had made up a suitable gun with eleven-groove rifling making a three-quarter turn in a 30in barrel, a back-action lock, iron furniture and a standing-block back sight with a single folding leaf.

While this gun was being tested by the Rifle Brigade, however, Berners sent Lovell a two-groove rifled musket. Though this could not use a standard paper cartridge, had a low muzzle velocity and was very heavy, it shot much better than expected.

A ·654-calibre short rifle was made on the Berners principle, rifled with two grooves making an entire turn in its 30in barrel. The gun weighed 9lb without its Baker-type sword bayonet. One major improvement was to move the attachment bar back so that the bayonet cross-guard lay behind the plane of the muzzle; one of the principal complaints against the Baker was that it could not be fired with the bayonet fixed, as the guard protruded ahead of the muzzle and blast strained the bayonet mounting. The experimental rifle was tested against a Baker on 26 December 1836. It proved as accurate at short range, but better at greater distances; it was handier; needed less cleaning; and the barrel, owing to the reduction in grooves, was reckoned to have a greater life.

The ·654-calibre Lovell-Brunswick had no sooner been approved for service than the calibre was changed to ·704 under the standardization programme. A new pattern was substituted on 4 August 1837 and the first order was passed to Enfield, whence, as production capacity was insufficient, work was sub-contracted to the gun trade. Thirteen gunmakers, including Lacy & Reynolds and R.E. Pritchett, subsequently participated.

The earliest mass-produced examples of Lovell's Improved Brunswick Rifle, as the weapon was officially known, had a back-action lock and a two-compartment patch box with a brass lid. The barrels were made of good quality twist-steel and had two-position back sights intended for 200 (standing block) and 300 yards (folding leaf). The stock had a straight wrist, while the low-comb butt lacked a cheek piece. Furniture was brass. Measuring about 46¼in overall, with a 30¼in barrel, the Bruswick weighed about 9lb 3oz without its sword bayonet. It was generally issued with 560-grain compressed lead balls, made on a machine patented by David Napier which eliminated air bubbles and regularized weight.

The back-action lock was abandoned in August 1841, but the replacement side-lock was not fitted to the Brunswick until 4,000 rifles were ordered on 31 October 1845. An improved bayonet fastening was submitted by Lacy & Reynolds in autumn 1847, and approved in June 1848. Its principal distinguishing feature was the locking notch, which lay approximately halfway along the upper edge of the attachment bar.

An inventory made in October 1852 showed that 11,530 Brunswick Rifles were in store or on issue. However, though a Brunswick Rifle with a P/53 Enfield side-lock was sealed in July 1864 to govern manufacture for the 'East India Government', the advent of the self-expanding bullet with the P/51 rifle-musket had rendered the belted ball moribund.

A few hundred Brunswick-type rifles were made for Serjeants of Foot Guards in 1840, a solitary later order — for a mere fifty with side-bars and rings — being delivered to Cape Colony in 1843. The Foot Guards rifle had a back-action lock, a 33in barrel and a socket bayonet; unusually, the bayonet stud lay under the muzzle to avoid the sight-line.

A few two-groove heavy rifles were made at Enfield in 1840–1 for the Royal Navy, distinguished by their large size and a bore diameter of ·796 for a 875-grain belted ball. The guns measured 48¾in overall, had 32½in barrels and weighed about 11lb 10oz. Bayonets were not used, the rifles being stocked to the muzzle, but there was a unique back sight with folding leaves for 300, 400 and 470 yards. Only a handful of these navy rifles was made, as the common Sea Service musket was preferred owing to the speed at which it could be loaded.

During its short service life, the Brunswick was probably cursed more than any other British service rifle. A gun that had performed so well in its trials proved a disaster in the field; indeed, it is hard to see it as an improvement on the flintlock Baker, except in certainty of ignition. Its accuracy was no better than its predecessor, largely because the belted balls deformed too easily in the soldiers' pouches.

Trials undertaken at Enfield in 1852 to determine the angle of departure of the belted ball at various ranges had to be abandoned beyond 500 yards, as the rifle had ceased to shoot consistently enough; there is little doubt that the maximum range at which a Brunswick-armed rifleman could reasonably expect to hit a man-size target was less than 250 yards. One of the testers commented that 'the loading...is so difficult that is wonderful how the rifle regiments can have continued to use it for so long'.

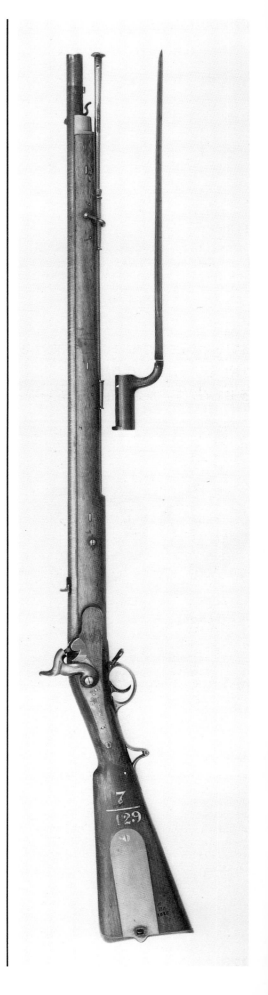

THE EXPANDING BALL

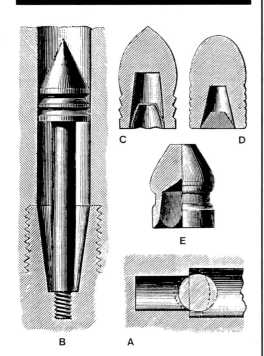

17 ABOVE

A is a Delvigne chamber breech, showing the deformation of the bullet – somewhat exaggerated! – required to seat it effectually. **B** is a Thouvenin 'à Tige' or pillar breech. Powder occupied the space between the pillar and the barrel wall. The three bullets are all expanding patterns – **C** is an original Minié, with an iron base-cup, **D** is an approximation of the British wood-plug version, and **E** represents the French Nessler. From Schott's *Grundriss der Waffenlehre* (1876).

The ribbed projectile had little other application in the British service. However, the exploits of John Jacob in India are worth mentioning. Jacob commanded the Scinde Irregular Horse, serving on the North West Frontier, and was greatly concerned about the poor long-range performance of the regulation firearms. Consequently, he had quantities of special double barrelled cap-lock rifles made by Manton, Swinburn & Son and Witton & Daw in the 1850s. The perfected version had 24in 32-bore barrels and accepted an impressive-looking sword bayonet with a 30in blade. Sights comprised a standing block with folding leaves for 200 and 300 yards, plus a bar-and-slider for ranges up to an unbelievable 2,000 yards. The cylindro-conoidal bullet had four short rhomboidal ribs to engage the rifling.

Performance proved to be very good, Jacob and his cronies amusing themselves by hitting targets at prodigious distances with explosive bullets, but the basic principle of the ribbed bullet was soon obsolete. Jacob's Rifles were raised in 1858, but the general died soon afterwards and his unit was subsequently incorporated in the 30th Regiment of Bombay Infantry (Jacob's Rifles) in 1861.

The belted ball and its near-relation, the ribbed slug, were an improvement on the patched ball; but care was still needed to ensure that belts and ribs mated satisfactorily with the rifling. However, the accuracy of the cap-lock Brunswick offered little improvement over the flintlock Baker. Loading was quicker than with patched balls, but by no means as easy as if the projectile could simply be dropped down the barrel. The problem was that the ball then had to be expanded into the rifling. Early attempts relied on gravity and the assistance of a heavy ramrod to distort the malleable lead sufficiently to fill the bore when the projectile stopped against a ring in the breech. This was an old idea, dating back to the Frenchman Deschamps (1718). It was briefly revived in Britain during the French Revolutionary Wars in the form of the Gardner Nail-breech and Nock Ring-breech, but experimentation had been abandoned in 1813.

When the idea of an expanding ball reappeared in France in 1826, a sturdy ramrod or a small mallet still sufficed to upset the projectile into the rifling. Delvigne's breech had a sub-calibre powder chamber, the ball being expanded against the shoulder at the chamber-mouth. It was superseded by Thouvenin's pillar ('à Tige') in which the projectile was expanded over a rod protruding centrally from the breech-face.

The pillar-breech system was championed in Britain by Charles Lancaster, who registered a suitable design in April 1848. Two years previously, the Board of Ordnance had asked Lancaster to prepare 24 pillar-breech rifles, stocked and locked in the manner of the Brunswick, in the hope that they would be able to shoot accurately to 1,200 yards. Though a few Lancaster rifles had been taken to the Kaffir War in southern Africa, trials had not been completed when the first Minié expanding balls rendered the pillar-breech obsolete virtually overnight.

As the projectiles were deformed by the blows necessary to force them into the rifling, systems such as Delvigne's and Thouvenin's were scarcely ideal. But shooting had improved perceptibly compared with their smooth-bore predecessors. In the late 1840s, the French army pitted Thouvenin pillar-breech rifles against infantry muskets at ranges varying from 200 to 1,000 metres. At the shortest range, a behatted-soldier target measuring two metres high and a half-metre broad was hit thirty per cent of the time by the musket and 62 per cent by the rifle; at the 500-metre target (two metres square) the

†In April 1855, Delvigne and Minié jointly petitioned that the P/51 and its successors should be known as 'Delvigne-Minié Muskets'. The British authorities simply ignored the request.

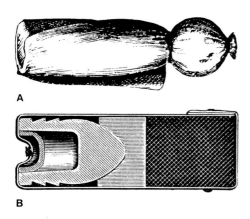

18 ABOVE

A typical paper or linen-wrapped ball cartridge (A), widely issued with flint- and cap-lock muskets. This is a Prussian cavalry carbine version. Drawing B shows a typical 'second generation' version, in this case for the Prussian M.1839/55 rifled musket. It contains a Minié expanding ball reversed onto the powder charge; to load, the cartridge was torn open, the powder emptied down the bore, the ball rammed down on top of it and the remnants of the packaging added as a wad. From Schott's *Grundriss der Waffenlehre* (1876).

figures were five and 52 per cent respectively. At longer ranges, however, the musket became useless while the rifle recorded 42 per cent on the 800-metre target (two metres high, four metres broad) and even 23 per cent at 1,000 metres, where the target was two metres high and six metres broad.

Where Delvigne and Thouvenin had led, others soon followed. The next stage was the self-expanding bullet, now generally credited to French army officer Claude-Etienne Minié, an instructor at the École Normale de Tir de Vincennes. However, Norton and Greener in Britain both claimed to have pre-empted him and Delvigne patented the basic principle in France in 1842.†

Minié's hollow-base bullet was simply dropped down the bore and was expanded into the rifling by the violent ignition of the main propellant charge. The system, which worked surprisingly well, was greatly improved by a plug set in the base to facilitate expansion — even though the iron cup of the original Minié bullet occasionally blasted through the body to leave a leaden annulus jammed in the breech. The perfected British Metford-Pritchett bullet of 1852–3 was expanded simply by a carefully contoured base cavity.

It was soon obvious that the expanding bullet was vastly superior to the chamber- and pillar-breech rifles, then generally confined to the French army. Almost immediately, every army attempted to follow Minié's lead.

Greener's ovoid ball, fitted with a conical base plug, had been rejected by the ordnance authorities in 1836 — a precipitate act that cost the Treasury £1,000 compensation twenty years later. Learning that good progress with the self-expanding ball was being made on the Continent, the British ordnance authorities despatched George Lovell on a European tour in the summer of 1850. In the Spring of 1851, French and Belgian Minié-type rifles were tested against a Carabine à Tige, the Lancaster pillar-breech rifle, a Dreyse needle-gun made at Enfield, a Brunswick and a P/42 musket. On 30 April 1851, the Small Arms Committee reported that the French rifle, in particular, had proved so superior that the Lancaster should be abandoned immediately.

Subsequently, several prototype rifle-muskets were made at Enfield, following the general lines of the Belgian weapon but rifled in the French manner. George Lovell was ordered to prepare bullet-making machinery in May 1851 and, on 13 October, the Small Arms Committee settled the salient features of the new rifle: a weight of 10lb 8¾oz with bayonet, and a ·702-calibre 39in barrel. The smooth-surfaced projectile, without cannlures, was to weigh 680 grains and be propelled by 2½ drams of powder. Alone among the debits was that the new gun could not accept the standard musket ball in an emergency.

Permission to introduce the Minié rifle had been elicited from the Commander-in-Chief, the octogenarian Duke of Wellington. In September 1851, just as the first trials rifles were being readied for issue, the Duke withdrew his consent. Though the Master-General of Ordnance, the Marquis of Anglesey, protested strongly enough to force a return to the original plan, the future of the Minié rifle-musket in the British service hung in the balance for some time.

The first five hundred guns were issued in February 1852, on a scale of fifty apiece, to the Battalion of Guards, the 1st Battalion of the Royals, seven line regiments and the Rifle Brigade (95th). Apart from complaints about poor sighting, and few minor grumbles about the ramrod and ball-drawer, they were extremely well received.

Orders for 23,000 new guns were then placed with the trade. Barrels made by Ezra Millward, Beazley & Sons, Deakin & Son, Henry Clive, William Millward, John Clive and Turner & Sons were subsequently stocked, locked and finished

The Grenadiers then took up a defensive formation and began to fire with great accuracy into the charging Russian mass. The Minié rifle did sterling work. Prince Gorchakov's horse was shot from under him; the Russians hesitated, and then began to retreat. Hard on their heels came the Guards regiments, until at last they mounted the wall of the Great Redoubt and found it deserted, save for dead and wounded.

Denis Judd, *The Crimean War*, describing part of the Battle of the Alma, 20 September 1854.

by Hollis & Sheath, Swinburn & Son, Tipping & Lawden and Thomas Turner.

The P/51 was a conventional-looking weapon, difficult to distinguish at a glance from the rifled P/42 musket with which it shared the side-action lock, ramrod and brass furniture. Its principal distinguishing characteristics were a leaf-and-slider back sight graduated to 900 yards, a barrel retained by keys (the later P/53 used bands), and a bore diameter of ·702 compared with ·758 for the rifled P/42. The P/51 is lighter than the P/42 – nominally 9lb 8oz compared with 10lb – but this is sometimes difficult to detect owing to variations in stock-wood density. The rifle-muskets measured 55in overall, had 39in barrels and their socket bayonets were retained by Lovell's Spring.

Large numbers of P/51 rifle-muskets had been delivered by the time war broke out in the Crimea. However, inefficiency and the chaotic state of transport ensured that many of the units engaged in the fighting – particularly in the early stages – were armed with P/42 smooth-bore muskets. By April 1855, only about half of the P/51 arms delivered into store had found their way into issue.

Compared with the smooth-bore muskets and the Brunswick, the rifle-musket was awesome. Tests undertaken with P/51 and P/42 arms, in which twenty men each fired ten rounds at a target 6ft high by 20ft broad, illustrated the margin of superiority. At 100 yards, the P/42 hit the target 149 times compared with 189 for the P/51. At 200 yards the figures were 85 and 160 respectively. At 400 yards, however, the P/42 recorded a mere nine hits from two hundred shots: the P/51 registered 105. It was also found that errant shots from the P/42 could fly anything up to fifty feet wide of the target at the farthest range, while those of the Minié all passed within a few feet.

Many paintings of the Battles of the Alma, Balaklava and Inkerman show the British troops with P/53 Enfields, none of which reached the Crimea until 1855. Thus the first 'Minnie', now comparatively rarely seen, made a genuine contribution to British military history.

The rifle-muskets proved to be much more accurate than the Brunswick, as well as infinitely easier to load. Greatly encouraged, the authorities decided to extend the principle to the P/42 and Sea Service muskets, the double-barrelled Cape Carbine, and the Paget cavalry carbine. The muskets were

THE PERFECTED RIFLE-MUSKET

20, 21 FAR RIGHT
The first British rifle-musket was the P/1851 Minié (20), with a 39in ·702-calibre barrel retained by keys. Note also the design of the back sight, which helps distinguish the P/51 from the externally similar P/42 rifled musket. The bayonet is retained by a Lovell's Spring. The perfected weapon was the ·577 P/1853 or 'Enfield' (21). Apart from generally lighter construction, the Enfield has a 'banded' barrel and accepts a socket bayonet with a locking ring. This gun is a second-pattern P/53, with solid bands and retaining springs. Courtesy of the Board of Trustees of the Royal Armouries, HM Tower of London.

‡The tail of the mainspring is connected to the cock with a link, rather than simply resting on the tail. Benefits included greater reliability and a reduction in friction.

* The weight of the P/53 steadily increased as the design was refined. The fourth pattern, with Baddeley Bands, weighed 8lb 13oz.

bored out to ·758 and shallowly rifled to avoid weakening the barrels. They fired an awesome 850-grain projectile with 3 drams of powder, and had a bone-breaking recoil even though muzzle velocity was greatly reduced. Not surprisingly, the conversions were universally disliked.

The P/51 with its socket bayonet and 60 cartridges weighed about 17½lb, greater than the Brunswick or P/42 smooth-bore. This was much too heavy, as the goal had originally been to reduce the infantryman's burden.

The excessive calibre of the British Army rifle-musket was largely due to the insistence of the Duke of Wellington, who would not countenance any reduction. However, even before the Duke died in 1852, the ordnance authorities had decided to fix bore size by projectile weight rather than calibre. As the standard musket ball weighed 480–485 grains, this was adopted for the new expanding bullet and, by working backward, the Small Arms Committee arrived at a calibre of ·577.

As early as January 1851, George Lovell was instructed to make two ·530-calibre small-bore Minié rifles to fire 480-grain projectiles. Attempts were then made to involve leading gunmakers in the project, James Wilkinson, Westley Richards, Charles Lancaster, James Purdey and William Greener all agreeing to supply guns for trial. The *Report of Experiments with Small Arms carried out at the Royal Manufactory, Enfield, 1852* was a voluminous document; the testers had been nothing if not thorough. As a by-product of the trials, a cylindro-conoidal bullet was developed for the P/51 to replace the older and less accurate conoidal pattern.

The most promising submission had been Lancaster's rifle, which had an oval bore. However, problems had arisen from its two-piece bullet, which sometimes trapped large enough pieces of cartridge paper in the joint to ruin accuracy. A new bullet had been developed to eliminate the trouble, but the trials had ended before it could be vindicated.

As none of the trials rifles had been acceptable, the Small Arms Committee drew up a specification. The new rifle musket was to weigh 9lb 3oz with its bayonet; have a 39in ·577-calibre barrel weighing 4lb 6oz, rifled with three grooves making one turn in 78in; incorporate a swivel-lock‡; and utilize three barrel bands, rather than traditional flat keys. The new socket bayonet was to have a locking ring, but a decision on the design of the sights was deferred. Some members of the committee considered that a simple standing block, with auxiliary leaves for 200 and 300 yards, would suffice; others wished to give Westley Richards' 800-yard elevating sight an extended trial.

Experimental Enfield-made ·577 rifle-muskets were first shot in December 1852, with special self-expanding bullets developed by Richard Pritchett from a prototype submitted by William Metford. The Metford-Pritchett bullet lacked a base plug, a carefully shaped cavity ensuring that the projectile expanded into the rifling. Shooting proved to be very good, all but one of twenty shots hitting a 12ft-square target at 800 yards. Consequently, 1,000 guns were ordered on 17 January 1853, details of sights and rifling still being omitted. Finally, trials resolved in favour of Lancaster's back sight, which combined a stepped sight bed (for ranges up to 400 yards) with a slider-and-leaf for longer distances.

The problem of rifling still exercised the committee, as Lancaster's oval-bore rifle-musket was still comprehensively outshooting the Government prototypes. In midsummer 1853, for example, a Lancaster had placed almost all its shots inside an 18in circle at 200 yards; at 500 yards, the group measured a mere 48in, while one in four shots from the Enfield had missed the

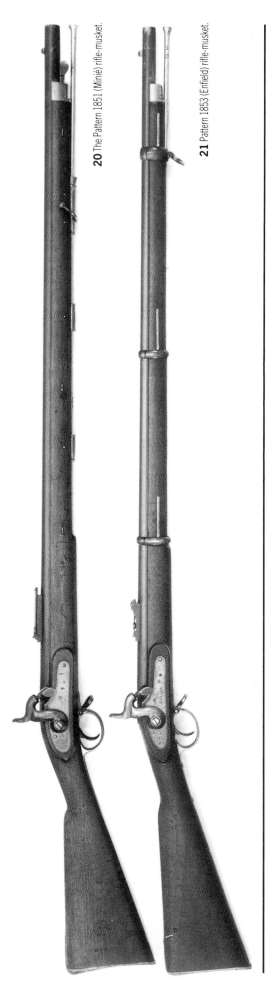

20 The Pattern 1851 (Minié) rifle-musket.

21 Pattern 1853 (Enfield) rifle-musket.

6ft-square target entirely. Trials dragged on, largely owing to fears that mass production would lead to declining quality. The simplicity of Lancaster's rifling was deceptive, as the bore was choked and the spiral increased progressively towards the muzzle.

Twenty thousand P/53 guns were ordered early in August 1853, but the rifling specification was still absent. Later the same month, the Lancaster rifle-musket defeated an oval-bore gun emanating from Enfield by placing all twenty shots inside a 26in circle at 300 yards. During a hundred-round trial at the same distance, the Lancaster hit the standard 6ft-square target 99 times compared with the Enfield's miserable 32.

Unfortunately for Lancaster, his rifles began to exhibit a tendency for the bullet to strip from the rifling. The cause could not be determined, but the problems were severe enough for the committee to recommend conventional three-groove Enfield rifling for the service weapon. To this day, no rational explanation has been put forward to explain the Lancaster's affliction, which did not affect the later oval-bore Sappers & Miners Carbine.

By the Spring of 1854, the rifle-musket manufacturing pattern had been settled. Projectile weight had increased to nearer 490 grains, owing to the use of compressing machinery, and the charge had been adjusted from 2¼ to 2½ drams. But manufacture was not to be as straightforward as the Board of Ordnance had hoped.

The 20,000 guns ordered from the gun trade in Birmingham in October 1853 were to be assembled ('set up' in British ordnance parlance) by four principal contractors, Hollis & Sheath, Swinburn & Son, Tipping & Lawden and Thomas Turner. However, the components were supplied by a legion of sub-contractors (see TECHNOLOGY, EMPIRE AND THE RIFLE-MUSKET below) and it was typical of the whole inefficient process that those responsible for the back sights − the four assemblers − should have failed to honour their obligations.

By the time the first P/53 rifle-muskets were accepted into store, the Crimean War was well underway. The new guns were badly needed to supplement supplies of the P/51 and replace ineffectual P/42 smooth-bore muskets that had been pressed into front-line service. Consequently, in addition to guns ordered in London and Birmingham, contracts were placed abroad − action only ever taken by the Board of Ordnance in dire emergency. Twenty thousand P/53 rifle-muskets were ordered in Liége on 31 October 1854; 25,000 from Robbins & Lawrence of Windsor, Vermont, USA, on 12 February 1855; and 20,000 in Saint-Étienne on 6 August 1855. The Belgian and French orders were successfully completed, if tardily, but Robbins & Lawrence soon went into liquidation. Only about 16,000 Enfields were made in the USA, 10,400 by Robbins & Lawrence and 5,600 by the Union Arms Company, before the contracts were cancelled.

Deliveries of the P/53, which had amounted to about 30,000 by the end of April 1855, peaked only after the Crimean War had ended; 211,288 were accepted from London and Birmingham alone between 31 May 1856 and 31 March 1858. The reliance traditionally placed on private contractors had clearly failed. The immediate solution was to accelerate production at Enfield, where 323,035 P/53 rifle-muskets were made between 1 April 1858 and 31 March 1864.

The P/53 was a conventional weapon, with a side-action lock and an elegant walnut stock. Measuring about 55in overall, with a 39in barrel rifled with three grooves making a turn in 78in, the P/53 originally weighed about 8lb 8oz.* For the first time in British service, the browned barrel was retained by bands instead of transverse keys. Swivels lay on the foremost or nose band, and through the front of the trigger guard. The earliest guns had their bands retained by screws, and the hammer-tip had a perceptible curl. In the Crimea, however, problems were encountered with the bands — which loosened during rapid fire or when the stock shrank — and the hammer proved too fragile. Spring-retained bands were substituted after the first orders had been fulfilled, but were then themselves superseded by the streamlined Baddeley Band in 1861. The hammer was reinforced, losing its curled tip, and changes to the heat treatment cured breakages.

So many changes were made to the basic P/53 that the 'Rifle Musquet Improved Pattern 1853' was sealed in December 1855. There were four differing nipples, several cleaning rods, differing sights, and changes to the butt. The most important are noted in the relevant section (see RIFLES).

The P/53 proved to be very successful, once the teething troubles had been overcome, and is regarded as one of the best (if not <u>the</u> best) of its type. Though only the guns made by the Royal Manufactory at Enfield and the London Armoury Company were regarded as interchangeable — both establishments were mechanized — virtually every gun accepted by the ordnance viewers displayed impeccable finish. The fit of wood to metal was also usually exemplary, guns made in the USA by Robbins & Lawrence being the poorest.

The P/53 laid the basis for four patterns of short rifle, three artillery carbines, three cavalry carbines, and a series of ·656 smooth-bores for India Service. As many of these were later converted to Snider-system breech-loaders, details will be found later in the book. The most fascinating of these cap-locks was the Pattern 1855 Sappers & Miners Carbine which, though

22 BELOW

Foot Guards on their return from the Crimea. A 'Sketch from Aldershot', engraved by Landells, published in the *Illustrated London News* in July 1856. The delineation of the rifle-muskets, presumably P/51 Minié if the lack of barrel bands can be trusted, leaves much to be desired. Courtesy of Philip J. Haythornthwaite.

23 BELOW RIGHT

'Metropolitan Rifle Corps Assembled in Hyde Park', a coloured lithograph published in the *Illustrated London News* in October 1860. The six men in the foreground represent (from left to right) the Working Men's College Rifle Corps, the South Middlesex Rifle Volunteers, the South Kensington Rifle Volunteers, the ordinary and kilted companies of the London Scottish Rifle Volunteers, and St George's Rifle Volunteers. In view of the acceptable accuracy with which the rifle-musket held by the kilted London Scottish rifleman is depicted, attention must be paid to the gun held by the Working Men's College Rifle Corpsman. Unusually, it is drawn with a back-action lock. Courtesy of Philip J. Haythornthwaite.

GUARDS RETURNED FROM THE CRIMEA.—A SKETCH FROM ALDERSHOTT.

externally similar to the short rifles, featured Lancaster's oval bore. Interestingly, the P/55 had a reputation for exemplary accuracy; it was never prone to the stripping that had caused Lancaster's rifling to fail against the three-groove Enfield type in 1853–4.

Great strides being made in machine-tool design and mass-production techniques permitted the expanding bullet to be issued to British line infantry in time for the Crimean War (1853–6). Typified by the British P/53 Enfield and US M1855 Springfield, the rifle-musket had become widespread by the commencement of the American Civil War in 1861.

This was largely due to the establishment of efficient government-owned smallarms factories, which, in Britain at least, broke much of the reliance that had traditionally been vested in the gun trade. The Royal Small Arms Factory at Enfield was mechanized in the mid 1850s to solve problems caused by this reliance. Such a shambles had been created during the Crimean War that the government, exasperated and forced to place contracts abroad, looked to a more permanent solution.

Typical of the fragmentation of British gunmaking was an order for 20,000 P/53 rifle-muskets placed with the Birmingham Trade on 6 October 1853. The guns were assembled, or 'set up', by only four companies: Hollis & Sheath, C.P. Swinburn & Son, Tipping & Lawden and Thomas Turner. However, the barrels were made by Beasley & Farmer, John Clive, William Millward, Ezra Millward, William Deakin & Sons, Henry Clive, and Joseph Turner & Son.

Locks came from William Corbett, John Duce, Joseph Brazier & Son, J. & E. Partridge, Samuel Sanders, James Francis, and R. & W. Aston. The rammers were made by James Francis, T. & C. Gilbert and R. & W. Aston. And as if this was not enough, the barrel bands were made by R. & W. Aston, while bayonets came from no fewer than seven contractors: Aston, S. Hill & Sons, Heighington & Lawrence, Geo. Salter & Co., G.W. & E. Roe, J. Roe & Son and William Deakin & Sons.

Minor parts have always been made by specialist sub-contractors. As far as the October P/53 order was concerned, nails, wood screws and triggers came from R. & W. Aston and James Grice, while the nipples were all made by J.B. Palmer. But the involvement of so many agencies courted disaster.

Even with this comparatively small order, the back-sight makers – ironically, the four assemblers – all defaulted on their obligations. Four others, including two new sub-contractors, were hastily recruited to make good the shortages. It was hardly surprising that deliveries were almost always late. When another order was placed in Birmingham in December 1854, for 27,400 P/53 rifle-muskets, no fewer than fourteen *new* assemblers were recruited.

Owing to the fitting necessary to ensure that parts made by largely by hand assembled into effectual guns, no Birmingham-made Enfield was classed as 'Interchangeable': the accolade was reserved exclusively for those made at Enfield or by the London Small Arms Company.

Increasing industrialization was matched by improvements in transport. Suddenly, politicians with expansionist goals could not only acquire sufficient guns to equip their growing armies, but also transport them virtually anywhere. With the USA seeking insularity, then immolating itself in the Civil War, the way was open for the leading European powers to seize what territory they could. Spain and Portugal were spent, great colonializers though they had been three centuries previously; the Italian states still bickered and jostled; united Germany had yet to be created. With the power and ambition of the Habsburgs confined to central Europe, only France and Britain had the will to

TECHNOLOGY, EMPIRE AND THE RIFLE-MUSKET

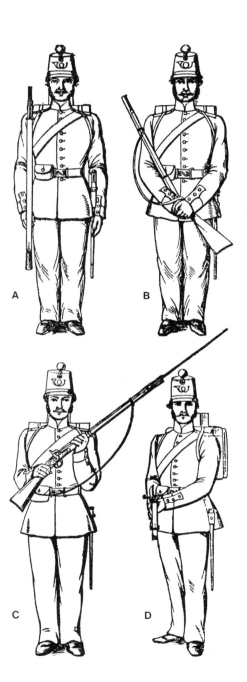

24 ABOVE

Illustrations from the British *Field Evolutions for Infantry*: **A** 'The Shoulder', **B** 'The Support', **C** 'The Port' and **D** 'The Charge'. Though the publication dates from 1867, it shows P/53 Enfield rifle-muskets. The Snider, though adopted approximately contemporaneously, had not reached service status.

‡Cattle were sacred to Hindus; pigs were anathema to Muslims. The suggestion that the cartridges could be loaded and fired without tearing them open is mistaken – the P/53 bullet was packed with its point towards the powder.

Gun performance, 1850-70

The trials undertaken with prototypes in the early 1850s often revealed impressive accuracy. This had been particularly true of the Lancaster oval-bore guns.

Tests undertaken in 1857 with a standard British P/53 obtained groups with diameters of 120in (FoM 2·24ft) at 500 yards, 220in (FoM 4·11ft) at 800 yards and 434in (FoM 8·04ft) at 1,100 yards. And though the P/53 was among the best of the weapons of its type, the small-bore cap-locks were capable of even finer shooting: the ·451-calibre Whitworth, with its special mechanically fitting projectile, recorded groups measuring 18·5in (FoM 4·1in) at 500 yards and 250in (FoM 4·62ft) at 1,400 yards – where the P/53 shot so wildly that results could not be recorded. At 100 yards, the Whitworth bullet penetrated 33 half-inch elm planks compared with only twelve for the P/53.

Unfortunately, the hexagonal bore was notoriously difficult to keep clear of propellant fouling; in a fouled state, the Whitworth's shooting deteriorated markedly and excessive force was needed to ram the projectile down the bore.

Owing to the many methods of assessing accuracy, it is difficult to express the accuracy potential of a P/53 rifle-musket in absolute terms. However, based on the results of trials undertaken in Britain, the chance of obtaining an incapacitating hit on a single man may be reckoned as thirteen per cent at 500 yards, seven per cent at 800 yards and four per cent at 1,100 yards. There was practically no chance of hitting such a target with a smooth-bore musket at more than 150 yards.

What is not so widely known is that the muzzle velocity of a rifle-musket was substantially less than the smooth-bores it replaced. In trials undertaken in the USA in the late 1850s, the then-new ·58-calibre M1855 – very similar to the P/53 Enfield – recorded 1,005fs⁻¹, compared with 954fs⁻¹ for a M1842 rifled musket firing a Minié bullet and 1,500fs⁻¹ for the old M1822 flintlock musket. The musket was most wasteful of powder, requiring 130 grains compared with only sixty for the M1855, and its high initial velocity was rapidly dissipated by poor ballistics. Musket balls had lost half their initial velocity by the time they reached 200 yards, comparable distances for the rifled M1842 and M1855 being about 930–950 yards. By this point the Minié projectiles were travelling more than twice as fast as the musket balls, and the stability owing to their rate-of-spin enhanced accuracy beyond comparison.

expand. Britain, politically more stable and with a head start in Africa and India, made the most of it.

Ironically, the Enfield rifle-musket – such an advance on antique muzzle-loaders – helped create a near-disaster. British troops in India were outnumbered by indigenous forces swearing allegiance to Queen Victoria. But nineteenth-century India was still a mixture of British possessions and princely states; peace sometimes hang by a thread. In 1857, three cavalry regiments mutinied in Meerut, slaughtering not only their European officers but also the officers' wives and children. What had begun as a local dispute soon spread across the sub-continent.

Largely confined north of a line drawn from Karachi in the west to Calcutta in the east, the discontent had several roots: resentment among Indian nobility, increasingly constricted by British administrators; indigenous troops dissatisfied with pay and conditions; and, at the lowest levels, concern that the new Enfield paper cartridge (which was usually torn open with the teeth before being rammed down the muzzle) contained pig and cow fat in its tallow coating.‡ It is probable that no-one in the Anglo-Indian establishment knew what the coating contained, but the religious taboos of Muslims and Hindus alike had been threatened at a stroke. Ironically, as the flash of the cap could penetrate the paper case, the cartridge could have been used simply by ramming it home – had not the ball been reversed.

The mutiny was suppressed by 1859, often with brutality and not before the siege of the Residency in Lucknow had passed into British military folklore. Once the dust had settled, the British were panicked into withdrawing rifled firearms from native units in favour of ·656 smooth-bore Enfields. Only the Sikhs were trusted sufficiently to receive rifles in the immediate post-Mutiny era, but had to make do first with Brunswicks drawn from store. When supplies ran short, a 'new pattern' Brunswick with a standard P/53 lock was sealed in 1864.

The widespread issue of rifle-muskets throughout Europe, as well as in the USA, should have distanced battle tactics from stereotyped geometry. Yet the major confrontations of the Crimean War, the opening stages of the US Civil War and even the Seven Weeks War (at least from the Austrian viewpoint) were fought in the classical manner.

The Enfield and its equivalents were still handicapped by problems that had affected the muskets of the Napoleonic Wars – slow loading, and powder that generated immense clouds of smoke. However, they were better long-range killers, their margin of superiority over conventional smooth-bores being tenfold. The rifled-musket and the expanding bullet challenged conventional military tactics, but had failed to convince senior commanders of the need to adapt. So, though the range of engagement increased perceptibly, lines and squares still slugged it out with squares and lines. Commanders simply shrugged aside the spiralling casualty rate as a natural consequence of war.

The distribution of new weapons throughout an entire standing army presented a difficult problem for most governments in the mid-nineteenth century. Great colonialists such as Britain had to find vast numbers of guns. There is a popular fallacy – particulaly widespread in Britain – that an industrial revolution occurred with such startling rapidity that cottage industries were transformed into mass-producers virtually overnight. But there were few industries in which the 'revolution' was anything other than accelerated progress, often spread over twenty years or more. The change from handwork to fully interchangeable machine-made parts took the British gunsmithing industry a hundred years.

Rates of change varied from country to country, depending on availability of capital and labour. The American firearms industry presents the best example of rapid growth, progressing from a backwoods base to satisfy the gargantuan needs of the Civil War within fifty years. In Britain, conversely, such a transition did not take place until the First World War: the gun trade in 1900 was still primitive. Large-scale manufacturing capability was restricted to a handful of agencies. The Royal Small Arms Factory at Enfield only began to mass-produce in the mid-1850s, using a large proportion of American-made machine tools; BSA was not founded until 1861; and companies such as Vickers, Sons & Maxim did not attain prominence until the end of the century.

Differences between American and British attitudes can be gauged by the reactions of BSA employees altering 20,000 Egyptian Remington rifles from rim- to centre-fire in the early 1870s. The men were incredulous when they realised that guns could be stripped and the parts piled indiscriminately, before being assembled at random with practically no handwork. Gunsmiths' 'crib boxes' were normally full of parts to juggle until one was found to fit.

Contemporary British workmanship was usually very good, but Britain was a small country with a comparatively large population; conversely, the USA had vast under-populated tracts and a shortage of skilled labour in all but some New England states. It is not entirely coincidental that the US gunmaking industry was confined to Connecticut, Massachussetts and New York State. Britain could afford labour-intensive production, but Americans had few options but to mechanize.

Enfields were very popular during the American Civil War, being sold in vast numbers to Federals and Confederates alike. The Federal government alone purchased 428,292 P/53 rifle-muskets and 8,034 P/58 Short Rifles, while many thousands more were bought for volunteer units. The Confederacy acquired 70,890 P/53 longarms and perhaps 10,000 short rifles from the London Armoury Company, regarded as the best arms issued south of the Mason-Dixon Line.

The P/58-type short rifle was very popular in the Confederacy, though less so in the north. Its sabre bayonet proved a boon to recruitment, but increased the clumsiness of the rifle in combat and was often relegated to the status of a sidearm.

25 RIGHT

The charge of the Foot Guards at the Battle of Inkerman, 5 November 1854, when 16,000 Anglo-French troops under Generals Lord Raglan and Pélissier prevented 42,000 Russians led by Prince Menshikov recapturing Sevastopol. The guns would have been P/51 Minié rifle-muskets. From a contemporary engraving. Courtesy of Philip J. Haythornthwaite.

THE FIRST BREECH-LOADER

26 RIGHT

An engraving of the breech-loading Ferguson rifle, from W.W. Greener's *The Gun and its Development* (1910). Note the multiple-leaf back sight and the rapid-pitch thread on the breech plug. It is only necessary to make a single turn of the trigger guard to expose the chamber; most previous guns of this class needed either several turns — which slowed loading appreciably — or, alternatively, a separate spanner.

If the American Civil War closed the brief heyday of the rifle-musket, it also testified to the efficacy of the breech-loading rifle and metallic-case cartridge. These vital advances in technology were not immediately recognized by military authorities, partly owing to conservatism but also because many guns chambered unique cartridges of widely differing calibre. But the lessons were clear to those who wished to heed them.

Rudiments of breech-loading can be seen in some of the earliest guns, in which separate cylindrical breech chambers were retained by a wedge. Ineffectual breech seals were a perpetual problem, however, and gas leaks were bad enough to delay the universal acceptance of breech-loading appreciably. Unsuccessful powder-and-ball repeaters were still appearing as late as 1840; early single-shot breech-loaders had better fortune.

The first rifle to achieve any notoriety in the British Army was designed by Patrick Ferguson, second son of James Ferguson of Pitfours.* A rotating trigger guard dropped a rapid-pitch threaded plug to gain access to the breech, whereupon a tight-fitting ball, wadding and a suitable powder charge could be inserted. The plug was then wound back to seal the breech. The Ferguson was well enough made to prevent excessive escape of gas at the breech, the minimal blowback being lost amongst priming smoke.

Its design was scarcely innovative; Ferguson claimed novelty only in the way in which his breech-plug was permanently retained in the gun, and in grooving the breech-plug screw to minimize the effects of propellant fouling. But the gun was less susceptible to damp than contemporary muskets, and underwent some spectacular public trials — often in the most adverse conditions† — before Major Ferguson and his men sailed for North America in 1777.

There were too few Ferguson rifles to revolutionize contemporary warfare. Badly wounded in a skirmish at Chadd's Ford, during the Battle of Brandywine (11 September 1777), Ferguson was sent back to Britain to convalesce and his picked riflemen became regular infantry. Still suffering from his wound — his right elbow had been shattered by a musket ball — the gallant officer returned to the fray in 1778.

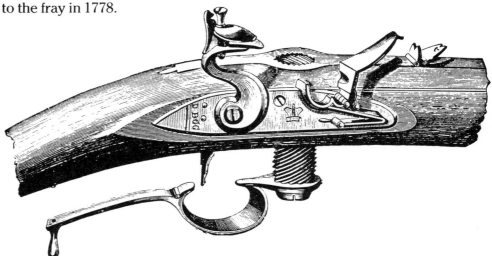

It is said that he had his breech-loaders taken out of store, and issued them to loyalist volunteers. Appointed Inspector-General of the Southern Provinces, he was killed while commanding Loyalist forces on King's Mountain, South Carolina, on 7 October 1780, before anything of value could be achieved.‡

The impact of his rifle on the British Army had been minimal, awaiting modern historians to restore its reputation. Only one survivor of the original hundred-plus Ferguson breech-loaders has been identified, currently in the Morristown National Park Museum; serial number 2, it is ·68-calibre, measures

49in overall and has a 34in eight-groove barrel. The greatest drawbacks of the Ferguson breech were that it weakened the stock alongside the breech plug, and could not handle standard musket cartridges.

British efforts subsequently centred on an adaptation of the Crespi breech-loader, extensively but unsuccessfully tested by the Austrian army in 1770–9. Made by Durs Egg with Hennem's Screwless Lock, an assortment of these chamber-loaders was tested in 1784–8. The Board of Ordnance then expressed concern that the breech would leak as badly as the Austrian prototypes had done when the chamber mouths began to wear, and the project was abandoned. Egg made a rifle, c.1788, in which removal of a stout pin set an automatic safety and allowed a chamber to be withdrawn backwards to receive powder and ball. James Wilkes' submission in 1801, based on the Baker flintlock rifle but hardly innovative, had a detachable plug screwed into the left side of the breech; and Hulme's rifle of 1807 had a vertical disc-type breech-block rotated by a lever on the left side of the barrel.

Predictably, nothing came of these early attempts. In Prussia, however, Johann Niklaus Dreyse made the first of his needle-fire pistols in the mid 1820s and a promising breech-loading needle gun was submitted to the Prussian War Ministry in 1836. The receiver supported a simple tubular bolt containing the needle, its drive spring and a locking catch; it was necessary only to press down on the locking catch and then pull catch and needle backward together until they locked. The operating handle was then turned to the left through about 30°, disengaging its massive base from the bridge of the body, and the entire bolt could be drawn rearward to expose the chamber. A cartridge was pushed into the chamber with the thumb, the bolt was closed and rotated to the right to lock the action. The closing stroke cocked the needle and the gun was ready to fire.

Prussia formally adopted the Dreyse needle-rifle (Zündnadelgewehr) on 4 December 1840, attempts to keep it secret finally being abandoned in 1855. They had never been worthwhile, as guns had been sent to Britain in 1849 and copies were made at Enfield in the early 1850s. High rate of fire and acceptable accuracy had been offset by operating problems when the mechanism became hot or foul, whereupon the Board of Ordnance had abandoned the Dreyse in favour of the P/51 Minié.

The principal problem afflicting the early needle guns was gas leakage, the periphery of the bolt-head and the mouth of the chamber rarely being concentric; Prussia was not among the leading industrial powers in 1850.

The successful development of the Enfield rifle-musket highlighted that the cavalry still carried the Victoria Carbine, accurately characterized as useless. Jenks' Carbine had been tested by the Board of Ordnance in 1841, but the guns had been made in Liége and failed to duplicate the impressive performances of the American pattern. It is probable that the standards of manufacture were inferior, as the cavalrymen to whom they were issued were singularly unimpressed.* Regulation patterns are covered in Part Two.

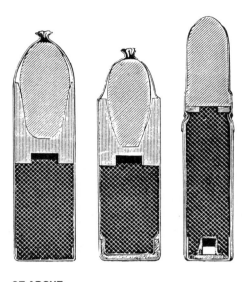

27 ABOVE
Three needle-rifle cartridges, from Schott's *Grundriss der Waffenlehre* (1876). **A** is an original 1855-pattern Prussian Zündnadel-Patrone; **B** is the improved version, for the Beck Transformation of 1869-70; and **C** is a French Mle.66 Chassepot. Note the vulnerable position of the Chassepot primer, and the poor ballistic shape of the Dreyse projectiles compared with Minié expanding bullets.

* The Jenks carbine, in its American-made form, was capable of outstanding performances. Typical of these was an endurance trial at Fort Adams in 1844, when one gun fired 14,813 shots – with virtually no trouble – until the nipple finally split. The Jenks was generally regarded as effectual, gas-tight, simple and compact; it is surprising, therefore, that the British should have formed such a low opinion of the design.

THE FIRST MACHINE-GUNS

The advent of the rifle-musket was accompanied by an appreciable increase in hitting power at long range. As this was still achieved at the expense of considerable numbers of men, inventors' thoughts returned to replacing these men in a single 'battery gun'. Apart from fascinating eccentricities such as the British Perkins Steam Gun of 1843, awesome but particularly unpractical, the first of the modern volley-guns was the Mitrailleuse. Credit for the re-discovery of the ancient ribauldequin is generally given to a Belgian artilleryman named Fafschamps, but his gun was refined for production by Josef Montigny and Louis Christophe; made in Montigny's factory in Fontaine l'Évêque, near Liége, the 37-barrel Montigny Mitrailleuse was extensively employed in Belgian strongpoints.

However, excepting the secrecy-obsessed French, few nineteenth-century Europeans regarded these multi-shot weapons with enthusiasm. When the American Civil War began, however, the attitudes of the field commanders differed greatly.

This was largely due to the employment of volunteers commanded by politicans and leaders of commerce instead of career soldiers. And as these 'civilian' generals were often prepared to listen to gimcrack schemes, so inventors were willing to propose them. Results included the Union Repeating Gun, the Billingshurst & Requa Battery Gun (the first to use self-contained metallic cartridges) and Ripley's Battery Gun.

28 BELOW

The French Canon à Balles de Reyffe, Mle.66, otherwise known as the 'Mitrailleuse'. The gun had 25 13mm-calibre barrels, the detachable loading block being shown in the detail views.

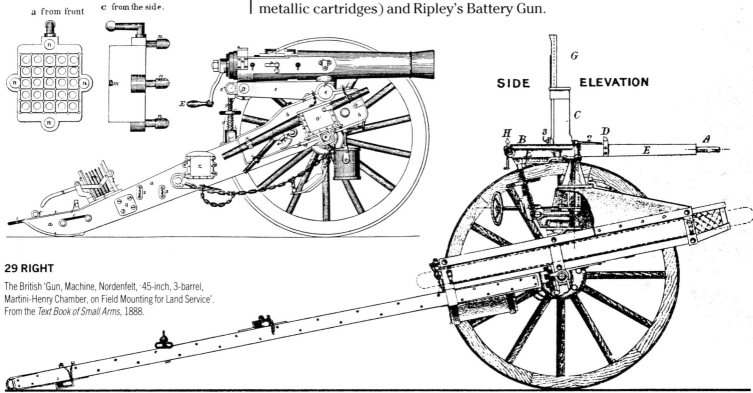

29 RIGHT

The British 'Gun, Machine, Nordenfelt, ·45-inch, 3-barrel, Martini-Henry Chamber, on Field Mounting for Land Service'. From the *Text Book of Small Arms*, 1888.

The Gatling Gun, patented in the USA in November 1862, fired standard ·58-calibre combustible cartridges inserted in integrally-capped carriers. It fired six times for each turn of the barrel cluster, each barrel firing when it reached a pre-determined position. The first Gatlings leaked gas severely, and the method of wedging the cartridge-carriers into the breech made the crank handle difficult to turn. Yet the weapon's potential was clear.

By the middle of the war, the Gatling had been adapted to handle ·58-calibre copper-case cartridges, still carried in separate cylindrical inserts. Unfortunately, accuracy remained poor and the guns were esteemed by neither the US Ordnance Department in general nor the notoriously conservative Chief of Ordnance, James W. 'Old Fogey' Ripley, in particular.

By 1870, the quality of metal-case cartridges had improved substantially and successful trials had been undertaken in many countries. Gatling's fortune was assured: guns had been sold to France, Prussia and Japan, and a production licence had been granted to Sir W.G. Armstrong & Co. Ltd.

A solitary Colt-made Gatling Gun was submitted to the War Office as early as February 1867. Tested against a 9pr field-gun, it was rejected as 'unsuited for service'. In August 1868, however, the British observer at official trials of

On the following day [3 January 1874] a little practice with the Gatling was held for the benefit of the Ashanti envoys, Captain Rait firing a drum of ammunition up the stream where the accuracy and force with which the bullets struck the water, at a range of some 500 yards, was shown by the fountain of spray that was thrown up . . . At one o'clock in the morning of the 5th, we were awakened by a shot fired in the hut where the Ashantis were under guard, and on visiting the hut it was found that one of the scouts had put the muzzle of his gun to his throat . . . At first the other messengers expressed ignorance as to the cause of the act, but a court of enquiry was held on the 5th and . . . one of the Ashantis said that the dead man . . . had expressed his opinion that all the scouts were going to be killed . . . and it appeared that they had all been more or less surprised and astonished at the firing of the Gatling.

Eye-witness report by Captain Henry Brackenbury RA, published in the *Journal of the Royal United Services Institution*, 1874.

30 RIGHT

A Model 1874 Gatling Gun on its field carriage. These guns incorporated improvements in the basic action, patented by Richard Gatling in April 1872 (US Patent 125,563). They fed from Broadwell drum magazines on top of the breech, the pintle mount being visible in the engraving. From Wahl & Toppel, *The Gatling Gun*.

the Belgian Montigny Mitrailleuse — Major G.V. Fosbery VC — reported most favourably. A committee was formed to test the Gatling and the Mitrailleuse in 1869.

Trials were undertaken at Shoeburyness in the summer of 1870, pitting ·42, ·65 and 1-inch Gatlings against breech- and muzzle-loading field-guns, the Montigny Mitrailleuse and a selection of infantry rifles. Though the Gatling and Mitrailleuse performed similarly on static targets, the former was easier to use. At 300 yards, for example, the Gatling had obtained 369 hits out of 616 shots in two minutes, compared with 171 out of only 185 for the Mitrailleuse. At 1,400 yards the figures had been 104 from 545 and 68 from 296 respectively. The Mitrailleuse proved more accurate, but the Gatling was better at sweeping a designated area.

A realistic trial then pitted each gun against individual man-size dummies, representing a column 'retiring in loose order'. The Gatling scored twice as many hits as the Mitrailleuse at 300 yards; at 950 yards, it obtained 177 hits compared with only nine. The clumsiness of the Belgian gun had finally been its undoing.

Not surprisingly, on 28 October 1870, the committee recommended adopting the Gatling for field and ship-board use. Forty ·45 and ·65-calibre guns were ordered from Armstrong in January 1872. Within two years, all had been delivered. Twelve were initially retained at Woolwich, the remainder being given to the Royal Navy. With a single exception, these guns — and all Gatlings used in Britain — chambered solid-drawn cartridge cases. Consequently, the popular opinion that British Gatlings jammed because they chambered rolled-case Martini-Henry cartridges is quite mistaken.

'The Naval Brigade with Gatling & Gardner Guns hard at it at the battle of Teb' – an on-the-spot sketch by the artist/correspondent Melton Prior for *The Graphic*, 1 March 1884. Visible are a ten-barrel Gatling and a five-barrel Gardner, borrowed for the campaign from the navy.

* In some parts of Africa, well into the twentieth century, even the Maxim was known as a 'Gatling Gun'.

31 LEFT

A stirring, but somewhat misleading view of the Battle of Majuba (27 February 1881), a disastrous defeat in the First South African War in which 500 Boers under General Petrus Joubert dislodged 647 Britons commanded by General Sir George Colley from a strong hilltop position. British loses were 223 dead and wounded, plus about fifty prisoners; the Boers lost little more than twenty men. Engraved for the *Illustrated London News* in May 1881, from a painting by R. Caton Woodville, it is remarkable for one major mistake: the Martini-Henry rifle being carried by the sailor (centre) has the cutlass bayonet on the wrong side of the barrel. Courtesy of Philip J. Haythornthwaite.

The British authorities subsequently agonized over their choice of machine-gun, testing Nordenfelt and Gardner guns against each other until the automatic Maxim rendered manually-operated guns obsolete in the late 1880s. However, though the Gatling was comparatively rapidly superseded, it had left a lasting impression on many native armies; the impact was so strong, indeed, that virtually all manually-actuated guns were 'Gatlings' to the uninitiated.* The machine-gun had become synonymous with imperial expansion.

The first use of the Gatling was during the Asante War of 1873–4, when a force despatched under the command of Sir Garnet Wolseley included two ·45 Armstrong-made Gatlings. Their wheeled carriages soon proved unsuited to rough tracks; one gun was adapted to an improvised (and very unsteady) narrow-track carriage, but the other was simply left behind at the base camp. The dreadful effects of even the earliest machine-gun on massed ranks at close range had yet to be witnessed, as the 'portable' Gatling Gun, left guarding a strategically important bridge, took no further part in the Asante War.

Gatlings accompanied Lord Chelmsford in his campaign to subdue Cetshwayo's Zulus in 1879. The war – brief, but very bloody and backed by the flimsiest pretexts – was chiefly remarkable for a series of battles fought by Europeans with breech-loading rifles, rockets, artillery and a few machine-guns against a disciplined and well-trained native army armed with little other than spears.

The results were not always predictable. Poor tactics, bad leadership and ineffectual ammunition supply led to the disaster of Isandhlwana (22 January 1879), where much of the first battalion of the 24th (2nd Warwickshire) Regiment of Foot was annihilated; and then, later the same day, when careful attention to detail allowed the a single company of the second battalion of the 24th to defend Rorke's Drift against Zulus outnumbering them thirty to one. After the battles of Kambula and Gingindhlovu, the Zulu impis were finally destroyed at the Battle of Ulundi (4 July 1879).

Though the effectiveness of the Gatlings was praised in the popular press, Chelmsford's admiration was more grudging. Writing in the *Journal of the Royal United Services Institution* in 1885, he noted that:

Two Gatling Guns accompanied the column, and at the battle of Ginginhlovo [sic] did considerable execution amongst the Zulus at the opening of their attack, which commenced on the north side of our position. The Zulus very soon, however, worked around to the west and south of our laager, and the Gatlings were not in action . . . for any length of time.

At Ulundi we also had two Gatlings in the centre of the front face of our square. They jammed several times in the action, but when in work proved a very valuable addition to the strength of our defence on that flank. Machine-guns are, I consider, most valuable weapons for expeditions such as that which we had to undertake in Zululand, where the odds against us must necessarily be great, and where it is necessary to leave small detachments in charge of posts along the lines of communications . . . If a machine gun can be invented that may safely be entrusted to infantry soldiers to work, and could be fired very much as one grinds an organ, I am satisfied of its great value. They should, however, be considered as essentially an infantry weapon . . .

At a time when the machine-gun was considered the prerogative of the artillery, encumbered by wheeled carriages, limbers and ammunition carts, Chelmsford was perceptive enought to see that its greatest value lay with the infantry.

Hand-operated machine-guns were prominent in several of the campaigns undertaken by the British Army in Africa in the late nineteenth century, though their contributions were often over-stated by the Press. At the battle of Tel-el-Kebir, fought between the British and Egyptian rebels on 12/13 September 1882, there were six Gatlings — as usual, borrowed from the navy. The *Army and Navy Gazette* reported:

The naval machine gun battery . . . reached the position assigned to it in the English lines on September 10th, and, on Tuesday, September 12th, received orders to advance. They came within easy range of the Tel-el-Kebir earthworks, and observed guns in front, guns to the right, guns to the left, and a living line of fire above them. Nothing daunted, the order, 'action front', was given . . . Round whisked the Gatlings, r-r-r-r-r-rum! r-r-r-r-r-rum! r-r-r-r-r-rum! That hellish noise the soldier so much detests in action, not for what it has done, so much as what it could do, rattled out . . . The parapets are swept. The embrasures are literally plugged with bullets. The flashes cease to come from them. With a cheer the blue jackets double over the dam, and dash over the parapet, only just in time to find their enemy in full retreat . . . The trenches were full of dead.

It was rare that machine-guns were employed to good effect against the British Army in this period. Even though Gatlings were recovered from Mahdist batteries after the Battle of El Teb, where the British had made good practice with Gatling and Gardner guns, there is no evidence that the Mahdists understood them. It became fashionable to regard with amusement the glorious futility with which Africans, particularly, threw themselves against Gatlings and then even the Maxim. No European army, observers reasoned, would be so stupid. The dangerous myth arose that machine-guns were fit only for colonial use, or in strongpoints. Incidents in the Russo-Japanese War clearly signposted the future, but few military minds grasped them. Many high-ranking officers — Buller and Haig amongst them — opined that cavalry would always overcome mere gunners. Unfortunately for the 'Cavalry School', the First World War showed how rare were cavalrymen who would press forward an attack against a well-sited machine-gun with plenty of ammunition. Technology had won in the end.

The Battle of Ulundi, fought on 4 July 1879 during the Zulu War, typified the average Briton's view of the British Army.

Chelmsford's army was advancing in a meticulously described hollow square, bands playing, colours flying, with the steady precision of parade-ground ceremonial. The imperial infantry, forming the sides of the rectangle, marched in sections of four, the front and rear wall deployed in extended line. In the leading wall were the 90th Foot, the Cameronians, the 94th, in the rear the 13th Foot, Somerset [Light Infantry], and 58th, on the right the 80th South Staffordshires, on the left a residue of the 94th and the 21st. In line with the walls trundled Gatlings.

33, 34 LEFT

A Vickers, Sons & Maxim machine-gun is seen here on a one-horse 'galloper' carriage. Probably dating from about 1900, these pictures show clearly why lofty shielded mounts were vulnerable to fire from Boer 1pr pom-poms during the South African War. Note that the gun can be detached from its mount and fitted to a pedestal on the limber. Note also the curiosity of the spectators in the first picture: two peer over the wall to the left, and two more observe from windows! By courtesy of Vickers Ltd.

THE BRITISH ARMY, 1870–90

35 ABOVE
Grenadier Guards in action during the Second South African War, 1900. Engraved after a painting by R. Caton Woodville. Note the Lee-Metford or Mk I Lee-Enfield rifles, which are surprisingly accurately observed – even though the rifle fired by the soldier kneeling (right) appears to lack a cocking piece. By courtesy of Philip Haythornthwaite.

†Most of the Anglo-Egyptian forces engaged at El Obeid, fought on 1–4 November 1883, carried 11mm Egyptian Remingtons. The defeat was largely due to an effectual encirclement by the Mahdists and poor tactics employed by Colonel William Hicks ('Hicks Pasha'). The nominal strength of the Anglo-Egyptians was some 5,000 Egyptian and 6,000 Sudanese troops, plus nine European officers and a handful of NCOs. Owing to mass desertion, the battle was really no more than a series of skirmishes and a final stand by something less than a thousand men. Only one European lived to tell the tale.

Within the square . . . jogged the 17th Lancers and Dragoon Guards . . . A low sun, glancing on enclosing ranks of scarlet infantry, the pennons of the Lancers in blue uniforms lapelled with white, the great standards inscribed in gold, glinted on bayonets, cannon-brass and blaring musical instruments. The band of the 21st was playing 'The British Grenadiers' . . . Years afterwards, Zulu veterans would tell their children of the 'devil's diagram', the geometry that sealed their destruction . . . Alan Lloyd, *The Zulu War*

Ulundi was a slaughterhouse, military melodrama purveyed to Victorian drawing rooms by the war correspondents and artists accompanying Chelmsford's army. The Zulus had dashed against the might of an unbroken square, dropped in swathes by volleys from ·45 Martini-Henry rifles, shrapnel from the 7pr and 9pr cannon, and the deadly rattle of two ten-barrel ·45 Gatling guns fed from Broadwell drum magazines. None of Cetshwayo's men breached the British ranks. When the smoke of battle cleared, the British had lost ten killed and 97 wounded; but a thousand native dead lay around the square alone. The power of the Zulus and their king had been broken in a morning.

Annihilating natives, however bravely they fought, was generally such easy sport that reverses such as Isandhlwana and El Obeid, where an Anglo-Egyptian force of 4,000 was obliterated in a defile, were quickly forgotten.† That African campaigns had little relevance to encounters with fellow Europeans was still to be learned, and the dangerous myth that European troops — cavalry, in particular — would not be vulnerable to machine-gun fire persisted even after the advent of the Maxim.

Great improvements in the organization of the British Army had been begun by Edward Cardwell, Secretary of State for War in 1866–74. Commitment for life, which had hindered recruitment, had been replaced by voluntary short-term service proposed by the Enlistment Act of 1870; purchase of commissions was abolished from 1871; and considerable advances had been made in weaponry, with the introduction by 1880 of effectual metallic cartridges, breech-loading rifles, the first machine-guns and rocket batteries. Regrouping of infantry regiments on a two-battalion establishment (suggested in the Localization Scheme of 1872) occured in 1881, a year in which flogging was finally abolished.

Yet the work of Cardwell and his successors could not replace an entire system based around its patrician officer corps overnight; social rank ruled promotion disproportionately as late as 1914, 'Indian' officers were regarded as inferiors, and any men who saw a future in technology were the butts of ridicule.

There was no particular lack of devoted or intelligent officers, but their talents were all too often directed largely towards perpetuating the existing system. This they did with such success that the reformers rarely made easy headway. A succession of ultra-conservative commanders-in-chief — the Duke of Wellington, Lord Hardinge, the Duke of Cambridge — had successively jeopardized the Minié rifle, the breech-loader and the machine-gun. Their views were faithfully reflected in the upper echelons of the British Army, and it took a brave man to rail against their recommendations. It was small wonder that dreadful mistakes were made, or that lessons passed unheeded.

The Second South African War (1899–1902) was to be the first turning point though, unhappily, most of the reforms were temporary.

During the First South African War, in 1881, the British had been ignominiously beaten by Boer farmers at Majuba and Laing's Nek. These isolated skirmishes showed that ponderous European geometry was easily beaten in unfavourable terrain by innovation — mounted riflemen, for example, or entrenched infantry supported by well-sited artillery. Majuba and Laing's Nek had little effect in the upper echelons of British military hierarchy. Too many comprehensive victories against ill-led hordes had followed, and a gloriously bonehead charge by the 21st Lancers at Omdurman in 1898 captured public imagination better than the defensive role of the Maxims, even though the machine-guns had wreaked havoc.

Not until Roberts — an artilleryman, and an 'Indian Soldier' — took command in South Africa in 1900 did efficiency begin to displace bravado in the British Army: a lesson still improperly heeded in 1914.

Colonial campaigns in Africa and on the North West Frontier in India emphasized need of firearms suited to a wide range of climatic conditions. Guns that worked perfectly on home service often fell short of perfection abroad.

The Snider was comparatively trouble-free once the improved 'Bolted Action' had been adopted to prevent the breech flying open, as it was simple and rugged. Extraction was facilitated by the short straight-sided cartridge case, even though the gun had be inverted to eject spent cases.

The Martini-Henry encountered severe extraction troubles in heat, sand and dust. The culprit was found to be the necked ·45 rolled-case cartridge, which was far more likely to stick in the chamber than the straight ·577. The Boxer case was expressly designed to unwind momentarily on firing, sealing the breech against the escape of gas, but this strength proved to be a weakness. In hot climates, especially with sand in the chamber, the case did not contract quickly enough. When the firer attempted to open the Martini breech, the case was often still held tightly against the chamber wall. The extractor then tore through the case-rim or detached the case head entirely, leaving the remnants of the case jammed in place. These stoppages were difficult to rectify, with the result that guns were often out of action when most needed.

36 ABOVE

A man of the Queen's Own Cameron Highlanders from a print after F. Teller. Though somewhat slender in the wrist, the Martini-Henry rifle is surprisingly well observed. Courtesy of Philip J. Haythornthwaite.

TRIALS AND TRIBULATIONS

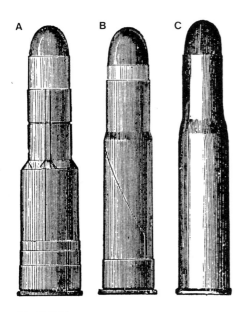

37 ABOVE

Alternative early metal-case cartridges, from W. Greener's *Modern Breech Loaders* (1871): **A** is the Government Boxer-type ·45 Martini-Henry with a wrapped and crimped brass case; **B** has a tin case, less complex than the Government Pattern but still 'built up'; and **C** is a solid-drawn brass case, which proved by far the most effectual.

*Also known as the Battle of Gubat, causing the mistaken identification of separate skirmishes.

†Under ideal conditions, the Soper, in particular, could be fired extremely rapidly; at Wimbledon in 1870, one gun was fired sixty times in two minutes and obtained 58 hits on a target 100 yards away. But whether the figure of forty rounds per minute for the Martini-Henry is realistic may be questioned. During government trials, the best 'unaimed' performance was twenty rounds in 48sec – 25 per minute. Greener's figures seem at least 30 per cent too high.

Extraction problems became public knowledge after the campaigns undertaken in the Sudan in 1884–5. At the battle of Abu Klea, fought on 17 January 1885, the Mahdists had managed to engage the British in fierce hand-to-hand combat. Superficially, the battle had been a British success; outnumbered about six to one, they had inflicted nearly a thousand casualties for the loss of 168 men. But the fact that the Mahdists had reached the British lines had been facilitated by lessening of rifle-fire. And this had been due to jamming.

It was estimated that one in three Martini-Henry rifles was out of action during this phase, and the problems recurred at the battle of Abu Kru* two days later. A trial in which 120 men were asked to fire ten rounds as rapidly as possible, ceasing fire after a jam, proved a disaster; more than half the soldiers had withdrawn after two rounds, and none fired all ten. A cartridge that had performed acceptably on home service, and even in the heat of battle at Rorke's Drift in 1879, was a liability in the Sudan.

Howard Blackmore, in his pioneering *British Military Firearms, 1650–1850*, records that firing ten shots from a flintlock musket in 3½ minutes was regarded as a reasonable performance. By the 1870s, rates had risen tremendously owing to the appearance of the metallic cartridge.

In *Modern Breech Loaders*, published in 1871, W.W. Greener suggested that the maximum fire-rate of the Soper rifle was an almost unbelievable fifty rounds per minute. He assessed the Martini-Henry at forty, followed by the Westley Richards and Henry rifles at 38.† The Remington he considered capable of thirty shots per minute; the Chassepot, nineteen; and the Snider, Braendlin-Albini and Berdan I eighteen apiece. The Dreyse needle-gun was rated at a mere nine.

These impressive rates of fire, of course, were usually obtained from demonstrations designed to impress the gullible; the firers were highly experienced, and the cartridges were lined up in readiness. Consequently, the figures had no particular relevance in battle, as the barrels rapidly heated to a point where they could not be touched.

High rates of fire have always troubled military planners, conscious that, unless discipline was maintained, ammunition would be wasted faster than it could be supplied. Minutely detailed, and often wildly conflicting studies were made by the champions and opponents of breech-loading. A typical deduction was that the Austrian, Saxon and Prussian armies involved during the Seven Weeks War in 1866 had used 1,854,000 rounds at an average of about 4½ per man. However, as this included non-combatants, the true usage was much higher. At the battle of Trautenau, men of Prussian Infanterie-Regiment Nr.43 expended 43 rounds per man, which was considered acceptable as the Prussian soldiers each carried sixty cartridges. At Königgrätz, however, the average expenditure in Prussian I.Armee – continuously engaged for more than four hours – had been 72 rounds per man, and ammunition had to be brought up to the line from the regimental reserves.

The planners' fears were not altogether groundless, as properly packed ammunition was very heavy and the ammunition wagons were too cumbersome to be brought up in support quickly. The 'Box, Ammunition, Small Arm, Rifle, 1,000 rounds (Mark XIII)', introduced in LoC 6153 of 10 May 1890 for Home Service, weighed about 670lb. A Gatling, Gardner or Nordenfelt machine-gun – or even a hundred riflemen firing comparatively leisurely – could expend a thousand rounds in a few minutes.

Replenishing ammunition was comparatively easy in European wars; battles were generally fought between approximately equal forces, often under traditional rules of engagement, and lines of supply were generally short. Colonial wars were different. European protagonists were often vastly outnumbered and hundreds of miles from their camps. To defeat huge, if ill-armed native armies, the Europeans relied on their superior firepower. But firepower depended on sufficient supplies of ammunition. Supplies of ammunition depended on effectual communications. Communications were almost always bad.

The British, the most committed colonizers in the last quarter of the nineteenth century, suffered some particularly humiliating reverses in Africa. It is an odd characteristic of the national psyche that such disasters have often been explained away as heroic irrelevancies. Very rarely were lessons learned anything but the hard way.

The battle of Isandhlwana (22 January 1879), during the Zulu War of 1879, was one of the worst defeats inflicted on the British Army in Africa. The cause is generally agreed to have been the decision of the commanding general, Lord Chelmsford, to depart on a questionable venture accompanied by half the force encamped at Isandhlwana. Chelmsford also failed to fortify the camp, and no clear chain of command was established before his foray. But the battle fought in his absence was close-run.

The men of the 24th (2nd Warwickshire) Regiment of Foot, armed with Martini-Henry rifles, held the Zulus at bay for some time. Then ammunition began to run low, particularly on the right wing where the Natal Native Horse had fewer supplies than the men of the 24th. Encouraged by the perceptible slackening of fire, the Zulus surged forward and hacked and stabbed their way through the defensive ring. As the right wing fell back, it exposed the men in the centre; the battle was effectively lost.‡

Few survived to relate the tale, but it was suggested that the quartermasters in charge of ammunition held for the 24th Foot had refused to supply the Natal Native Horse; and, in addition, that too few ammunition boxes had been opened in readiness for the battle. Men had hammered at the boxes with rifle butts; cursed them; tried to break the stout straps with their bayonets; but had not been able to get sufficient cartridges back to the line in time. There was too great a distance between wagons and hard-pressed soldiers attempting to hold an unnecessarily broad perimeter.

A European detachment, many times outnumbered but armed with the latest breech-loading rifles, had been bested by a spear-wielding native army. The expenditure of ammunition had been a key factor, though not, perhaps, the decisive one. Yet if better precautions had been taken, and if the supply wagons had been nearer the front line, Isandhlwana might have been simply a battle honour on the colours of the 24th Foot instead of a blot in the annals of Victorian military history.

The much lesser battle of Rorke's Drift, fought later that same evening, was largely responsible for the immediate reduction of Isandhlwana to the status of a minor mishap. The defenders of the hospital and mission station, 137 men, were mainly drawn from B Company, 2nd Battalion, 24th Regiment of Foot. Under the command of two subalterns – Chard of the Royal Engineers and Bromhead of 2/24th – ramparts of mealie bags were built, and ammunition boxes were broken open in readiness.

As there was also a cogent defensive plan, a handful of regulars beat off attacks mounted by 4,500 Zulus. For the loss of fifteen dead and two dying, the Britons inflicted casualties variously estimated between 450 and 1,000.* Rorke's Drift gained its defenders eleven Victoria Crosses and six Distinguished Conduct Medals to divert public attention from the catastrophe at Isandhlwana.

‡Lieutenant-Colonel Henry Pulleine of the 24th Foot, the senior officer left by Chelmsford at Isandhlwana, commanded 822 Europeans and 431 Africans – most of the former from the 1st Battalion of the 24th Foot and the latter from the 1st Natal Native Contingent. Lieutenant-Colonel Anthony Durnford of the Royal Engineers, senior officer of the Natal Native Horse, is believed to have had about 475 men. Thus the total of roughly 1,730 faced an estimated 18,000–20,000 Zulus. Only ten men of the 24th Foot survived, plus 45–50 others. The battle lasted two hours.

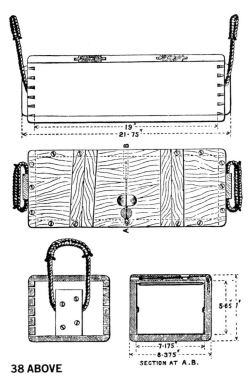

38 ABOVE

The sturdy construction of a standard British 'Box ammunition, Small Arm, wood, with tin lining, Mark XII'. From the *Text Book of Small Arms*, 1888.

* The figures most widely accepted are about 480 dead and 300 seriously wounded.

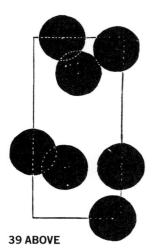

39 ABOVE

A typical group obtained at 100 yards from a ·45 Martini-Henry (actual size). From Greener's *The Gun and its Development*.

*The alternative 'danger zones' were sometimes quoted instead. Trajectory was divided in an initial danger zone, then a safe zone and lastly the terminal danger zone.

†These mid-range figures are used for convenience. Owing to the shape of the flight path, which air resistance prevents being symmetrical, the vertex lies a short distance past the half-way point.

‡Continual improvements in manufacturing quality ensured that the shooting of mass-produced guns improved steadily. However, the trend was not so obvious in the Queen's Prize (shot at Wimbledon and then Bisley). Prior to 1873, when the format changed, the best scores had been 71×84 (84·5 per cent) with a 'Government Whitworth' and 68×84 (81·0 per cent) with a Martini-Henry. The best result in 1874−81 was 86×105 (81·9 per cent) with a Martini-Henry. The ranges were changed in 1882, 1885 and 1886, and then again in 1898; in the intervening period, the best Martini-Henry score was 283×330 (85·8 per cent). The first ·303 Lee-Metford victory came in 1897, with an excellent score of 304×330 (92·1 per cent). Owing to continual changes of range, however, these figures cannot be compared directly.

*The acceptance tests were later changed so that the guns were required to place nine out of ten shots inside a 20in-diameter circle at 500 yards.

THE MAGAZINE RIFLE

Gun performance, 1870–1900

TRAJECTORY

The height of projectile trajectories has always been important in a military context, as a flat bullet path greatly reduces the significance of range-gauging errors. The Dreyse needle rifles, owing to their low muzzle velocity, were inferior to the standard rifle-muskets in this respect; they were also vastly poorer than the French Chassepot, which compared favourably with the contemporary metallic-cartridge rifles – for example, the Martini-Henry – though its accuracy was generally inferior.

Most sources quote differing ways of assessing the flatness of trajectory, though most were based on calculations of the 'safe zones'* for infantry and cavalrymen in each bullet path. These naturally varied according to distance, and whether the marksman was standing, kneeling or prone. There were two basic ways of quantifying the results: by safe-zone limits or by stating a maximum range at which no safe zone existed.

The goal was to keep the maximum height ('vertex') of a bullet fired from ground level below the height of standing soldier. This entirely eliminated the safe zone.

The steady reduction in calibre in 1865−1900, together with increasing velocity, flattened trajectory appreciably until the 'safe zone' disappeared at normal combat ranges. With the sights set for 500 yards, the 250-yard vertices for the ·577 Snider, ·45 Martini-Henry and ·303 Lee-Metford were 11·5ft, 8·6ft and 3·9ft respectively.† Consequently, the ·303 effectively eliminated the safe zone at 500 yards, being never greater than 4ft above the bore axis. Owing to their looping trajectories, neither the Snider nor the Martini-Henry could perform similarly. With the sights set for 500 yards, their bullets were above 'man height' for a substantial portion of flight. The safe zone for the ·577 Snider lay between 90 and 430 yards, and between 120 and 400 yards for the ·45 Martini-Henry.

ACCURACY

It may be difficult to compare figures surviving from nineteenth-century trials directly; some are 50 per cent dispersions – ignoring the fall of half the shots – while others, particularly those emanating from Britain, were expressed as 'Figures of Merit'. As related in the preface, this particular system can be related to group diameter with some success; the keys to similar arbitrary systems, unfortunately, have often been lost.

Few of the earliest metallic-cartridge breech loaders were more accurate than the best of the preceding rifled-muskets, assuming the latter were kept clean. By 1880, however, accuracy had improved significantly.‡ British government trials with the early Martini-Henry returned average Figures of Merit of 6·8in at 300 yards, 1·63ft at 800 yards and 3·46ft at 1,200 (equating to group diameters of about 31in, 88in and 187in respectively). The best Figures of Merit at these distances had been 5·6in, 1·29ft and 2·28ft.

Trials against a Chassepot revealed the superiority of the metallic cartridge, the Martini returning an average Figure of Merit of 1·15ft, with a best of 0·96ft, compared with 2·74ft and 2·38ft for the French rifle. It must be remembered that these trials were undertaken with government ammunition, supported by no more than a shoulder rest, and that far better figures could be obtained by clamping barrels in a machine-rest. On one such occasion, a ·45 Henry barrel placed twenty shots in a square measuring a mere 26in at 1,200 yards.

Accuracy achieved on trials was very rarely attained in service. Not only were the series-made guns often poorly sighted, but the sights themselves were very coarse. As few soldiers were crack shots – annual practice was limited by miserly issues of ammunition – the results were predictable. The British Army and most of its Continental rivals, with the possible exception of the Prussians, were geared to fighting against massed formations. Attempts to engage individual targets were almost always doomed, even when the first Lee-Metfords were introduced. The acceptance tests simply required batches of rifles, selected at random and fired from a shoulder rest, to return Figures of Merit bettering 8in at 500 yards (a potential group diameter of about 36in). As no notice of the *position* of the group on the target was taken, no check on the efficacy of the sights was kept.*

Traditional European battles, and most of those fought in the American Civil War, camouflaged this shortcoming with clouds of black powder smoke. Volley-firing was effectual enough, as individual targets could not be ascertained after the few first shots. As the British were to find to their cost in the early stages of the Second South African War, smokeless cartridges enabled marksmen to select individual targets for the entire duration of an engagement.

Within a short period, the bitter memory of the latter was finally excised by the Battle of Ulundi, a classic demonstration of how difficult it was for native hordes to defeat the breech-loading rifle and well-organized European geometry.

Improvements in the quality and education of the British soldier had been matched by contemporaneous advances in smallarms design. Cardwell's reforms had been mooted just as the Snider was reaching service, and the implementation of his most important recommendations – grouping of the regiments on a two battalion system, for example – was approximately contemporary with the perfection of the Martini-Henry.

By the time of the Franco-Prussian War, the single-shot breech-loader was well established. Most armies had replaced their rifle-musket conversions; little Switzerland had even adopted the 10·4mm Vetterli bolt-action *repeating* rifle in August 1869. The way ahead was plainly signalled. The Vetterli infantry rifle had a twelve-round tube magazine under the barrel and could carry a thirteenth cartridge on the elevator. Though long and heavy, it conferred a considerable advantage on the Swiss infantryman. Yet most armies remained ultra-conservative, fearful of the effects on their exchequers of univeral re-

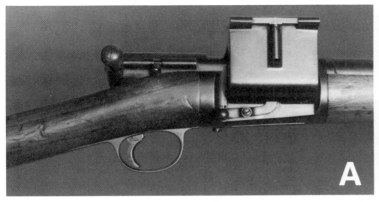

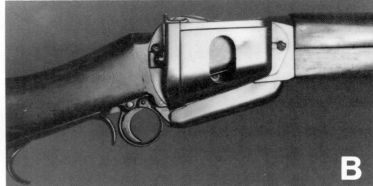

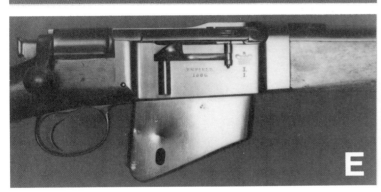

40-45 ABOVE

The adoption of the ·303 Magazine Rifle Mk I, later known as the Lee-Metford, was preceded by experiments lasting a decade. The three principal competitors were the box-magazine 1879-model Lee; the hopper-magazine Bethel Burton (**A**); and the quirky block-action Owen Jones (**B**). The Owen Jones was rejected, which left a contest between the ·402 Enfield-Lee (**C**) – replaced by the ·43 Remington-Lee for troop trials – and the Enfield-made ·402 Lee-Burton (**D**). **E** is an experimental ·402 Enfield-Lee with a two-piece stock; **F** is the Magazine Rifle Mk I (Lee-Metford). Courtesy of the MoD Pattern Room Collection, Royal Ordnance plc, Nottingham; photographs by John Walter.

equipment. Italy adopted the Vetterli in 1871, for example, but insisted on a single-shot derivative of the Swiss magazine rifle.

Though magazine breech-loaders were widespread by the late 1880s, some offering the virtues of reduced calibre, the European scene was in disarray. Colonel C.G. Slade, commanding the 2nd Battalion of the Rifle Brigade, wrote on 13 January 1887 that:

An examination of the state of affairs both at home and abroad shows clearly that the weapon of the future has yet to be found. The Germans have only adopted the Mauser in order to get a magazine arm as quickly as possible, and for economical reasons. The Austrians are taking up the Manlicher [sic] in a half-hearted way, and at the last moment may change it. The French are still carrying on exhaustive trials with the 'Normale' [Lebel] which may not turn out satisfactory after all. The Italians are giving up the Vetterli and substituting the Vitali. The Russians and the Turks are, perhaps prudently, holding their hands. In England, the delay that has taken place has probably saved the country from prematurely adopting an imperfect weapon.

In 1887, the French introduced the first serviceable small-calibre military rifle, firing an 8mm cartridge loaded with smokeless 'Poudre B', and everyone scrambled to follow France's lead; no self-respecting world power, Britain included, could afford to defer to the French.

The Lebel rifle had an archaic, potentially dangerous tube magazine in which centre-fire cartridges could be ignited prematurely (even by slamming the butt hard on the ground) if a bullet-nose smashed into the primer of the round ahead of it. But though the rifle offered no real advance on contemporary 11mm clip-loaded Austrian Mannlichers, its cartridge was a huge

LEE-METFORD AND LEE-ENFIELD

advance. No less lethal than the big black powder patterns it replaced, it performed far better at long ranges and was so much lighter that many more cartridges could be carried for a given weight.

The introduction of the Magazine Rifle Mk I, or Lee-Metford as it was soon renamed, has often been the subject of criticism. Certainly, the gun trade viewed it with jaundiced disapproval.

In 1888, however, the Small Arms Committee could have not achieved better without abandoning the work of the previous nine years. Many people — wise after the event — criticized the authorities for failing to heed the merits of the Mauser. However, the Mausers submitted to the trials had either been unacceptable tube-magazine guns or the quirky C/88 prototype. The latter was the *newest* Mauser in 1888. It was a very clumsy gun, even though the action may have been stronger than a Lee. Judged as a service weapon, the Small Arms Committee was justified in rejecting the C/88. Critics have since pointed to the emergence of the near-contemporaneous Belgian Mle 89, Argentine Mo.91 and Spanish Mo.93 Mausers as evidence that the British efforts were laggardly. This was simply not so; the Belgian rifle was only perfected after the Lee-Metford had been introduced, and did not reach service until February 1892.

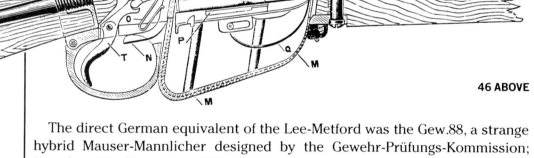

46 ABOVE

A longitudinal section of the Mark II Lee-Metford magazine rifle (note the absence of a safety catch on the cocking piece). The parts are: A, body; B, bolt; B1, bolt head; C, chamber; E, stock bolt; H, cocking piece; L, sear; M, magazine; N, magazine catch; O, combined magazine-catch and sear spring; P, cartridge platform; Q, platform spring; S, striker; and T, trigger. From Greener's *The Gun and its Development* (1910).

The direct German equivalent of the Lee-Metford was the Gew.88, a strange hybrid Mauser-Mannlicher designed by the Gewehr-Prüfungs-Kommission; introduced in November 1888, this rifle was inferior in many respects to the Lee-Metford. Not until 1898 — a decade later, with the experience of other armies as a guide — did the Germans adopt a better weapon.

This is not to say that the Lee-Metford was perfect, but merely that it should be judged by the standards of its precise time. In common with many military weapons, its development had been lengthy — even unnecessarily protracted. Rifle design moved so quickly that it was overtaken within ten years. Arguments that the Lee bolt system was obsolescent even in 1888 are unreasonable. Even the principle of rear-locking lugs, so often vilified in comparison with the Mauser, can be defended on several grounds.‡

Thus it is inappropriate to judge the Lee-Metford rifle by the standards of 1898 instead of 1888. A survey of the rifles being used by Britain's rivals in 1893 would have revealed that the Austrians still had an ineffectual straight-pull Mannlicher, with a clip-loaded magazine and a weak breech lock; the French had the Lebel, with an archaic tube magazine; and the Germans had the Gew.88, with its clip-loaded magazine and weak barrel jacket. The Italians were still experimenting with the Mannlicher-Carcano, and the Belgian army had only just received the first Mle.89 Mausers — the best of these rifles, but by no means flawless.

‡Among the advantages of rear locking is that cartridges may be fed almost directly into the chamber, rather than having to bypass the locking-lug recesses. Most modern rear-locking rifles — notably the Steyr-Mannlichers — have a reputation for smooth feed-strokes.

Admittedly the Lee-Metford had faults, true of all new military rifles introduced before or since. As few designs are truly settled until the lessons of active service have been digested, perfection may be delayed for a decade or more.

Lee-Metford rifles entered service during one of the British Army's few respites in the late nineteenth century from colonial wars against weakly armed and naively led opponents. One of the first major opportunities to try the rifles in combat came in the Sudan campaign of 1898. Fought on 2 September 1898 between the dervishes of the Khalifa, Abd Allah ibn Muhammad,* and Anglo-Egyptians commanded by General Sir Herbert Kitchener, the Battle of Omdurman showed that the introduction of the magazine rifle and the advent of smokeless powder were a considerable advance on the old single-shot breech-loaders.

The 2nd Brigade were to open fire with their Lee Metfords as soon as the brigadier thought it justified. Hurriedly, Lt. Grenfell got the range from the nearby gunners. Just over 2000 yards. It was a long shot but probably worth it. At 6.35, ten minutes after the field guns had opened fire, the Guards fired their first volley. A few seconds later the Warwicks joined in; then, as the wing of the dervish army began to draw near the zariba [encampment], the Highlanders and the Lincolns began to play their part. And so the action moved across to embrace Maxwell's 2nd Egyptian brigade, each regimental commander ordering fire as the quality of his weapons and his men's marksmanship made expedient. Last of these to fire was Townshend with the XIIth Egyptians. 'I determined that not a trigger should be pulled until they were 400 yards from us. Many of the men kept looking round to me as much as to say "Let us fire now!"...' In the end...the XIIth Egyptians [with Martini-Henry rifles] were allowed to open fire when the dervishes were still a generous 600 yards away.

Most battles since the invention of gunpowder have been in part at least shrouded in a pall of smoke. On September 2, 1898, there was a curious clarity. The prevailing wind, perhaps, took much of the smoke away; the Lee Metfords using cordite anyway produced little, the Egyptian infantry did not fire their antiquated Martini-Henrys fast enough to yield the thick white cloud which they could produce in more experienced hands. The whole battlefield lay exposed to Kitchener and his staff as they took up their positions...   Philip Ziegler, *Omdurman*.

Omdurman was another in a long series of one-sided African battles, the imbalance between the Mahdists and the Anglo-Egyptians being heightened by the presence of magazine rifles and Maxim machine-guns. Casualties among the Khalifa's army, which mustered more than sixty thousand men, were appalling: perhaps 9,800 dead and 18,000—20,000 wounded. Kitchener's force of 8,000 Europeans and 18,000 Egyptians and Sudanese lost 48 dead and 434 wounded.†

It took the Second South African War (1899—1902) to shake the foundations of the army establishment. Initially outnumbered by the burgher armies of the Zuid Afrikaansche Republiek and the Oranje Vrij Staat—better known in Britain as the Transvaal and Orange Free State respectively—where tens of thousands of 1895-type 7mm Mauser rifles had been held in readiness,‡ the British were comprehensively outshot and often outmanoeuvred.

Many of the Boers were experienced fieldsmen and their leaders realised that engaging the British in set-piece battles courted disaster. Playing to their strengths, the Boers fought in open order behind as much cover as they could find. Often fighting as mounted infantry, a style of warfare to which they were particularly well suited, the Boers' defensive positions were chosen most carefully. Their movements were greatly aided by their knowledge of terrain for which the British lacked even the most basic maps. Familiarity with their weapons was also greatly in the burghers' favour. The British soon fell in awe of Boer marksmanship, which was simply due to the fact that many of the farmers were practised shots and—most importantly—knew the characteristics of their rifles intimately.

47 ABOVE
A corporal of the King's Own (Royal Lancaster) Regiment, pictured *c.*1903 – note that he wears both Queen's and King's South Africa Medals. The proportions of the long Lee-Enfield rifle are adequate, except that the bolt mechanism is poorly observed. From a contemporary print. Courtesy of Philip J. Haythornthwaite.

TO WAR AGAIN

* The Khalīfa ('successor' in Arabic) had succeeded Muḥammad Aḥmad ibn as-Sayyid 'Abd Allāh, better known as 'al-Mahdī', on the latter's death in 1885.

†Some of the wounded subsequently died of their injuries, or from disease. It is generally agreed that as many as five thousand dervishes were fatally injured, but no accurate count was ever made.

‡In the period immediately after the Jameson Raid, the ZAR acquired 36,000 Martini-Henrys from Britain (at least some of which were made by Westley Richards), 6,000 Guedes rifles from Austria, and 37,000 Mausers from Germany. Larger weapons included ten Creusot guns from France, twelve from Krupp in Germany, and twenty 1pr Maxim pom-poms from France. OVS Mauser purchases are believed to have amounted to about 20,000.

48 ABOVE

Men of the 12th (Prince of Wales's Royal) Lancers are pictured in an encampment at Paarl in Cape Colony, shortly after the Second South African War. One man wears both the Queen's and King's South Africa Medals, which means the picture cannot date earlier than 1902. The long Lee-Enfield rifles appear to be Mk I*, the safety-catch thumb piece being visible on the rifle carried by the man on the left. None of the guns has a cleaning rod. Note that the butts are in buckets attached to the saddle, with muzzles secured by straps passing over the troopers' shoulders. Courtesy of Elex archives.

49 FAR LEFT

'Cavalry Ambushed', engraved for *The Graphic* after a 1900-vintage original by J.J. Waugh. Though the panic of the scene is caught effectually, the drawing of the weapons is open to criticism; the bolt of the Lee-Enfield rifle appears to be sliding on top of the receiver, and the trigger guard would scarcely admit the firer's finger! Courtesy of Philip J. Haythornthwaite.

50 LEFT

'The Backbone of the Navy'. A coloured postcard by Millar & Lang, Art Publishers, Glasgow and London. Set against a crudely faked jetty and horizon, this sailor is armed with a Mark I* Lee-Enfield rifle and a P/88 sword bayonet. Courtesy of Elex archives.

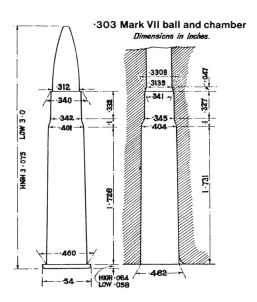

·303 Mark VII ball and chamber
Dimensions in inches.

51 ABOVE

52 BELOW

Taken during a demonstration for the benefit of the Chinese ambassador Li Huang Chang – pictured centre right, with Sigmund Loewe and then Hiram Maxim to his left – this picture is remarkable for the array of contemporary weaponry. A tripod-mounted light Maxim (left) lies behind a three-barrel Nordenfelt, on a wheeled carriage with a pole trail, with a five-barrel Nordenfelt and its limber in the foreground. A water-cooled Maxim on a light wheeled carriage stands in the group to the right. Courtesy of Vickers Ltd.

British rifles were quite popular among the Boers, especially those armed with nothing other than single-shot Martini-Henry, Westley Richards or Guedes dropping-block patterns. There is no evidence that a Lee was ever preferred to the Mauser, though many men liked the eight-round magazine and long range sights of the British weapon.

The fighting was a complex, rambling affair best appreciated from books such as Thomas Pakenham's magisterial study *The Boer War*. Though the British had the best of opening exchanges such as Talana Hill and Elandslaagte, even the most minor tactical successes were dearly bought. Attempts to take Boer positions by frontal attacks, often characterized by lack of cover and poor intelligence, were catastrophic.

The depths were plumbed when three British generals attacked strong Boer defensive positions without so much as a cursory reconnaissance. During 'Black Week', 10–15 December 1899, Gatacre was repulsed at the Battle of Stormberg, Methuen experienced disaster at Magersfontein and Buller was rebuffed at Colenso. None of these battles was large, compared with Omdurman or most of those fought during the First World War. But Magersfontein, particularly, showed that the geometry of battle was easily dominated by the magazine rifle.

The British attempted an artillery barrage on the Boer position, but had succeeded only in wounding three of General Piet Cronje's men. Methuen then ordered the Highland Brigade to make a night march across the intervening veldt on the basis of a compass held by Major Benson of the Royal Artillery, who had previously reconnoitred the ground on foot as best he could. The awkwardness of the task, and the effect on the compass bearings of local lodestone, delayed progress. As the order to deploy was finally givem, the leading ranks stumbled over trip-wires strung out ahead of the Boer intrenchment — which was 250 yards ahead of the ridge at which the British barrage had been directed. Predictably, the massed ranks of the Highlanders were rapidly thinned: in less that ten minutes, the Boer riflemen had inflicted five

53 ABOVE

'The Late Field Marshal Lord Roberts. Commander of the Overseas Forces, 1914' – a postcard published by Raphael Tuck & Sons in 'The European War. Notabilities Series' (no. 4307, series II). Frederick Sleigh Roberts (1832–1914), first Earl Roberts, was commissioned into the Bengal artillery, winning the Victoria Cross in the Indian Mutiny. The much-loved hero of Kandahar, 'Bobs' had commanded the British forces in the later stages of the Second South African War; afterwards, he had encouraged the development of the SMLE. After retiring as commander-in-chief in 1905, he devoted himself to the development of marksmanship in the army. Appointed Colonel-in-Chief of the Indian Forces serving in the BEF on the eve of war, Roberts died on his way to visit his men. Courtesy of Elex archives.

* The Second South African War claimed the lives of 20,721 British troops, according to the official history: 7,582 killed in action, and 13,139 dead of wounds and disease. Boer fatalities amounted to about 4,000, but no accurate record survives. The official history records that 87,465 men served the ZAR and OVS, including volunteers from Cape Colony and Natal but possibly something of an exaggeration. The staggering total of 448,435 British, Australian, Canadian, New Zealand and South African troops were engaged, though not all at the same time.

† These trials were undertaken by the King's Own (Royal Lancaster Regiment) at extreme range. They were spoiled by a strong headwind; only 47 from 2,000 shots hit the target-screens placed at 3,100 yards, the majority falling between 2,650 and 2,870 yards. Many of the Lee-Metford rifles were worn sufficiently to reduce their maximum range, but it is interesting that bullets striking the ground around the screens still had sufficient energy to penetrate inch-thick pine boards.

hundred casualties. The Black Watch, in the van, were cut to ribands. When the units were finally relieved, only six men of the three leading companies were unhurt.

War Office patience finally snapped; General Lord Roberts – 'Roberts of Kandahar' – was sent to South Africa after Colenso, with Kitchener as chief-of-staff, and a new phase began. Even though Warren and Buller were beaten back at Spion Kop and Vaal Krantz, Roberts gradually gained the upper hand. Forced to rely on guerrilla tactics, the Boers were slowly isolated. On 30 May 1902, the Treaty of Vereeniging ended the war.*

The most worrying deficiency of the Lee-Metford and Lee-Enfield rifles was their poorly regulated sights. A deviation of twenty inches from the sight-line at 500 yards had meant little against the densely packed dervishes at Omdurman, only a year earlier; but now it was the difference between a hit and a miss on Boers in loose order. This particular problem was not due to the design of the rifle, but to a detail that could (and should) have been rectified in the period between issue of the guns and their use in southern Africa.

Typical of the comments made in response to a 1900-vintage War Office questionnaire was that of Thorneycroft's Mounted Infantry, a composite unit armed with a collection of Martini-Enfield, Lee-Metford and Lee-Enfield rifles. No complaints were made about the accuracy of the guns, but the consensus of opinion was that they shot 12in high at 200 yards, the error increasing with range. Most of the guns also shot markedly to the right; the front sights were agreed to be too coarse; the back sights needed improvement; and some form of charger- or clip-loading was requested. Longer hand guards were needed to reduce the mirage caused by hot barrels, as well as making the guns easier to handle. Some of the butts had shrunk, worked loose and even fallen out of their sockets. This was more serious than it seemed, as the special screwdrivers necessary to re-tighten the stock bolt were in short supply.

The maximum effective range of individual rifles was regarded, unbelievably, as 1,800 yards. Useful volley-firing had been reported at distances between 2,000 and 3,000 yards, provided the range had been established.

The long-range sights had been useful at Omdurman, where fire had been opened at 2,000 yards, but were the subject of much debate in South Africa. Some authorities recommended their deletion, as they were comparatively delicate. Others, mindful of the value of long-range harassing fire in the era before machine-guns became commonplace, wanted to retain them.

A special trial was undertaken at Aldershot in October 1900, when men of the Highland Light Infantry fired 2,000 rounds at a series of khaki-colour canvas screens placed at twenty-yard intervals. Each screen was 30 yards broad and 4ft 2in high. They were mounted eighteen inches clear of the ground, the nearest being 2,200 yards from the firing point. The officers in charge reported that the nearest screens could only just be seen unaided, the remainder being hidden by falling ground. Amazingly, 17 per cent of the shots registered hits, markers in the butt noting that a little over half the shots fell among the targets. The official report concluded that 'A bullet striking a man direct at this range would no doubt kill or wound him. Owing to the sharp angle of descent of the bullet it would be difficult for a man to find cover. The bullet had, however, lost a great deal of its penetrating power and any cover which could be found need not be very thick'. A subsequent trial, which was something of a failure,† proved that descending bullets would pierce a one-inch pine plank at ranges approaching 3,000 yards.

Modified back sights, with the central sighting 'V' offset ·03in to the left, were issued after January 1900. Long-term solutions included offsetting the front sight ·02 to the left of the bore axis on all new guns, or substituting a removable pinned-in sight on guns returned to Sparkbrook (Birmingham) for repairs. These rifles displayed a star on the front-sight block or the back-sight leaf.

Detailed experiments revealed that the sights, which were not adjusted for any particular range, allowed a lateral deviation of 18−30in at 500 yards. The deflection was greatly influenced by the fit of the lugs against their resisting shoulders in the body. Impact of the bullet above the predicted strike-point, 3−6in at 200 yards, was largely due to interference between the stock and barrel. It was very susceptible to sudden changes in temperature.

By midsummer 1900, sufficient experimentation had been completed to enable the Small Arms Committee to recommend that faults inherent in the Lee-Enfield should be rectified in a new rifle. The service rifle's faults included excessive weight and unnecessary complexity; a weak damage-prone bolt head; capricious bearing between the bolt lugs and the body; the cock-on-closing feature, which was widely disliked; a flimsy magazine incapable of charger- or clip-loading; and an unsophisticated trigger.

A SHORT RIFLE

54 RIGHT

Men of the Honourable Artillery Company are seen at Fargo Camp in this 1914-vintage photo-postcard by Wm. May & Co. Ltd of Aldershot. The rifles are Charger Loading Lee-Enfields, converted from original Mk I* examples (note safety catches). Courtesy of Elex archives.

The development of the short rifle is considered in greater detail in the relevant section in Part Two. While the ordnance authorities were toying with Lee-Enfield derivatives, several interesting rifles were developed privately. Each was developed in answer to problems that had become obvious in the South African War; and each attempted to shorten the basic action so that a single gun – the 'universal rifle' – could serve cavalry and infantry alike. Whether this originally came from the army, or the army espoused it only after approaches had been made privately, remains open to question. The former seems more likely but, as the proposers of the rifles were often military men, the answer may not be clear-cut.

The Godsal was probably the oldest. Dating from 1901, but made in varying forms prior to 1914, it was the work of Major P.T. Godsal. Commissioned into the 52nd Regiment in 1860, he had retired his commission in 1880 to become adjutant of the Eton College Volunteers. His rifle embodied a 'travelling block', really no more than a short bolt (a term for which Godsal had no great love) running in tracks on the upper edge of the combless butt. Its twin lugs, mounted on the bolt-handle base, locked into the breech.

The Thorneycroft was somewhat similar to, and apparently also contemporaneous with the Godsal. Its bolt/block unit had a carefully shaped wooden shroud; and the back sight was usually comparable with that of the SMLE. As

the bayonet fits onto a boss at the muzzle, the surviving gun probably dates from 1903 or later. It was specifically developed for cavalry, hence the care with which everything was clothed in wood.

Like the Godsal, the Thorneycroft had a magazine in the wrist of the butt immediately behind the trigger. However, though this permitted a long barrel, it restricted the capacity of the magazine to five rounds. In addition, the Godsal and the Thorneycroft were both difficult to handle; not only was aim disturbed to reload after each shot, owing to the position of the bolt, but the grip for the trigger-finger hand was very uncomfortable.

The Gamwell rifle, said to have been developed in 1901−2 but not patented by H. & C. Gamwell until April 1904 (British Patent 8,759/04), featured a different approach to the problem of accommodating a long barrel in a short gun. The rifle was built on a standard Lee-Metford action, with the bolt mechanism running back along the butt comb and the trigger moved forward ahead of the chamber. A double magazine − two standard ten-round patterns brazed together − was inserted in the underside of the butt.

The Gamwell rifle was an extraordinary design. Perhaps the first of the voguish bullpups, it had little to commend itself to the Small Arms Committee. Not only was it clumsy and badly balanced when laden with twenty rounds, but the bolt handle was awkwardly placed. The proximity of the chamber to the firer's cheek vibrated the cheekbone each time the gun fired.

None of these interesting private experiments stood any chance of adoption, interesting though they were, and tests performed on rifles gleaned from abroad were rarely especially meritorious. Quite reasonably, therefore, the Small Arms Committee continued work on the Short Magazine Lee-Enfield.

The gun trade remained united in its opposition. In its November 1908 issue, *Arms & Explosives* summarized some of the major points of contention. Reading the *Minutes of the Proceedings of the Small Arms Committee*, more that eighty years after the event, shows that the authorities did not deserve the abuse heaped on them. As much − perhaps more − than any other army, the British took their own weapons and those of their likely opponents very seriously indeed, conducting trials with a maniacal attention to detail.

These minutes were not available to public scrutiny in 1908, leaving the field open for speculation and allowing *Arms & Explosives* to confuse details of the standard 8mm German service **cartridge** with those of the smaller 7mm pattern chambered by the Spanish Mauser rifles. The periodical had casti- gated the British for lagging behind the other Great Powers, while con- veniently ignoring that the service rifles of France, Austria-Hungary and

THE FIRST WORLD WAR

* Though the great Haldane reforms of 1906–12 had replaced the previous system of militia, yeomanry and volunteers with the Territorial Army, there had been comparatively little increase in size. The mobilization strength in 1900 was reckoned to have been about 684,000 – comprising 236,000 regulars, 108,000 reservists and 320,000 irregulars.

57, 58 BELOW

Patriotic cards produced during the early years of the First World War took many forms. These, by Raphael Tuck & Sons in the 'Oilette' range, are the work of Harry Payne; from the 'Colonial Badges and Their Wearers' series, both are numbered '3160'. Payne was a popular military artist of the day, though his depictions of weapons were generally unsatisfactory; the action of the New Zealander's SMLE is very crudely observed, while the angle between the bore and the butt of the Canadian's rifle is much too great. In neither case is the butt-socket drawn, though this is a most obvious characteristic of all British Lee-Enfields.

Russia (to name but three) were vastly inferior; forgot that simple changes of bullet meant wholesale changes of sights, which usually took several years to complete; and conveniently overlooked the legions of 'improved' rifles that the Small Arms Committee had quite reasonably rejected.

When the British Army went to war in August 1914, it still relied on the Lee-Enfield, the Webley revolver and the Vickers Gun.

The British Expeditionary Force, mustering some 160,000 men, if deficient technically, was enthusiastic and well trained. As the British Army was recruited entirely from volunteers until the advent of conscription in 1916, it was much more professional than the European conscript armies of 1914. The major problem was that the pool of trained reserves was very small; the combined strength of the regular and territorial units on 1 August 1914, a mere 733,514, had scarcely changed since the end of the South African War.‡

The standard infantry rifle was the ·303 Mark III SMLE. Though the ·276 P/13 had been provisionally approved, problems with this sturdy amalgam of the best Mauser, Lee-Enfield and Springfield features had not been overcome. No production contracts had been let, and only a thousand trials guns had been forthcoming by the summer of 1914.

Despite widespread opinion that the war would be over by Christmas 1914, steps were rapidly taken to assure long-term supply of weapons. Enfield, BSA

NEW ZEALAND INFANTRY.

CANADIAN INFANTRY

and the London Small Arms Company (LSA) were requested to accelerate production of short Lee-Enfield rifles. Vickers was given piecemeal orders for Vickers Guns, and tentative approaches were made abroad for other weapons.

Christmas 1914 soon passed; campaigns dragged on into 1915, with no end in sight. In October 1914, Kitchener, who had unpopularly predicted a three-year conflict, appealed for volunteers. So many men flocked to the colours that supplies of guns, uniforms and accoutrements proved woefully inadequate. Blue-serge uniforms were hastily made to answer shortages of khaki; storerooms were ransacked for old Martini and Lee-Metford rifles; ·303 Trade Patterns and a variety of sporting rifles were impressed; and manufacturers of war matériel were exhorted to ever greater efforts with the promise of open 'for the duration' contracts.

THE AGE OF THE MACHINE-GUN

Losses of equipment on the Western Front proved to be much greater than had been anticipated. In addition, imaginative use of Maxim Guns by the Germans showed that the British Army had seriously under-estimated the potential of automatic weapons. British infantrymen fell in swathes until all bowed to the emergent technology of war but the most diehard cavalry-men, who clung to the belief that élite horsemen would simply ride down mere machine-gunners.

The opening day of the Battle of the Somme, Saturday 1 July 1916, epitomized the folly of matching man against Maxim. In some parts of the line the attack began with a carnival atmosphere; several platoons of the East Surrey Regiment, for example, kicked footballs towards the German trenches and set off in pursuit. But it was to be a carnival of death, as British generals rarely admitted a mistake by abandoning an attack.

Most had to form up in their waves and walk into the fire-swept zone. They met fear-crazed survivors running back, and badly wounded men dragging themselves along. They had to step over the bodies of the dead, torn-off limbs and torsos mangled by shell fire, or rows of bodies hardly marked but the victims of machine-gun fire . . . Some did not get far. As with the leading waves, unsubdued German machine-guns soon found their range and whole waves of men were shot down.

59 RIGHT

The 'Gun, Machine, Vickers, ·303-inch Mark I' on the Mark IV tripod mount, with ammunition box, steam pipe and condensing can. Note the distinctive webbing ammunition belt, with three brass eyelets between each cartridge. Courtesy of Ian Hogg.

*According to Major-General T.J. Mitchell and G.M. Smith, *Official History of the Great War. Casualties and Medical Statistics* (HMSO, London, 1931), the final returns revealed 19,240 killed or dead of wounds, 35,493 wounded, 585 prisoners and 2,152 'missing' (mostly untraced dead): the total of 57,470 comprised 2,438 officers and 55,032 men. German losses have been estimated as 7,500–8,000.

60 BELOW

'Sir John French' – a photo-postcard by Beagles (no.691.B) after an original by Bassano, London. John Denton Pinkstone French, first Earl of Ypres (1852–1925), was gazetted to the 8th Hussars in 1874. Commander-in-Chief of the British Expeditionary Force until relieved by Haig in December 1915, he was another of the many cavalrymen who had so little faith in machine-guns that thousands of men went unwittingly to their doom. This photograph was taken in 1913–14, as French carries a field marshal's baton. Courtesy of Elex archives.

61 RIGHT

Cheerful British soldiers pose for the camera in this photograph, taken on the Western Front during the First World War – probably during the summer of 1917, as the man centre front wears shorts. In addition to the SMLE rifles and P/07 bayonets, the leader carries a large revolver – probably a .455 Smith & Wesson. Examination of the original photograph suggests that these men may be from the Duke of Wellington's (West Riding Regiment). Author's archives.

The first day of the Somme brought the greatest number of casualties sustained by the British Army in any single day in the First World War. By nightfall, twenty thousand Britons lay dead; nearly forty thousand more were missing, wounded or in enemy hands.* Some units had lost eight men in every ten through sheer thoughtlessness.

Precisely on time the Tyneside Irish Brigade, 3,000 men strong, rose . . . They had to cover nearly one mile of completely open ground *before* they reached the original British front line.

Behind the German front line the defenders of La Boisselle had not been destroyed by the bombardment and the German machine-gunners there dominated all the surrounding ground. As soon as they saw these long lines of men coming down the hillside in front of them, they raised their machine-gun sights and opened fire . . .

Furiously the German machine-gunners fired belt after belt into this fantastic target. The first to be extinguished were the two left-hand battalions, the 2nd and 3rd Tyneside Irish; very few of these *ever reached the British front line* . . . Martin Middlebrook, *The First Day on the Somme.*

When the rolls were mustered after the battle, the cost became obvious. From establishments nominally of a little over a thousand apiece (but generally at least ten per cent under strength), the 4th Tyneside Scottish alone had suffered 629 casualties and the 1st Tyneside Irish had lost 620.

Though they were ruthlessly efficient, Maxim and Vickers Guns were difficult and expensive to make. Production could not be accelerated to the levels demanded by the army without recruiting other contractors.

Facilities in the Royal Small Arms factory at Enfield Lock, where Maxims had been made in tiny quantities, were diverted to the Hotchkiss light machine-gun programme in 1915. This left only Vickers making water-cooled machine-guns. A solution was found in the pan-fed Lewis Gun, developed in the USA but licensed to BSA in 1913. As the Lewis Gun was comparatively easily made, Vickers Guns could be withdrawn from infantry battalions and grouped in Machine Gun Corps. This was universally beneficial. It enabled the guns most suited to sustained support fire to be commanded by men who understood them, and infantrymen received light machine-guns they could carry.

The Lewis was prone to jamming, as its spring-feed magazine was delicate and capricious, but the men accepted this failing in return for its mobility. If a magazine jammed, it was simply discarded in favour of the next one. Defective pans were repaired when (or if) their firers got back to British trenches.

Conscription was introduced in 1916, creating whole new divisions from untutored civilians. These impressed men were given the most rudimentary insight into military life and packed off to the front. But they needed weapons in vast numbers, and strained supply lines almost to breaking point.

53. THE "FIGHTING FIFTH" (NORTHUMBERLAND FUSILIERS) AFTER THE BATTLE OF ST. ELOI

SMLE production was accelerated by recruiting legions of sub-contractors (see Part Two), but demand greatly outstripped supply. The problem had been complicated by the discovery that the vaunted Canadian Ross rifles performed badly in adverse conditions. Though 118,000 ·303 Ross rifles, Marks IIIA and IIIB, were purchased by the British for training purposes, those serving Canadian units on the Western Front had to be withdrawn in favour of the SMLE.

This was savagely ironic, as the Ross had been preferred to the SMLE in Canada partly through national pride but, equally, because it answered criticisms of the short Lee-Enfield made by armchair soldiers, embittered gunsmiths and civilian marksmen who expected military rifles to win honours on the target range. The performance of the Ross as a military weapon had always been doubted by the Small Arms Committee.

Apart from making best use of existing production lines – Enfield, BSA and LSA – comparatively little could be achieved in Britain. The Standard Small Arms Company promised much, but ultimately delivered little, and the achievements of the 'peddled' rifle scheme were minor. No sooner had war begun than the British government looked abroad, mindful that it would take months or even years for production to begin.

Japan was only involved in the peripheries of the First World War and could supply rifles to order; the USA had immense production potential that had yet

65 ABOVE
Portuguese troops of the 23rd regiment, with British helmets and equipment, pose in front of their rockets. Note the breech cover on the SMLE, which was very useful in trench warfare. Courtesy of Elex archives.

66 ABOVE RIGHT
An Australian sergeant examines German MG.08 abandoned when their position was in danger of being overrun. Many thousands of Allied troops perished during the First World War in the face of guns such as these, well sited and stoutly manned. Both guns are mounted on improvised parapet mounts rather than the standard sledge, which suggests that this picture was taken towards the end of the war. Both have been disabled; the gun on the left lacks the feed block, while its companion lacks the feed block and top cover. Courtesy of Elex archives.

A WORLD AT PEACE

†According to the official history, the status at 11 November 1918 was 907,371 dead, 2,090,212 wounded and 191,652 missing or prisoners of war from 8,904,567 men mobilized in 1914–18. Many of the missing men were subsequently regarded to have been killed.

67 RIGHT
'London welcomes Her Very Own Boys': King George V takes the salute of a celebratory march-past of the London Regiments, pictured outside the gates of Buckingham Palace on 5 July 1919 in a photo-postcard (no.168U) by J. Beagles & Co. Ltd of London. Courtesy of Elex archives.

to be harnessed. It seemed that only the USA would be able to produce ·303-calibre rifles quickly enough, though many 6·5mm Arisaka rifles and a few ·44–40 1894-model Winchesters were purchased for training or to free naval Lee-Enfields for the army. Arisakas also later armed the RAF.

These were seen purely as expedients pending the distribution of sufficient ·303 rifles, and many of the Arisakas were subsequently shipped to Russia.

The role of the sniper – and the counter-sniper – assumed a new significance as soon as the dynamic warfare of 1914 had been replaced by the static entrenchment of 1915. Sniping was widely regarded as ungentlemanly in the British Army but, faced with mounting casualty lists, even senior officers were forced to admit its advantages. As there was an impossible shortage of suitable rifles, Mannlicher, Mauser and Ross sporters – and some long Lee-Enfields – were impressed until sufficient P/14 and the otherwise temperamental Canadian Ross Mark III rifles had been converted. The P/14 usually received British Aldis optical sights, while the Ross took the cumbersome American-made Warner & Swazey Telescopic Musket Sights of 1908 and 1913.

The horror of the Great War, which had cost Britain nearly a million dead,† was succeeded by what was optimistically expected to be the Great Peace. Most of the guns being developed in 1918 were promptly abandoned.

Little had been learned during the war from the French, whose ordnance was something of a shambles in 1918. And though the American Expeditionary Force had introduced the M1917 Browning to Europe, perhaps the best of all

68 ABOVE

This picture typifies the parsimony of the army towards re-equipment – and of the Treasury towards the army – that characterized the 1930s. Taken during exercises on Salisbury Plain on 27 August 1935, men of the 3rd Carabiniers (Prince of Wales's Dragoon Guards) participate in a 'decisive battle for the Army manoeuvres'. Note the Bren Gun, making one of its earliest appearances, and the 'fire simulator' rattle to save ammunition! The rifle is an SMLE Mk III, with a cut-off. Courtesy of Brian L. Davis.

the water-cooled medium machine-guns, its advantages over the Vickers Gun were not great enough to force a change in British policy.

Most of the efforts were devoted to perfecting aircraft and armoured vehicles. During the 1930s, the Royal Air Force had been able to approve the Vickers Gas Operated and Colt-Browning machine-guns for aerial use. The army, starved of funding, had been content to develop the Bren light machine-gun from Czechoslovakian prototypes and to refine the SMLE of the First World War into the simplified Rifle No.4 Mk I. By 1939, however, Bren Guns were only just beginning to supplant the Lewis Gun in general service and the No.1 Mk III (SMLE) had yet to be challenged. Production of the new No.4 rifle in an equally new BSA factory had not even begun. For the first months of the war, therefore, BSA made No 1 Mk III and III* rifles in its Birmingham (Small Heath) factory as well as the No.4 Mk I in Shirley.

The greatest advance in the 1930s was made by the US Army, where, after trials lasting more than a decade, the ·30 Rifle M1 ('Garand') had been approved in 1936. The M1 was the first auto-loading rifle to be regarded as universal issue. It was also attracted considerable criticism, failing the standard British dust and mud tests, but combat soon showed that its advantages considerably outweighed its drawbacks.

The worst feature of the Garand was the idiosyncratic magazine, which accepted nothing but an eight-round clip. In terms of rate of fire and – most importantly – ease and comfort of firing, the Garand was a vast improvement on the bolt-action ·30 M1903 Springfield. It eliminated the considerable physical effort needed to manipulate a bolt, which minimized the fatigue, muscle tremors and increases in blood pressure that caused accuracy to deteriorate.

Though the British had made little visible advance in their smallarms, this did not signify inactivity. Experiments had been undertaken with Gerlich and Janaček high velocity systems, many auto-loading rifles had been examined in minute detail, and attempts had been made to develop yet another infantry rifle to replace the Lee-Enfield. Unfortunately, the British were still obsessed with long-range accuracy; added to optimistic armour-piercing requirements, some of the projects verged on lunacy. In April 1937, for example, the Small Arms Committee had considered a selection of guns made to Enfield Design Department project 2012 ('DD[E]2012'). One BSA-made survivor embodies a recoil-absorbing butt plate and a massive Mauser-type action, derived from the P/14, chambering a rimless ·276 cartridge. The muzzle velocity of the 104-grain bullet was a stupefying $4,000\text{fs}^{-1}$, allowing infantrymen to broach 14mm-thick armour plate at 500 yards.

THE SECOND WORLD WAR

In the autumn of 1939, as had been done a quarter-century previously, the government optimistically ordered the British Expeditionary Force (BEF) to France. The subsequent events are etched indelibly into the annals of British military history, as the 'Phoney War' was shattered by the German invasion of France by way of the Low Countries. Despite spirited resistance from the BEF and sections of the French Army, the Germans ground inexorably onward until the British were pinned back against the Channel coast.

Author's archives.

69-71 ABOVE

The progression of the Lee-Enfield. **A** The SMLE Mark 1 of 1902. Note the two-piece charger guide, with one part on the receiver and the other on the bolt head. **B** The SMLE Mk V, 20,000 of which were made for troop trials in 1922–4. Note that the cut off has been reinstated, a leaf-and-aperture back sight lies on top of the receiver, and a auxiliary barrel band has been added. **C** The Rifle No.4 Mk 2, the perfected postwar pattern. Compared with the SMLE Mk V, the back sight position has been retained, the cut off is omitted, and the nose cap has been greatly simplified.

Desperate situations required desperate solutions, virtually anything afloat in the South of England endeavouring to take men off the beaches at Dunkirk (26 May–4 June 1940). The evacuation was simultaneously a bitter disappointment and an incredible achievement – J.B. Priestley spoke on 5 June of beginning the war by 'snatching glory out of defeat' – that brought 338,226 Anglo-French troops safely back to Britain. Subsequent 'Little Dunkirks' staged along the French and Belgian coasts rescued 136,000 more.

The greatest post-Dunkirk problem was not the loss of men, nor even the noticeable decline in morale among returnees, but tremendous losses in matériel. The BEF had been the pick of the British Army, and its equipment had been the most modern; six hundred tanks had been left behind in France, plus many large-calibre guns. According to one assessment, only 2,130 Bren Guns remained to defend Britain.

It had been obvious for several weeks prior to Dunkirk that the Germans would be difficult to stop, and that Britain would be threatened should France fall. During a broadcast on 14 May 1940, Anthony Eden, Secretary of State for War, had announced the formation of the Local Defence Volunteers (LDV).

‡The upper age limit proved particularly elastic; many men were entitled to wear Matabeleland Campaign or South African War medals, and a national search for the most senior LDV man discovered a Scots serjeant-major who had served in the Suakin Campaign of 1884–5. The nationality restriction was later relaxed to include men of dual nationality who had served the British armed forces in 1914–18, or who had satisfactorily completed three years or more of regular service prior to 1939.

72 BELOW

Punjabi riflemen advance behind a Sherman tank towards Meiktila during the campaign to liberate Burma from the Japanese in the Spring of 1945. Note the Mk III* SMLE being carried by the man on the right, and the cumbersome full-length P/07 bayonet.

The requirements were simply that recruits should be aged between 17 and 65, reasonably fit, and hold sole British nationality.‡

Within 24 hours a quarter-million men had volunteered for service, and the total had risen to 1·5 million by the middle of June. Winston Churchill subsequently referred to the LDV as the 'Home Guard', the change of name being regularized at the end of July 1940.

The problems of arming vast numbers of keen, but untrained civilians had not even been considered. It proved an unjustifiable supposition that volunteers would be farmers, gamekeepers and countrymen who could each contribute a shotgun. An overwhelming response from the urban areas was quite unexpected.

At first, a lucky few . . . were given Short Lee Enfield rifles, which had been standard in the First World War. But even in Berkshire, a vulnerable enough area, one battalion received, as its first issue of arms, four rifles per one hundred men and only ten rounds per rifle. In any case, after Dunkirk, these were surrendered to the army. A fowling piece was a pretty superior item of equipment in the L.D.V. Picks, pickaxes, crowbars, niblicks, choppers, or even dummy rifles which might bluff paratroopers into submission, were taken out on the first all-night patrols. One Lancashire battalion borrowed a quantity of rifles which had been used in the Crimean War and the Indian Mutiny; another provided each man with a six-foot spear and a heavily weighted truncheon. Engineering workers turned out coshes and sticking knives after finishing a day's shift; in one Derbyshire colliery, the miners invented their own bizarre but serviceable anti-tank gun. Nigel Calder, *The People's War*

The advent of this people's army led to a series of bizarre emergency weapons. The gloriously named Bates Eight Barrel Bottle Thrower was intended to saturate an area with 'No.76 Grenades', which were simply bottles filled with a self-igniting phosphorus compound. Very few of these projects concerned smallarms, though the origins of the Sten Gun may be traced to this stressful episode.

73 ABOVE
Indian troops of 8th Army advance after establishing a bridgehead across the river Sillaro in northern Italy – most likely posed specially for the photographer, owing to the lack of caution with which the ridge is being approached. The man nearest the camera has a flamethrower, the remainder carrying SMLE rifles and P/07 bayonets. Author's archives.

A 4in gun was fitted on the poop and two rings for high-angle anti-aircraft guns were fitted, though no guns were available. Eight Ross ·303 rifles arrived . . . A Royal Marine sergeant was appointed gunner and he and I decided to test the Ross rifles, and found that only two were serviceable; the other six had to have their bolts clouted with a hammer as the springs were too weak to fire the pin.

Alec Niblock, 'When the War was Young and we had not learned to Hate', in *Sea Breezes*, vol.64 no.533 (May 1990), describing his experiences aboard the Elders & Fyffes steamer *Corrales*.

* The Ulster Volunteer Force, 80,000 strong at its height, was formed shortly before the First World War to oppose the Home Rule Bill. The organisation was legal, but unarmed until substantial quantities of rifles were imported — illegally — from Germany. These included 20,000 Austrian 'M1904' Mannlichers and German Gew.88, plus an unknown quantity of old Italian Vetterli rifles. Many of these subsequently were used for training purposes.

The efficiency of Home Guard units in 1940 may be questioned, but their enthusiasm and dedication most certainly cannot. Even so, during one day-time 'parachutist alert' in Croydon, the local battalion commander managed to muster a mere fifteen men, a rifle with ten rounds, an old revolver and a 12-bore shotgun!

During the summer of 1940, a large consignment of ·30 M1917 ('Enfield') rifles arrived from the USA. Together with even greater numbers of British ·303 P/14 rifles refurbished from store, these provided the backbone of the Home Guard until the volunteers were formally stood down on 1 November 1944. M1917 rifles displayed broad red stripes around the fore-end, on the chamber or across the butt to remind firers that they chambered rimless ·30 cartridges instead of the rimmed ·303.

Huge quantities of submachine-guns were acquired from the Auto-Ordnance Corporation, deliveries of ·45-calibre Model 21 and 28 Thompsons totalling 541,000 by October 1942. The first hundred thousand, which had been accompanied by more than 800,000 drum and 1·46 million box magazines, was distributed to the needy: 56,000 to the army, compensating for losses of automatic weapons at Dunkirk; 12,000 to the RAF, for airfield defence; 5,000 each to the Dominions, India and the Home Guard; and 2,000 for special operations. The remaining 15,000 were held for emergencies.

Among other weapons supplied from North America were 75,000 Canadian ·303 Ross rifles; 1,280 ·30 M1903 Springfields; 30,000 ·30 M1 Garands; and at least 4,200 (possibly 9,200) 7·65mm Belgian Mausers, made during the First World War by Hopkins & Allen but never delivered.

Westley Richards refurbished 475 M1888 Austrian Mannlicher rifles in 1940–1, the guns apparently being part of pre-1914 consignments to the Ulster Volunteer Force,* and surprising numbers of sporting guns were retrieved from the gun trade. The Contract Books record the purchase of 12,450 ·22-calibre guns between 4 April 1940 and 29 January 1943. They ranged from 2,066 assorted bolt-action, pump-action and semi-automatic Winchesters, acquired from Parker-Hale in October 1941, to a single Winchester Model 68

†Including 339 Air Rifles No.1 Mk I and I* (BSA gunnery trainers) and twelve examples of the Webley No.3 Mk I.

purchased for £1.14.0d from J. Braddell & Son on 19 November 1941. Approximately 8,430 12-bore shotguns – mostly Greener Police Guns – were acquired in the same period, together with 2,608 assorted air rifles.†

It is difficult to imagine what the average German parachutist, perhaps a veteran of the attack on Fort Eben-Emael, would have made of the Home Guard. Pitting shotguns, choppers and six-foot spears against well-trained men armed with Maschinenpistolen and efficient machine-guns courted disaster.

Yet the LDV and Home Guard fulfilled a vital role in the defence of Britain, freeing many thousands of regular soldiers from guard duties. As the war ran its course and the Home Guard began to receive better weapons, increasingly professional training raised the fighting potential of the irregulars immeasurably. This was helped by the development of submachine-guns such as the Sten, which could be mass-produced in even the most ill-equipped machine-shop, and by the acquisition of effectual weapons under Lend-Lease. The latter included nearly 80,000 machine-guns.

74 BELOW
The Hefah V machine-gun, an emergency design approved for adoption during the Second World War as an anti-aircaft gun for merchant shipping. The guns were intended to be mounted in pairs and fired by a receiver-top linkage.

By courtesy of Ian Hogg.

SLOW PROGRESS

‡It is sometimes suggested that the Light Rifle was developed at British requests. However, the relevant patents were filed on behalf of Edward S. Pomeroy on 23–28 June 1939. It seems clear, therefore, that the project was originally a simple commercial speculation.

The standard British infantry weapons in 1945 remained Lee-Enfield rifles, Webley-type revolvers, Bren and Vickers Guns. These had been joined by millions of cheap Sten Guns and an assortment of American equipment, but not all procurement had been successful.

A notable failure had been the Smith & Wesson Model 40 light rifle, a 9mm auto-loader offered to the British Purchasing Commission in 1940.‡ Smith & Wesson accepted a million-dollar advance payment, but the rifle failed the British proof tests and was rejected. Only 1,010 were made before the project was abandoned. Understandably, the British demanded that the advances be returned. To do so would have ruined the company, so an offer of ·38/200 revolvers in payment of the debt was accepted instead.

Few efforts were made to develop simplified weapons in Britain, though an all-metal version of the No.4 rifle was made by Adams Bros & Burnley in the summer of 1943 and a 'Pressed Steel Bren' (the Besal) was actually approved for service in the same period. However, excepting the Sten Gun, which remained in production until 1945, the need for emergency weapons had passed by 1943. Thus the British had not gained experience of the advanced fabricating techniques being incorporated in contemporary German automatic weapons – a deficiency which was to blight the British metalworking industry in the immediate postwar period.

THE MODERN ERA

Though the Russians soon copied the German assault rifle, which fired a short 7·9mm cartridge, the Western Allies remained firmly wedded to long-range accuracy and striking power. Some sections of the US Army were particularly hostile to reductions in bullet weight or propellant capacity, refusing to countenance 500-yard limitations on effective engagement range.

Immediately after the war, using a mixture of German, Polish emigré and indigenous research, the British produced the EM-1 (Thorpe) and EM-2 (Janson) rifles around a special ·280in cartridge whose bullet, weighing 140

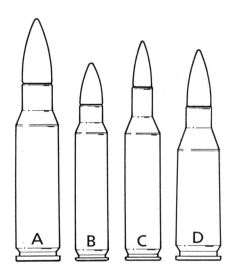

75 ABOVE

Comparative cartridges: **A** 7·62X51 NATO, **B** 5·56X45mm, **C** 4·85X49 (UK experimental) and **D** 6·25X43 (UK experimental).

grains, reached a muzzle velocity of $2,535\text{fs}^{-1}$. This was less powerful than the ·303, German 7·9mm or US ·30−06, but developed greater energy than the German intermediate 7·9mm and had a longer effective range.

The advent of the EM-1 and EM-2 heralded an appreciable change in British ordnance circles. Previously, smallarms had often originated abroad: Jacob Snider, James Lee and Hiram Maxim had all been American, Friedrich von Martini was Swiss, and the father of the Bren Gun, Václav Holek, was Czechoslovakian.* This pragmatic approach undoubtedly minimized development costs, and avoided the worst excesses of nationalism that had characterized smallarms history in − for example − France and Italy.

The establishment of the Small Arms Group at Cheshunt during the Second World War disturbed the balance. Greatly influenced by Belgian, Czechoslovakian and Polish technicians, the post-war British attitude changed to one of self-sufficiency. It was also created a feeling of superiority; though the British have always blamed the US Army for the demise of the EM-2, British authorities proved just as obstructive by adopting the ·280 cartridge.

Locked by modified Friberg-Kjellman flaps, the EM-2 was entered in NATO standardization trials in 1950. Its opponents were the ·280 Belgian FAL, designed by Dieudonné Saive and made by Fabrique Nationale d'Armes de Guerre, and Earle Harvey's T25. The American rifle chambered the experimental ·30 T65 cartridge.

Among the advantages claimed for the British 'bull-pup' design, with its magazine behind the pistol grip, was that a full-length barrel could be fitted into an otherwise compact design. This no-one disputed. However, trials undertaken at Aberdeen Proving Ground in 1950 revealed that the EM-2 was too complicated, awkward and not particularly accurate.

76 ABOVE

A longitudinal section of the EM-2, from the official manual – *Provisional Notes for users of Rifle, Automatic, 280-inch EM-2 (C.E.A.D.)* – published by the Ministry of Supply in 1950.

Criticisms of similar magnitude (differing in detail) were made of the FAL and the T25, but US Army refused to accept the ·280 cartridge in preference to the ·30 T65. France agreed with the US Army, while Canada was willing to accept a majority decision.

Neither for the first nor last time in its ordnance history, Britain stood alone. In 1951, the EM-2 was officially approved by the Labour Government of the day as the 'Rifle 7mm No 9 Mk 1'. Soon it had been cancelled by the Conservatives in favour of the FAL.

There were many recriminations, particularly in the British Press, and searching questions were asked in parliament in attempts to reveal the truth. It is highly likely that the replies only contained parts of the truth. Though one most interesting modern account exists (T. B. Dugelby, *EM-2 Concept &*

Design, 1980), it was forced to rely too greatly on secondary sources by restrictions placed on official documents. A balanced narrative account, devoting space to those who felt the EM-2 to be irredeemably flawed, has yet to be written.

A few EM-2 rifles had been chambered for the 7·62mm T65 and even the larger ·30−06, but the design disappeared into history in the early 1950s. Owing to the curious circumstances of its demise, the EM-2 has attained a mythical place in British smallarms history. Whether it was really so badly treated is difficult to determine. As early as 1951, a British Army technical commission appointed to report on relative merits had overwhelmingly favoured the FAL over the EM-2. A user trial in the summer of 1951 had been inconclusive, but rapid development of the Belgian gun had tipped the balance by 1953.

The EM-2 design clearly had more potential than was ever exploited, but was complicated and costly. The basic 'bullpup' layout − still controversial − has reappeared in the current L85A1, though direct links with the EM-2 project are tenuous.†

†The L85A1 is locked by a rotary bolt adapted from the Armalite series; comparisons with the EM-2, therefore, are misleading in all respects other than layout and the concept of a standard-issue optical sight.

Unwilling to take an American rifle, the British accepted the perfected Belgian Fusil Automatique Léger (FAL), tooling for the modified Rifle L1A1 beginning in the Royal Small Arms Factory and at BSA Guns Ltd in 1956. Compared with the EM-2, the FAL was long and heavy. Owing to its conventional construction, however, it handled much better than its unorthodox rival and has given more than thirty years of satisfactory service.

The FAL was subsequently joined by other Belgian-designed weapons. By 1970, therefore, the British soldier's firearms − L1A1 rifles, L4A4 (Bren) and L7A1 machine-guns, plus the L9A1 pistol − were once again largely imports. Only the L2A3 Sterling submachine-gun and the L42A1 (Lee-Enfield) sniper rifle went against the trend. Interestingly, standardizing on the Belgian-designed guns has led to decades of comparative stability. Though the L7A1 and L7A2 are none too popular with their users, this is due more to the continued presence of the Bren Gun than defective design.

THE KOREAN WAR

77 BELOW

The US M1 Garand rifle was occasionally used by British troops serving in Europe after D-Day (6 June 1944) and later in Korea. This is an M1C sniper rifle with a Weaver M84 sight. The prong flash suppressor was not found on pre-1953 guns, most of which had a simple cone.

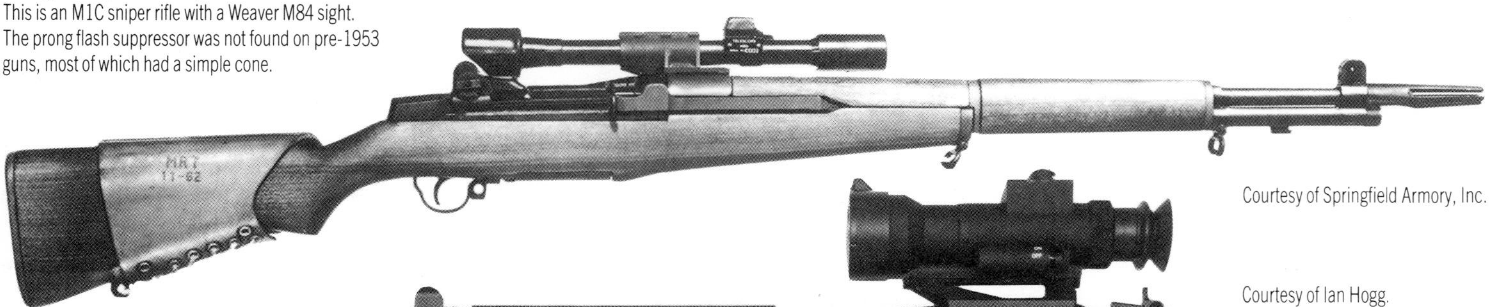

The campaigns of 1950−3 were largely an American affair, though United Nations forces, two British infantry brigades and Commonwealth contingents were committed to supporting South Korea in an ugly, sprawling war against North Koreans and Chinese. The British 27 and 29 Brigades, raised in Hong Kong and the United Kingdom respectively, were supported by 45 Field Regiment, Royal Artillery, and the Royal Navy. Compared with the 1.319 million

Courtesy of Springfield Armory, Inc.

Courtesy of Ian Hogg.

78 ABOVE
This picture shows a Litton Industries Model 845 image-intensifying sight mounted on a commercial FN FAL rifle (note the chambering mark '·308 MATCH').

Americans who served in Korea, British participation was minor.‡ It is remarkable principally for the Battle of Imjin River (22–25 April 1951), in which units of the Gloucestershire Regiment, the Royal Ulster Rifles and the Northumberland Fusiliers were sacrificed to hold a vital position against three divisions of the Chinese 63rd Army. The Gloucesters, in particular, emerged with great glory from what many observers deemed an unnecessary catastrophe. Only 169 men out of a battalion strength of eight hundred mustered for roll-call after the final withdrawal.

The first British unit to arrive in Korea, 41 Independent Commando Brigade, Royal Marines, had been equipped entirely with American weaponry. It was common to encounter British infantry armed with US Garands and M1 Carbines in addition to traditional equipment – Sten, Bren and Vickers Guns, and No.4 rifles. Browning machine-guns were also popular.

Many Britons, particular officers and senior NCOs, coveted the US ·30 M1 Carbine. Originally conceived to arm non-combatants, the lightweight M1 Carbine was roundly condemned by US Army ordnance experts owing to its lack of stopping power in combat! At close range, however, it was much more powerful than a pistol and far more accurate than a submachine-gun. Consequently, the M1 Carbine was extremely popular in the field, and photographs taken in Korea often show it serving alongside Sten Guns and No.4 rifles.

THE CHANGING FACE OF WAR

Confrontation between major powers has become increasingly rare since 1953 – apart from the conflict in Vietnam, the Arab-Israeli Wars, the brief war between India and Pakistan, and the Gulf War between Iran and Iraq. Korea was also saw the last war to be fought with the weapons of the Second World War. The advent of battlefield radar, missiles and tactical nuclear weapons has since changed the rules of engagement irreversibly.*

As major colonial empires have fallen apart, so interminable guerrilla campaigns, skirmishes and 'Brush Wars' have changed the face of war. They have also changed the basic infantry rifle, as even the US Army finally accepted the subordination of long-range performance to short-range firepower.

The deconstruction of the British Empire, begun with grants of independence to India and Pakistan (1947–8), was not always peaceable. Prior to the conflict with Argentina in 1982, the most serious incidents occurred in Malaya and Borneo.

The Malayan Emergency (1948–60) arose from the disenfranchisement of Malaya's sizable Chinese minority, many of whom had actively resisted the Japanese, in favour of the largely supine Malays. Though the guerrilla force, rarely greater than 7,000 strong, managed at one stage to involve 170,000 British and Malay troops, emphasis in fighting the insurgents on their own terms eventually paid dividends. Yet it still took nine years to reduce the nuisance to a level where the Federated States of Malaya could be granted independence. When the end of the emergency was declared in 1960,† it had cost the lives of 637 British, Gurkha and Malay soldiers, 1,346 Malay policemen and at least 6,700 guerrillas.

Sterling submachine-guns and shotguns were deemed better jungle-fighting weapons than the ponderous No.4 Lee-Enfield or an L1A1. This unsurprising discovery led to purchases of the 5·56mm M16 rifle for Limited Theatre use by the British Army, the American rifle being particularly popular in Borneo owing to its light weight and rot-proof synthetic stock. The campaign against Indonesian insurgents (1963–6) drew great inspiration from the Malayan Emergency, though jungle-fighting and the tactical use of helicopters had been considerably refined.

More than 30,000 British, Gurkha and Malay soldiers were eventually committed with great success against insurgents and Indonesian regulars. Denis Healey, then Minister of Defence, opined in the House of Commons that the campaign had been 'one of the most efficient uses of military forces in the history of the world'. For a loss of 69 British and Gurkha dead, the Indonesians had been repulsed with a loss estimated at 2,000 men.

Intent on developing a rifle of its own, rather than adapting the best available design, the British Army embarked in the late 1960s on another 'calibre controversy' by promoting a new 4·85mm round. In the NATO standardization trials of 1977−9, the British repeated the mistakes of the EM-2. All the participants had entered 5·56mm rifles, with the exception of the Germans,‡ and it was clear that the 4·85×49 cartridge would not be acceptable to the majority even before testing began. Its undoubted merits were simply not enough to displace the rival American 5·56mm.

The trials unexpectedly led to the standardization of the Belgian-designed 5·56mm SS109 bullet, heavier than the US M193, slower moving and fired from a faster rifling twist to increase rotation-speed and improve stability.* The US M16 box magazine was also standardized, despite being difficult to mass produce, and the French grenade-launcher attachment was approved.

Britain came away with nothing, except the need to convert the 4·85mm XL70 Infantry Weapon to 5·56mm. This was successfully achieved during the early 1980s, and allowed the adoption of the L85A1. The new bullpup is reaching the troops, but service issue has been plagued with teething troubles. Whether these are simply due to poor manufacture or defects in the concept has already been argued forcefully in the specialist press, but it is too early to attempt a balanced summary. The SUSAT optical sight is a great asset, improving the standards of marksmanship appreciably, but the SA-80/L85A1 rarely performs better than the Steyr AUG or the FN FNC in competitive trials.

NEW DEVELOPMENTS

‡The Bundeswehr entered the 4·75mm Heckler & Koch G11, which fired a unique caseless cartridge. The Germans had little expectation of success, other than to promote what may yet become the next generation of smallarms.

* The SS109 carries farther, but its lethality is reduced in pursuit of accuracy compared with the US Ball M193.

79 BELOW

Two pre-production versions of the SA-80, now officially designated L85A1: note their 'XL70E3' marks and UI-series numbers. The farther gun, in Light Support Weapon ('LSW') guise, offers a bipod and a heavy barrel. Courtesy of Ian Hogg.

HANDGUNS

Though substantial numbers of pepperboxes were made in Britain in the 1840s, and even small numbers of the first Colts had been sold on the British market, little interest was evinced in the revolver until the Great Exhibition of 1851.

An impressive display of machine-made Colts in the Crystal Palace was devalued by the appearance of a solid-frame self-cocking revolver on the stand of Deane, Adams & Deane. This was made to Robert Adams's British Patent 13,527 of 1851, one of those all-embracing specifications that also protected breech-loading sporting rifles. The revolver may even have been added as an afterthought; but, though accorded no prominence in the catalogues of the Great Exhibition, it was to be the cornerstone of Adams's success. To Colt's chagrin, Deane, Adams & Deane received a prize medal for its 'double & single guns & pistols properly finished'. The Colonel received nothing.

The advent of the revolvers had not passed without interest. *The Times* reported on 27 June 1851 that 25 Colts had been purchased by officers of the 12th Lancers, soon to depart for Cape Colony, and a Select Committee assembled at Woolwich on 10 September 1851 to test a hefty ·44 six-shot Dragoon Colt (Model of 1848) against a lighter 32-bore five-shot Adams. The tests were repeated at the Royal Manufactory, Enfield, later that month and then again at Woolwich (13–21 October) under the supervision of Lieutenant-Colonel Chalmers of the Royal Artillery. There was little to choose between the guns. The Colt was clumsier; and the Adams, owing to its double-action lock, could be shot faster. However, Adams's mechanism was more fragile.

Little was achieved by the earliest trials. When the Crimean War began at the end of 1853, however, a letter appeared in *The Times* drawing attention to a 'decision' of the Russian navy to arm its men with Colt copies made in Tula. Whether or not there was truth in the claim, which may have been penned by a Colt stooge, the Admiralty resolved to take immediate action. On 8 March 1854, Colt was asked to supply four thousand 1851 or Navy-pattern ·36-calibre revolvers. Another 5,500 were ordered in late summer 1854, and then the army sought 14,000 in 1855. Unfortunately for the cavalrymen, to whom the guns would have been most useful, the Commander-in-Chief refused to sanction such issues.* Instead, the Colts benefitted infantry officers, serjeants-major, and curiously-named irregulars such as Count Zamoyski's Cossacks of the Sultan.

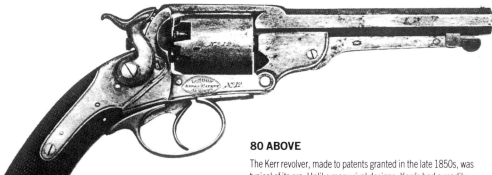

80 ABOVE
The Kerr revolver, made to patents granted in the late 1850s, was typical of its era. Unlike many rival designs, Kerr's had a readily detachable lock to facilitate maintenance. Courtesy of the Board of Trustees of the Royal Armouries, HM Tower of London.

Many of the Navy Colts were withdrawn after the war, inventories indicating 17,344 at home and a mere 713 abroad on 1 January 1859. Survivors were still in store in 1868; indeed, the combustible cartridge – 'Cartridge, Small Arm, Ball, Pistol, Revolver, Colt's, Skin' – was not declared obsolete until LoC 5344 of 8 November 1887.

The original self-cocking Adams revolver, though its one-piece frame was extremely sturdy, had two important disadvantages: it lacked a hammer spur, preventing thumb-cocking, and the absence of a rammer hindered loading. The bullet had to be seated in the chamber by thumb pressure alone, and sometimes jarred forward to leave a gap between its base and the powder. In addition, as the chamber diameter was greater than the bore, the bullet needed to accelerate very rapidly to engage the rifling effectually. Adams's guns worked perfectly when properly loaded, but attempts to use coarse or slow-burning powder were often disastrous.

It was not that the guns were structurally weak; pressures simply rose far above normal levels. But it was a problem that attracted adverse comment, especially in trials undertaken in the colonies where the quality of propellant was less predictable. The Colt had a powerful rammer that seated each bullet firmly down on to the powder charge. Excessive pressures were rarely generated and the guns attained a reputation for excellent accuracy. Maximum range exceeded 600 yards.

Experience in the Crimea, however, showed that the ·36 Colt bullet was a poor man-stopper compared with the appreciably larger Adams patterns.

While Colt's star waned, Robert Adams had made substantial improvements to his basic design. Among them had been rammers designed by John Rigby, Adams himself and James Kerr. These were patented in September 1854, 1855 and July 1855 respectively. The original Rigby rammer is rarely seen, the pattern currently identified with this particular patentee being Adams's despite its 'Rigby Patent' marks. It lies on the left side of the frame above the trigger guard. The effectual Colt-like Kerr rammer was mounted on the left side of the barrel rather than underneath.†

If the rammer improved Adams's revolver appreciably, then new lockwork credited to Lieutenant Frederick Beaumont of the Royal Engineers was the difference between commercial obscurity and military approval. At last, the Adams could be thumb-cocked. Now that it offered single- and double-action to accompany its sturdy solid frame, and had a satisfactory rammer, the War Department substituted the ·442 (54-bore) Adams for the ·36 Colt in British service. The first orders were placed in October 1855, but war in the Crimea ended before many could be delivered. Return of peace lessened the urgency, and only 19,123 Adams revolvers had been purchased by December 1860. Guns were sent to the USA during the American Civil War, though in no great quantity. A licence to make the Beaumont-Adams revolver had been granted to the Massachussetts Arms Company in the mid 1850s, but production, never large, had ceased in the USA prior to the war.‡

* This was apparently on the grounds that he considered a revolver to be a source of danger to a trooper on a skittish horse.

†The best of the rammers was probably Joseph Brazier's, the subject of British Patent 760 of 5 April 1855. However, this was confined to guns sold by Brazier, Wilkinson and a few other gunsmiths; it does not appear on any of the service revolvers, which all featured Kerr's rammer (Patent 1,722/55).

‡Small numbers of ·36 Belt and ·31 Pocket Model Beaumont-Adams revolvers were made by the licensee in 1857–8. Between 11 November 1861 and 23 April 1862, the Federal authorities purchased 623 assorted Adams revolvers from Schuyler, Hartley & Graham of New York.

Robert Adams soon parted with the London Armoury Company, which had been founded in 1856 specifically to make the Beaumont-Adams revolver. To avoid wrangling over Adams's patents, the armoury immediately substituted the Kerr revolver; soon, however, rifle-musket contracts for the Confederacy relegated the manufacture of handguns to the background.

Though many cap-lock revolvers were produced by Webley, Tranter, Daw and many other gunsmiths in this period, often to be bought privately by army officers, none achieved official service status in the British Army. The revolver was still regarded with suspicion by many senior officers, and sufficient Colt or Beaumont-Adams guns remained to answer immediate needs.

The advent of the metallic cartridge brought the first change of heart. The lead came from the Royal Navy when, on 20 November 1868, the Admiralty sanctioned the conversion of existing Beaumont-Adams revolvers for centre-fire cartridges. Most of these guns had been made by the London Armoury Company in 1856–8. The guns can be identified by their solid frame; however, they have a plain-surface cylinder, hammers modified for centre-fire cartridges, and an ejector rod on the right side of the barrel. They usually display the dates of conversion (e.g., 'C/69' or '-/69') on the frame.

The new revolver had been patented by John Adams, Robert Adams's younger brother. Made by, or more probably on behalf of Adams's Patent Small Arms Co. Ltd, its built-up frame (patent 1,758/61) avoided infringing the patents sought previously by Robert Adams. A patent granted in July 1866 (no.1,959/66) improved the frame design, and a loading gate and ejector rod were added by British Patent 2,961/67. These features appear on all John Adams's service revolvers. An improved ejector system, patented in 1872, did not.

On 22 February 1872, the army approved the Pistol, Revolver, Breech-Loading, Adams, ·450-inch, Interchangeable, (Mark II), the converted percussion guns becoming 'Mark I' even though their design differed considerably from that of the new weapons. The Adams Mark III, approved on 24 August 1872, was simply a Mark II with an improved extractor; and the Mark IV was a Mark I with strengthened lockwork.

Though production of Mark III Adams was sufficient to allow guns to be sold commercially and despatched to colonial agencies, a shortage of handguns in the British Army existed by 1878. For once, problems had been foreseen and five hundred assorted Colt, Tranter and Webley revolvers had been ordered in time for the Zulu War of 1879.

The Colts are believed to have been the so-called double-action 'Model 1878', but confirmation is currently lacking. The Pistol, Revolver, Breech-Loading, Tranter, ·450-inch, Interchangeable (Mark I), approved on 19 July 1878, was a sturdy solid-frame gun with an ejector rod on the right side of the barrel, a hinged loading gate on the right side of the frame behind the cylinder, and a double action trigger system. The Webleys are believed to have been the well-known Royal Irish Constabulary Model.

The standard of these guns depressed the War Department greatly — one gun in four was rejected by the inspectorate — and a decision was taken to make revolvers at Enfield. It is assumed that a competition was held in the late 1870s, though information is currently lacking. In the end, the government seized on a quirky revolver patented by a Welsh-born Philadelphian mechanic named Owen Jones. A combination of the Jones extraction system and Warnant lockwork, the Pistol, Revolver, Breech-Loading, Enfield, ·476-inch (Mark I), adopted in August 1880, was an odd combination of a hinged barrel and sliding cylinder.

The action of the Mark II Enfield, approved in March 1882, is described in the 1888 edition of the *Text Book of Small Arms*.

Unfortunately, despite best intentions, the committee-designed Enfield revolver was no great success. It was very cumbersome compared with many contemporary designs, shot poorly owing to a reliance on standard Martini-Henry rifling, and often failed to extract properly. The lowermost case sometimes had to be prised loose before reloading. The original gun had rifled chamber mouths, which not only clogged with lead fragments but also failed to align with the rifling in the bore. Bullets were cut, and accuracy was reduced. Nickel plating on the lockwork flaked badly enough to jam the action, and the joint between the barrel and the frame worked loose.

Approval of the Mark II notwithstanding, the Enfield was doomed. It was soon discovered that the guns could be fired if the hammer was struck sharply when in the rebound position. A safety device was announced in LoC 5317 (28 July 1887) as "a pawl and spring catch

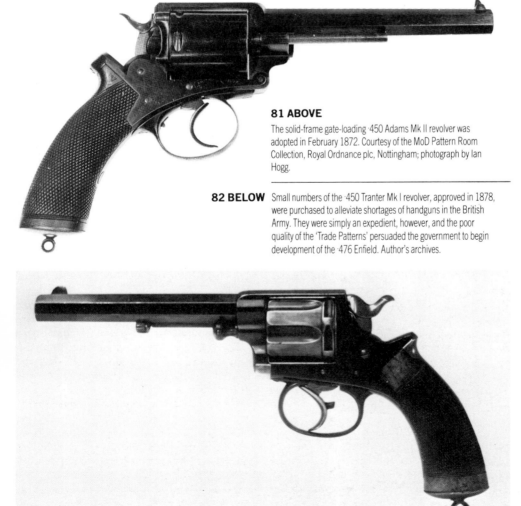

81 ABOVE

The solid-frame gate-loading ·450 Adams Mk II revolver was adopted in February 1872. Courtesy of the MoD Pattern Room Collection, Royal Ordnance plc, Nottingham; photograph by Ian Hogg.

82 BELOW Small numbers of the ·450 Tranter Mk I revolver, approved in 1878, were purchased to alleviate shortages of handguns in the British Army. They were simply an expedient, however, and the poor quality of the 'Trade Patterns' persuaded the government to begin development of the ·476 Enfield. Author's archives.

83 LEFT
The ·476 Enfield Mk II revolver was approved in March 1882.
Courtesy of the MoD Pattern Room Collection, Royal Ordnance plc,
Nottingham; photograph by Ian Hogg.

84 LEFT
A ·450 solid-frame Webley No.5 revolver. Note the 'OVS' mark
(Oranje Vrij Staat, Orange Free State) pressed into the grip.
Courtesy of the MoD Pattern Room Collection, Royal Ordnance plc,
Nottingham; photograph by Ian Hogg.

85, 86 BELOW
Variants of the ·476 Webley 'WG' revolver, the Model 1886
(top) with a Pryse-pattern cylinder retainer, and the later Model
1892 (bottom) with a Whiting design. Note the perfected stirrup-
type locking catch, which was adopted for the government Mk I
Webley revolver in 1887. Courtesy of Richard Milner.

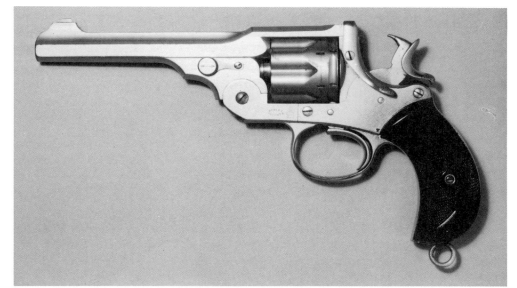

attached to the outside of the lock plate; this
catch is acted on by the pawl, keeping it free
from the hammer when at full cock, and allowing it to return in front of the hammer when
the latter is at the 'rebound' position".

The expedient was short-lived, as a Pistol,
Breech-Loading, Revolver, Enfield, with safety
catch (Mark II) was approved in December
1888. Announced in LoC 5671 on 8 January
1889, the new catch comprised a small arm
pivoted on the trigger lever, with a pin on the
arm to interpose between the hammer and the
hammer-seat unless the hammer had been
released from full-cock. Modified guns have a
large 'S' on the left side of the frame beneath
the barrel catch. The earlier safety system was
declared obsolete, all issue guns being recalled for modification.

THE FIRST WEBLEYS

By 1886, it was clear that the Enfield revolver
was not a success. Experiments began to find
a better weapon, eventually narrowing to a
choice between Webley's Government Revolver (or 'W.G. Model 1886') and a break-
action Smith & Wesson.

Sensibly, as there was little to choose
between the guns, the Small Arms Committee
recommended the indigenous Webley. The
company had been making revolvers for many
years, beginning with the so-called 'Longspur'
cap-lock revolver contemporaneously with
the self-cocking Adams. The approval in January 1868 of a sturdy solid-frame ·442 centre-
fire cartridge revolver by the Royal Irish Constabulary had assured Webley's success.
Gradually, guns based on the Constabulary
pattern and a series of break-action designs
enabled Webley to eclipse its rivals.

The first hinged-frame Webley appears to
have been made in the early 1870s, to the
designs of Edward N. Wood, but the first commercially successful gun was the so-called

Webley-Pryse or No.4. This included a cylinder-locking bolt patented by Charles Pryse the Younger in November 1876 (no.4,421/76).

Though Pryse illustrated the device attached to an appropriate revolver, he should not be credited as the originator of the break-action system. This was already well established in Europe and North America and could scarcely have been regarded as innovative in 1876.

The Webley No.4 was soon supplemented by the 'Webley Improved Government Revolver' of 1882, embodying several patents granted to Michael Kaufmann. These included an elegant trigger mechanism with only five components, patented in October 1880 (British Patent 4,302/80), and a three-piece transverse locking bolt dating from November 1881 (no.3,313/81). Webley paid Kaufmann a royalty on each gun bearing the patentee's distinctive mark – an MK monogram within a triangle, on the right side of the frame. Several modifications were made to the gun during its production life, culminating in an improved stirrup fastener patented by Henry Webley and John Carter on 31 March 1885.

The subject of British Patent 4,070/85, the stirrup remains the subject of controversy. A well-known gunmaker, Edwinson Green of Cheltenham, subsequently claimed to have originated the stirrup catch two years before Webley filed the patent specifications. There followed an acrimonious exchange of correspondence in *The Field*, in which Webley attempted to rebut Green's claims. Unfortunately, the modern revision of William Chipchase Dowell's classic *The Webley Story*, by Bruce & Reinhart, makes no attempt to unravel the mystery. Perhaps nothing survives, though one well-known British arms authority claims to have seen the papers in the possession of the Green family. The only demonstrable fact is that Green's design was not patented until 1889.

Green apparently filed suit against Webley but the case, if case there was, never became public. Webley allegedly settled out of court. Yet did Webley pay Green a royalty on all guns marked 'W.G.' just as the company had done on Kaufmann's 'MK' patterns ...?

The 'Improved Government' Webley was superseded by the Webley Government Revolver, also known as the Model of 1886. Fitted with a special ferrule on the cylinder axis pin, patented by William Whiting in February 1886 (no.1,923/86), the revolver was originally offered only in ·455/·476 and had the 'church steeple' cylinder flutes associated with the government Enfield. It had vulcanite bird's head grips, measured 11¼in overall with a 6in barrel, and weighed a fraction over 40oz.

Until the end of the century, Webley constantly changed model dates without necessarily upgrading the pattern. However, the W.G. Model 1893 had a spring-loaded firing pin in the frame rather than utilising a pin in the nose of the hammer, and the Model 1896 featured an improved cylinder retainer.*

It was against this background that Webley entered the British Army trials in the mid 1880s. Solid-frame Webley revolvers had been accepted by the Royal Irish Constabulary in 1868; by the Director-General, India Stores,

* The W.G. series was supplemented in 1902–3 by the 'W.S.', or Webley Service revolver. Claimed to have been specially developed for mounted regiments, this gun had a squared butt; when fitted with a 6in barrel, it bore a close resemblance to the later Mark VI service pattern.

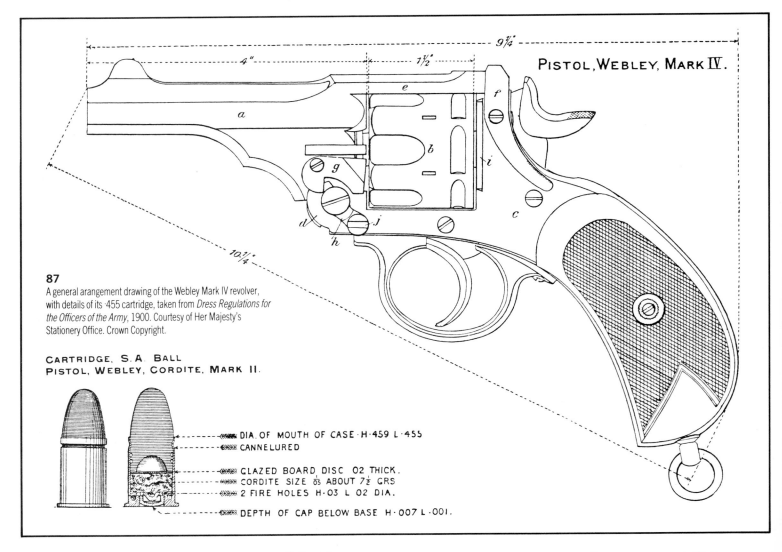

87
A general arangement drawing of the Webley Mark IV revolver, with details of its ·455 cartridge, taken from *Dress Regulations for the Officers of the Army*, 1900. Courtesy of Her Majesty's Stationery Office. Crown Copyright.

who had purchased several hundred ·476 RIC No.3 revolvers in November 1883; by the Metropolitan Police (931 of the 'MP Model' being taken in 1883–4); and by police, volunteer and paramilitary organisations throughout the Empire. Substantial quantities of the New Model No.5 Army Express had gone to the Orange Free State in the 1880s, but none of the break-action guns had seen British service other than in the hands of officers. These had simply been purchased privately.

THE BRITISH ARMY WEBLEYS

Finally, the Pistol, Breech-Loading, Revolver, Webley (Mark I) was sealed on 8 November 1887 and announced in LoC 6075 on 12 July 1890. An initial order confirmed by the Director of Army Contracts as early as 18 July 1887 had called for the manufacture of ten thousand guns.

The Mark I was a minor adaptation of the W.G. revolver, with a 4in barrel and an overall

88 ABOVE
The ·455 Mark IV Webley service revolver of 1899 could be distinguished by its short barrel and rounded bird's head butt. Courtesy of the MoD Pattern Room Collection, Royal Ordnance plc, Nottingham; photograph by Ian Hogg.

89 LEFT
Photographed sometime prior to the First World War, this Household Cavalry Corporal of Horse, identified only as 'Bill', wears a Sam Browne Belt, a holstered short-barrel Webley revolver (probably a Mk IV), and a P/97 infantry officer's sword with a post-1899 leather-body scabbard. Close examination of the original photograph suggests that the sword guard displays the cypher of Edward VII (reigned 1901–10). Courtesy of Elex archives.

length of about 9¼in. It weighed about 35oz unladen. The cylinder assembly was retained by a large transverse screw on the barrel lug, and the grips were vulcanite. The single-action trigger pull was about 7lb, the double action requiring initially fifteen and later 13lb.

No sooner had work commenced than the bore diameter was changed from ·441 to ·446 in June 1888. Confusingly, the gun actually accepted the government ·455 Webley and ·476 Enfield cartridges. By the time LoC 6580 was issued in the autumn of 1891, the 'Stirrup Fastener' had been renamed 'Barrel Catch' and its associated parts re-designated accordingly. An extractor lever spring and pin were added at the same time.

The first holster was approved as the 'Case, Brown, Pistol, Land Service (Mark II)': LoC 6985, published in March 1893. The holster was an open-top pattern with a strap, stitched to the back, which passed over the pistol behind the hammer spur and then latched over a stud on the body-front. The 'Case, Brown, Pistol, Webley, Naval', announced in LoC 6434 of 23 January 1891, had a flap covering the pistol butt.

Issues of holsters suggest that the Webleys reached the troops several years after they had been authorized. As John Carter patented a safety device in this period, to prevent the gun firing from the rebound position (British Patent 16,638/88), and Carter & Whiting sought protection on a two-point cylinder lock (5,778/88), it seems that series production did not commence until 1889; both improvements are incorporated in the Mark I.

Two cleaning rods had been sealed by the time guns were issued, details appearing in LoC 6480 of 20 October 1890. The army type, made of an alloy known as 'delta metal', had a 7½in rod and a single slot for the cleaning patch; the navy version, 10⅛in long, was twisted so that its two slots lay at right angles. Navy pistols generally display a large 'N' on the backstrap.

A leather cleaning rod holder was stitched onto the back of Mk II Land Service holsters towards the end of 1896, strips of leather being issued to regimental artificers to modify holsters that had already been issued. The Mark III holster, subject of LoC 9040 of 21 January 1898, was made with a rod pocket. Its belt loop was stitched so that the holster was carried at an angle, preceding patterns hanging vertically.

The introduction of the 'Sam Browne' belt, sealed on 4 January 1900, led to a change in the holster. The 'Case, Pistol, Sam Browne Belt, Land Service (Mark I)', the subject of LoC 10440 of 28 December 1900, had a closing flap inspired by the naval patterns. However, the retaining strap came up from the lower back of the body in the region of the pistol trigger-guard before slipping over the retaining stud.†

†As officers were permitted to purchase their own revolvers, provided they chambered service ammunition, no holster pattern was sealed specifically for use with the Sam Browne belt. This should be remembered when attempting to identify guns visible in contemporary photographs.

This was subsequently found to inhibit drawing the revolver, and the flap was replaced by a second strap carrying the retaining stud. This holster, the Mark II, was announced in LoC 11202 of 25 June 1902. Though the thickness of the leather in the belt and holster were subsequently reduced, little was done to the holster until 6in-barrelled guns appeared during the First World War. A temporary elongation of the Marks I and II was permitted by LoC 17176 (8 March 1915) pending the introduction of the perfected Mark III holster for the Mark VI revolver.

The Webley Mk I revolver proved durable, *The Field* reporting in May 1889 that one gun had fired 2,330 rounds between 3 December 1888 and 15 April 1889 without cleaning. After firing additional rounds during a demonstration, making 2,392 in all, the Webley had been clamped in a rest. Twelve consecutive shots were put inside a 3in bull's eye at 20 yards.

Sealed in the autumn of 1894, the Mark II Webley revolver was announced in LoC 7816 of 1 October. Several changes had been made to the action. Erosion was found to enlarge the firing-pin hole in the standing breech, so the original fixed shield was replaced by a detachable pattern retained by a dovetail and a screw. A modified hammer with a sturdier striker was fitted; the hump on the Mk I backstrap was removed; the shape of the trigger guard was refined and its edges rounded; the extractor lever, previously a single piece of spring-steel, became a separate component powered by a small coil spring; the V-spring powering the hammer catch was substituted by a coil; and the size of the hammer thumb-piece (or 'spur') was reduced.

The Mark I*, sealed at the same time as the Mk II, was simply an original Mk I fitted with a detachable shield, the new hammer, and a rounded grip. LoC 8002 of 22 October 1895 amended the earlier instructions to indicate that the striker hole in the frame of the Mark I revolver had to be relieved to admit the nose of the Mk II hammer.

Variants of these early guns included the Mark II* N (Naval Service), approved in 1899, which had a Mark IV hammer assembly. The Mark I** N and Mark II** N, approved on 27 April 1915, were Mks I, I* or II revolvers fitted with Mk III cylinders and Mk IV barrels. They had new cylinder cams, cam levers and joint-axis pins, and an additional hole for the cam-lever retaining screw was drilled on the left side of the body hinge. Guns made after 5 June 1915 received 6in barrels instead of the older 4in pattern.

The Mark III, sealed on 5 October 1897, had a new barrel and cylinder. The cylinder axis pin had become an integral part of the barrel forging, a modified bearing reducing friction. A spiral groove cut in the cylinder pin reduced the accumulation of fouling and prevented

PISTOL, REVOLVER, ·455 INCH, WEBLEY,
WITH 6 INCH BARREL, MARK VI

90 ABOVE
General arrangement and longitudinal sectional drawings of the ·455 Webley Mk VI revolver, taken from the 1929 edition of the *Text Book of Small Arms*. Courtesy of Her Majesty's Stationery Office. Crown Copyright.

jamming. An improved method of retaining the cylinder – the 'cylinder cam' – had been patented by William Whiting in February 1891 and then improved in August 1896 (British Patents 3,427/91 and 17,291/96).

The Mark IV, sealed on 21 July 1899, was issued in time for the Second South African War. Revisions were minimal and largely internal. The body, barrel and cylinder were made of a special grade of mild steel, the ratchet on the extractor was case-hardened and the point of the lifting pawl was water-hardened to increase its life. Externally, the hammer-spur was lightened to reduce lock time, the cylinder locking slots were broadened and the edges of the body were rounded. A total of 36,756 Mk IV revolvers was made in 1899–1904.

The Mark V, sealed on 9 December 1913 and approved for manufacture in June 1914, was strengthened for nitrocellulose-propellant ammunition. Consequently, its cylinder had a diameter of 1·745in instead of 1·718in, and the body was appropriately relieved. The rear edge of the cylinder was rounded instead of squared. Many Mk III and Mk IV revolvers were upgraded to Mk V standard when returned for repair, which required parts of the frame to be cut away at the bottom of the cylinder aper-

ture. After May 1915, Land Service guns were given 6in barrels and a new 9½in cleaning rod was approved. It is believed that about 20,000 of an original order for 23,600 Mk V revolvers were made in 1914–15.

Approved on 5 May 1915, the Mk VI ·455 Webley revolver is the most common of the series, production exceeding 300,000 during the First World War. It differed from the Mk V principally in having a squared butt and a modified barrel catch. The front sight was detachable. Some guns will be encountered with the Prideaux Quick Loader, patented in 1893 and then, in an improved form, in 1914.‡ Others may even be accompanied by a shoulder stock, shared with the contemporary signal pistol.

Three butts were introduced in July 1919 – small, medium and large – but the largest was declared obsolete early in 1924. Production of Mk VI revolvers began at Enfield in 1921, continuing until 1932, though few were made after 1928; they have A-prefix numbers, and lack Webley marks. The Mk VI revolver, subsequently renamed Pistol No.1 Mk VI, was a

‡The 'Rapid Loader' was patented by William de Courcy Prideaux on 17 February 1893 (no.3,560/93) and 17 November 1914 (22,653/14). Similar ideas were patented by other inventors, but few reached production status.

Parts Legend

1. Barrel
2. Barrel latch/rear sight
3. Barrel latch screw
4. Barrel latch spring
5. Cylinder
6. Cylinder cam lever
7. Cylinder cam lever lock screw
8. Cylinder cam lever screw
9. Cylinder cam
10. Cylinder cam screw (2)
11. Extractor lever
12. Extractor lever cam
13. Extractor lever cam pin
14. Extractor lever cam spring
15. Extractor rod retainer
16. Extractor spring
17. Extractor/ratchet
18. Extractor/ratchet index pin
19. Frame
20. Front sight blade
21. Front sight blade screw
22. Stock panel, left
23. Stock panel pin (2)
24. Stock panel, right
25. Stock screw
26. Stock screw escutcheon, left
27. Stock screw escutcheon, right
28. Hammer
29. Hammer catch/sear
30. Hammer catch screw
31. Hammer catch spring
32. Hammer pivot screw
33. Hammer swivel/stirrup
34. Hammer swivel screw
35. Hinge pin
36. Hinge pin screw
37. Lanyard ring
38. Mainspring
39. Mainspring auxiliary lever
40. Pawl/hand
41. Recoil plate
42. Recoil plate screw
43. Trigger
44. Trigger catch/cylinder stop
45. Trigger catch spring
46. Trigger catch spring screw
47. Trigger guard
48. Trigger guard screw (2)
49. Trigger pivot screw

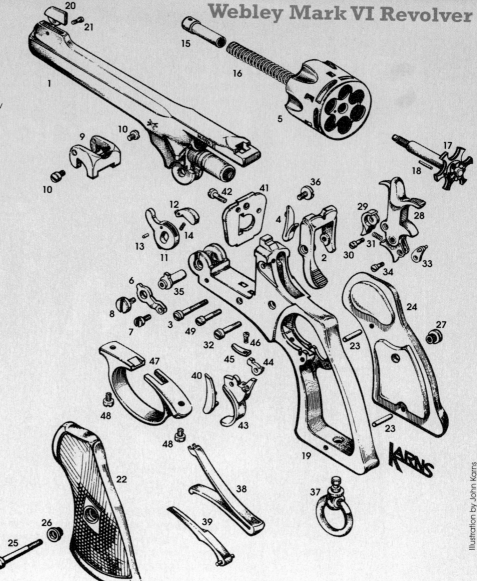

Illustration by John Karns

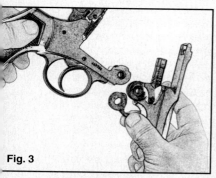

Fig. 3

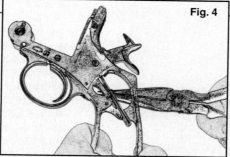

Fig. 4

the frame by pulling its integral securing pin from the hole in the right side of the frame **(Fig. 4)**.

Compress the barrel latch spring (4) using padded pliers and unscrew the barrel latch screw (3) while the spring is compressed. The barrel latch and barrel latch spring may now be taken from the frame by moving the latch down and to the rear and freeing the spring from its retaining hole in the recoil plate (41). Remove the recoil plate screw (42) and drift the recoil plate sideways out of the frame.

Remove the trigger guard screws (48) to free the trigger guard (47). Unscrew the hammer pivot screw (32) and slide the hammer from the frame. Remove the trigger pivot screw (49) and trigger (43). Separate the pawl/hand (40) from its recess and take out the trigger catch spring screw (46) to remove the trigger catch (44) and trigger catch spring (45). Reassemble the revolver in the reverse order.

I'd Like To Thank The *Academy* ...

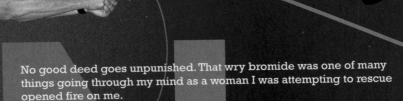

No good deed goes unpunished. That wry bromide was one of many things going through my mind as a woman I was attempting to rescue opened fire on me.

I had been trying to make my way to my car when I heard her screams in the dark garage and went to investigate. Shining my high-intensity flashlight on the scene, I saw a large man atop the woman, pinning her by her shoulders while she screamed bloody murder. I drew my pistol and yelled for him to get off of her as two more men came up on my right, their hands concealed. I swung the beam of light toward the men, yelled for them to stop and demanded they show me their hands. My pistol at the low ready no doubt contributed to their rapid compliance. Returning my attention to the man struggling with the woman, I observed that he hadn't gotten off of her. I continued yelling at him over her loud screams. They were too close together for me to fire at him without endangering her, and he really didn't seem to be doing anything more than holding her. I closed distance, intent on putting my gun close enough to him that he could see it and back off or, worst case scenario, I could fire without threat to the woman.

With a quick check to make sure that the men on my flank hadn't moved, I approached the couple. The man suddenly disengaged and backed off, and that's when the woman drew and began firing. My first thought was that she was shooting at *him*, which concerned me because he was backing away. Then I realized she was shooting at *me* and that concerned me even more.

continued on p. 86

Webley Mark VI Revolver

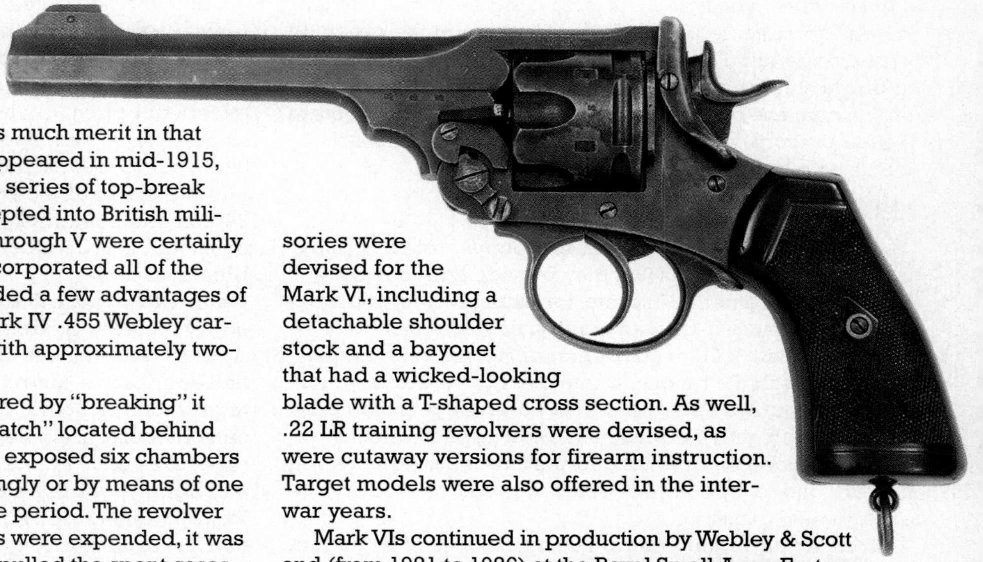

Many firearm experts have called the Webley Mark VI "the finest military revolver ever designed," and there is much merit in that statement. The Mark VI, which first appeared in mid-1915, was actually the final installment in a series of top-break service revolvers that were first accepted into British military service in 1887. While Marks I through V were certainly reliable, robust arms, the Mark VI incorporated all of the virtues of the earlier models and added a few advantages of its own. It was chambered for the Mark IV .455 Webley cartridge, a smokeless-powder round with approximately two-thirds the puissance of a .45 ACP.

The revolver was loaded and cleared by "breaking" it open via a thumb-operated "stirrup latch" located behind the recoil shield. Dropping the frame exposed six chambers where cartridges could be loaded singly or by means of one of the patented "quick-loaders" of the period. The revolver was then closed and when the rounds were expended, it was again opened where a star extractor pulled the spent cases clear of the cylinder.

The gun was double-action, but could be thumb-cocked for deliberate shooting. The stocks were made of checkered vulcanite and were of a squared configuration rather than the rounded bird's head style of the earlier Marks. The finish was blue. The barrel measured 6" and was fitted with a removable front sight, the rear sight being fashioned out of a notch on the top of the stirrup latch.

The Mark VI became a staple during World War I, and, while earlier Webleys were still seen in the trenches, it became the pre-eminent sidearm of the British soldier in that conflict. By the end of the war, approximately 280,000 Mark VIs had been manufactured. Some accessories were devised for the Mark VI, including a detachable shoulder stock and a bayonet that had a wicked-looking blade with a T-shaped cross section. As well, .22 LR training revolvers were devised, as were cutaway versions for firearm instruction. Target models were also offered in the interwar years.

Mark VIs continued in production by Webley & Scott and (from 1921 to 1926) at the Royal Small Arms Factory, Enfield. Despite being replaced by a smaller, less powerful .380/200 cal. revolver in 1928, the popular .455s were still being cataloged by W&S for civilian use as late as 1939.

Renamed "No. 1, Mark VI," the Mark VI saw some use during World War II (and beyond) with British and Commonwealth forces where a good number of officers and men preferred it over the issue Enfield No. 2 Mark I.

Many thousands of Webley Mark VIs have been imported into the United States over the years. Some have had the rears of their cylinders ground down 1/16" in order to accept .45 ACP ammunition in half moon clips or .45 Auto Rim cartridges, and while this practice makes the gun more convenient and inexpensive to shoot, it does reduce collector value and interest.

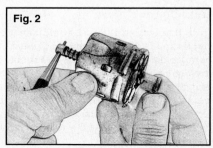

Fig. 1

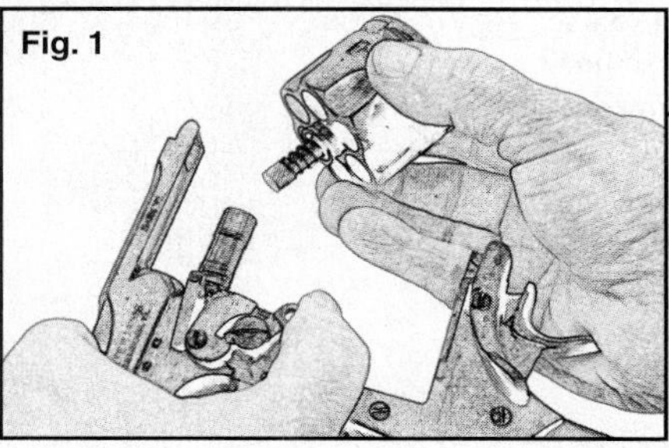

Disassembly

To disassemble the unloaded Mark VI, press the stirrup barrel latch (2) forward, open the revolver and ensure it is unloaded. Unscrew the cylinder cam lever lock screw (7) and rotate the cam lever (6) to depress the cylinder cam (9). The cylinder (5) may now be removed from the barrel assembly (1) **(Fig. 1)**. Remove the cylinder cam lever by unscrewing the cylinder cam lever screw (8). Place a dowel or fired case in a chamber to protect the extractor/ratchet pin (18), insert a punch or nail into the disassembly hole in the extractor rod retainer (15) and turn it counter-clockwise **(Fig. 2)**. The rod retainer and spring (16) may now be removed from the front cylinder and the extractor/ratchet (17) from the rear.

The barrel is removed from the frame by unscrewing the hinge pin screw (36) and pushing the hinge pin (35) out to the left. Separate the barrel from the frame taking care not to drop the extractor lever cam (12) **(Fig. 3)**.

Remove the right and left cylinder cam screws (10) and slide the cylinder cam from the barrel assembly. Remove the front sight blade (20) by turning out the front sight blade screw (21).

To take out the mainspring (38), unscrew the stock screw (25), remove the right and left stock panels (22, 24) and put the hammer (28) on full cock. Take a piece of wire and slide it through the forward portion of the mainspring. Using a pair of needle-nose pliers, twist the wire until the mainspring is held captive in the compressed state. Lower the hammer and disengage the spring's hooks from the hammer swivel/stirrup (33). The mainspring may now be cleared from the left side of

Fig. 2

dark. Conversely, if the exit pupil is larger than the eye pupil, the extra light contained therein will be blocked by the iris of the eye and will, therefore, be wasted. As if that weren't complicated enough, the diameter of the eye pupil varies, depending on ambient light levels, from about 2 mm in bright sunshine to about 7 mm at night. Since the pupil of a normal eye cannot open larger than about 7 mm, there is little practical advantage in designing viewing instruments with larger exit pupils.

Easier Eye Alignment

Another advantage of larger exit pupils, which applies in all light conditions, is that they provide added leeway for lateral movements. Assume, for example, that you are glassing for mule deer with high-quality compact binoculars, such as an 8x20 or 10x25 model, having 2.5 mm exit pupils. Though the binocular may be up to the task, you'll soon find yourself struggling to keep your eye pupils perfectly aligned with the binocular's exit pupils, which is very tiring if done for extended periods. This explains why hunters who carry compact binoculars seldom spend enough time glassing.

If, on the other hand, you are using a binocular with 5 mm exit pupils, your eyes can be considerably off-center in the exit pupils without any loss of optical effectiveness. The larger the exit pupil, the less critical the eye alignment, and vice versa.

Room for Eye Rotation

A similar problem is that small exit pupils leave very little room for eye rotation. People often complain that compact binoculars have excessively narrow fields of view (FOV), which often is not the case. For example, Swarovski's petite 8x20 pocket binocular has a 345-ft. FOV at 1,000 yds., which is exactly the same as its king-sized 8x56 binocular. Although, in side-by-side comparisons you'd swear that the latter had a much larger FOV. The reason is that the larger 7 mm exit pupils of the 8x56 allow the eye pupils to rotate much farther off axis before beginning to lose sight of the exit pupils.

That happens because the eye pupil is not located at the center of rotation of the eye, but roughly 10 mm farther back, near the center of the eyeball—thus, causing the eye pupils to rotate out of the exit pupils when attempting to view objects near the edge of the FOV. The result, particularly with the small exit pupils of compact binoculars, is that you must continually rotate your head, along with the binocular, to clearly view off-axis objects. This also occurs with spotting scopes but seldom with telescopic sights because of their inherently narrower FOV and larger exit pupils, particularly at lower powers.

Wise Compromises

If given my druthers, I would never use optics with exit pupils smaller than 7 mm, which, alas, is impractical. Thus, compromises are called for—especially considering the inverse relationships that exist between an instrument's exit-pupil diameter and its size and weight. Magnifications being equal, the larger the exit pupils, the larger and heavier the instruments, and vice versa. Here, beginning with binoculars, is how the various types of instruments measure up.

Daytime Binoculars: These include so-called mini and compact models with exit pupils of from 2 mm to about 3.5 mm, the usefulness of which is limited to the hours between sunrise and sunset. Given the tendency of game to be active in low light, I can't recommend anything in this class for serious hunting. But, assuming excellent optical quality, such binoculars perform astoundingly well. Typical models include: 7x21, 8x20, 8x25, 10x25, 10x32 and 12x25. Differences of one or two millimeters in objective diameters, such as between 24 mm and 25 mm, are insignificant. Also, I can't, in good conscience, recommend variable magnification binoculars.

General-Purpose Binoculars: This extremely broad category includes models with exit pupils of from 3.5 mm to 5 mm, the usefulness of which ranges from roughly one-half hour before sunrise to one-half hour after sunset (i.e., legal shooting hours). These are widely preferred by serious binocular users because, except for models with objectives of 50 mm or larger, they are reasonably small and lightweight. Specification numbers include: 7x30, 7x35, 8x32, 8x36, 8x42, 8-12x42, 8.5x42, 9x35, 10x42, 10x50, 12x50 and 15x56.

continued on p. 95

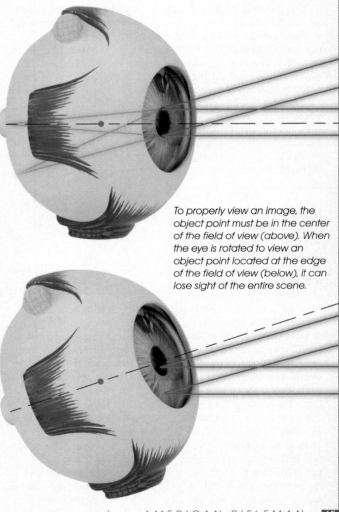

To properly view an image, the object point must be in the center of the field of view (above). When the eye is rotated to view an object point located at the edge of the field of view (below), it can lose sight of the entire scene.

sturdy and durable weapon with extremely good knock-down capabilities. Its efficacy had been proven during the First World War, in conditions ranging from the mud of the Somme to the deserts of Mesopotamia. Though the Webleys were widely criticised, this was generally on the grounds of poor accuracy rather than durability.

In addition to serving the British Army and the armed forces of the principal colonies, the Mk VI was issued to the police of the Irish Republic (Garda Siochana) from 1922, to the Royal Canadian Mounted Police in the 1930s, and to police in South Africa from 1935.

THE LATER REVOLVERS

The First World War found the British Army short of all types of weapon, handguns included. The shortages were rectified by accelerating production of Webleys, but also by

91 BELOW

Cheery British soldiers dig-in on the Western Front, probably in 1917–18. The men appear to be from an Irish regiment or the London Scottish – at least two are wearing plain kilts – but are not otherwise identifiable. Six SMLE rifles and a Lewis Gun are visible, while the moustachioed officer standing in the shallow trench next to the machine-gun has a large revolver. The shape of the butt suggests that it is a ·455 Smith & Wesson or a Colt rather than a Webley. Courtesy of Elex archives.

purchasing Smith & Wesson and Colt ·455 revolvers. Orders were even placed in Spain, two suitable revolvers being approved on 8 November 1915. Declared obsolete in 1921, the Pistols, Revolver, ·455, Ordnance Pattern* were made in Eibar by Garate, Anitua y Cia (No.1 Mk I) and Trocaola, Aranzabal y Cia (No.2 Mk I). The two guns were essentially similar, though the Garate pattern had a square-backed trigger guard and a humped back strap. Its bakelite grips ended some way above the lanyard ring. The Trocaola version had a rounded back strap and trigger guard, and its plain chequered grips extended to the full depth of the butt.

The ·455 Webley Mk VI, renamed Pistol, Revolver, No.1 Mk VI in 1926, was a sturdy and dependable weapon. However, owing to the power of its cartridge, novices found it difficult to shoot accurately. This suggested to the British authorities that a reduction could be made to ·38 with beneficial effects: as the handgun was essentially an ultra-short range weapon, generally used as a last resort, the reduction in 'stopping power' was more than offset by lower recoil.

Instead of ordering guns from Webley, and probably mindful that all patents and licensing agreements had lapsed, the government decided to instal a production line in the Enfield factory while the Small Arms Committee developed a satisfactory design. Pre-production guns were made in small quantities in 1928–31. After satisfactory troop trials, the

Pistol, Revolver, ·38 No.2 Mk I was approved on 2 June 1932. Apart from a reduction in size compared with the old ·455 No.1 Mk VI, the new gun had a replaceable firing pin in the hammer nose and a detachable side plate giving access to the lockwork. No.2 revolvers measured 10·3in overall, had 5in barrels and weighed 1lb 9oz. The cylinder contained six rounds. The grips were originally squared walnut, but the pattern was later changed to rounded walnut and then to bakelite with thumb recesses.

The No.2 Mk I was followed by the No.2 Mk I*, approved on 22 June 1938. Developed principally for use in armoured vehicles, the Mk I* lacked the hammer spur and the single-action cocking notch on the hammer body. It was only capable of double-action fire. The No.2 Mk I** of July 1942 was simply a Mk I** without the hammer safety stop.

About 250,000 No.2 or 'Enfield' revolvers were made by the Royal Small Arms Factory in 1936–45, including 1,000 for Iraq. Albion Motors of Yoker, Glasgow, made 21,422 guns from contracts totalling 42,516 placed from May 1940 onward; the remainder of the order was subsequently given to Coventry Gauge & Tool Co. Ltd, freeing Albion's facilities for more important tasks.

Large numbers of components were made by the Singer Sewing Machine Co. Ltd of Clydebank, and then assembled at Enfield.

* Also sometimes known as 'Pistols, Revolver, ·455 Old Pattern'; the term 'Ordnance Pattern' is believed to be correct.

92 RIGHT

The Webley-Fosbery was an interesting self-cocking revolver, favoured by officers but not reliable enough to attract more than cursory official attention. This ·455-calibre cased example dates from c.1908. Courtesy of Wallis & Wallis, Lewes.

These are marked 'SM' or 'SSM', or with the area code 'N67'. Enfield revolvers lasted in British service until replaced by the L9A1 (FN GP) pistol in 1957. They were declared obsolete in June 1963.

The Second World War caught the authorities short of weapons. Thousands of No.1 Mk VI revolvers were refurbished (mainly at Enfield), and 105,066 'Pistols, Revolver, Webley, ·38 Mk IV' were ordered in the period from May 1940 until November 1944.† The ·38 Webleys were formally approved 'for the record' in September 1945 and declared obsolete only in June 1963. They were very similar to the government No.2 Mk I, but had commercial-grade finish and bakelite grips bearing the manufacturer's trademark.

Large numbers of ·38 revolvers were acquired from North America, the Smith & Wesson K200 (or ·38/200) being supplied to repay monies advanced against the abortive Light Rifle. The Contract Books suggest that 277,125 ·38 K200 S&W and 37,100 ·38 Colt revolvers were ordered but, with Lend-Lease supplies, the actual quantity issued in Britain was far greater. In addition, at least 105,250 assorted ·32, ·38 and ·45 revolvers were also forthcoming from 'trade sources'.

THE AUTOMATICS

The British Army was very fond of the revolver prior to 1945, accepting automatic pistols only as a last resort.

The Small Arms Committee had tested many automatics prior to 1914, but none had met the Small Arms Committee criteria. The major problem had been excessive demands on bullet weight and muzzle velocity. The simplest or most effectual guns – such as the FN Brownings – were too low powered, while the only guns that approached the power requirements (e.g., the clumsy Gabbett-Fairfax 'Mars' series of 1901–3) were impossibly complicated and awkward to handle.*

After the final rejection of the Mars, interest centred on the Colt and Webley pistols. The first ·38 Colt had been submitted in December 1902, passing so admirable a test that the Chief Inspector of Small Arms had recorded it as 'the best pistol yet submitted'. Trials of a ·45 version in January 1906 were similarly impressive.

An improved ·45 pistol appeared in July 1910, but a 'drop safety' or rough usage test undertaken by HMS *Excellent* in August proved the Colt's undoing. Dropped onto hard ground, the hammer persistently jarred out of contact with the sear and fell on an empty chamber. Damage caused to the lockwork then caused the Colt to fire the next magazine-full automatically. As the competing Webley had performed impeccably in the rough usage test, the navy immediately (and mistakenly) rejected the Colt.

The first ·45 Webley pistol, designed by William Whiting, had been submitted to the Chief Inspector of Small Arms in October 1904. Trials had been disappointing, however, and a ·38 blowback submitted in April 1909 was equally unacceptable. When an improved ·45-calibre gun appeared in the summer of 1909, locked by displacing the barrel block diagonally down and back, opinions changed after the gun had passed a stringent trial with only nine failures in 1,254 shots. Though CISA rejected the Webley in March 1910, as 'unsuitable for service', the Royal Navy was determined to adopt it.

The Pistol, Self Loading, Webley, Naval Service, ·455 Mark I was approved in January 1912, first guns being delivered in 1913.

* See Peter Labbett, 'British Automatic Pistol Trials, 1900–1914' in *Guns Review*, August–October 1964; Jim Stonley, 'The ·455 Automatic Pistol in the British Services', in *Guns Review*, December 1978–February 1979 (with addenda in January 1980 and March 1987); and John Walter, *Luger* (1977), pp 57–60 and 62–3.

93 RIGHT

A Sealed Pattern 'Pistol, Self-Loading, Webley & Scott, ·455-inch Mk I No.2' is shown here with its detachable butt. Note the special back sight, which distinguishes the No.2 from the simpler No.1. Courtesy of the MoD Pattern Room Collection, Royal Ordnance plc, Nottingham; photograph by Ian Hogg.

†Ian Skennerton, in *British Small Arms of World War 2*, suggests the total ordered between May 1940 and September 1945 to have been 120,120.

94, 95 RIGHT

A ·45 Colt M1911. Substantial numbers of near-identical guns were acquired by the British Army during the First World War, often chambered for the ·455 Webley pistol cartridge. Author's archives.

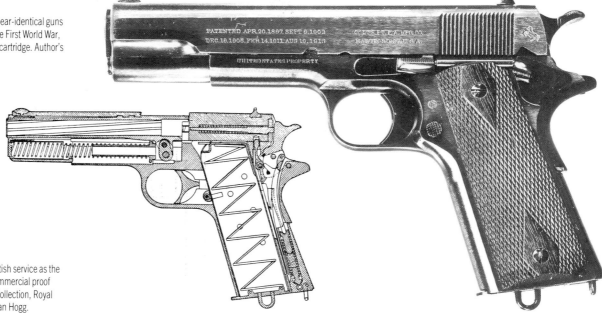

96 BELOW RIGHT

An FN-made GP Mle.35 pistol, issued in British service as the L9A1. This is a pre-war gun with Belgian commercial proof marks. Courtesy of the MoD Pattern Room Collection, Royal Ordnance plc, Nottingham; photograph by Ian Hogg.

In June 1912, the army authorities, mindful that the navy had adopted the Webley pistol, had a sudden change of heart and decided to issue a hundred guns for trials with the Royal Horse Artillery. These had an adjustable back sight designed by W.J. Whiting (patent 201 of 1913) and were numbered in a block taken from the navy series. The first fifty were cut for shoulder stocks, the remainder having plain back straps.

Little came of the trials, owing to the start of the First World War. The ·455 Webley pistol was subsequently found to be unreliable in adverse conditions, jamming as easily from the effects of mud and dust as from excessive fouling produced by its cordite-loaded ammunition.

The Pistol No. 2 Mk 1 was approved for the Royal Flying Corps in April 1915, similar to the experimental RHA guns (with an adjustable drum-type back sight and a board-type shoulder stock) but clearly marked 'Mark I No.2 1915' instead of 'Mark I 1913'.

The recoil-operated Webley was about 8·5in overall, had a 5in barrel and weighed 2lb 7oz. It fed from a seven-round detachable box magazine in the butt and locked by displacing the barrel diagonally downward to release the slide. Very cumbersome, though not unpleasant to shoot, the design proved unsuited to service. Production was small, apparently amounting to a little over eight thousand service weapons and 1,248 commercial examples. Claims that tens of thousands were made arise from the serial numbers of commercial versions, which were intermixed with the other Webley auto-loaders.

The Webleys were supplemented by ·455 M1911 Colts, distinguished by W-prefix numbers, which were ordered in the USA during the First World War; standard ·45 Colts were issue in the Canadian Army.

It is not clear how many ·455 pistols were acquired in 1916–18, though the commonly accepted total is 13,150. They were apparently confined to officers, the Royal Flying Corps (later the RAF) and the navy. The ·455 rimless pistol cartridge would chamber in a standard ·455 revolver, developing pressures greater than the revolver proof round, so attempts were made to keep it out of the trenches. Most RAF Colts were apparently withdrawn to arm the crews of air/sea resuce craft after 1942, and then sold back to American wholesalers in the 1950s.

Though the service handgun in 1939 remained the ·38 Enfield revolver, substantial numbers of Canadian Inglis-made FN-Browning GP pistols were impressed after 1942. They proved particularly popular with the Special Forces, largely owing to the thirteen-round magazines, and were sealed for British service in September 1944 as Pistols, Browning, FN, 9mm, HP, No.2 Mk 1*. Ultimately, the post-war Belgian made version was approved for universal issue as the Pistol, 9mm L9A1 (1957). Guns have since been bought from Fabrique Nationale when required.

Limited quantities of Mauser and Astra machine pistols came from the gun trade in 1940–5, together with 1,700 ·45 and 2,200 ·32 Colt automatics. Ballester Molina pistols were purchased from Argentina and Stars, amongst others, came from Spain.

RIFLES

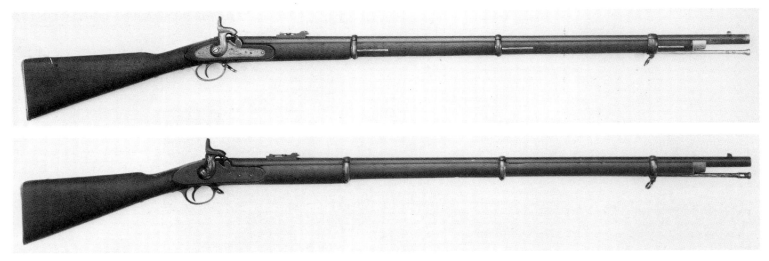

THE ENFIELD RIFLE-MUSKET

The first 20,000 P/53 Enfields were ordered
from the gun trade in Birmingham on 6
October 1853, to be assembled from sub-
contracted parts by Hollis & Sheath, Swinburn
& Son, Tipping & Lawden and Thomas Turner.
The process was not without hazard, as the
gunmakers entrusted with the back sights
(ironically enough, the four assemblers) failed
to honour their obligations.

Eventually, with outside help, difficulties
were resolved. The London trade agreed to set
up 1,500 guns on 12 May 1854, and Enfield had
contributed its first thousand by the end of
March 1855. Other guns were ordered overseas.

Twenty thousand were sought in Liége in
October 1854, followed by an additional contract in c.1855; 28,139 guns had been accepted
by 31 March 1859, whereupon 5,000 more
were ordered in June.

25,000 rifle-muskets were ordered from
Robbins & Lawrence of Windsor, Vermont,
USA, in February 1855 through the agency of
Fox, Henderson & Company. The manufacturer went into liquidation after delivering
10,400; nearly six thousand additional guns
were supplied by the Union Arms Company,
but the incomplete US contract was cancelled.
Better luck was experienced with an order for
20,000 given to Escoffier of Saint-Étienne in
August 1855, as 19,603 Enfields had been accepted by 31 March 1857.

Small numbers of P/53 rifle-muskets were
despatched to the Crimea to serve alongside
the P/51 Minié, though the orders contracted
at home and abroad were completed only
after hostilities had finished. In the period 31
May 1856–31 March 1859, for example,
Birmingham and London contractors had
delivered 211,298 guns into store.

The standard ·577-calibre P/53 Rifle-musket
was an elegant weapon, with a conventional
cap-lock, a walnut stock with a straight wrist,
and a browned barrel retained by three bands.
It measured 55in overall, had a 39in barrel
rifled with three clockwise-twisting grooves
making a turn in 78in, and originally weighed
about 8lb 8oz.* Progressive-depth rifling,
·13in deep at the breech but only ·005 at the
muzzle, was adopted in 1858.

Not surprisingly, minor problems were encountered in the Crimea. So many improvements had been made by December 1855 that
the 'Rifle Musquet Improved Pattern 1853'
had to be re-sealed to guide the contractors.

The most visible change, apart from a
strengthened hammer substituted in December 1855 and a one-inch reduction in butt
length in 1859,† concerned the barrel bands.
Service in the Crimea showed that the original
screwed pattern worked loose during rapid
fire or if the stock shrank. It was superseded
by a solid version retained by a spring let into
the right side of the fore-end. Suggested by
Westley Richards, this system was loathed by
the cavalry. Bands still loosened in adverse
conditions, and the springs caught on clothing
and equipment. The perfected Baddeley Band,
retained by screws but streamlined, was accepted on 3 June 1861 to most soldiers' relief.

There were also four types of adjustable
tangent-leaf back sight. Pattern No.1 was

immediately recognizable by its convex sides.
It was replaced c.1856 by Pattern No.2, identical but flat sided; Pattern No.3 of 1859 had an
additional 450-yard V-notch in the bottom of
the leaf. Pattern No.4 of November 1861 was
graduated to 1,000 yards instead of 900, had
shallower V-notches in the cap and leaf, and
the shoulders of the leaf were cut back to
enable the slider to go below the 500-yard
setting.

Less obvious changes concerned the
nipple – a coned-channel or venturi pattern
was provisionally adopted in May 1861 – and
behind the lock plate, where a strengthened
swivel had been substituted as early as
December 1854 and an under-cut stud had
replaced the mainspring pin.

The first P/53 rammer had a swell head, but
never stayed in place properly. Smith's roller-
spring retainer was approved in the autumn of
1855, but replaced from January 1857 by
Burton's perfected spoon spring.

The rise of the Volunteer movement produced a series of P/53 lookalikes, often with
bores measuring a mere ·448–·452. Made by
gunsmiths such as Beasley, Bissell, Henry,
Newton, Rigby and Turner, each offered minor
variations in rifling and furniture. Some barrels were conventionally grooved, some were
polygonal and others had a ratchet profile;
some shot better than others, though the
standards were generally very high.

There was even a small-bore Lancaster,
with an oval bore measuring ·447 and ·459 on
its minor and major axes. Though this gun was
often prone to stripping when clean, it rather
oddly shot incredibly well when foul. One trial
returned a mean 'thousand shots uncleaned'
Figure of Merit of 7·08in at 500 yards for the
Lancaster, compared with 8·88in for a Whitworth that had been regularly scoured.

* This had increased to 8lb 14½oz by 1861, and the
adoption of the Baddeley bands.
†The short-butt pattern gun was not released until August 1860,
and guns made in Liége or by the London Armoury Company
all had long (14in) butts. The butt-toe was modified in May
1864, being cut straight instead of shaped.

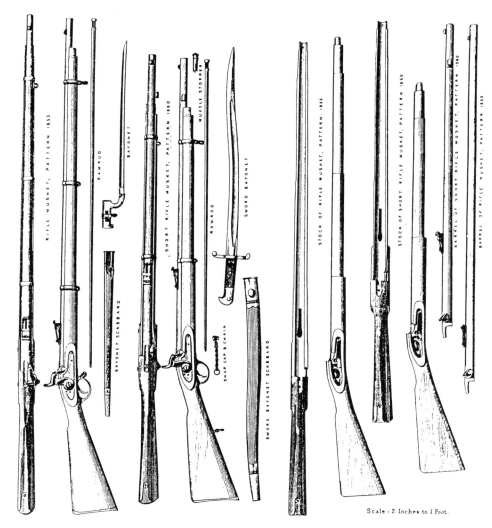

An engraving of the P/53 rifle-musket and P/60 Short Rifle, their bayonets, barrels and stocks. From *Equipment of Infantry* ('forming Part V. of the Series of Army Equipments'), 1865. Courtesy of Her Majesty's Stationery Office. Crown Copyright.

100, 101 BELOW

The upper illustration shows a P/58 Short Rifle, with the bayonet bar on the upper band. Made at Enfield, this example has a plain lock plate. The lower gun is a P/60 Short Rifle, with the bayonet bar on the barrel. It also has five-groove rapid-twist rifling.

Volunteer rifles, which deviated from the official patterns, are not regarded as regulation weapons. Details of the best of them will be found in material listed in the bibliography.

THE SHORT RIFLES

The P/53 proved a great success, once the initial teething troubles were overcome, but was too long for specialist applications. As accuracy suffered little from reducing the length of the barrel, the Pattern No.1 Short Rifle (or P/56) was sealed in 1856 to arm the Rifle Brigade, the 60th Regiment of Foot, the Cape Mounted and Royal Canadian Rifles, and serjeants of line regiments on Home Service. The short rifle had an improved high-quality lock, two barrel bands, and carried the bar for its sabre bayonet on the right side of the barrel at the muzzle. It was 49in overall, had a 33in barrel, weighed 8lb 2½oz and was sighted to 1,100 yards. Progressive rifling was adopted on guns made after 1858–9.

Sealed on 6 July 1858, the Pattern No.2 (or P/58) short rifle was essentially similar to its predecessor, but was stocked practically to the muzzle and had a bayonet bar on the upper band. Weight was about 8lb 8oz, measurably heavier than the P/56. It was superseded by the Pattern No.3 or P/60 short rifle, sealed on 6 November 1860. The principal changes were the substitution of five-groove rifling for the older three-groove version and a reversion to a bayonet bar on the barrel. The last short rifle, Pattern No.4 (P/61), was sealed in August 1861. It had a back sight graduated to 1,250 yards for J2 powder, and a Baddeley lower band. The bayonet bar remained on the barrel. Pattern No.4 rifles are now very rarely seen in their

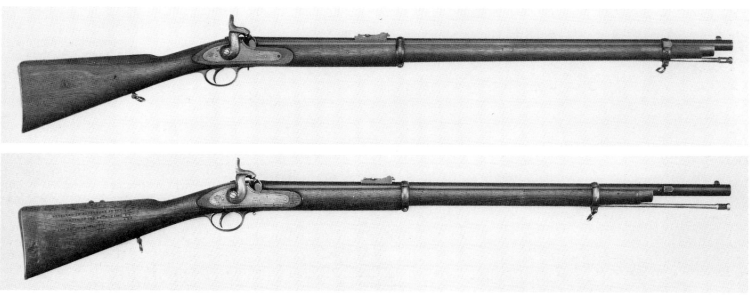

original cap-lock form, as most were converted to Sniders.

There was also a Pattern No.1 Naval Rifle (P/58), sealed in November 1857. Outwardly similar to the P/56, it had a special heavy barrel with five-groove rifling making a turn in 48in, accepted a heavy cutlass bayonet on a bar attached to the barrel, and had a sling swivel ahead of the trigger guard instead of beneath the butt.‡ The naval rifle had a standard P/53 lock, brass furniture, and was stocked in inferior sapwood.

‡ Marine artillery examples had conventional butt swivels.

ENFIELD CARBINES

The Pattern No.1 Artillery Carbine, or P/53, was the first ultra-short derivative of the rifle-musket to be approved. Sealed on 23 January 1853, it measured 40in overall and weighed about 7lb 9oz. There was a 24in barrel, P/53 lock and furniture, a butt swivel, and a simple two-leaf 300-yard back sight. Distinguished by a long auxiliary tenon, the bar on the barrel accepted a special brass-hilted sabre bayonet.

A P/58 or Pattern No.2 carbine, was sealed in March 1858 and a Pattern No.3 version followed in December 1861. The No.2 had progressive-depth rifling, a ramrod spring and a bayonet bar without tenon; No.3 carbines had Baddeley lower bands, five-groove barrels and 600-yard sights.

The Royal Sappers & Miners Carbine (P/55), sealed on 15 January 1855, had Lancaster's oval bore with a progressive or gain-twist, a minor axis measuring ·577 at the muzzle and a major axis of ·593. It was 48in overall, had a 31½in barrel and weighed 7lb 6¼oz.

Issued with a special brass-mounted sword bayonet and a brass-sheathed swell rammer, the P/55 had a reputation for excellent accuracy and was sighted accordingly. The back sight was graduated to 400 yards on its base-wings, and then to 1,100 on a leaf hinged at the front end of the base-block. Interestingly, despite problems with the full-length oval bore rifles, there was never any evidence that bullets stripped the carbine rifling.

The perfected Pattern No.1 Cavalry Carbine, or P/56, was sealed on 11 August 1856 – apparently originally for the East India Company. It was 37in long, had a 21in barrel, and weighed about 6¾lb. Standard fittings included a swivel ramrod, two screwed bands, brass furniture and a P/53 lock. The simplified back sight had a standing block for 100 yards, plus folding leaves for 200 and 300 yards. The Pattern No.2 carbine of March 1861 was similar, but had Baddeley bands; and the No.3 of October 1861 had a five-groove barrel, a rounded lockplate and an improved step-and-slider sight graduated to 600 yards. Virtually all cavalry carbines had a side-bar and ring on the left side of the breech, and those remaining in issue after May 1862 were fitted to receive a leather back sight protector. Most P/61 examples were subsequently converted to Sniders.

Inventory returns revealed that, on 1 January 1862 and excluding guns in India, the British Army possessed 283,364 P/53 rifle-muskets, 24,714 P/56 and P/60 short rifles, 37,009 'P/56' (sic) naval rifles, 5,961 P/53 artillery carbines, 6,409 P/55 Lancaster Sappers & Miners carbines, and a mere 1,352 'East India' P/56 cavalry carbines. There were also 422 P/51 rifle-muskets and 18,895 rifled P/42 and Sea Service muskets. Reserve stocks included 41,164 P/51 and P/53 rifle-muskets, mostly

repaired and reduced to second-class status, plus nearly 200,000 assorted smooth-bore cap-lock muskets. There were even 6,438 Brunswicks and more than 22,000 *flintlock* longarms.

INDIA PATTERNS

Panicked by the Indian Mutiny, the British withdrew rifle-muskets from native troops in the late 1850s. They were replaced by a series of smooth-bore derivatives made at Enfield from 1858 until c.1872.

Ironically, the first India Service gun had been the "Serjeant's Fusil, Native Regiments, Rifled, P/56 (for India)", sealed in May 1856. This gun weighed 8lb 10oz without its socket bayonet, and had a 33in ·577-calibre barrel. It was quickly superseded by a ·656-calibre Pattern 1858 smooth-bore version, which weighed only about 8lb 5oz owing to its lightened barrel.

The Pattern 1858 ·656 smooth-bore musket, sealed in August 1858, weighed 8lb 8½oz, accepted a socket bayonet and had a simple standing-block back sight. Its 3lb 7oz barrel proved to be too fragile, so the Pattern 1859 was sealed in May 1859. The new barrel weighed a fraction over 4lb, raising the gun weight to 8lb 13oz even though stock and furniture had been lightened. Owing to the rapidity with which the P/59 replaced the P/58, the older gun is now very rarely encountered. Excepting sights, it is all but indistinguishable externally from P/53 Enfields.

A rifled ·577-calibre India Service P/57 Engineers Carbine had been approved in August 1856, amalgamating an Enfield-rifled barrel with the sights and bayonet of the

Lancaster Sappers & Miners Carbine P/55. It measured 47¾in overall and weighed 8lb 3oz. Surviving P/57 carbines were replaced after the mutiny by the ·656 smooth-bore P/58 Engineers Carbine, sealed on 14 October 1858, which weighed 7lb 15oz and had a standing-block back sight.

There were four distinctive ·656-calibre smooth-bore India Service carbines – the Native Foot Police Pattern of October 1858 (31½in banded barrel, weight 7lb 9oz); a Constabulary Pattern of October 1858 (29in pinned barrel, 7lb 9oz); the Mounted Police Pattern of December 1858 (21in banded barel, 6lb 9oz); and a Bengal Native Cavalry Pattern of February 1867. All these guns were newly made except the Mounted Police version, which was made by shortening condemned P/53 rifle-muskets and fitting brass mounts, slide-bars and swivel rammers.

BREECH-LOADING CARBINES

The first serious trials were undertaken with a cap-lock submitted by James Leetch, a London gunmaker. The laterally hinged breech-block, locked by a lever, received a combustible cartridge from the front. A safety unit incorporated in the back-action lock prevented the gun firing prematurely. A short rifle with a 33in barrel was successfully tested at Woolwich in June 1854, whereafter an 18in-barrel Leetch Carbine was tried against a Sharps. The subsequent report offered no recommendation, though the Leetch Carbine had fired 130 rounds without a misfire. A board of cavalry officers, impressed by its handiness and the ease of loading, recommended adoption. This was formally approved on 19 July 1855 by Lord Hardinge, the Commander in Chief, and an order for 15,000 guns was passed to the Royal Manufactory at Enfield. There the Superintendent rebelled, drawing attention to potential flaws in the Leetch design. Spilled powder grains could prevent the breech closing or, alternatively, the bullet could be jarred forward across the joint of the breech-block and barrel. This was of particular concern to a cavalryman, whose carbine was scabbarded muzzle downward; it effectively locked the action shut.

The official order was reduced to a mere two thousand guns in January 1856, but very few were actually made: none had been received into store by the Spring of 1859.

The Superintendent of the Royal Manufactory, Captain William Dixon, preferred Sharps' Carbine to the Leetch. Originally patented by Christian Sharps in September 1848 (US Patent 5,763), a specimen had been submitted to the Sub-Committee on Small Arms in April 1854; another, fitted with a Maynard Tape Primer, had been favourably tested at Hythe in February 1855. Though many observers considered the dropping-block action too complex for service, twelve experimental carbines were made at Enfield in the Spring of 1855 and issued to the East Kent Mounted Rifles in July. They proved so successful that Dixon recommended that 1,500–2,000 be acquired for large-scale trials. An order for six thousand guns was placed in the USA in January 1856, the guns being delivered into store by 31 March 1858. Five cavalry regiments in India, together with their home depots, subsequently received Sharps Carbines for extended trials.

Made for the Sharps Rifle Manufacturing Company by Robbins & Lawrence of Windsor, Vermont, British carbines existed in two patterns. The earlier had standard ·577 Enfield three-groove rifling making a turn in 78in; overall length was about 37¾in, the barrel measured 20½in and the guns weighed 7lb 9oz. The second pattern had an 18in ·551 calibre barrel, the rifling made a turn in 48in, overall length was 35½in and the weight was about 7lb 6oz. The Sharps had P/53-type nipples, standard except for a longer thread, and were fitted with Maynard Tape Primers. The four-leaf back sight was graduated to 600 yards, the barrel was retained by a single band, and the furniture was brass. A sling bar and ring lay on the left side of the breech. The breech-block slid diagonally forward when the operating lever was pushed down, exposing the chamber to receive a cartridge. Closing the action sheared the base of the cartridge open, but usually scattered loose powder grains on top of the action block. Cocking the hammer automatically fed the next primer over the nipple.

The Sharps Carbine was easy to use, but the earliest patterns leaked gas too badly. As the Maynard priming system gave more misfires than percussion caps, the Sharps were never adopted officially. Though an improved gun was tested against a Westley Richards carbine in January 1860, it was considered 'inferior in simplicity, precision and range'.†

Lord Hardinge – who had initially favoured the Leetch Carbine – turned briefly to the Prince system, featuring a vertical operating handle in front of the trigger-guard to push the barrel assembly forward. His attention then

---

†The Sharps Carbine tested in 1860 is assumed to have been one of the original guns acquired by Britain in the mid-1850s, rather than a perfected 1859 model. The latter was the first to feature a vertically moving breech-block (previous patterns had moved slightly diagonally) and had a Conant gas-check system improved by Richard Lawrence.

---

102 LEFT

The P/55 Royal Sappers & Miners Carbine featured Lancaster's oval bore. Note the bayonet bar on the muzzle and that the back sight leaf is hinged at the front of the block rather than the rear. Courtesy of the Board of Trustees of the Royal Armouries, HM Tower of London.

103 BELOW LEFT

This P/61 cavalry carbine, made at Enfield in 1862, has Baddeley-patent bands, a swivel rammer and a distinctive leather back sight cover. (Note that the rammer of this particular specimen is lacking its head.) Courtesy of the Board of Trustees of the Royal Armouries, HM Tower of London.

104 RIGHT

Drawings from Christian Sharps' US Patent 5,763 of 12 September 1848. The gun had a vertically sliding breech-block operated by a lever that locked around the trigger guard; production guns combined the trigger-guard and operating lever, simplifying production.

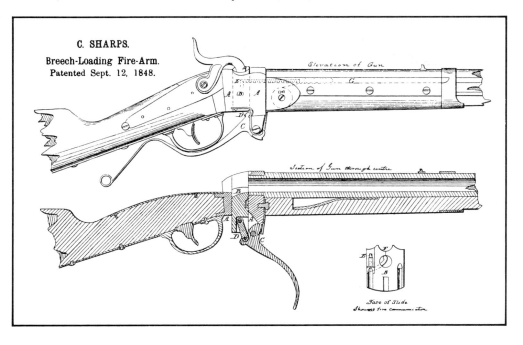

C. SHARPS.
Breech-Loading Fire-Arm.
Patented Sept. 12, 1848.

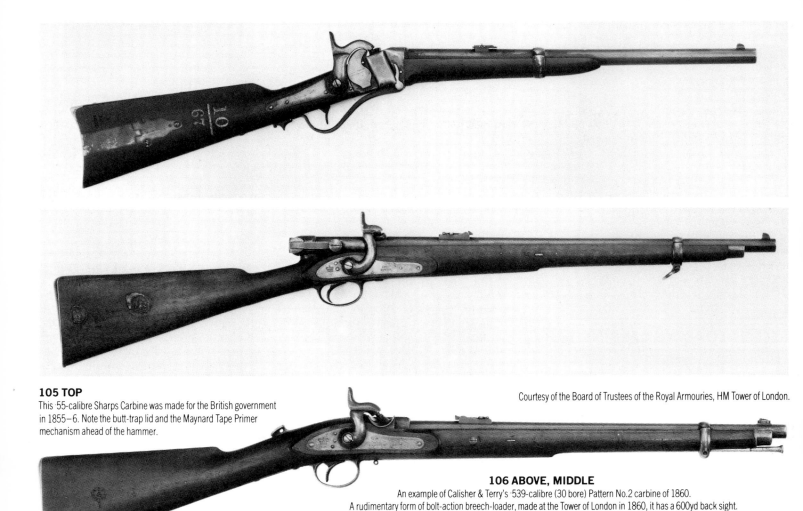

105 TOP
This ·55-calibre Sharps Carbine was made for the British government in 1855–6. Note the butt-trap lid and the Maynard Tape Primer mechanism ahead of the hammer.

106 ABOVE, MIDDLE
An example of Calisher & Terry's ·539-calibre (30 bore) Pattern No.2 carbine of 1860.
A rudimentary form of bolt-action breech-loader, made at the Tower of London in 1860, it has a 600yd back sight.

107 ABOVE
This ·451-calibre Pattern No.5 Westley Richards carbine was made at Enfield in 1866. Note the tail of the breech lever protruding from the butt wrist. This specimen lacks the leather back sight cover, though the retaining stud is visible.

focussed on the Sharps and, when its problems became obvious, seized on the Greene.

Patented by John Durell Greene in June 1854 (US Patent 11,157), the Greene Carbine was made by the Massachussetts Arms Company of Chicopee Falls. A gun fitted with a Maynard Tape Primer was successfully tested at Hythe in the summer of 1855. Accuracy up to 400 yards proved to be as good as any carbine that had been submitted, there was no gas leak and, even after firing nearly three hundred rounds without cleaning, a fire-rate of nine rounds per minute was still possible. Two thousand guns were ordered in 1856, being delivered into store by March 1858. They had ·55-calibre 18in barrels, rifled with three grooves making a turn in 78in, and measured 34½in overall. The back sights were graduated to 600 yards. To load the gun, it was only necessary to press the front trigger and rotate the barrel slightly to the right to disengage the locking lugs. The barrel was then pulled forward to clear the standing breech and swung over to the right.

A hollow spike projected from the standing breech to pierce the cartridge when the action closed. This feature proved to be the worst flaw of an otherwise effectual design; trials at Enfield and Woolwich failed to produce a cartridge strong enough to withstand the rigours of service yet pierce easily. The Greene Carbines spent many years in store until, apparently, being sold back to the Federals during the American Civil War.‡

If the Greene was unlucky, the same could not be said of the Terry Carbine. Made by Calisher & Terry of Birmingham to the design of William Terry (British Patent 843 of 1856) and recommended for service by the Small Arms Committee, 'under the pressure of the moment', on 23 August 1858, this was a crude bolt-action design in which a breech cover

‡The sale of Greene's Carbines to the USA has never been authenticated. Owing to the lack of information in *Statement of ordnance and ordnance stores purchased by the Ordnance Department from January 1, 1861, to June 30, 1866*, unless hidden in the entry '10,051 foreign carbines', it is suspected that the ex-British guns were sold to a wholesaler and thence to militia or volunteer units.

(pivoted to the bolt) was pulled outward then rotated to disengage the retaining lugs. Pulling the bolt back then exposed the chamber. Though the Terry bolt head had an obturating pad, this rapidly deteriorated to a point where excessive gas leakage could blow the breech cover open. Terry's Carbine was heartily disliked by the troops.

Sealed on 21 December 1858, Pattern No.1 featured a ·568-calibre 19½in barrel, rifled with three grooves making a turn in 78in and held in the stock with two bands. The guns were 36¾in long and weighed about 6½lb. Their back sights were graduated to 500 yards, a sling bar was anchored to the left side of the stock with two side-nails, and the furniture was iron. The carbines were issued to the 18th Hussars in sufficient numbers to be considered a regulation pattern.

Pattern No.2 was sealed in November 1860, featuring a ·539-calibre 21in barrel, and five-groove rifling making a turn in 36in. Measuring 38in overall, the gun weighed 6lb 3½oz. It had a single barrel band and a back sight similar to that of the contemporary P/61 cavalry carbine. The Pattern No.3 (sealed on 9 March 1861) was identical, but lacked the upper band swivel and had a Baddeley band. Neither small-bore Terry carbine was issued in quantity.

First submitted in the Spring of 1858 and intitally patented in March 1858 (British Patent 633/58), the Westley Richards Carbine was refined in several stages. The action consisted of an open-topped box-like barrel extension into which a breech-bolt attached to the actuating lever could be swung. The shape of the lever soon earned the sobriquet 'Monkey Tail'. The system was simple and effectual; though the earliest guns could be fired with the lever slightly open, potentially very dangerous, a safety system was soon added. The first guns also had a hook on the obturating pad to pull the cartridge base-wad out of the breech when the action opened.

Later guns had a plain coned bolt-head, obturation being achieved by the cartridge base wad. The wad was simply pushed out of the muzzle by the next shot. Design of the carbine had stabilized by 1860, its ·450 octagonal bore making a turn in 20in. Firing a 420-grain ·457 bullet ahead of 2¼ drams of FG powder, a Figure of Merit of 3·86ft at 800 yards was obtained.

Pattern No.1 was sealed on 29 April 1861, two thousand guns being ordered from Westley Richards. Unfortunately, it was subsequently discovered that the chambers were too long. Eventually, 404 guns had been completed to the existing design, Pattern No.1; 544 were finished to Pattern No.2, 387 to Pattern No.3 and 665 to Pattern No.4. No.2 was simply No.1 with a correct short chamber, and No.3 was No.2 with minor improvements. Sealed on 3 January 1862, Pattern No.4 exhibited many detail changes – the nipple was moved forward, a fence added to the nipple-lump, round studs were used on the trigger plate, the front sight bed became oval, and a 4in tongue on the modified nose cap was let into the rammer channel.

The Westley Richards carbine was very popular with the troops, so 20,000 were ordered from Enfield in the autumn of 1864. Made to Pattern No.5 (sealed in March 1866 after protracted wrangling), these were machine-made and, therefore, classed as 'Interchangeable'; 19,000 were received into store by 31 March 1867. They had 20in ·451-calibre octagonally rifled barrels, measured a fraction short of 36in overall and weighed 6lb 8oz. The 402-grain ·467 bullet was fired with a charge of 2 drams of FG powder, accuracy being in the region of a Figure of Merit of 2·50ft at 500 yards. The barrel was retained by a bolt and a single Baddeley band, furniture was iron, and the butt was drilled longitudinally for the breech scraper and rammer-tip.

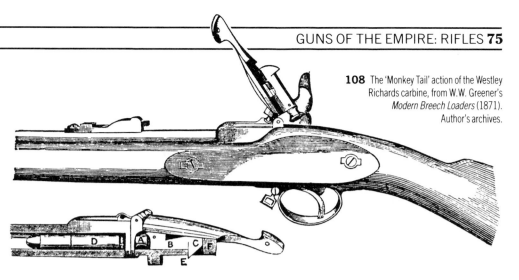

108 The 'Monkey Tail' action of the Westley Richards carbine, from W.W. Greener's *Modern Breech Loaders* (1871). Author's archives.

Hinged at the front, the ramp-and-leaf back sight was graduated to 800 yards. Studs projecting from the fore-end beneath the sight accepted the standard leather protector.

Monkey Tail carbines worked satisfactorily, except that breeches leaked gas when in bad repair. The action could be stiff in extremely cold conditions, when lubricants froze and cartridges had to be forced into the breech with sticks. The weapons' misfortune was to appear at a time when metal-case ammunition was being perfected; suggestions that the Westley Richards carbines should be replaced with Sniders were being heard as early as August 1866.

THE WHITWORTHS

The idea of a mechanically fitting projectile, rather than one that was simply expanded into the rifling by the propellant, had been suggested in Robert Moore's rifle of 1843. This had been brought to the attention of Isambard Brunel, who in turn mentioned it to Westley Richards. Richards made a prototype ·451-calibre polygonal-bore rifle in 1854, through which Joseph Whitworth became involved in the project.

Tests began in 1857 against the P/53, but the results were disallowed as the Whitworth polygonal-bore rifle could not use service ammunition. By 1859, these trials had intermixed with attempts to discover whether the conventional three-groove rifling used in the P/53 rifle-muskets, which made a turn in 78in, was worth retaining. They proved that the existing rifling was among the poorest alternatives, and a five-groove 48in-twist pattern was hastily substituted.

A ·572/·580 Lancaster oval-bore rifle appeared in 1861, proving better than the P/53 when clean or foul. The absence of conventional rifling grooves made the Lancaster particularly easy to clean. A ·564 Whitworth eventually appeared in 1864; firing Whitworth-Metford bullets, it comprehensively out-shot the government Enfield by returning a Figure

of Merit of ·68ft at 500 yards compared with 1·60ft. Unfortunately, concurrent experiments with small-bore guns made the larger Lancasters and Whitworths irrelevant.

The Secretary of State for War had authorized the manufacture of a thousand ·451 Whitworths in the Spring of 1861. These guns had 36in barrels weighing nearly 5lb apiece, the hexagonal twist making a turn in a mere 20in. The experimental rifles had P/60 Short Rifle locks, three Baddeley bands apiece, recurved trigger guards and platinum-lined nipples. Their special back sights were graduated to 1,350 yards for Whitworth ammunition and 1,250 for common bullets.

Trials revealed no real problems, so the purchase of 8,000 'P/63' Whitworth short rifles was authorized. Made at Enfield in 1864, these had 33in 5lb 1oz barrels and weighed 9lb 14oz. Rifled with uniform hexagonal twist, making a turn in 20in, they had a calibre of ·4495 measured across the flats. The back sight was much the same as the experimental P/62, but the sight ramps were carried inside the broadened leaf. The upper band was retained by an additional cross-pin to prevent the bayonet straining the barrel in hand-to-hand combat. P/63 rifles were subjected to lengthy field trials by twelve Home Service units – including the Grenadier Guards, the Scots Fusilier Guards and the Rifle Brigade – as well as five regiments stationed in India.

Service soon revealed that the guns were extremely temperamental in hot and dry conditions, fouling so quickly than no more than six shots could be fired before the bore had to be scoured. Experiments with mechanically-fitting projectiles, therefore, were abandoned in 1865.

THE SNIDER

The adoption of breech-loading rifles in some Continental European armies, and the success of guns such as the Spencer and Sharps rifles in the American Civil War, persuaded the War Office to appoint a Select Committee under

109 RIGHT

General arrangement drawings of the Snider rifles, long and short, from *Field Exercises and Evolutions of Infantry* (1867).

Courtesy of Her Majesty's Stationery Office. Crown Copyright.

the presidency of Major-General Russell. Several meetings were held in the summer of 1864, at which opinions veered from unhesitatingly recommending breech-loading to condemning it outright. Brevet-Colonel William Dixon RA, Superintendent of the Royal Small Arms Factory, and Major Young RA, who had witnessed the 1861 field manoeuvres of the Prussian army, were both strongly opposed to the breech-loader owing to difficulties of obtaining satisfactory ammunition.

The committee examined the bizarre Troubridge Regulator, developed to limit the fire-rate of the Westley Richards 'Monkey Tail' carbine, and considered the influence of five European designs – the Prussian needle-rifle, the Norwegian-designed Swedish army rifle, the Swedish navy rifle, the French Fusil de Rempart and the Belgian cavalry carbine – before deciding that there was sufficient merit in breech-loading to promote an open competition.

Notice of this was made public, requesting that guns should be submitted by 20 September 1864. On the due date, 47 differing rifles were available; nine were selected for trial, eleven were set aside for further examination and the others – which included prototypes from Needham, John Adams, Antoine Chassepot, Hollis, Leetch, Soper and Garcia Saez – were firmly rejected.

After the withdrawal of the rifle developed by the Royal Manufactory at Enfield, whose ammunition proved unacceptable, the eight triallists were the American-designed Storm, submitted by Charles Phelps, which had a tipping chamber designed for the standard service or a special skin cartridge; a bolt-action rifle submitted by C.E. & J. Green, which required a special combustible cartridge; a modified Westley Richards 'Monkey Tail' rifle in which even its inventor professed little faith; the American Joslyn, which was to be submitted by E.H. Newby when the samples arrived from the USA; two rifles submitted by Clarence Shephard, one adapted to fire combustible cartridges and the other firing rimfire cartridges; a gun with a laterally swinging block submitted by Messrs Aston on behalf of Jacob Snider the Younger; and a bolt-action gun championed by Thomas Wilson.

By the middle of January 1865, all guns – excepting the Joslyn, held up in New York docks – had been delivered to Enfield and trials began immediately. A rapidity-of-fire test indicated that all the breech-loaders were far superior to the P/53, the best being the Green (2 minutes 26 seconds to fire twenty rounds)

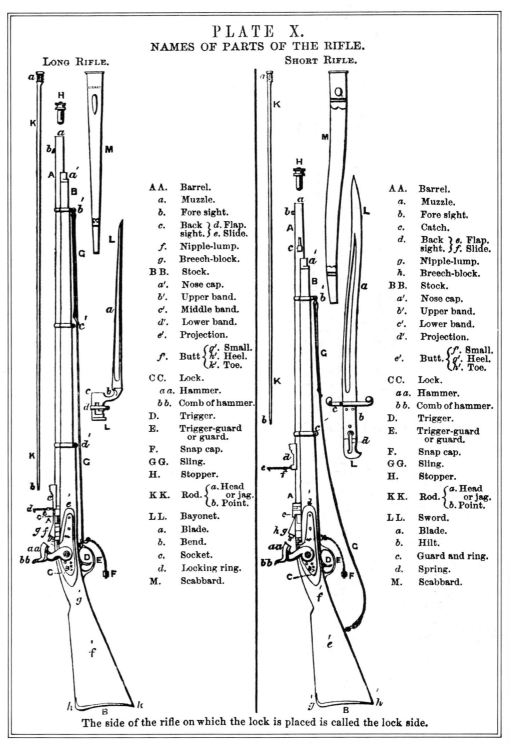

PLATE X.
NAMES OF PARTS OF THE RIFLE.

LONG RIFLE.

A A.	Barrel.
a.	Muzzle.
b.	Fore sight.
c.	Back sight. } *d.* Flap. } *e.* Slide.
f.	Nipple-lump.
g.	Breech-block.
B B.	Stock.
a'.	Nose cap.
b'.	Upper band.
c'.	Middle band.
d'.	Lower band.
e'.	Projection.
f.	Butt. { *g'.* Small. { *h'.* Heel. { *k'.* Toe.
C C.	Lock.
a a.	Hammer.
b b.	Comb of hammer.
D.	Trigger.
E.	Trigger-guard or guard.
F.	Snap cap.
G G.	Sling.
H.	Stopper.
K K.	Rod. { *a.* Head or jag. { *b.* Point.
L L.	Bayonet.
a.	Blade.
b.	Bend.
c.	Socket.
d.	Locking ring.
M.	Scabbard.

SHORT RIFLE.

A A.	Barrel.
a.	Muzzle.
b.	Fore sight.
c.	Catch.
d.	Back sight. } *e.* Flap. } *f.* Slide.
g.	Nipple-lump.
h.	Breech-block.
B B.	Stock.
a'.	Nose cap.
b'.	Upper band.
c'.	Lower band.
d'.	Projection.
e'.	Butt. { *f.* Small. { *g'.* Heel. { *h'.* Toe.
C C.	Lock.
a a.	Hammer.
b b.	Comb of hammer.
D.	Trigger.
E.	Trigger-guard or guard.
F.	Snap cap.
G G.	Sling.
H.	Stopper.
K K.	Rod. { *a.* Head or jag. { *b.* Point.
L L.	Sword.
a.	Blade.
b.	Hilt.
c.	Guard and ring.
d.	Spring.
M.	Scabbard.

The side of the rifle on which the lock is placed is called the lock side.

and the worst the Westley Richards (3 minutes 29 seconds). However, even the latter was an improvement on the rifle-musket, which had taken nearly seven minutes. After endurance and exposure trials, an appraisal of accuracy revealed that the P/53 was closely followed by the Westley Richards and Wilson; the Snider, made by Potts & Hunt and firing French Pottet cartridges, was by far the worst. There had been very few jams, the only two in the whole trial occurring in one of the Wilsons and a Snider.

Penetration experiments had greatly favoured the Westley Richards rifle, which fired a hardened bullet, while the others had been roughly comparable. However, both the Westley Richards stocks, together with one of the Wilsons and a Storm, had broken on trial; the Snider was adjudged the most desirable, requiring least removal of wood.

The exclusion of Shepard's guns and the non-appearance of the Joslyn left the way open for the Snider, the only remaining metal cartridge design. The committee offered its inventor a thousand P/53 rifle-muskets for conversion so that troop trials could be undertaken. However, the Secretary of State preferred the Storm on the grounds that it could be loaded from the muzzle in an emergency and accepted standard combustible cartridges.

As even the trials committee had praised it as the best of the capping breech-loaders, no objections were raised to the procurement of 3,000 P/53 rifle-muskets converted to the Storm breech system.

Meanwhile, Colonel Edward Boxer RA had solved the poor accuracy of the Snider by redesigning the French cartridge. So great was the change that the Snider, instead of being markedly inferior to the standard P/53, suddenly began to shoot considerably better. Though a Storm cartridge was sealed on 16 September 1865 to govern manufacture of a trial series, it was soon seen to be incapable of improvement.

A pattern to govern conversion of ten P/53 rifles to Snider's breech was sealed on 25 November 1865, and an order to manufacture 10,000 cartridges was passed to the Royal Laboratory at Woolwich. It had become clear that the Snider stood such a good chance of being adopted that lucrative government contracts would be involved. Predictably, many additional guns were offered to the British authorities; all were rejected, including the Spencer and Peabody rifles. Undaunted, spurned inventors suddenly decided that Snider's design infringed theirs. However, though litigation subsequently ensued between Snider and several appellants, only Thomas Wilson managed to prove his case.*

Before comparative trials could be undertaken, the Storm conversions exhibited an unduly high failure rate at proof. As the entire batch of contract-made skin cartridges had been rejected, the whole project was abandoned. Snider had the field to himself.

The first ten guns (numbered H1 to H10) arrived at the end of March 1866. Their accuracy proved better than the P/53, rapidity of fire was three times that of the rifle-musket, fouling was minimal, and practically no misfires or jamming occurred. The results were so pleasing that the Duke of Cambridge, the Army Commander-in-Chief, approved the conversion of 20,000 P/53 rifle-muskets at Enfield in the 1866–7 fiscal year.

Concurrently, ten converted P/58 naval rifles had been tested at HMS *Excellent* with encouraging results. The navy had actually requested three Remington rifles for comparative trials, but these had not been forthcoming and experience with the Sniders was deemed satisfactory enough. By the end of the summer of 1866, therefore, experimental conversions of the P/61 cavalry carbines and the oval-bored Engineer Carbines were also being tried. On 18 September 1866, the Snider breech was formally adopted.

Unfortunately, Snider had fallen desperately ill earlier in the year and did not live to see his ultimate triumph. On 4 August 1866 his representative, Colonel Roden, requested an immediate settlement of Snider's outstanding account with the War Office. Only £1,000 of this was remitted prior to the inventor's death, the remainder being paid to his widow together with £15,000 to acquire the production licence and benefit of royalties.

THE SERVICE WEAPONS

The basic hinged block action had been developed by Jacob Snider the Younger in association with François Eugene Schneider of Paris.† It had been patented in Britain in June 1862, but protection had been allowed to expire. Jacob Snider subsequently filed a number of variations alone. The relevant patents – so far as the British rifles were concerned – were 2,741/1864 and 2,912/1864, the essence of which was an improved sideways-tipping block which could be retracted on its axis pin to extract the spent case.

The Musket, rifled, Enfield, P/1853, converted to a breech-loader on Snider's Principles (Pattern I) was officially approved on 18 September 1866, conversion contracts immediately being placed with the Birmingham Small Arms Company ('BSA') and the London Small Arms Company ('LSA') to supplement the output of Enfield. BSA was to convert 100,000 rifle-muskets by 31 March 1868; LSA, 50,000 by 30 June 1867.

The Snider long rifle greatly resembled its muzzle-loading predecessor, apart from the

---

* Wilson was granted one tenth of the initial royalty payments in settlement.
†Possibly a cousin, despite the different spelling of the surname.

110 ABOVE

A ·577 Mk I* Snider rifle. The date on the lock plate shows that it was converted from a P/53 Enfield rifle-musket. Courtesy of the MoD Pattern Room Collection, Royal Ordnance plc, Nottingham.

111 RIGHT

Men of the 42nd (The Royal Highland) Regiment of Foot (The Black Watch) advance to the battle of Amoaful, fought on 31 January 1874 during the Asante War. Five thousand British troops commanded by General Sir Garnet Wolseley successfully repulsed 20,000 Fante tribesmen, though the fighting was bitter. The 42nd, which had been in the van, suffered 114 of the 190 British casualties. This contemporary engraving pays little attention to the Snider rifles! Courtesy of Philip J. Haythornthwaite.

replacement of the original breech by the new receiver and breech block unit (called a 'shoe' in contemporary terminology); like the P/53, it accepted the standard socket bayonet. On 30 October 1866, the first of the short rifles was sealed – a conversion of Lancaster's oval-bore P/55 Engineer Carbine (LoC 1374) – and conversion of existing guns began in the government's factory at Pimlico. By this time, a minor change had been made to the snap-cap and a retaining chain had been attached to the front of the trigger guard.

Problems had also arisen with the original Snider cartridge, whose narrow base was apt to rupture, and a new long-base Mark II was adopted in November 1866. The case-rim was squared rather than rounded, whereupon alterations were made in the rifle. Apart from squaring the countersink for the case groove, the shape and size of the extractor were changed, the underside of the breech block was extended to cover the entire case-head, the receiver ('shoe') dimensions were revised, and the nipple was shortened. Unfortunately, these revisions were introduced gradually; for a time there was great confusion over the pattern of the service rifle.

By early 1867 there were four differing guns – Patterns I, I*, II* and II** – with, respectively, the original rounded rim countersink; a partially squared countersink achieved by converting existing guns; the new squared countersink, but no other improvements; and the new countersink plus all the prescribed changes. The guns all shared the same type of action, however, as the improvements were largely internal. Only standard long rifles and Lancaster oval-bores were subject to this variety, as the basic design had been settled before additional conversions were sanctioned.

Accuracy problems were traced to the differences between the 525-grain Mark II and the 480-grain Mk III bullets, which suited the short rifles and long rifles respectively but performed badly if their roles were reversed. The differences were so marked that supplies of Mark II ammunition were restricted to rifle regiments and the Royal Navy, while the new Mark IV (which performed more like the Mk III) was issued to the remainder of the troops.

A conversion of the P/60 short rifle to the Snider system was approved on 6 March 1867, to be followed on 2nd May by the P/61 artillery carbine and an adaptation of the P/56 cavalry carbine. These all used the Pattern II** breech, though the cavalry gun had been given a half-stock and the appearance of a new design. Its two-piece cleaning rod was carried in a butt-trap. Next came the converted P/58 naval rifle (essentially similar to the standard Serjeant's P/61 but with brass mounts), approved on 7 August 1867 for issue with a cutlass bayonet.

112
Courtesy of Her Majesty's
Stationery Office.
Crown Copyright.

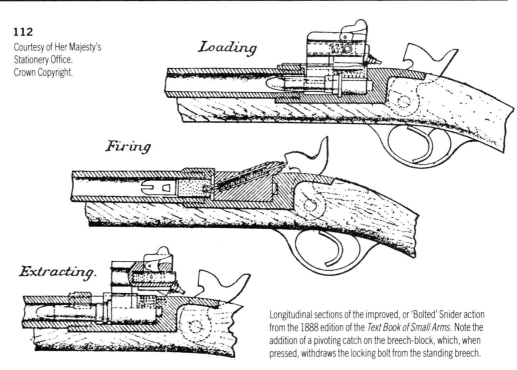

Loading

Firing

Extracting.

Longitudinal sections of the improved, or 'Bolted' Snider action from the 1888 edition of the *Text Book of Small Arms*. Note the addition of a pivoting catch on the breech-block, which, when pressed, withdraws the locking bolt from the standing breech.

On 31 March 1868, the Royal Small Arms Factory reported that it had converted 47,000 P/53 long rifles; 14,114 P/60 short rifles; 15,600 P/58 naval rifles; 11,980 cavalry carbines; 15,219 P/61 artillery carbines; 4,500 Lancaster oval-bore carbines; 7,900 P/56 short rifles into Irish Constabulary Carbines; and 330 P/53 rifle-muskets to Convict Guard Carbines. In addition, 92,000 long rifles had been supplied by BSA and LSA.

Experiments undertaken in the Spring of 1868 with ·5-calibre ammunition, anticipating the flat trajectory of the then-experimental ·45-inch cartridges combined with the resistance to fouling shown by the standard ·577, soon failed. Contemporaneously, Mark V ·577 ammunition was approved. As this shot nearly as well as the Mk II in short rifles, it was immediately adopted by the Navy for universal issue. However, its thin case ruptured too easily, and the Mark V was substituted by the heavier Mk VI; the latter was distinguished by a broad black band around the middle of the case-body.

Premature breech-opening began to happen with exasperating frequency once the Snider breeches had begun to wear. As large numbers of new guns would be needed while a new small-calibre breech-loader was being developed, the opportunity was taken to experiment with three differing locking catches. The design of Edward Bond, Managing Director of the London Small Arms Company, was subsequently adopted with the Rifle, P/53, Snider (Improved Action, 1868), Interchangeable on 13 January 1869.

Rifles embodying the new Pattern III or 'Bolted Action' also had a steel barrel, a strengthened receiver and a squared-off hammer face. Their actions were easily recognizable by the knurled-head latch set into the left side of the breech block.

The first guns embodying the Bolted Action were not issued until the late summer of 1870, when supplies reached the Scots Fusilier Guards. Several thousand Sniders had accompanied the Abyssinian Expedition in 1867, to subdue Emperor Theodore, and some had even been carried during the highly successful assault on Magdala fortress (April 1868). They had all embodied the old Pattern II** action.

Production of newly-made Sniders had totalled 60,017 by 30 June 1870. The quality of the trade products had proved very good, few inspection problems occurring. In August 1871, 12,000 naval P/58 Sniders were released from store for the army reserve, the sole change being the fractional enlargement of the muzzle-ring of the yataghan bayonets for the new guns.‡ An inventory made at the end of 1871 revealed that 650,905 assorted Sniders were on issue and 225,247 in store.

By 1872, progress with the Martini-Henry indicated that the Snider would soon be superseded; production slowed accordingly. By the end of January 1873, a total of 589,678 conversions and 292,424 new guns had been made. Virtually all had been the work of Enfield or the principal trade manufacturers, BSA and LSA, though most of the oval-bore Lancasters were converted in Pimlico.

Issues of Martini-Henry rifles began in 1874, involving the home infantry regiments, but the changes soon gathered momentum: overseas infantry units received theirs in 1875, the Royal Navy and the Royal Marines in 1876, the

‡This allowed the naval cutlass bayonets to be retained for the new Martini-Henry (when finally forthcoming).

cavalry in 1878–9 and the field and garrison artillery in 1880. By 1 April 1885, Sniders had been recalled from volunteers and 165,432 placed in store. Many had been sold to India; others had been auctioned at Weedon in the mid-1870s, seriously damaging the profitability of the Birmingham Small Arms & Metal Company (as BSA had become in February 1873). Together with LSA, BSA&M had banked on supplying colonial needs for some years. By retaining the Snider production line intact – the only one of the three major manufacturers to do so – BSA&M was subsequently able to supply guns to Portugal, India and New Zealand.

The last service-pattern Snider to be adopted was the impressively named Carbine, breech-loading, rifled, with cleaning rod, Snider, Yeomanry, Interchangeable, with cover, leather, back sight, Mk I (!). Sealed on 19 July 1880 and announced in LoC 3774, it was converted from P/53 Snider long rifles; it lacked side-nail cups for the saddle bar, and was an inch longer in the butt than standard carbines. As late as May 1887, a few long Sniders were converted to artillery-carbine stan-

dards, but the first ·303 magazine rifle was approaching perfection and the single-shot hinged-block rifle was obsolescent.

Some Sniders will be found marked 'L.A.C.' for the London Armoury Company, predecessor of LSA, while others will bear the marks of C.G. Bonehill of Birmingham. Sniders intended for commercial sale normally display a large 'S' transfixed by an arrow.

QUEST FOR A NEW GUN

The Snider was nothing more than an expedient, ideal for converting thousands of Enfield rifle-muskets but with few long-term prospects. Even as work to perfect the P/53 conversion was proceeding, new breech-loading rifle trials were announced. The 'Advertisement to Gunmakers and Others' was signed by Major-General James St George, Director of Ordnance, on 21 June 1865.

The advertisement was accompanied by an explanatory memorandum enlarging some of the details, such as the construction of the

sights. Papers were sent to as many interested parties as possible, and, by the time the Ordnance Select Committee had convened, 24 rifles had been submitted.

The eight 'recommended for trial' included the Henry, submitted on behalf of Alexander Henry of Edinburgh. The rifle was a single-shot external-hammer breechloader 'not unlike Sharps' and chambered metallic-case cartridges. The dropping block, actuated by a trigger-guard lever, was adapted to cam the cartridges hard into the breech and had an auxiliary extractor.

The Josyln, submitted by E.H. Newby, featured a side-hinged block and an external hammer. The gun was patented by Benjamin Joslyn of Worcester, Massachussetts, in the 1860s. The British trial gun chambered a necked metal-case cartridge.

The Lindner, patented by Edward Lindner of New York on 29 March 1859 (US Patent no.23,378). The action combined a percussion lock with an interrupted-screw breech later adopted in Bavaria.

To complete transatlantic interest, the Snider had a breech 'similar to that of the

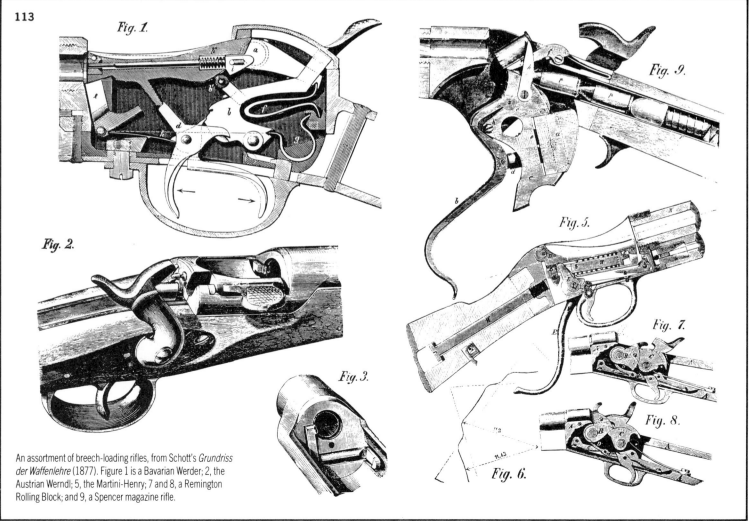

An assortment of breech-loading rifles, from Schott's *Grundriss der Waffenlehre* (1877). Figure 1 is a Bavarian Werder; 2, the Austrian Werndl; 5, the Martini-Henry; 7 and 8, a Remington Rolling Block; and 9, a Spencer magazine rifle.

Enfield Rifles converted by Mr Snider' (protected by US Patent 69,941 of 15 October 1867). One Snider chambered a Lefaucheux-style pinfire cartridge, but the final ·450 trials gun was centre-fire.

The British Byrnes & Benjamin rifle, one of those 'set aside for further examination', was essentially similar to the Westley Richards Monkey Tail pattern with a locking bolt (or 'plunger') actuated by a lever inlet in the small of the stock. It fired a paper cartridge by means of a conventional side-hammer. Owing to the difficulty of dismantling the locking bolt for maintenance, the rifle was disqualified.

The three ·450 Millar rifles fired metal-case rimfire cartridges, one having an external hammer and two coil-spring powered strikers. Operating the Millar breech proved troublesome, and the spring-catch extractor was inefficient.

The action of the ·50-calibre Peabody rifle, submitted on behalf of Henry Peabody of Boston, Massachusetts, was already well known. Made to US Patent 35,947 of 22 July 1862, the pivoting-block action was controlled by the trigger-guard lever. An external hammer struck a firing pin running through the block. The Peabody action was well proven and immensely strong; however, the British were concerned about susceptibility to jamming, the inherent weakness of the two-piece stock and the unacceptable design of the rimfire cartridge.

The first series of trials resolved in favour of the ·450 Snider, but even this fell short of the War Office's hopes. After circulating requests for information among leading members of the gun trade, the Director of Ordnance decided to hold another competition in the Spring of 1867. Accordingly, another advertisement was circulated to interested parties.

A trial of magazine rifles was to be held concurrently, the prizes being £1,000 for the best single-shot rifle, £600 for the best breech mechanism, £400 for the best cartridge, and £300 for the best magazine rifle. The Director of Ordnance added a further inducement: 'if the rifle to which the first prize is awarded is adopted into the service, it will bear the inventor's name'. Who could overlook such a chance of glory?

Trials were protracted and exhaustive. Finally, on 11 June 1867, the Ordnance Select Sub-committee reported on the progress of no fewer than 104 submissions. These had been split into two groups – conforming with the specification and failing to do so – and thence into sub-classes. Of the 37 guns that conformed to the specification, and were admissible for the prize competition, 21 had been rejected immediately; seven failed the second stage, leaving a mere nine to be tested. The successful submissions had been the Albini & Braendlin, two Burtons, the Fosbery, the

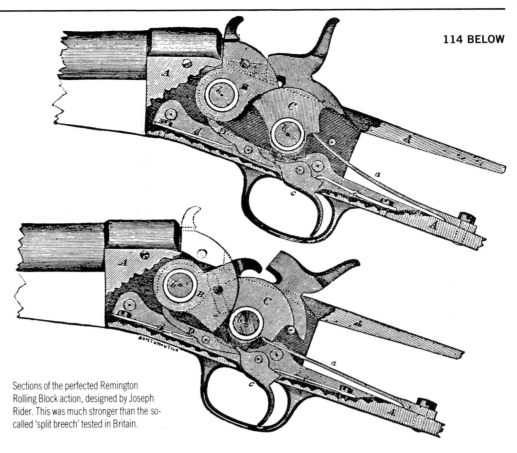

Sections of the perfected Remington Rolling Block action, designed by Joseph Rider. This was much stronger than the so-called 'split breech' tested in Britain.

Henry, the Joslyn, the Martini, the Peabody and the Remington.

On 22 June 1867, the promoters of the approved rifles were requested to submit six guns of each pattern together with a thousand rounds per gun.

Eleven of the guns that had failed to comply with the competition specifications were 'retained for consideration' until the results of the prize competition were known: Berdan, Carter & Edwards No.3, Fosbery No.4, Greve & Dowling No.4, Hammond, Needham No.1, Poultney, Westley Richards No.3B and 11,[*] Sharp and Wilson.

The Ordnance Select Sub-committee reconvened late in October 1867, only to find that the Martini rifles had been delayed on the Franco-Swiss border and John Burton was requesting additional time on the grounds that he had to prepare twelve guns rather than six.

Finally, on 28 November 1867, testing that was to last into February 1868 began. It was undertaken with the thoroughness that characterized British ordnance affairs, and also with considerable enthusiasm. Though the details are too protracted to be related in detail,[†] the accuracy trials proved particularly interesting. The committee had set optimal Figures of Merit of 0·50ft at 300 yards and 1ft at 500. At the shorter range, however, only the Burton No.2 and the Albini & Braendlin – which recorded 0·63ft and 0·69ft respectively – beat the Snider navy rifle being used as

a control (0·75ft). At 500 yards, the Burton No.2 (1·27ft) again beat the Henry (1·41ft), with the Snider recording 1·37ft and the Martini only 2·01; the Fosbery, Joslyn, Peabody and Remington had been excluded after their comparatively poor performance at short range.

It was clear that only three guns were more accurate than the Snider, so both the Burtons and the Henry were tested at 800 yards. To the committee's surprise, the Henry recorded 2·38ft to the Burton's 3·14ft and 3·76ft for the Snider. As the Burton No.1 gave a poor 5·23ft, it was excluded from the subsequent 1,000 yard trial. At the longest distance, the Henry (3·45ft) increased its superiority over both the Burton No.2 (5·77ft) and the Snider (6·92ft). All rifles had been fired sufficiently rapidly, and none had exceeded the recoil limits. But only the Remington, Joslyn, Henry, Peabody and the Albini & Braendlin passed the penetration tests (in that order), with the Martini and the Burton No.1 failing narrowly while the Burton No.2, Fosbery and Snider failed by steadily increasing margins.

The Martini, the Henry and the Albini & Braendlin met the trajectory requirements, while only the Burton No.2 and the Snider – and the Henry, with reservations – passed the

*According to the trial reports. It is now known why Westley Richards numbered one gun as high as '11'.

†The relevant portions of Temple & Skennerton, *A Treatise on the British Military Martini, 1869– c.1900* relate the story in far greater detail.

fouling test. Most of the rifles were deemed superior to the Snider in durability, and only the Joslyn and the Remington breeches showed any distress with over-loaded cartridges.‡

However, such great problems had been encountered with the ammunition that the committee found 'considerable difficulty in instituting a fair comparison between the different breech-loading systems, owing to the great variety in ammunition and in the calibre of the arms submitted'. The Albini & Braendlin and the Martini, in particular, were plagued with cartridge problems.

Finally, the committee ranked the rifles in descending order of preference: Henry, Burton No.2, Albini & Braendlin, Fosbery, Burton No.1, Peabody, Martini, Remington and Joslyn. However, though the Henry had almost managed to satisfy the War Office criteria, it was compromised by its cartridge; similarly, Burton No.2, which had much to commend it, was insufficiently accurate at long range. The £1,000 prize was withheld, £600 for the best breech mechanism being awarded to Alexander Henry. In this category, his rifle had placed ahead of the Burton No.2, the Albini & Braendlin and the Burton No.1.

Worried that the terms of reference had been too narrow, even while the trials were being undertaken, the Ordnance Select Committee decided to extend them to encompass virtually any rifle that was potentially military. It was also obvious that progress would not be made until a barrel design had been perfected. Accordingly, on 3 March 1868, letters were sent to Joseph Whitworth, Westley Richards, Charles Lancaster, William Metford, John Rigby and Alexander Henry inviting them to participate. Metford declined and Rigby subsequently withdrew, but ·450-calibre barrels were submitted on behalf of the remainder. Excepting Westley Richards' products, which were allied with an improved form of his falling-block breech to test simultaneously, the barrels were all fitted to Henry actions. For comparison, Colonel Dixon submitted two ·500-calibre Sniders made at Enfield. Apart from one of the Westley Richards rifles, which chambered special solid-drawn ammunition, the rifles all chambered Boxer-pattern rolled-case cartridges.

The sub-committee reported on 11 February 1869 that the ·450 Henry had proved superior to its rivals, competition coming only from the government-sponsored ·500 Snider.

However, though neither cartridge was prone to fouling, the Henry bullet had a flatter trajectory out to 500 yards, was markedly superior in crosswinds and offered better penetration. Henry rifling was approved, reservations about the great length of the cartridge – 3·75in compared with 2·56in for the ·577 Snider – being referred to the Royal Laboratory, Woolwich, for action.

‡ It was an example of the early Geiger-patent 'Split Breech' pattern, which lacked the strength of the later Rolling Blocks perfected by Joseph Rider.

115 BELOW LEFT
Men of the 66th (Berkshire) Regiment of Foot in Afghanistan in 1880. This engraving, after an illustration by R. Caton Woodville, was published in the *Illustrated London News* in August 1880. Note the revolver holster and the Martini-Henry rifles; Caton Woodville generally took care over the proportions of the weapons, but was not always well served by engravers. Courtesy of Philip J. Haythornthwaite.

116 BELOW
Indian cavalrymen in Egypt: an engraving after an illustration by R. Caton Woodville, published in the *Illustrated London News* in September 1882. Note the Martini-Henry cavalry carbine. Courtesy of Philip J. Haythornthwaite.

Breech-mechanism trials began almost immediately the Henry barrel had emerged victorious. Once again, there were dozens of hopeful entrants: the nine guns selected for the prize competition were joined by those non-standard designs that had been set aside for consideration, together with new rifles submitted prior to 26 October 1868. Soon, all but ten guns had been excluded.

Only the Bacon, Berdan (block action), Carter & Edwards, Henry, Kerr, Martini, Money-Walker, Westley Richards Nos.1 and 2, and Wilson were retained. Six of these – Berdan, Henry, Martini, Money-Walker and Westley Richards – incorporated block-locks, the remaining four being bolt-action.

The sub-committee was concerned by the design of the bolt actions, allowing them to participate only under protest until a special sensitive-cartridge test could determine the safety margins. This was undertaken with defective cartridges loaded with coal-dust, the intention being to discover whether the priming compound would ignite when the breech was slammed shut. The resulting explosions would be so minor that no damage would be done to gun or firer. Though the Carter & Edwards rifle passed the test successfully, Kerr's and Berdan's showed signs of the firing pins striking the primer. The Bacon actually fired some of its cartridges before the breech was closed.

The bolt-action rifles were subsequently allowed in the endurance trials, but a serious premature explosion occurred – predictably – as the Bacon breech closed, and the whole genre was excluded on the grounds of suspect safety. The exposure trials also undid the Berdan, the Money-Walker and the Westley Richards elevating-block rifle.

Now just three guns remained. The Martini was considered to have the best extraction, while the Henry was effectual if somewhat complicated; the Westley Richards falling-block rifle had rusted badly in the exposure trials, despite its promoter's special lubricant. Richards requested that a modified rifle be considered, but then withdrew from the competition on 2 November 1868. In light of his later condemnation of the Martini-Henry as being inferior to his own designs, the results of his participation in 1868 are worth remembering.

Trials that had begun three years previously had reduced the choice to Martini or Henry rifles. A modified Martini rifle was subsequently made at Enfield, latterly under the supervision of Friedrich Martini personally, while Henry worked to improve his rifle for the eliminator.

Final trials proved that there was little to choose between the performance of the two guns. However, the Martini was more compact and its breech contained thirty parts compared with the Henry's 49. As the committee was also concerned that the Henry side-lock weakened the stock, the final conclusion was that after

a careful consideration of the relative advantages and disadvantages of the two systems, and of the results of the many trials to which both have been subjected, the committee decide [sic] on giving the preference to the Martini, and on recommending it as the one best qualified for a military arm of any that has been brought before them.

THE MARTINI-HENRY

Resolution of the trials allowed the Royal Small Arms Factory to make four prototype Martini-Henry rifles early in 1869, similar in concept but differing in detail. All had the so-called Whitworth Sights, with a deep broad V on the back sight leaf. Trials of seven- and nine-groove barrels had favoured the former, which had a flatter trajectory, and a 380-grain bullet had been rejected as too light. Apart from a weakness in the cartridge indicator, the rifles had worked well.

Martini, meanwhile, had patented his rifle in Britain (Letters Patent 2,305/68 of 22 July 1868); the first rumblings of discontent were also beginning to be heard, the most serious of which was an allegation of plagiarism made on behalf of Henry Peabody. Recently, this charge has been subjected to much scrutiny by enthusiasts – such as Temple & Skennerton, in *A Treatise on the British Military Martini*.

I am less convinced. The basic principles of the two guns seem too similar to be coincidental and it seems fair to describe the Martini breech, as Martini himself had once done, as 'an improvement on the Peabody'. But it has to be admitted that it is a *considerable* improvement. Attention has been drawn to the fact that Peabody or his agents never sued Martini, but dropping-block rifles operated by an underlever were scarcely new in the 1860s. It is difficult to see how litigation could have been successful.

The controversy appears to have weakened the War Office's resolve to adopt the rifle, even though the Special Committee on Breech Loading Rifles was formally dissolved on 31 March 1869.† While the authorities vacillated, the Council of Ordnance ordered Enfield to make two hundred guns for trial. These were to be issued to an infantry battalion in Aldershot, the Royal Engineers in Gravesend, the School of Musketry in Hythe, Curragh Camp in Dublin, and the Director of Naval Ordnance at Portsmouth.

Some of the Portsmouth guns were to be despatched to ships on overseas service,

† The military members of the committee were retained for several weeks to resolve the few remaining problems.

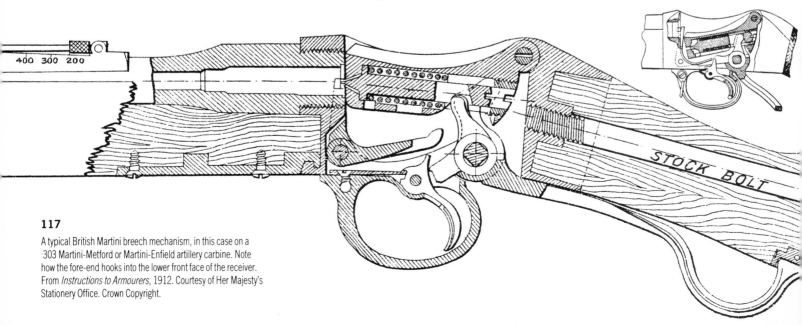

117
A typical British Martini breech mechanism, in this case on a ·303 Martini-Metford or Martini-Enfield artillery carbine. Note how the fore-end hooks into the lower front face of the receiver. From *Instructions to Armourers*, 1912. Courtesy of Her Majesty's Stationery Office. Crown Copyright.

118 ABOVE

An 1874-vintage ·450 Mk I Martini-Henry. Note that this gun lacks the safety catch encountered above the trigger of rifles made prior to 1873. Courtesy of the MoD Pattern Room Collection, Royal Ordnance plc, Nottingham.

119 The 'Cartridge, Small Arm, Ball, Martini-Henry Rifle, Solid Case, Mk II' (left) and the Mk II Martini-Henry buckshot round (right). From the 1888 edition of the *Text Book of Small Arms*. Courtesy of Her Majesty's Stationery Office. Crown Copyright.

while rifles were also sent to Cape Colony, Canada and India in an attempt to make the experiments as wide-ranging as possible. The British Army held a unique brief, and it was important that its firearms should work effectually in extremes of climate.

The two hundred rifles chambered an exceptionally long cartridge. However, even as they were being made, notice arrived that William Eley had perfected a necked case that gave the same powder capacity as an original Martini-Henry round while greatly reducing its overall length. As the new cartridge promised to be much more durable — it was less likely to bend — ten suitable rifles were prepared to test it. Eight shared the long action of the 200 trials guns, the other two being specially shortened.

Trials dragged on through the summer into the autumn of 1869. The reports were generally satisfactory, though a few of the flaws that were to plague the early service career of the Martini-Henry were highlighted. Among the worst were broken strikers; the unsuitable design of the butt; excessive recoil compared with the Snider; and the poor trigger pull, which was never entirely solved. The most worrying problem, not immediately identified, was the tendency of the rifle to fire as the breech was being closed. Owing to the sturdy breech block, this caused the firers little more than shock. However, it could have fatal consequences among onlookers. Though the incidents were dismissed in the earliest reports as soldiers' errors, they were due to débris getting in behind the trigger lever or into the notch (or 'bent') on the tumbler. These reduced the contact between trigger and tumbler until a sudden jerk — such as shutting the breech — released the striker.

A brace of new short action guns was made to cure manufacturing problems, being about a half-inch longer in the body than their predecessors, and it seemed that the pattern had been sealed. Ammunition trials occupied much of early 1870, a period in which 24 additional 'perfected' short-chamber rifles had been made. The final report of the Martini-Henry Rifle Committee, made on 8 February 1871, opined that the short-chamber gun

should be adopted for service. On 30 March 1871, at a meeting of the Council of Ordnance chaired by Lord Northbrook, Under-Secretary of State for War, the rifle was finally approved.

Though the leading students of the Martini-Henry recognise fourteen separate experimental patterns from this period, only the long-chamber trials gun is likely to be encountered; the others are rarely seen outside official collections. The long-chamber pattern, sealed on 1 October 1869, measured 51in overall and weighed about 9lb 5½oz without its bayonet. The barrel was 35in long, weighed 4lb 6oz, and was rifled with seven-groove twist. There were swivels on the fore-end, trigger guard and butt. A cocking indicator lay on the right side of the action, and a pivoting safety catch protruded from the right side of the trigger guard ahead of the trigger lever. Pushed forward, it enabled the action to fire.

The most obvious features were the minimal butt wrist and the projection of the action body ahead of the trigger guard; the standard service-rifle body ended virtually in line with the trigger-guard swivel. Internally, the action incorporated a tumbler rest, added by Enfield to Martini's original design but subsequently abandoned.

A long-butt version of the Rifle, Breech-Loading, Martini-Henry (Mk I) was sealed on 3 June 1871 together with its cleaning rod, muzzle cover, jag and muzzle protector. The 'Sword bayonet, Elcho pattern' and its scabbard were approved simultaneously. The rifles measured 49in overall, weighed 8lb 7½oz and had a 3lb 6¼oz barrel. Excepting a prototype or two, this rifle was never made; a modified trigger system was approved by the Secretary of State for War on 21 November 1871, even though the appropriate pattern was not sealed until September 1872. And finally, after more experiments, the third or 'Approved' pattern was accepted by the authorities on 17 July 1874.

Long-butt rifles measured 49½in overall, weighed 8lb 12oz, and had a 33$\frac{7}{32}$in barrel weighing 3lb 6oz. Announced in LoC 2659 of 1 October 1874, the 'Rifle, Breech-loading, Martini-Henry (Mark I)' was accompanied by the Jag Mk I; Protector, foresight and muzzle, Mk I; Rod, cleaning, Mk I; and Bayonet, Mk I. The Elcho sword bayonet had been replaced by a conventional socket pattern, approved by the Secretary of State for War in November 1872. The new bayonet was initially made simply by sleeving P/53 examples.

Compared with its immediate predecessor, the Approved Mk I rifle had a split-steel block axis pin, a modified cleaning rod, a longer butt, and a plain butt plate. The edges of the trigger guard had been rounded and the safety catch was discarded. The sling swivel on the butt was eliminated on 20 January 1875, only the Rifle Brigade and the 60th Rifles protesting vigorously enough to retain them.

The first issues of the new rifle had been made in 1874. On 4 November 1875, however, the Director of Artillery directed that the pattern arm (which had been altered) should not be sealed; trouble with the trigger system had become serious enough for a modified gun to be tested.

Sealed on 25 April 1877, the Mark II rifle was announced in LoC 3193 on 1 November 1877 (as 'Arm, Interchangeable, Rifle, Breech-loading, Martini-Henry, with cleaning rod [Mark II]'). Many changes had been made, including the omission of the tumbler rest and tumbler-rest axis screw. The upper surface of the breech block was browned to eliminate reflections, and the V-notches in the backsight slider and leaf were deepened. An entirely new trigger mechanism had been developed, the trigger-guard plate shrouding the trigger lever well enough to reduce jamming caused by débris. Changes were made to the trigger screw and trigger spring, and the pull-off was improved.

Improvements in the trigger and the lengthened butts – which now measured 14 and 14½in – were appreciated by the firers, and complaints of excessive recoil began to decline. The new trigger also eliminated the occasional tendency of the Mk I to fire when the breech was being closed.

Mark II rifles measured 49½in overall and weighed 8lb 10½oz; their 3lb 6oz barrels were 33³⁄₁₆in long. Guns were only made by the Royal Small Arms Factory, Enfield, until the approval of the Mark III in August 1879. However, the trade continued to deliver Mark II Martini-Henrys until the last gun ordered from BSA in 1887 was delivered.

120–5 BELOW

A selection of block-action rifles. **A** is one of the original Martini guns submitted to British trials. Note the distinctive Swiss-type tangent back sight and the large cocking indicator. **B** is a Henry, made by the National Arms & Ammunition Co. Ltd in the 1870s. This example has a non-standard left-hand lock. **C** is a Soper, possibly made by BSA about 1871. Pressing the lever downward flips the breech up. **D** is a standard ·450 Martini-Henry Rifle Mk I, made at Enfield in 1874. **E** shows a Westley Richards Martini-type rifle, of a pattern patented in 1870. Note the distinctive two-piece stock. **F** is an example of Field's patent military rifle, probably made by Westley Richards. The action is cocked and the block dropped by pulling the side lever backward. Courtesy of the MoD Pattern Room Collection, Royal Ordnance plc, Nottingham; photographs by John Walter.

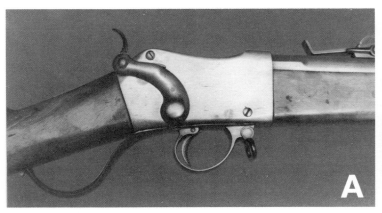

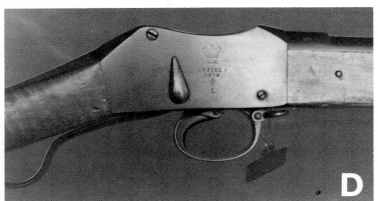

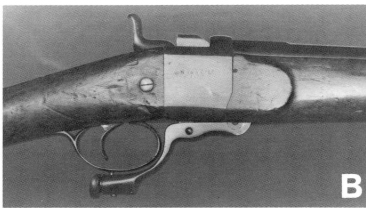

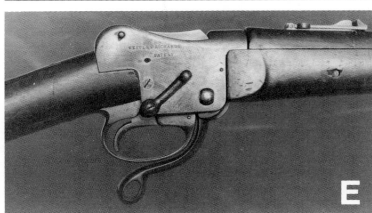

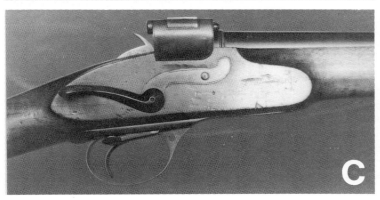

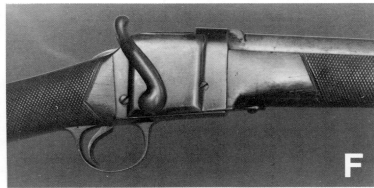

126 RIGHT
Mounted infantrymen of the 90th Perthshire Light Infantry, pictured during the Zulu War of 1879. Note that they are armed with Swinburn-Henry carbines; the hump-back action, cocking lever and plain fore-end are most distinctive. The 90th was amalgamated with the 26th in 1881, forming the Cameronians (Scottish Rifles). By courtesy of the Africana Museum, Johannesburg.

The advent of the new rifles upset the cavalry, which considered itself to be the élite. Though experimental cavalry and artillery carbines had been tested at Enfield in June 1871, little had been done. Many cavalrymen had expressed a preference for the Snider, a test of a third-pattern Martini-Henry trials carbine in May 1873 arousing criticism of its strong recoil and poorly shaped stock.

Efforts were made to reduce the cartridge loading, initially to 70 grains of powder driving a 380-grain bullet (compared with 85 and 480 for the standard rifle round). Though recoil declined, so did accuracy at ranges greater than 500 yards. An intermediate 'light rifle' load – 80 grains of powder and a 410-grain bullet – also failed to satisfy the cavalry, so trials dragged on into the mid 1870s. Finally, after fifty guns had been issued to the hussars at the end of May 1875, the sixth-and-last experimental carbine was approved by the Secretary of State for War on 15 June 1876.

Fully stocked, with two bands and a distinctive nose cap, the carbine was issued to representatives of cavalry and artillery, as well as to the School of Musketry, Hythe. It had a very distinctive half-cock thumb-piece on the right side of the body above the cocking indicator, the latter being reduced in size to allow the thumb-piece to rotate unhindered.

The half-cock system, potentially dangerous, was abandoned before the weapon was approved for service as the Carbine, Breech-loading, Martini-Henry (Mark I) and sealed on 24 September 1877.‡ Compared with the contemporary Mark II rifle, it offered several improvements: the fore-end was retained by a hook, instead of a stud and pin; the cocking indicator was greatly reduced in size; two reinforces appeared on the breech instead of one; and a new striker and breech-block assembly minimized striker breakages. Weighing about 7½lb, the carbine was 37¹¹⁄₁₆in long and had a 2lb 4¾oz barrel measuring 21⅜in.

A leather back-sight cover was adopted in April 1879, anchored over screws protruding from the fore-end. These cut into the carbine scabbard so quickly that their heads were speedily rounded off – LoC 3566 of 1

127 BELOW

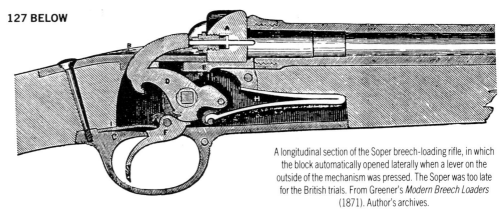

A longitudinal section of the Soper breech-loading rifle, in which the block automatically opened laterally when a lever on the outside of the mechanism was pressed. The Soper was too late for the British trials. From Greener's *Modern Breech Loaders* (1871). Author's archives.

August 1879. The shape of the fore-end retaining hook was changed in August 1880, necessitating a change in the Pattern Arm, and swivels were reinstated in August 1882 to accept a sling and steadying strap.

A Garrison Artillery Carbine was approved for issue on 9 April 1878, but was never made in quantity. It would have been similar to the cavalry carbine, excepting that it accepted a sword bayonet. It was substituted by the Carbine, Breech-loading, Rifled, with Cleaning Rod, Martini-Henry, Interchangeable, Artillery (Mark I), sealed on 21 July 1879, though near-identical guns had been made for some time. The carbine was essentially similar to the abortive Garrison Artillery design, but had swivels on the butt and upper band. It weighed 7lb 10½oz and measured 37¹¹⁄₁₆in overall; or, with its sword bayonet, 9lb 4¾oz and 63⅜in respectively. A total of 57,208 guns was made at Enfield.

Many artillery carbines were converted from Martini-Henry rifles, the Mark II pattern (sealed on 16 June 1892) being originally a Mark II rifle.* The barrel and fore-end had been shortened, and the muzzle turned down

to receive the crossguard ring of the sword bayonet. The fore-end finished about one inch from the muzzle, which distinguishes the Mk II from the otherwise comparable Mk III. A new upper band carried the bayonet lug. The back sight, swivels, butt disc and cleaning rod were all new. 38,407 rifles were modified at Enfield in the 1890s, but the resulting Mk II artillery carbines were rapidly reduced to Drill Purpose status after the Second South African War.

The Mark III artillery carbine, supposedly converted from Mk III rifles, was never sealed. It had a special cleaning rod, retained the original rifle front sight, and had a fore-end terminating about 2in from the muzzle.

The Mk III Martini-Henry rifle, sealed on 22 August 1879, was refined from the Mark II and described in LoC 3998 of 1st March 1882.

Long-butt Mark III Martini-Henry rifles measured 49½in overall and weighed 9lb 1oz. Their barrels measured 33³⁄₁₆in and weighed 3lb 6oz without the back sight.

MARTINI-HENRY RIVALS

By the time the Mark I rifle finally reached the troops – in 1874 – unfavourable opinions had already formed. Everyone in officialdom, from the Secretary of State for War downward, had been castigated for accepting an 'inferior' rifle. Much of the derision had come, not unexpectedly, from gunmakers whose submissions had been rejected.

In 1874, however, the Martini was at least the equal of the rifles being issued in other armies. And the critics, so quick to condemn, always overlooked that foreign armies were often experiencing far worse trouble with their firearms. The length of time the Martini had taken to perfect was by no means unique. The French were frantically converting the Chassepot needle rifle to take a centre-fire metallic cartridge; the Austro-Hungarians were labouring with the drum-breech Werndl, which jammed when it got hot; and the US Army had only just accepted the clumsy 'Trap-door Springfield', which was slow to operate and prone to extraction failures.

By eliminating bolt-action rifles from the trials undertaken in 1868, critics claimed, the relevant sub-committee had effectively hamstrung itself. But none of the perfected designs had appeared in time, and problems common

in the earliest weapons – in particular, premature ignition – had not been solved by 1870. Delays caused by protracted trials had been unfortunate, but it is hard to accept that the British trials had been in any way unfair or ineffectual.

Among the most vocal critics of the Martini breech was Westley Richards, who, after the committee had looked likely to place his rifle third (behind the Martini and the Henry) had withdrawn from competition voluntarily in 1868. Great claims were also made for the Soper rifle, which had appeared too late to be included.

Few rifles tested in Britain in 1866–9 – often the most interesting designs – were superior to the perfected Martini-Henry. Consequently, few were made in quantity. Service with the British Army would undoubtedly have revealed weaknesses; complication and fragility were common to many, and it is unlikely that any of the competing block-action designs offered better extraction than the Martini (even if their triggers were often superior).

Outstanding among the Martini-Henry's competitors were the various Westley Richards 'improved Martini' rifles. The basic design had been patented in Britain in 1868 (no.1,931/68), but had been withdrawn from the trials when likely to place third. Its promoter then filed several patents of addition, before perfecting the design in the early 1870s;

excepting sales to the South African Republic,† Westley Richards's block-action weapons achieved comparatively little. Though the breech mechanism was simpler than the Martini, the efficacy of its springs under service conditions (notably the curiously bent sear spring) may be questioned.

Also generally made by Westley Richards, the Field rifles had an operating lever on the right side of the body. Pushed forward, this opened the breech and cocked the hammer. The guns were made to British Patent 1,927/77 of 1877, granted to William Field of Birmingham. However, though Field's design was compact, lack of mechanical advantage in the operating lever would have promoted extraction problems with rolled-case Boxer ammunition.

Alexander Henry made quantities of his external-hammer gun, which had come so near to success in the government trials, but then proceeded to a complicated and less durable hammerless design. Guns by Farquharson and Soper, so highly regarded by enthusiasts, had no military application.

Apart from the Westley Richards 'Improved Martini', the principal military-pattern rifle was the Swinburn, which was a basically a Martini modified by the substitution of a V-spring for the coil pattern. Swinburns were carried by many locally-raised units during

†These are usually marked 'Z.A.R.', for Zuid Afikaansche Republiek.

---

the Zulu War of 1879 and the First South African War (1881). Several differing guns were made, six relevant patents being granted to John Swinburn in 1872–7.‡

The perfected rifle is sometimes known as the 'Model 1877'. Its principal distinguishing external feature is a lever on the right side of the body, in much the same place as the Martini-Henry cocking indicator, with which the action could be re-cocked in the event of a misfire. Internally, the Swinburn striker was struck by a hammer propelled by a V-spring; owing to the conventional butt construction, attached to the body by means of tangs, there was ample space to house the trigger and mainspring behind the body. Though the

‡Specifically, British patents 110/1872, 1,895/1872, 3,635/1875, 3,689/1876 and 2,206/1877.

Swinburn was not as compact as the Martini-Henry, it had a far better trigger.

Comparatively large numbers of Swinburn-Henry rifles, chambering the government ·450 cartridge, were acquired by the authorities in Natal during the crisis that precipitated the Zulu War in 1879. Whether they were available from stock, or whether Swinburn accepted a 'rush order' is not known; it is likely that they were made by a sub-contractor, possibly even Westley Richards. Many survivors are marked 'N. & J. Blakemore, London', apparently the Natal purchasing agency. Rifles and carbines were issued to volunteer corps such as the Natal Carabiniers, Victoria Mounted Rifles and Border Mounted Rifles in 1878–9. The Swinburn-Henry remained issue until the advent of Martini-Metfords in 1895, its passing apparently unmourned. Surviving rifles were placed in store, returns for 1905 still showing 145 rifles and 582 carbines.

It is surmised that the Swinburns – much more complicated that the Martini-Henry – were less durable than the government rifle and at least equally prone to jamming.

The Swinburn never served with regular troops. Though some were associated with Lord Chelmsford's units, and some are said to have been used at the Battle of Isandhlwana, these were usually carried by native drivers and volunteer units raised in Natal. Measuring 49½in overall and weighing 9lb 5oz, the

·450 Swinburn-Henry resembled the contemporary Martini-Henry Mk II. However, the rear of the body was noticeably different; an auxiliary cocking lever replaced the Martini-Henry indicator; and the underlever was practically straight between the action and the finger loop. In addition, the Swinburn rifle accepted a sword bayonet instead of a socket pattern. Sights and fittings otherwise duplicated the service types.

The Swinburn-Henry carbine shared the rifle action, but had a plain fore-end without bands or nose cap. The fore-end was retained by a cross-pin at the breech and a swivel-eye running up into the underside of the barrel. The gun accepted a sword bayonet and a leather back sight cover, measured 39·3in overall and weighed 7lb 8oz.

LATER MARTINI-HENRY RIFLES

British authorities always paid close attention to events abroad, worried lest their soldiers should face better-armed European adversaries.

A committee was formed in December 1880 to investigate the development of a universal cartridge for rifles and machine-guns; to test whether the Martini-Henry was as badly under-sighted as complaints had suggested; to develop long-range sights; to report whether a new breech system should be adopted; and to experiment with magazine rifles.

After meeting early in 1881, the committee recommended adapting fifty Martini-Henry rifles to accept the ·45 Gatling machine-gun cartridge. It was clear that this would be better than adapting the Martini-Henry pattern for machine-guns. The Machine Gun Committee had reported that

From experience of the working of machine guns ... much of the difficulty with the service cartridge arises not only from its weak construction, but also from its shape, which does not lend itself to the exigencies of rapid feeding, and, when expanded on discharge, the cylindrical portion of the case adheres to the cylindrical chamber with a large bearing surface, causing great frictional resistance to extraction.

Forty Martini-Henry rifles were altered in 1881, simply by inserting an annular bush in a reamed-out chamber.

A report received from the Inspector-General of Musketry in May 1881 stated that there had been many mis- and hang-fires (56 in 1,288 rounds),* and blustery conditions on the firing range at Hythe had reduced the value of accuracy trials appreciably.

Accuracy of the original and converted guns had been comparable. At 500 yards, a standard rifle had returned a Figure of Merit of 1ft, compared with 1·01ft for the ·450 Gatling-cartridge gun and 1·07ft for the ·451 version. Results at 1,000 yards had been 2·86ft for the standard rifle, compared with 2·57ft and 2·58ft for its rivals.

Trials at 1,400 yards had been reduced to counting the numbers of hits obtained from 25 rounds. The standard Martini-Henry scored only five, its two rivals scoring fourteen (·450) and eighteen (·451). Tentatively, Hythe's staff concluded that the relieved-bore rifle firing Gatling ammunition performed best at long range, but that there was little difference at normal distances. Gatling ammunition raised muzzle velocity by 60–70fs, and recoil had increased perceptibly.

Accuracy improved still further when the bore was enlarged to ·452 in July 1882. Trials continued with the modified ammunition being used in the then-experimental Gardner Guns. These cartridges had a thicker rim than the Gatling type and were eventually approved for service in September 1881. Performance in the modified Martini-Henry rifles was very satisfactory, with only a single failure in 3,500 rounds.

However, though results had been encouraging and a new 'Martini-Henry Mk IV' had been approved on 1 October 1881, issuing two practically identical but non-interchangeable cartridges made no sense. In mid-January 1882, therefore, the Secretary of State for War suspended introduction of the Mk IV rifle.

* Hang-fires were subsequently attributed to the headspace, which had been adjusted for cartridges with a thicker rim than the standard ·45 Gatling pattern. Consequently, the striker blow was not as effectual as in Martini-Henry service rifles.

THE FIRST SMALL-BORE RIFLES

The desire to flatten trajectory led to experiments with reduced-calibre cartridges, for which a suitable rifle was required. The immediate result was the Pattern 1882 experimental ·40 Martini-pattern rifle, 53 of which were made. Though this gun will never be encountered – all but two were apparently converted to P/83 standards† – it had an important effect on the later Enfield-Martini. Measuring 49in overall, its 33⁹⁄₁₆in barrel rifled with nine 'ratchet' grooves making a

†One unaltered gun is kept in the Tower of London; the other is believed to be lost.

130 BELOW FAR LEFT

A trooper of the 3rd (Prince of Wales's) Dragoon Guards. This print after an original by Simpkin, probably dating from the turn of the century, shows the Martini-Henry Cavalry Carbine clearly enough for the leather back sight protector to be discerned. Courtesy of Philip J. Haythornthwaite.

131 BELOW LEFT

A sergeant of the Royal Sussex Regiment, a print after a painting by F. Teller. Though the design of the nose cap and upper band has defeated the artist, the remainder of the rifle is passably accurately drawn. Courtesy of Philip J. Haythornthwaite.

132 BELOW

The King's Royal Rifle Corps (60th Rifles) at Kindji Osman, 5 August 1882. An engraving after a painting by W.H. Overend, published in the *Illustrated London News*. Note that the sabre bayonets are shown, correctly, on the right side of the Martini-Henry muzzles, though the engraver has failed to distinguish between the wood fore-end and the metal receiver on the serjeant's rifle. Courtesy of Philip J. Haythornthwaite.

133 BELOW RIGHT

The advance of the 46th (South Devonshire) Regiment of Foot; Egypt, 5 August 1882. An engraving after a painting by Frederick Villiers, published in the *Illustrated London News* in August 1882. Courtesy of Philip J. Haythornthwaite.

turn in 15in, the rifle weighed 9lb 2¾oz without its bayonet.

The first ·40 cartridge had a gently tapering neck, a 384-grain bullet and an 85-grain powder charge that gave a muzzle velocity of about 1,570fs. Vertex of trajectory proved to be 6·7ft at a distance of 500 yards, or 39ft at 1,000 yards.

The rifle looked strange. It had a combless butt, and the body was cut away behind the block axis pin to facilitate grip. A laterally-pivoting long-range leaf appeared on the left side of the back sight base, and a detachable bar-type front sight could be attached to the left side of the upper band. The fore-end was cut down so that the barrel merely rested on top of it, to prevent moisture seeping down through the gap between the conventional fore-end and barrel. Though the operating lever was the same length as that of the Martini-Henry Mk III rifle, an extraordinary safety disc pivoted in the trigger guard.

The rifles were tested by HMS *Cambridge* (Devonport) and HMS *Excellent* (Portsmouth), by the Grenadier Guards and Highland Light Infantry, and at the School of Musketry. Complaints were few, though the back sight was considered too close to the eye and the safety catch was universally condemned.

Alterations created the Pattern 1883 rifle, to which all but two of the previous pattern were converted. Two differing patterns of rifling were tried — the standard nine-groove ratchet and a seven-groove 'improved' derivative — and the hand guard was revised. The lower band was solid rather than split, the long-range sights were refined, and a safety bolt was added. A bracket for an Enfield-pattern quick-loader* was held to the right side of the body by four screws.

P/83 rifles were eventually distributed to the units that had tested their predecessor, though the Highland Light Infantry had gone to the Sudan and was replaced by the 3rd Battalion of the Rifle Brigade.

The P/83 measured 49in overall, had a 33⁹⁄₁₆in barrel and weighed 9lb 6¾oz without the detachable long-range sight. Trials were successful enough for a modified version to be recommended for adoption. In its final report, made on 30 April 1884, the Committee on Martini-Henry Rifles and Ammunition suggested the features to be included in a new rifle.

* Developed in 1882, after the failure of trials with Mayhew's, Perry's, Speed's and Warry's experimental designs. The Enfield box was approved as the 'Body, Quick Loader, with spring, Rifle' on 17 April 1886. However, trials with quick-loaders and detachable magazines continued until 1887.

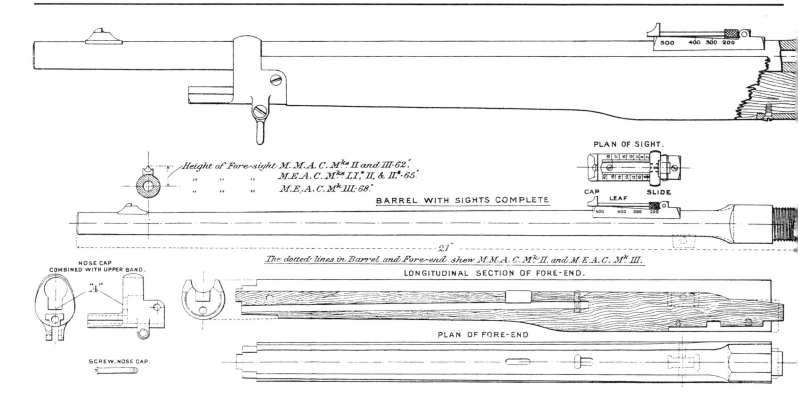

Height of Fore-sight M.M.A.C. M^{ks} II and III ·62."
" " " M.E.A.C. M^{ks} I, I,* II, & II,* ·65."
" " " M.E.A.C. M^k III ·68."

BARREL WITH SIGHTS COMPLETE

PLAN OF SIGHT.
CAP   LEAF   SLIDE
500 400 300 200

NOSE CAP COMBINED WITH UPPER BAND.
"4"

SCREW, NOSE CAP.

The dotted lines in Barrel and Fore-end shew M.M.A.C. M^k II. and M.E.A.C. M^k III.

LONGITUDINAL SECTION OF FORE-END.

PLAN OF FORE-END.

The Rifle, Enfield-Martini, ·402-inch (Mark I), with cleaning rod was sealed on 17 April 1886 to guide manufacture of a thousand guns for troop trials. It was similar to the P/83, but the long-range sights were sensibly abandoned in favour of an elevating leaf graduated from 400 to 2,000 yards. A standing-block 100-yard battle sight, with a folding leaf for 300 yards, appeared on the barrel immediately ahead of the body. The safety bolt, narrowed butt and idiosyncratic fore-end were all retained, though the shape of the wooden hand guard was refined.

Anxious to get new guns into the hands of the troops, the Secretary of State for War authorized large-scale production of the Enfield-Martini even before the final trial reports had been submitted. This proved to be a mistake: complaints soon filtered back to the committee. The hand guard was too bulky; the fore-end gave too little support to the barrel; the quick-loader sometimes jammed, and was awkward to carry when detached; the unpopular safety bolt had caused some accidental discharges; and extraction had often been troublesome. The under-barrel bayonet attachment, designed to prevent the additional weight moving the point of impact laterally, had its own problem: rifles now shot 18in high at 100 yards.

Though production of the first series-made rifles had begun – 21,732 were made in 1887–8 – the sealed pattern was cancelled in favour of a Pattern No.2 rifle. Approved on 13 May 1887, this reverted to the standard Martini-Henry fore-end. The bayonet bar was moved back to the right side of the upper band, and the battle sight became part of the back-sight slider. The wind gauge was discarded.

Obvious external changes included the replacement of the safety bolt by a cocking indicator and the absence of the quick-loader attachment plate. The operating lever was lengthened to give more power to the extractor, the lower arm of which was suitably extended.

Though 42,902 Pattern No.2 ·402 Enfield-Martini rifles were made in 1887–8, almost all were subsequently converted to ·45; it had finally dawned on the British authorities that the days of the single-shot breech-loader and black powder propellant were numbered.

Abandoning the ·402 cartridge in favour of ·303 left the authorities with 65,000 Enfield-Martini rifles in varying stages of completion. However, as the external profile of their barrels had been similar to those of their Martini-Henry predecessors, re-boring to ·45 was sanctioned on 15 September 1887. The Rifle, Martini-Henry, ·45 (Mark IV), Pattern A, was converted from the first Enfield-Martini; Pattern B was originally a second-type Enfield-Martini; and Pattern C was made by assembling stockpiled parts.

Pattern A was a major reconstruction, salvaging only the butt, furniture, hand guard, barrel and block of the original ·402 rifle. The body was a new second-pattern component taken from store. Pattern B rifles are difficult to distinguish from the rebuilt 'A', sharing a similar body, but their front sights lie on a short ramp. Pattern C is distinguished by its knoxform – longer than either A or B – and by

the 33³⁄₁₆in barrel. The converted guns lost an eighth of an inch from the breech during the re-chambering process; consequently, they have a short knoxform and a 33¹⁄₁₆in barrel. A total of 35,344 new or Pattern C rifles was made at Enfield in 1888–9.

THE FIRST ·303 MARTINI

Approved by the Secretary of State for War on 30 July 1889, the Rifle, Martini-Henry, ·303-inch (Mark V) was converted from the ·45 Mark III. The barrel, breech block, striker, extractor, sights and many minor components were exchanged. Fitting the fore-end, bands and nose-cap of the new ·303 magazine rifle meant that the Mk V accepted the P/88 sword bayonet. Lewes sights were standard, the back sight being graduated to 1,900 yards for black powder ammunition.

The Mk V measured 49³⁄₄in overall, had a 33¹⁄₄in barrel and weighed 8lb 12½oz. Though reclassified 'Rifle, Martini-Metford, ·303-inch (Mark I)' with effect from 8 August 1891, it was a complex transformation and only prototypes seem to have been made.

The Mark VI, converted from the Mk II Martini-Henry rifle, differed from Mk V in having a ·303 barrel with the same external contours as the ·45 version it replaced. As the existing bands and furniture could be retained, the rifle accepted the P/87 bayonet instead of the P/88.

Approved by the Secretary of State for War on 10 January 1890, but not sealed until 18

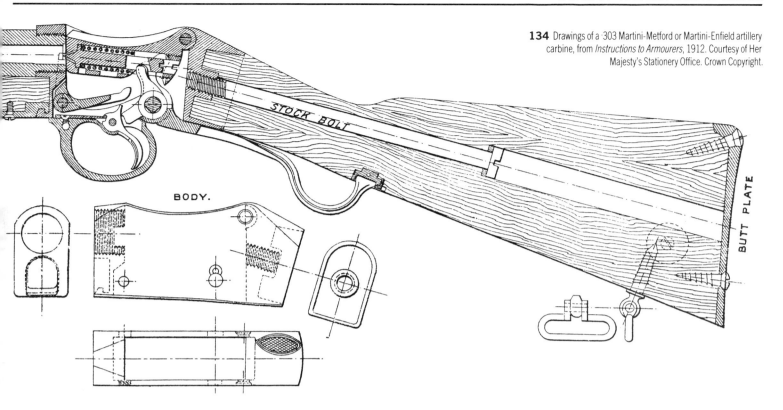

BODY.

STOCK BOLT

BUTT PLATE

June 1891 (and re-christened Martini-Metford Rifle Mk II a few weeks later), the gun measured 49¾in overall and weighed 9lb 11oz. The additional weight was due to reducing the bore diameter while retaining the original barrel contours. Only a single contract for 9,600 guns is known to have been placed, with the Birmingham Small Arms & Metal Company in 1889.

Few Martini-Metford rifles had been made by the time the Lewes sights were replaced by a conventional V-and-barleycorn pattern in the Spring of 1892. The back sights, which had been graduated to 1,900 yards, were changed to 1,600 yards (for black powder) and subsequently to 1,800 yards for cordite ammunition. However, as many Martini-Metfords were sent directly to the Colonies, black-powder sights were being fitted as late as 1895.

Five hundred guns went to South Australia in 1891–3, and 700 to Western Australia in 1894. These all had butt traps for the jag and oil bottle, the South Australian pattern being iron while Western Australia's was brass. A thousand rifles sighted for black powder went to Canada in 1894, but the 760 or more sent to Natal in 1895–6 were sighted for cordite. Natal guns also displayed a short wooden hand guard running from the breech to the back sight base.

MARTINI-METFORD CARBINES

In July 1889, the Commander-in-Chief sanctioned the development of magazine carbines for cavalry and conversions of the Martini-Henry patterns for the field and horse artillerymen.

The Carbine, Martini-Metford, Cavalry, ·303-inch (Mark I), approved on 2 May 1892, was converted from the Martini-Henry Cavalry Carbine Mk I. Its new barrel shared the profile of the original, but the nose-cap was shortened and the cleaning rod replaced. Approximately 11,150, supplied by the Henry Rifled Barrel Company, were issued in 1893–4. Carbine, Martini-Metford, Cavalry, ·303-inch (Mark II) was a conversion of the Martini-Henry Artillery Carbine Mk I, 850 being transformed at Enfield for the horse and field artillery. The sword bar was removed from the upper band, the rear swivel was removed from the under-edge of the butt and its hole was plugged. Sight-cover retaining screws were added on the fore-end sides beneath the back sight. The new carbines were all 37⅝in long and had 21⅜in barrels; the Mark I weighed 8lb 1½oz, the Mark II being 2½oz heavier.

Many of the cavalry carbines converted after a suitable pattern was sealed in October 1893 had front sight protectors. These were known as Mark I* and Mark II* (see LoC 7354), earlier guns often being upgraded when they returned for repair.

The Carbine, Martini-Metford, Artillery, ·303-inch (Mark I) was approved in May 1892, but re-sealed in June 1893 after front sight protectors had been added. Converted from the Mk I Martini-Henry artillery carbine, it had a new barrel, new bands, a nose-cap taking the P/88 bayonet, and differently graduated sights.

Like the Martini-Metford cavalry carbines, the back sight was graduated to 1,000 yards (Lewes and V-and-barleycorn patterns), or to 1,400 for cordite ammunition.

The Mk III cavalry carbine and the Mks II, II* and III for the artillery all had new lightweight barrels. The front edge of the body was ground down to enable the rifle-type sights to be seen at their lowest elevations, and brass marking discs were added to the butt.†

The Carbine, Martini-Metford, Cavalry, ·303-inch (Mark III), approved in July 1892 and then re-sealed in December 1892 with front sight protectors, had a new breech block. Tests subsequently showed that the original ·45 block could be retained with cordite ammunition, which would probably have led to the guns with new blocks being re-classified 'Mark III*' after the first five thousand had been converted. However, as only 4,296 are known to have been made, the designation was never changed. Many guns were fitted with wooden hand guards, running forward from the back sight base, and were despatched to Natal in 1895–6.

The Mark II and Mark II* artillery carbines (approved on 11 October and 2 August 1893 respectively) were identical, excepting that the Mk II* would have used specially-made breech blocks; once realization dawned that original components could be retained, the Mk II* was declared obsolete. The Mk II was identical with the Mk III Metford-barrelled cavalry carbine, except that it accepted a sword

†Many older guns were similarly treated when returning for repair, or after being reduced to Drill Purpose status.

bayonet and weighed about 7lb 1oz; 2,750 guns were converted at Enfield in 1894–6.

The Carbine, Martini-Metford, Artillery, ·303-inch (Mark III), approved on 8 March 1894 but modified and re-sealed in December 1894, was a conversion of the Martini-Henry Mk III rifle. Its fore-end was retained by a hook rather than a pin. Announced in LoC 7430 of 1 June 1894, it weighed 7lb 3oz. About 47,000 guns were converted by Enfield, the Birmingham Small Arms & Metal Company and the London Small Arms Company in 1895–8.

THE ·303 MARTINI-ENFIELDS

The substitution of Enfield rifling for the polygonal Metford type in the magazine rifles was faithfully reflected in the Martini series.

Approved on 4 October 1895, the Rifle, Martini-Enfield, ·303-inch (Mark I) was converted from the Mk III Martini-Henry rifle. It was given a new barrel, sighted to 1,800 yards for cordite ammunition,‡ and a hand guard ran forward to the back-sight base from the breech. Swivels lay on the butt and lower band, with an open piling swivel on the upper band. The P/95 socket bayonet was issued with these guns, 48,610 of which were transformed in 1896–1903. They measured 46½in overall, had 30³⁄₁₆in barrels and weighed 8lb 5oz.

The Mark II Martini-Enfield rifle was converted from Mark II ·45 Martini-Henry rifles. Approved on 11 February 1896 and announced in LoC 8196 of 1 April, it can be distinguished from the Mk I Martini-Enfield by the large cocking indicator. Enfield transformed 33,023 guns between 1896 and 1903, while a batch of seven thousand was modified by the Beardmore Engineering Company ('B.E.Co.') during the Second South African War.

Reports from the colonies subsequently alleged that Martini-Enfields shot markedly to the left, leading to approval on 12 February 1903 of three laterally adjustable front sights (High, Normal and Low). The designation of rifles fitted with these advanced to Mark I* and Mark II*.

There were five Martini-Enfield carbines – Marks I and II for the cavalry, and Marks I, II and III for the artillery. All were conversions,

and are often difficult to distinguish from Metford-barrelled patterns.

The Carbine, Martini-Enfield, Cavalry, ·303-inch (Mark I) differs from the very similar Martini-Metford only in its rifling and the revisions to its sights. Approved on 20 August 1896 and announced in LoC 8389 of 1 October, it measured 37⁵⁄₁₆in overall and weighed 6lb 11oz. Slightly under six thousand guns were converted from Mk II Martini-Henry rifles at Enfield in 1898–1900, plain solid fore-ends distinguishing those completed after clearing rods were abolished on 11 May 1899. The Mark II Martini-Enfield cavalry carbine was made only for New South Wales, 965 being despatched in 1903–4. The basis for the conversion was the Martini-Henry Mark I artillery carbine.

Carbines, Martini-Enfield, Artillery, ·303-inch (Mark I) were converted from Mark III Martini-Henry rifles. Approved on 6 November 1895, they accepted the P/88 bayonet. Fourteen thousand were converted by the Henry Rifled Barrel Company in 1896–7, then an additional 30,718 at Enfield in 1898–9. They measured 37⁵⁄₁₆in overall, had 21in barrels and weighed 7lb 4½oz.

Sealed on 6 December 1897 and announced in LoC 9018 of April 1898, the Mark II Martini-Enfield artillery carbine was converted from the Mark I Martini-Henry pattern. Its fore-end was pinned rather then being retained by a hook. A little over 26,000 guns were transformed by the Henry Rifled Barrel Company and at Enfield in 1898–1900. The Mark III, converted from the Mark II Martini-Henry rifle, was originally sealed in July 1899 and announced in LoC 9786 (1 October 1899) before being re-sealed with an offset front sight in protective wings. It was essentially similar to the Mark II Martini-Metford artillery carbine, but had a new Enfield barrel and modified sights. Owing to its advent after the abolition of clearing rods, this pattern had a solid fore-end. 32,535 guns were converted by Beardmore (7,500, 1900–1) and at Enfield (25,035 in 1900–4).

Martini-Metford Mark II cavalry carbines with replacement Enfield-rifled barrels became 'Martini-Enfield Mark I'; Martini-Metford artillery carbines Mk I and Mk II became Martini-Enfield Mk III and Mk II respectively.

Contact between the barrel and the fore-end or nose-cap was prevented from October

1901 in an effort to improve accuracy. Martini-Enfield rifles and carbines were so treated in addition to the magazine rifles.

‡Several hundred guns sent to Western Australia in 1898–1900 were sighted to 1,600 yards, for black powder ammunition, and five hundred guns sent to Queensland in 1899 accepted the P/87 sword bayonet. So-called 'Trade Pattern' (i.e., unofficial) conversions often take the P/88.

THE FIRST MAGAZINE RIFLES

On 23 October 1879, the Machine Gun Committee was asked to consider whether a magazine breech loader should be considered for the British Army, and whether submissions should be tested with their standard cartridges rather than nothing but the British service pattern.

Trials began on 29 March 1880, when three examples of the Kropatschek, Hotchkiss, Winchester, Lee, Gardner, Green and Vetterli rifles were available, together with three Lee carbines. Two German Mausers were subsequently acquired with detachable side-feed magazines. Martini-Henry rifles with Krnka and Mayhew quickloaders acted as control weapons. Godwin and Warry rifles had also been examined, but had been excluded. Shortly after the trials had begun, however, a cartridge exploded in the magazine of one of the 1876-pattern ·45 centre-fire Winchesters. The firer was so severely injured that the committee immediately withdrew Kropatschek, Hotchkiss and Winchester rifles.

If the glued paper cartridge holder of Krnka's quickloader tore too easily, the leather Mayhew pattern was appreciably more effectual. Not only did it substantially increase the rate of fire, but it also reduced the chances of dropping cartridges. Though the army was determined to have a magazine rifle, the Mayhew device was granted further trials by the Royal Navy.

The Lee rifles and carbines chambered the standard British ·45 drawn-case Gatling

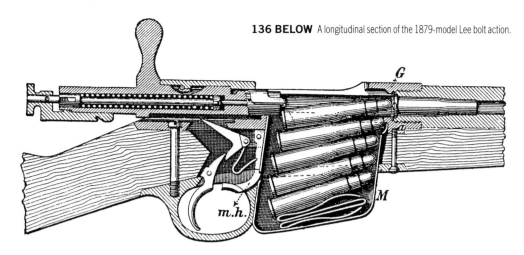

136 BELOW A longitudinal section of the 1879-model Lee bolt action.

cartridge, which gave extraction difficulties, but had five-round detachable box magazines with which twenty rounds could be fired in less than a minute even by an untrained man. Submitted by the designer of the machine-gun, the Gardner rifle was withdrawn before it could be perfected. The Green rifle, promoted by the Henry Rifled Barrel Company, suffered persistent extraction problems and was rejected after modifications failed to eliminate them. The Vetterli, with a ten-round magazine, was successfully tested at Woolwich in September 1880; its tube magazine was regarded with suspicion, even though rimfire cartridges were used, and it was ultimately rejected.

By the end of 1880, therefore, only the Lee, the Mauser with Lee's magazine and the Green were considered worthy of additional testing. The final report made on 21 March 1881 noted that, despite niggling extraction problems and a cracked stock on one of the rifles, the ·45 Lee had performed the best; however, the committee was opposed to bolt-actions, a prejudice dating back to troubles with the Bacon rifle some fifteen years earlier.

Though the Machine Gun Committee had not shown particular enthusiasm for magazine rifles, the Royal Navy was keen to adopt a rapid-firing gun even if accuracy was compro-

mised at long range. By lobbying the War Department incessantly, the Admiralty managed to get a sub-committee appointed to investigate the matter in August 1882. By November, Chaffee-Reece, Gardner, Jarmann, Improved-Lee, Mannlicher, Schulhof and Spencer-Lee rifles had been forthcoming. Attempts were then made to acquire the latest guns from America and Europe, and a new Small Arms Committee formed in March 1883.

Drawn from the army, with one navy representative and the superintendent of the Royal Small Arms Factory, its goals were to examine the submissions as soon as possible to determine whether any were suitable for service. The haste was necessary as 'the Lords Commissioner of the Admiralty [had] expressed a strong opinion that such an arm is necessary for the Navy, and press for an early decision in the matter'.

The trial reports mention more than forty rifles, but not all were available for inspection. Fewer still were actually fired.

A new Lee rifle chambering the ·45−70 US Army cartridge was tested at Enfield in April 1883. The Small Arms Committee opined that several features could be improved, requesting permission to make the alterations at Enfield. Subsequently, an 'Improved Lee' was

built for the experimental ·402 (Enfield-Martini) cartridge, together with another Lee rifle with a Bethel Burton hopper magazine on the right side of the action.

These rifles were the pick of the triallists, together with Owen Jones's anachronistic adaptation of the Martini-Henry. Jones deserves credit for the only effectual repeating transformation of the Martini block action. His hopper-magazine rifle was actuated by a slide under the butt, but was complicated and delicate. It had 113 parts and weighed a fraction under ten pounds, compared with only 82 components in the 9lb 6oz Improved Lee.

The Improved Lee was the only gun with a one-piece stock, though all three guns had the quirky fore-end characteristic of the original Enfield-Martini. At 53in overall, they were several inches longer than succeeding trials rifles of comparable pattern.

Rapidity trials showed that the Owen Jones had a slight superiority over the Lee patterns, but also that the Martini-Henry was at no real disadvantage when the rifles were used as single loaders. By 1885, the Owen Jones had been simplified by modifying the magazine, eliminating the cartridge elevator and 21 of the original 113 components. Surprisingly, the Small Arms Committee recommended the Owen Jones – though the Superintendent of the Royal Small Arms Factory protested that troop trials should be undertaken before a decision was taken. However, the Navy had obtained sufficient funds and provisional orders for a batch of Owen Jones rifles were placed with Enfield. The total of 5,000 was soon reduced to 2,000.

137, 138 BELOW

Two of the experimental predecessors of the Lee-Metford; a ·402 Lee action with a five-round Burton hopper magazine (top), and a ·43 Remington-Lee with a conventional detachable five-round box magazine . About 325 Lee-Burton rifles were made at Enfield in 1886−7 for trials against 300 Remington-Lee guns imported from the USA in April 1887. Courtesy of the MoD Pattern Room Collection, Royal Ordnance plc, Nottingham.

Colonel Arbuthnot, Superintendent of the Royal Small Arms Factory, stoutly maintained that the Owen Jones was much too complicated and delicate. Eventually, the Duke of Cambridge – the Commander-in-Chief – broke the deadlock. Without cancelling the navy's 2,000-gun order, he decided that the Owen Jones and the Improved Lee were to undergo exhaustive troop trials. The sample series-made Owen Jones was despatched to the Admiralty from Enfield on 1 October 1886, whereupon the Special Committee for Small Arms informed the Director of Naval Ordnance that the Owen Jones was less serviceable than the Improved Lee! Trials by HMS *Excellent* subsequently highlighted the superiority of the Lee-Burton and the Owen Jones was abandoned.

Late in 1886, 'Rubini' and Schulhof rifles arrived for trial. The former excited much interest not for its basic design – it was simply a modified Vetterli – but for its remarkable ·298-calibre bullet, set in a tapered straight-sided case with a notable step at the mouth. Meeting in January 1887, the Special Committee finally eliminated the Owen Jones rifle. The Schulhof, the 'Compound Gun' (an Enfield-made Rubin with a Burton hopper magazine) and the latest Improved Lee remained under consideration. The most important problem was whether the small-calibre Rubin bullet was more effectual than ·402, and whether smokeless powder should be considered.

The British authorities worried that the Special Committee on Small Arms might delay decisions too long, allowing the Europeans to steal a technical lead and place British troops at a disadvantage. In February 1887, therefore, the Director of Artillery tersely ordered the Special Committee to abandon the Rubin and the Schulhof; the Lee bolt and Metford rifling were to be adopted, he said, and no change made either to the ·402 calibre or the standard cartridge. The committee had simply to decide on either the Lee box or Burton hopper magazine as quickly as possible.

The Rubin bolt had already proved suspect, and the Schulhof had been rejected as much too complex. A new Remington-made Lee rifle in ·43 (11mm Spanish) had passed an outstanding test. Its action had been simplified, sacrificing nothing in efficiency, and was subsequently patented in Britain in August 1887 (11,319/87). 300 Lee rifles were ordered in the USA, receiving the War Department property mark ('W↑D') on the right side of the butt immediately they arrived in Britain.

Large-scale trials involving 300 Enfield-made .402 Lee-Burton rifles and the ·43 Improved Lee rifles were then programmed for April 1887, each being issued with a hundred ball and ten dummy rounds. There had not been time to convert the Remingtons for British service cartridges, so ·43 ammunition had also been imported from the USA.

The trials resolved so greatly in favour of the Improved Lee that the Burton hopper magazine was finally eliminated; the action and magazine for the prospective British service rifle had been settled. Surviving rifles were returned to Enfield – where 327 Lee-Burtons were made in 1887–8 – and placed in store, to be used in experiments.

Advances being made in France, where the smokeless 8mm cartridge was being perfected, persuaded even the most conservative elements in the British Army hierarchy that ·402 was doomed; a trial in June 1887 had confirmed that the 216-grain jacketed round-nose ·298 Rubin bullet had a flatter trajectory, better accuracy and better penetration than the 384-grain lead ·402. In addition, a hundred Rubin cartridges weighed only 6lb 9oz, four pounds less than their rival. Immediate development of a small-calibre cartridge began.

THE MAGAZINE RIFLE MARK I

The outcome of all the trials undertaken in 1883–7 was an experimental ·303-calibre rifle chambering a Rubin straight-case cartridge. Authorized in the Spring of 1888, 350 rifles and fifty carbines were made up at Enfield. They had a very distinctive butt with a continuous comb and a straight wrist: the prototype of virtually every subsequent British service rifle stock. The butt was drilled for an oil bottle and a jag. The action differed appreciably from its Lee antecedents, with a bolt-head release catch on the right side of the receiver and a long ejector let into the left side of the bolt-way. The seven-round box magazine and cut-off had been patented by Joseph Speed, Manager of the Royal Small Arms Factory (patents 6,335/87, 17,944/87 and 15,786/88), as had the unique long-range or dial sight on the left side of the fore-end

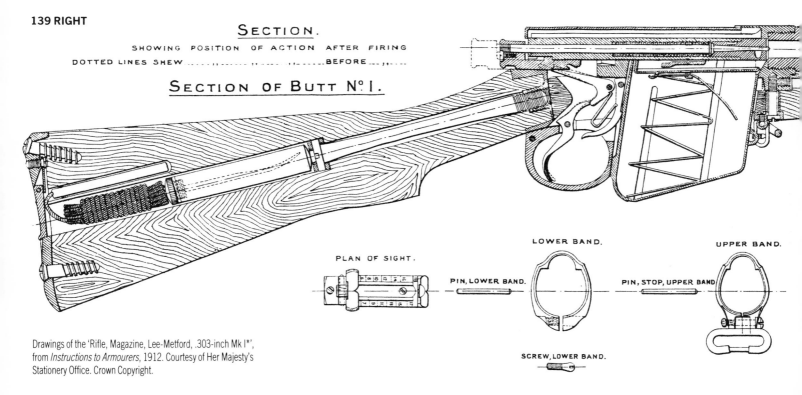

139 RIGHT

SECTION.

SHOWING POSITION OF ACTION AFTER FIRING

DOTTED LINES SHEW .... BEFORE ....

SECTION OF BUTT N.º I.

PLAN OF SIGHT.

LOWER BAND.

UPPER BAND.

PIN, LOWER BAND.

PIN, STOP, UPPER BAND

SCREW, LOWER BAND.

Drawings of the 'Rifle, Magazine, Lee-Metford, .303-inch Mk I*', from *Instructions to Armourers*, 1912. Courtesy of Her Majesty's Stationery Office. Crown Copyright.

The Church Militant? Members of the 4th Brighton (Hove) Company of the Boys Brigade pose with their leaders, 1920. Note the ·303 **140** Martini-Enfield artillery carbines. Courtesy of Elex archives.

(no. 13,335/87). A Martini-style upper band accepted a special sword bayonet; the leaf sight was graduated from 200 to 1,600 yards. The rifle measured 49⅞in overall, with a 29½in seven-groove Metford barrel, and weighed about 9lb 1½oz. Total production amounted to 437 1888-pattern rifles – fifty with Morris's Patent Magazines – and 51 carbines. The guns were issued to troops stationed from Brighton to Bombay.

Reports submitted by the early summer of 1888 were very satisfactory. Experiments continued throughout the autumn of 1888 with a selection of rimmed, rimless and semi-rim necked cartridge cases: the brass mouth-piece of the straight-taper Rubin type was fallible, and the two-piece Morse case was impossible to waterproof. Many minor changes were also made to the rifle, which gained Rigby's patented nose-cap (16,321/88) and its most distinctive bayonet. Lewes's sights (British Patent 14,093/88) were fitted, the ejector was simplified, a safety catch appeared on the left side of the receiver, a hand guard was added

behind the back sight, and an eight-round single-row magazine was substituted for the original seven-round version.

The Rifle, Magazine, ·303-inch (Mark I) was sealed on 12 December 1888 and announced in LoC 5877 together with the Bottle, Oil, Mark I; Jag (Mark I); Sword-Bayonet, Pattern 1888 (Mark I); Scabbard, Sword-Bayonet, Pattern 1888 (Mark I); Protector, Front Sight, Rifle, Magazine (Mark I); and a Muzzle, Naval. It measured 49½in overall, had a 30⁷⁄₃₂in Metford rifled barrel, weighed 9½lb and had 82 parts. There were two different butts, 'long' and 'short' (differing by ⅜in); the leaf sight was graduated from 300 to 1,900 yards; and the dial sight was designed for ranges from 1,800 to an amazingly optimistic 3,500 yards.*

Pattern guns were passed in January 1889 to the principal private contractors, Birmingham Small Arms & Metal Co. Ltd (mark: 'B.S.A.& M.' or 'B.S.A.& M.Co.') and London Small Arms Co. Ltd ('L.S.A.', 'L.S.A.Co.'). Tooling began immediately. The contracts totalled 200,000 and 100,000 respectively, but guns were also made by the Royal Small Arms Factory. The first BSA-made gun was completed on 16 June 1890, production reaching a thousand per week by October. Issues to the Aldershot garrison battalions occurred in December 1889, and then to the Guards in February 1890.

The Committee on Magazine Rifles was formed on 5 August 1890 to deal with the problems that would inevitably result from

†This was virtually the maximum range; there was no guarantee that a projectile would reach it, as there was a considerable variation in strike-point at extreme distances.

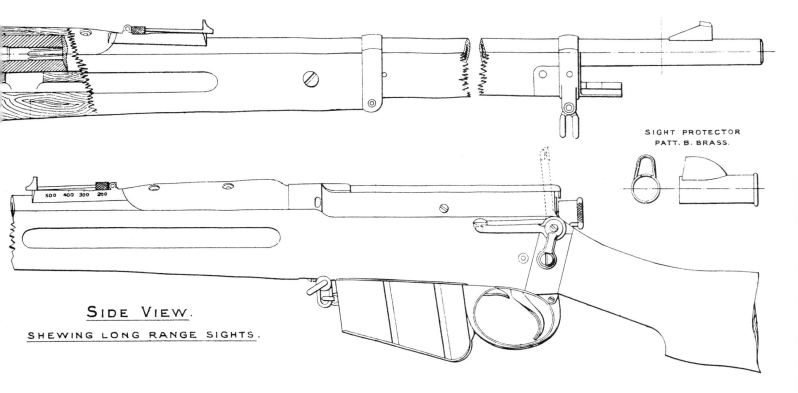

SIGHT PROTECTOR
PATT. B. BRASS.

SIDE VIEW.
SHEWING LONG RANGE SIGHTS.

issue of the new rifle. Reports from the troops revealed many problems, the most serious concerning the Lewes-pattern sights and the occasional tendency of commercially-loaded ·303 ammunition to strip the nickel bullet jackets in the bore. Other complaints centred on the failure of the magazine spring (strengthened from 22 August 1890), the design of the piling swivel, and the frequency with which the bolt head worked loose. Several methods of retaining the bolt head were tried, until the Deeley-Penn threaded head was adopted.†

A return to V-and-barleycorn sights was made in the Spring of 1892, despite Lewes's vocal protestations. This pleased the navy, whose representatives to the Small Arms Committee had always opposed the Lewes design.

Sights had been graduated on the assumption that smokeless propellant would be available immediately, but the adoption of the first cordite load was delayed until 3 November 1891; in the interim, cartridges were loaded with black powder, reducing muzzle velocity. The first back-sight leaves were graduated for the slower bullets, taking the opportunity to use large figures on alternate edges instead of minuscule stampings confined to the right side of the leaf. Jags were replaced by a pull-

through, and what had been the cleaning rod was redesignated *clearing* rod. A combination of the rod and the pull-through could be used to punch out a spent case jammed in the chamber.

The fore-end grasping groove was abandoned after complaints that the wood was too thin to facilitate grip; minor changes were made to prevent hand guards breaking; a disc for regimental markings was added to the butt with effect from 30 September 1890; and a combined front-sight protector and muzzle-stop was adopted in January 1891. Omitting the safety catch from 31 December 1890 permitted the designation to advance to Rifle, Magazine, .303-inch (Mark I*). Finally, on 8 April 1891, the rifles were officially re-named Lee-Metfords Mark I and Mk I*.

†The improved bolt-head was the subject of British Patent 19,145/90, granted to John Deeley and Frederick Penn. BSA adopted it on Trade Pattern rifles — suitably reimbursing the patentees — and it was then approved.

THE LATER LEE-METFORDS

The first prototype of the Mark II Lee-Metford, incorporating the lessons learned with the

earlier guns, appeared in September 1890. It had no rear barrel band, but featured a lightened barrel and a ten-round staggered-row box magazine patented in Britain by James Lee in 1889 (no.8,117/89). The safety catch was omitted; the bolt-head was radically revised; the bolt-cover was modified; a new cut-off was adopted; and the clearing rod was shortened so that two were required to clear a jam. The back sight was improved so that the leaf-block sufficed for 200 yards. Its bed was graduated for 300−500, the sight-leaf marks ran up to 1,600 and the dial sight displayed ranges as great as 2,800 yards.

A hundred trials rifles appeared in October 1890, ten with sights calibrated for cordite and the remainder for black powder. The former were graduated to 1,800 yards on the leaf and 2,900 yards on the dial. A C-type magazine spring replaced the former zig-zag pattern in February, but bolt covers still worked loose and a retaining screw was added from 6 March 1891. This screw also helped to retain the bolt-head.

Trials of the experimental rifle were completed in April 1891, whereupon survivors were returned to Enfield for modification. A new self-sprung bolt-cover was devised, the magazine catch and sear were improved; and

'Infantry of the Line for the Front'. A postcard produced by Raphael Tuck & Sons in 'The European War, 1914' series ('On Service', Photogravure Postcard No. 4318). These men of the London Division of the Territorial Army carry Charger Loading Lee-Enfield rifles. Courtesy of Elex archives.

the hollow beneath the cut off finger-piece was abandoned. The Deeley-Penn bolt head was approved, and the lower band returned so that rifle battalions could retain their traditional sling-anchor positions. The result was the Rifle, Magazine, Lee-Metford, ·303-inch (Mark II), sealed on 30 January 1892 and again on 12 April 1893 after changes had been made.

The principal contractors, informed of the changes in pattern, were assembling Mk II rifles by October 1892. By the Spring of 1894, the combined weekly output of BSA and LSA

had reached a thousand guns. BSA, indeed, had been offering Lee-type sporting rifles since early 1892, the 'Trade Patterns' displaying the legend LEE-SPEED PATENTS instead of government marks. Several thousands of these guns were sold to the British South Africa Company between December 1894 and September 1895, just in time for many to be lost on the abortive Jameson Raid into the Transvaal in 1896.‡ About 3,400 Mk II BSA Trade Pattern rifles were also supplied to Afghanistan in this period.

The Mark II* Lee-Metford rifle was similar to the Mk II, but had the carbine-type safety catch on the cocking piece. It was approved on 22 April 1895 and introduced in LoC 7879 of 1 August.

Most Lee-Metfords subsequently received Enfield-rifled barrels when the original polygonal design wore out, proving less resistant to cordite erosion than had been expected. Rebarrelled guns were marked 'E.I*' on the knoxform if originally Mk I or I*, or simply 'E.' if Mk II or II*. As modified Lee-Metford Mk II and II* rifles were practically identical with the Lee-Enfields, they were re-designated 'Lee-Enfield Mk I' if they retained the original clearing-rod fore-end or 'Mk I*' if they had received the later solid fore-end.

On 17 February 1890, the final report of the Special Committee on Small Arms noted that experimental cavalry and artillery carbines had been submitted, but had not been tested. The committee then disbanded, and the matter lay unattended until experimental Lee-Metford carbines were made in 1892–3. The

‡ Trade Pattern guns were purchased on behalf of the volunteers, and will often be found with improved back sight or non-standard retailers' markings.

141 LEFT

A Simkin print of line infantrymen at practice with their Lee-Metford or Lee-Enfield rifles. As the rifles have clearing rods, and as the bolt handles are wrongly drawn horizontally, it is suspected that the illustration dates from the early period of the magazine rifles. Courtesy of Philip J. Haythornthwaite.

142 FAR LEFT

Men of the Coldstream Guards are on the march in this Simkin print, with their Lee-type rifles at the slope. Like picture 139 (q.v.), the mistakenly-drawn horizontal bolt handle suggests this print originated in the early 1890s. Courtesy of Philip J. Haythornthwaite.

144 RIGHT

The breech of the Lee-system cavalry carbine (top), showing the six-round magazine and the safety catch mounted on the cocking piece. The lower illustrations show the standard long-range sights.

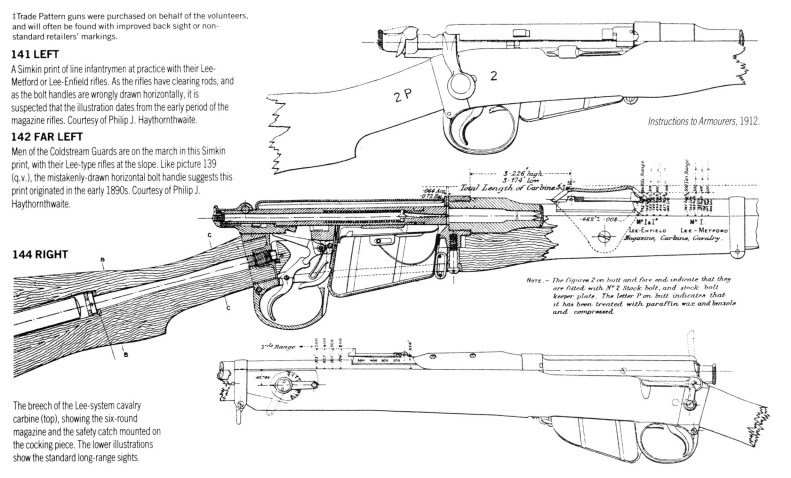

Instructions to Armourers, 1912.

NOTE.– The figures 2 on butt and fore end indicate that they are fitted with Nº 2 Stock bolt, and stock bolt keeper plate. The letter P on butt indicates that it has been treated with paraffin wax and benzole and compressed

perfected pattern was not sealed until 20 September 1894.

The Carbine, Magazine, Lee-Metford, ·303-inch (Mark I) measured 39¹⁵⁄₁₆in overall, had a 20¾in barrel and weighed 7lb 7oz. A safety catch was mounted on the cocking piece; the bolt handle was turned downward; and the special nose cap had ears protecting the front-sight blade. There was a full-length hand guard, and the small butt displayed a sling bar let into the right side behind the marking disc. A sling loop lay on the left side of the receiver. Long-range sights were omitted, the leaf of the back sight being graduated from 600 to 2,000 yards.

The flush-fitting six-round magazine and smoothed contours of the fore-end and nose cap facilitated insertion into the saddle scabbard.

Series production began at Enfield in 1894, but only a few guns were made before the Lee-Metford was replaced by the Lee-Enfield. A leather back sight cover was approved in 1895, and the sling loop was discarded from 6 March 1896.

Many Lee-Metford carbines received Enfield-rifled barrels as their Metford types wore out. Those guns with new barrels and the nose-cap ears drawn to the full Lee-Enfield height were re-classified as 'Lee-Enfield Carbines Mk I' from January 1902 onwards.

THE LEE-ENFIELD

The intention had always been to issue smokeless ammunition with the Lee-Metford, but delays in perfecting cordite forced the adoption of two ball cartridges – Mk I of February 1889 and Mk II of July 1890 – loaded with compressed black powder.

Problems arose soon after the Mk I Cordite load had been approved on 3 November 1890. Metford's segmental rifling had been created specifically to minimize black powder fouling, which it did admirably. Cordite gave very little residue, but the heat of combustion was so high that Metford-rifled barrels were completely useless after 6,000 rounds.

Bore-wear had become so severe by 1893 that experimental barrels were tested at Enfield. These led to approval of 'No.5' rifling, previously adopted for Maxim machine-guns: a concentric pattern with five square-shouldered grooves, each 0·0055in deep. The land width was increased from 0·023 to 0·0936 inches, the pitch remaining one turn in 10in.

The Rifle, Magazine, Lee-Enfield, ·303-inch (Mark I) was sealed on 11 November 1895 and announced in LoC 8117. It differed from the Lee-Metford Mk II only in the rifling and the front sight, which was moved a little farther to the left. The marking on the right side of the butt socket read 'L.E.' instead of 'L.M.'. The Mark I* Lee-Enfield, sealed on 7 August 1899, lacked a clearing rod, the abolition of which had been authorized three months previously. Consequently, the Mk I* has no rod-groove in the underside of the fore-end; Mk I rifles modified to Mk I* standards have a fillet of wood in the groove, glued and sometimes pinned in place. However, some Lee-Metfords assembled at the turn of the century – for colonial service, or from stockpiled parts – will also be encountered with the new fore-ends.

Guns repaired in the early twentieth century often display later parts; in the 1904 fiscal year, for example, nearly 10,000 Mk I* Lee-Enfields were fitted with Mk I SMLE butts – which had sheet-steel butt plates, but lacked the butt-trap. With effect from February 1906, the pull-off was lightened to 6± 1lb to match that of the SMLE; three months later, a special back-sight slide with a wind gauge was

approved for all Martini-Enfield, Lee-Metford and Lee-Enfield rifles, but was only supplied when specifically requested and never became standard issue.

Many Lee-Enfields were converted to the ·22 rimfire Aiming Tube system in 1907–8, the guns (and some of their parts) being marked 'A.T.': some subsequently reverted to ·303, probably for home defence purposes in 1940.

A single-shot Lee-Enfield rifle was approved by the Secretary of State for India in December 1909, two thousand being converted at Enfield in 1911–12. They were issued to Frontier Levies in India with effect from 31 August 1912. The magazine well was filled with a special wood block, and a modified trigger-guard/floor plate was fitted.

Most full-length Lee-Enfields were discarded after the First World War, the patterns being declared obsolete in 1926. However, a

147 RIGHT

A colour serjeant of the Royal Fusiliers carries a somewhat crudely drawn long Lee-Enfield rifle in this print, which dates from c.1900. Note that the gun appears to have a clearing rod. Courtesy of Philip J. Haythornthwaite.

148 FAR RIGHT

The long Lee-Enfield rifle held by a line infantryman, in this early twentieth century print, is surprisingly well drawn – even to the muzzle protector. As the soldier wears the Queen's and King's South Africa Medals, the illustration must post-date 1902. It was probably based on a photograph. Courtesy of Philip J. Haythornthwaite.

few survived to be used for home defence in the Second World War – during which both BSA and Parker Hale Ltd made replacement bolts.

THE LEE-ENFIELD CARBINES

The Carbine, Magazine, Lee-Enfield, ·303-inch (Mark I) was sealed on 17 August 1896 and introduced by LoC 8390 (October 1896). Though similar to the previous Lee-Metford pattern, it lacked the sling bar on the left side of the butt socket and had different back-sight graduations; the designation on the left side of the socket read 'L.E.C.'. The carbines were supposed to be issued with a leather back-sight cover, though many made at Enfield – the sole agency – were not so equipped. The Mark I* Lee-Enfield carbine, sealed on 7 August 1899, was identical with its predecessor apart from lacking a clearing rod. The differences between a Mk I carbine upgraded to Mk I* standards and a true Mk I* can be difficult to detect without removing the nose cap. The older gun will have a hole drilled into the fore-end; the Mk I* will not.

The 'Carbine, Magazine, Lee-Enfield, fitted to receive P/88 Sword-bayonet' was sealed for New Zealand in 1900 (LoC 10220). The muzzle diameter was increased to accept the sword bayonet crossguard-ring and the sights duplicated those of the Martini-Enfield Artillery Carbine Mk III. The guns measured 40^{5}/$_{16}$in overall, had 21in barrels and weighed about 7½lb. 1,500 were supplied to New Zealand in 1901–3; their butts generally display 'N↑Z' and a rack number above the date (e.g., '1135' over '1903').

Carbine sights were altered in this period by narrowing the back sight leaf and reducing the height of the sight block; these leaves will be encountered with 'E.C./88' in the lower right corner.

The Royal Irish Constabulary Carbine, ten thousand of which were converted from obsolescent guns at Enfield in 1905–6, also accepted the P/88 sword bayonet. However, it has a very distinctive nose cap, and feathers of wood are generally inlet in the fore-end. The butt discs display 'R.I.C.'.

THE SOUTH AFRICAN WAR

No sooner had hostilities begun than complaints began to filter back to Britain, where a new Small Arms Committee was formed in January 1900. The principal problems concerned poor sighting; Sparkbrook rifles – the worst tested – were subsequently found to shoot as far as twenty inches to the right at 200 yards. The sights were also under-sighted by up to seventy yards at 600.

Errors of this magnitude made little difference against massed ranks, such as at the Battle of Omdurman in 1898, but were important against men in loose order.

Replacement back-sight leaves with off-centre notches were rushed to South Africa, and the sighting of new guns was suspended while the problems were thoroughly investigated. An adjustable front sight was subsequently recommended for rifles that were already in service, but the front sights of new guns would simply be offset less to the left than previously. Three front sights – high, normal and low – minimized inherent errors.† It was also decided to test each gun individually, rather than select batches at random.

In May 1900, respondents to a War Office questionnaire complained that the Lee-Enfield bolt was too complicated; the magazine was too flimsy and difficult to fill quickly; actuating the magazine catch and trigger with the same spring was unwise; the gun was much too heavy; and the action contained too many springs.

Men fighting in South Africa understandably preferred the charger-loading capability and the double-pull trigger of the Boer Mausers, though the Boers had a liking for the Lee-Enfield's 10-round magazine. However, whether any Boer saw the Lee-Enfield as an improvement on 1893-pattern Mausers may be disputed. The Transvaal and the Orange Free State had purchased sufficient Mausers to arm their front-line units, but had no reserves. Substantial quantities of the Westley Richards 'Improved Martini' had been purchased

†Owing to variations in manufacturing tolerances, and especially in stocking-up, no two guns shot identically.

149 RIGHT
Dating from the First World War, this marksmanship trainer allowed 'shooting' to take place without expending ammunition. The recruit aligned the sights of the rifle – in this case, an old SMLE with a bolt-mounted charger guide – on a distant mark and pressed the trigger. A small needle darted forward to pierce a target at the front of the bed-plate, after which the accuracy of aim could be assessed by the instructor. Courtesy of Wallis & Wallis, Lewes.

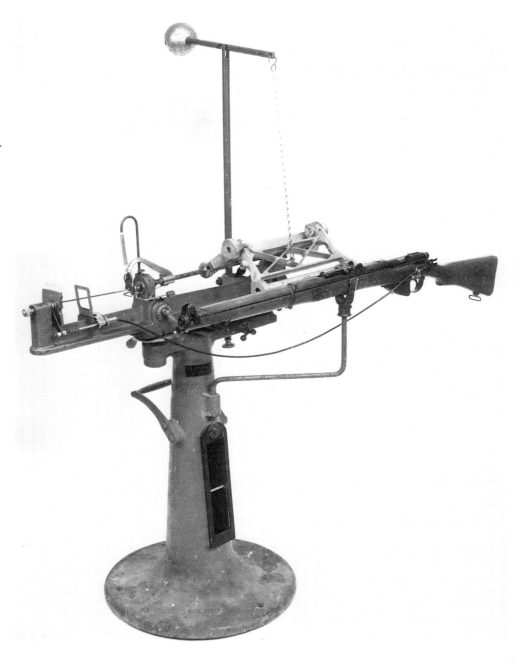

shortly before relations with Britain deteriorated, but captured Lee-Metfords and Lee-Enfields were infinitely preferable to single-shot rifles.

The butts of the Lee-Metford and Lee-Enfield rifles tended to shrink in hot climates. To combat the problem, the Small Arms Committee developed a modified butt-tip (marked 'P') that had been soaked in a mixture of benzole and paraffin wax, and then compressed. The stock-retaining bolt was lengthened to fit into a keeper plate let into the back of the fore-end; the improved stocks were marked 'No.2'. Short and long butts (marked 'S' and 'L' respectively) were introduced in September 1901 to help firers of differing stature. Each varied from the standard unmarked version by a half-inch.

A SHORT RIFLE: FIRST STEPS

After considering radical solutions – a smaller calibre, or even an automatic rifle – the Small Arms Committee produced a new variant of the Lee-Enfield incorporating lessons learned from the South African War.

The 'No.1 Improved Rifle' of February 1901 had a lightened barrel and butt, a full-length hand guard, and an improved nose cap to remove the strain of a fixed bayonet from the barrel. It had refined sights, a double pull-off and revised safety catch. The charger system

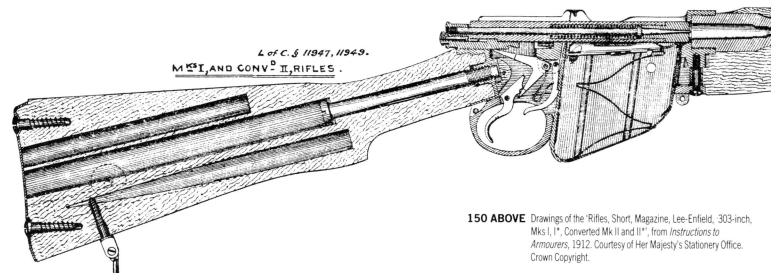

150 ABOVE Drawings of the 'Rifles, Short, Magazine, Lee-Enfield, ·303-inch, Mks I, I*, Converted Mk II and II*', from *Instructions to Armourers*, 1912. Courtesy of Her Majesty's Stationery Office. Crown Copyright.

was patented in 1901 by Henry Watkin, Superintendent of the Royal Small Arms Factory, and factory manager Joseph Speed (14,162/01); and the nose cap and modified trigger by Watkin alone (14,163/01). Though otherwise comparable with the long Lee-Enfield, the rifle weighed a mere 8lb 6oz.

Two patterns of the Improved No.1 rifle were tested, one with the Watkin & Speed charger system and the other with Harris's controlled platform magazine (patents 10,239/00, 16,284/00, 14,640/01 and 17,870/01). However, together with similar Ross patterns, the Harris magazine was soon discarded.

Finally, once the pull-off had been altered and the barrel allowed to float in the stock, the improved rifle was re-tested in December 1901. Apart from a few minor operating problems and the large back sight, which was susceptible to knocks, the new Lee-Enfield was well liked.

A suggestion that a short rifle could replace both the infantry rifle and the cavalry carbine then attracted attention. As this would simplify logistics, it was vociferously supported by Field Marshal Lord Roberts. Roberts had been Commander-in-Chief in South Africa; he knew that the length and weight of the Lee-Enfield had hindered accurate rapid fire, and that poor accuracy and unpleasant muzzle blast had characterized the carbines.

THE PERFECTED SHORT RIFLE

During the winter of 1901, 1,055 'Rifles, Magazine, Lee-Enfield, Modified (Shortened)' were made at Enfield for trials alongside the service weapons. The rifles were similar to the full-length No.1 Improved, but incorporated the latest refinements. The principal differences concerned the back sights, Pattern A being a

front-hinged tangent design patented by Watkin & Speed (6743/01) and graduated from 200 to 2,000 yards, while Pattern B had a conventional rear-hinged leaf. The safety was new and the barrel band, patented by Watkin & Speed (no.6,744/01), was carried internally. Rifling deepened towards the muzzle in an attempt to maintain velocity above 2,000fs^{-1}. Three different butts (short, normal and long) and two different bayonets were to be tested.

The shortened rifles were popular; safety catches had broken too frequently, but few serious problems had been reported. The Rifle Association and the gun trade, however, vehemently opposed the short rifle concept on the grounds that accuracy would be seriously compromised. Trials between the new SMLE, a Lee-Enfield Mk I*, a Charger-Loading Lee-Enfield with SMLE sights, and a shortened Lee-Enfield with SMLE sights subsequently revealed little difference. The most accurate gun had been the shortened Lee-Enfield with Short Rifle-type sights, but the margin of superiority was small.

Most of the original trial rifles were rebuilt to SMLE standards, and then converted for Aiming Tube rimfire ammunition in 1906–7.

151 ABOVE
The action of the SMLE Mk III. Note that the bolt handle has been raised to emphasize the engagement surfaces of the locking rib (arrowed). Courtesy of the MoD Pattern Room Collection, Royal Ordnance plc, Nottingham; photograph by Ian Hogg.

An improved rifle had been submitted to the Small Arms Committee by December 1902, incorporating the changes suggested by the troop trials – an adjustable barleycorn front sight; a deeper magazine; modified charger guides; reinstatement of the cut-off, at the navy's request; omission of the wind gauge on the back sight; an 'eared' rather than hooded front sight; and a modified hand guard. This rifle subsequently became the Rifle, Short, Magazine, Lee-Enfield, ·303-inch (Mark I) on 23 December 1902 and was announced in LoC 11715. Measuring 44⁹⁄₁₆in overall with the standard butt, the SMLE Mk I had a five-groove 25³⁄₁₆in barrel and weighed 8lb 2½oz. Production began immediately – 961 guns were made at Enfield in 1903 and 77,000 at Enfield and Sparkbrook in 1904 – but the first issues soon revealed problems. The wind gauge was reinstated, screws replaced rivets in the hand guard and back sight protector,

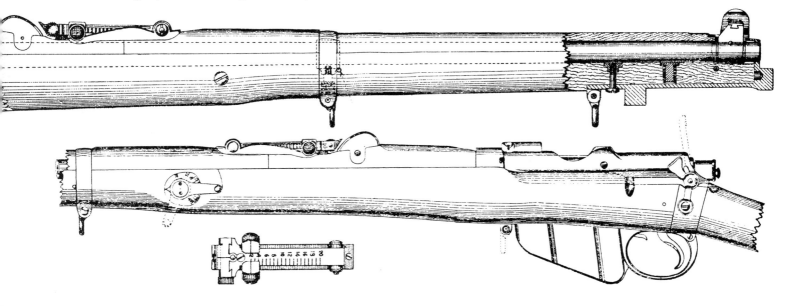

152 ABOVE

A Sealed Pattern tag dangles from the butt wrist of this SMLE Converted Mk II, made from Lee-Metfords Mk II and II*, in addition to Mk I and (later) Mk I* Lee-Enfields. The rifle shown here is the original version, approved in 1903. Courtesy of the MoD Pattern Room Collection, Royal Ordnance plc, Nottingham; photograph by Ian Hogg.

and the rear hand guard was modified. As a result of the revisions, the pattern was re-sealed on 14 September 1903 (LoC 11947, 1904).

Once the guns had seen widespread service, complaints began to filter back about their accuracy. This was by no means unusual, nor unique to Britain. Tests of Wallace-Metford rifling in the summer of 1904 showed no improvement over the standard Enfield type, though a shortened lead from the chamber to the bore improved accuracy; discovered almost accidentally, this was approved for SMLE barrels in 1906 and extended to Lee-Metford/ Lee-Enfield replacements two years later. Relieving the last fourteen inches of the barrel was found to degrade accuracy, the practice being stopped even though progressive rifling was retained until 1917. A U-notch replaced the 'V' in 1907 to improve the sight picture.

The SMLE Converted Mk I, an adaptation of the Lee-Metford Mk I*, was finally sealed on 2 November 1903 (LoC 11948); however, the transformation was so complicated that the rifle was declared obsolete in 1906. No more than a handful had been made. It was superseded by the SMLE Converted Mk II, initially sealed on 16 January 1903 but not finally approved until November. This was an adaptation of Lee-Enfields Mks I and I*, plus a few Lee-Metfords Mks II and II*. The guns received new short barrels, charger guides on the receiver and bolt head, new sights, and a greatly modified stock. Some SMLE Mk I and Converted Mk II rifles were fitted with cut offs (approved for naval service in August 1903, LoC 11850). The programme was extended to land service from 25 October 1906. A cut off featured on all new guns made prior to 1916, and was reinstated after the end of the First World War.

The SMLE Converted Mk II* was approved on 15 March 1906 (LoC 13578), transformed from Lee-Metfords Mk II and II* or the Lee-Enfields Mk I and I*. It foretold improvements being made to the contemporary SMLE, the Mark I* of which was eventually approved on 27 March 1906 (LoC 13577). The gunmetal butt plate had a trap for the oiler and pull-through,

a swivel was added to the butt, changes were made to the magazine to facilitate loading,* and the striker keeper-screw was slotted to facilitate removal.

So many minor changes were being made to the first short rifles that the Mk I and Converted Mk II Pattern Arms were re-sealed on 26 September 1906. Among the alterations were the approval of five differing front sight heights; a new fine adjustment screw on the back sight; a modified hand-guard retaining spring; a new trigger guard with a sling swivel ahead of the magazine aperture, but without the magazine link loop; a stronger striker keeper-screw; a stud and spring inside the fore-end to bear on the barrel near the muzzle; shorter swivels; and the addition of a piling swivel to the nose cap of all guns except those destined for mounted troops.

A persistent complaint about the bolt-head charger guide, which loosened in service, led to tests of experimental monoblock bridge-type guides in the Spring of 1906. The Enfield pattern proved most effectual in long-term trials. The new guides and an improved back sight, patented by Watkin & Speed in February 1906, were subsequently adopted for the new SMLE Mark III, sealed on 26 January 1907 (LoC 13853). Its nose cap had been lightened, the sight protectors on the rear hand guard were altered; many minor machining operations were revised. Weight rose to 8lb 10½oz unladen.

The SMLE Converted Mark IV was sealed on 17 June 1907 (LoC 13854). It was basically a Converted Mk II upgraded to SMLE Mk III standards, but weighed 8lb 14½oz.

Nose caps and fore-ends were numbered to match the receiver, barrel, bolt and back sights from the end of November 1901. Though the parts were completely interchangeable, the shooting of each *combination* of parts inevitably varied.

Between 4 January and 5 July 1908, three short rifle conversions were accepted for naval service. The SMLE Converted Mark I**, Mark I** and Mark II*** (LoC 14936) differed from the remainder of the series. Despite their Mk III sights and coin-slotted striker keeper-

screws, they retained the two-piece charger guides of pre-1907 guns. Converted by the Royal Naval Ordnance Depots in Chatham, Plymouth and Portsmouth, the designation marks on the receiver had an additional 'star', rarely aligning with the originals, and a large 'N' on the left side of the receiver shoe.

To confuse matters further, many naval conversions were re-sighted for Mk VII ball ammunition after 29 May (C.Mk I**) and 12 August 1912 (C.Mks II** and II***). Bridge-type charger guides were fitted, changes were made in the stock, the incurving front sight protectors were straightened, and a fore-end stud/spring unit was fitted. Some guns were transformed at Enfield, and others by the naval depots. By then approximating to the Mk III and C.Mk IV, the naval guns were transferred to land service in August 1915. Any that had survived in their original condition were immediately upgraded.

October 1910 brought adoption of the Mk VII cartridge, with its 174-grain ogival bullet. As this developed 2,440fs⁻¹, compared with only 2,230 for its 215-grain round-nose predecessor, the back sight base was lowered and re-shaped for the different trajectory of the new projectile. From 6 July 1911 (LoC 15638), changes were also made to the magazine and the receiver body to ensure the pointed bullet fed properly. The original dial sight was revised, either by altering the existing graduations or by replacing the dial plate; new plates are clearly marked 'L.E.S.2'. Shooting Mk VII ammunition loosened screws, particularly in the front of the trigger guard, the sear and the sight bed; permission was granted in March 1912 for these to be staked in place.

The last pre-war SMLE was the Mark I***, sealed on 22 August 1914 to guide conversion of the earlier Mk I* for Mk VII cartridges. The guns displayed a U-notch with a new wind gauge on the back sight, and had a blade front sight instead of a barleycorn. Most rifles retained the original Mk I charger guides, but those repaired during the war received the bridge type.

CHARGER-LOADING RIFLES

The adoption of the SMLE forced the modernization of many Lee-Metford and Lee-Enfield rifles. The first conversion from Lee-Metford Mk I* and II rifles, developed in 1904 for India Service, formed the basis for subsequent work in Ishapur arsenal. The original bolt-cover was replaced by a Mark I-pattern SMLE charger guide, and an SMLE bolt head was fitted.

The first truly British version was the Rifle, Charger Loading, Lee-Metford, ·303-inch (Mark II), approved early in 1907. Though a few surviving Lee-Metfords were transformed, the project was abandoned in 1909; the guns were then converted to Lee-Enfield standards before receiving charger guides and SMLE-type sights. Supplies of Metford-rifled barrels were exhausted by 1910.

A bridge-type charger guide was developed for the Lee-Enfield in March 1907, allowing the authorities to seal patterns for the Charger-Loading Lee-Enfield Mk II and Lee-Metford Mk II rifles on 1 July 1907 (LoC 13992) – the former being converted from Mk I and I* Lee-Enfields or Mk II* Lee-Metfords, while the latter was formerly the Lee-Metford Mk II. More than 300,000 rifles were converted by Enfield, Vickers, BSA and LSA in 1908–13.

The last of the full-length Lee-Enfield conversions produced the Rifle, Magazine, Charger-Loading, Lee-Enfield, Naval Service, ·303-inch (Mark I), approved c.1914. This was similar to the earlier Mk I*, with an identical charger bridge, but had Lee-Enfield-type sights altered for Mk VII ammunition. The leaf was graduated to 1,900 yards and bore 'C.L.' in the bottom left corner. A similar modification was made to the Mark I* rifles, approved on 2 October 1914 (LoC 17011).

By August 1914, Enfield, BSA and Westley Richards had re-sighted 251,985 rifles.

THE PATTERN 1913 RIFLE

The perfection of the Short Magazine Lee-Enfield rifle, which many army authorities believed to have occurred with the Mark III in 1907, heralded dismay among the gun trade.

Whether these views were altogether altruistic may be questioned, however. It had

153 ABOVE
Pictured on the Western Front, probably in 1917 though the photograph is not dated, this cavalryman spurs his mount forward from a stream. Note the SMLE carried in a full-length saddle scabbard. Courtesy of Elex archives.

been fashionable ever since the adoption of the 'foreign' Martini to criticise the government's actions. Prominent among objectors were spurned inventors, convinced that their superior designs had not been given a sporting chance, and gunsmiths who viewed the establishment of government rifle factories as a threat to their livelihood.

It was well known that the Lee action, even in the form embodied in the SMLE Mark III, did not have the basic strength of the most advanced Mauser.* From a purely military viewpoint, the SMLE had much to commend it; it had a more capacious box magazine than the German service rifle, the Gew.98, and was certainly much more handy. The short barrel was a great asset to cavalry, but no real handicap to an infantryman; and only a single pattern need be made for universal issue, instead of the traditional compromise of long rifle and carbine.

* Of course, the Lee pre-dated the Mauser by some years; it had been argued – even by Lee, in a famous lawsuit – that the Mauser succeeded only because it had copied the American's box magazine.

As part of the process of monitoring the weapons of other armies, however, the British became increasingly concerned by the German Mauser, the Japanese Arisaka and the US Springfield. The Japanese and US rifles were, in fact, modified Mausers; by 1908, it was widely appreciated that this particular action contained much that was commendable. Trials had shown that it was practically impossible to wreck it, unless grossly overloaded, and that the firer was generally well protected from blown primers or separated case heads.

The German and US rifles also developed considerably greater muzzle velocities than the short Lee-Enfield, which worried the authorities greatly. The early twentieth century goals were the highest velocity and lowest trajectory vertices attainable within an infantry rifle of acceptable length and weight – in practice, agreed to be maxima of 48in and 9lb respectively.

By August 1910, the War Office had allowed itself to be persuaded that the drawbacks of the Lee-Enfield outweighed its advantages. The Small Arms Committee was asked to list features to be incorporated in an entirely new gun, responding on 2 September. Not surprisingly, many SMLE features were still approved – including the provision of a single rifle for universal issue; a butt-plate trap for the cleaning equipment; the nose cap and bayonet boss; a full length hand guard; a detachable ten-round box magazine; and charger loading.

The new gun was to embody a one-piece stock and a Mauser action chambering a rimless cartridge. The trigger was to be attached to the body instead of the trigger guard, the safety catch was to lock the bolt in both fired and cocked positions, and an aperture back sight was to replace the open-notch pattern. The length, weight and recoil of the SMLE were all to be retained, assuming weight could be saved in the action to allow a heavier barrel to be fitted.

Trials with small-calibre rimless and semi-rim cartridges had begun several years earlier in an attempt to breach the 2,800fs⁻¹ barrier. It was soon obvious that the existing ·303 cartridge could not be loaded to the desired level, as pressures climbed much too high for the Lee-Enfield action unless the bullets were unacceptably light. The simplest solution was to reduce the calibre, the first experiments being inspired by the 6·5mm (·256) Japanese cartridge. However, contemporary Japanese ammunition was loaded to give only about 2,350fs⁻¹ and the Design Department at Woolwich was forced to increase cartridge-case capacity appreciably to hold sufficient MDS Cordite propellant; the increase in case diameter created problems in necking the cases satisfactorily, so a change was soon made to ·276 (7mm). This calibre – pioneered by the Spanish and other 7mm Mausers – has been a popular 'all purpose' solution to many problems of the type faced by the British Army in 1908, a view that has subsequently been been reaffirmed more than once.†

Made by the Royal Laboratory, Woolwich, with the help of sub-contractors Kynoch, the perfected cartridge was issued for troop trials in 1913. The ball round had a 2·35in rimless case loaded with a 165-grain lead core bullet, which gave an overall length of about 3·23in. Inspectors' and Drill dummies, proof and blank rounds were also made.

The Small Arms Committee, meanwhile, was hard at work on the new rifle. As the US Springfield rifle was stocked in an approved manner, and as it was basically a Mauser, the committee elected to save time by rechambering one such gun in the Enfield Tool Room for a ·276 cartridge firing a 150-grain bullet. This rifle was eventually submitted to trials in the Royal Small Arms Factory and the School of Musketry, Hythe, in competition with similar rifles developed by BSA. The earliest BSA – apparently submitted in April 1911 – was a Mauser chambered for 7mm Eley Special (·276), fully stocked with conventional British long-range sights.

†For example, during the early 1930s (with the ·276 Pedersen) and then with the ·280 round developed after the end of the Second World War.

154 TOP
This group photograph of men from 469 (S) Battery of the Royal Garrison Artillery is remarkable chiefly for the proliferation of bandoliers, though there is not a rifle in sight. The absence of weapons from pictures of this type is very typically British; contemporary German equivalents, conversely, almost always include rifles. Courtesy of Elex archives.

155 ABOVE
The open action of the P/14 rifle, showing the Mauser-type front-locking bolt and the rocking safety catch on the right rear side immediately behind the bolt-handle seat. Note the design of the back sight, protected by its sturdy wings. Courtesy of the MoD Pattern Room Collection, Royal Ordnance plc, Nottingham; photograph by Ian Hogg.

It was followed by a Norman-system inclined-bolt rifle, the first specimen being examined by the Small Arms Committee in March 1912 without enthusiasm. The perfected version of the BSA-Norman had an aperture back sight above the rear of the action as well as the long-range sights. As neither of the BSA rifles proved effectual, a modified form of the 'Enfield-Springfield' was recommended for troop trials in the Spring of 1912.

Unfortunately, the government-developed ·276 cartridge, which had replaced the 7mm Eley Special, was proving troublesome: on 10 May, the Small Arms Committee noted that 'no cartridge has yet been produced for the ·276-in. rifle which does not give such metallic fouling as to quite preclude its being tried by the troops'. The fouling was believed to arise from a combination of the cupro-nickel barrel jacket, mirror-polished bore, high chamber pressure and the excessive combustion temperature of Cordite MDT.

Inconclusive experiments to determine the basic cause were abandoned when a harder grade of barrel-steel, lubricating the bullet and substituting a nickelled steel jacket for cupro-nickel appeared to reduce the problem within acceptable bounds.

Trials with the ·276 Mark I cartridge in comparison with special high-quality ·303 Mark VII ammunition, undertaken at Hythe in the autumn of 1912, showed that the new cartridge – though far from perfect – was good enough to be issued experimentally. As it had also proved to be acceptably lethal, production began at Woolwich. Concurrently, rifles were being made at Enfield.‡

Early in 1913, the thousand trials rifles – now generally known as 'Rifles, Magazine, ·276-inch, Pattern 1913' – were issued at home and abroad, more than a hundred going to South Africa and Egypt. The guns had heavy 26in barrels with five-groove left-hand Enfield

‡Some components, apparently including the bolts, were made in Birmingham by BSA.

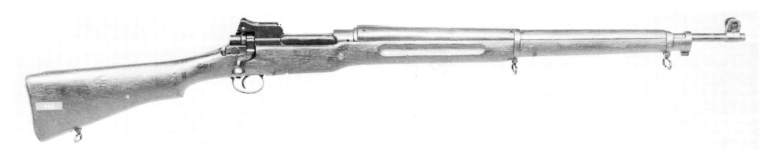

The ·303 Pattern 1914 rifle was an emergency adaptation of the experimental P/13. Made in the USA during the First World War, it proved durable and accurate. Though largely withheld from the front line, where the SMLE was standardized, the P/14 was popular with snipers. It also provided the basis for the US Army's ·30 M1917 ('Enfield') rifle. Courtesy of Ian Hogg.

rifling, lands and grooves of equal width making one turn in 10in. They were 46¼in long and weighed about 8lb 11oz without the sword bayonet, which was practically identical with the P/07 SMLE type excepting that the cross-guard ring fitted over the muzzle rather than a separate bayonet boss in an effort to reduce the weight of the nose cap. The front-sight blade was detachable and an aperture back sight lay between prominent protectors above the rear of the body ahead of the bolt handle. The leaf was graduated from 400 to 1,900 yards, with a fixed aperture for 600 yards and a long-range dial sight on the left side of the stock. The stock was made in one piece and the charger-loaded magazine, carried internally, held five rounds.

Each cartridge was loaded with 49·3 grains of Cordite MDT and a 165-grain spitzer bullet with a lead/antimony core. The bullet envelope was cupro-nickelled steel. Muzzle velocity and 800yd trajectory vertex proved to be 2,785fs⁻¹ and 5·23ft respectively, compared with 2,440fs⁻¹ and 9ft for ·303 Mark VII ball ammunition.

The rifle was undoubtedly stronger than the SMLE, could be stripped without tools, and balanced nearer its centre of gravity owing to the lightened nose cap. Its one-piece stock corrected the tendency of the separate SMLE butt to come loose. The magazine platform held the action open when the last round had been ejected, and the aperture 'battle sight' was generally approved. To its debit, the P/13 rifle was several inches longer than the SMLE and somewhat less handy, and the elimination of fine adjustments on the back sight could be regarded as retrograde. Enveloping the maga-zine in the stock, whatever improvement it may have been in theory, halved the magazine capacity; this was not immediately popular with the rank-and-file.

The rifles were widely approved after the trials, problems being comparatively minor — some guns tended to misfire, the numerals on the back sight were indistinct, the edges of the butt plate were sharp and the charger guides were not precise enough. Only poor magazine feed gave cause for concern.

The experimental rifles have four short grasping grooves on each side of the fore-end immediately ahead of the breech. Uniquely, these slope diagonally — and were universally disliked by the firers. Compared with the later and essentially similar ·303 P/14, the P/13 is lighter and has differing back-sight protector contours.

Ammunition had proved the greatest worry. Fouling may have been conquered, but the barrels wore out with frightening rapidity: most were badly worn after firing 2,500−3,000 rounds, and some even failed to last beyond the first thousand. Chambers had heated so quickly during rapid fire that at least one serious accident had occurred, a cartridge igniting from heat effects alone before the bolt had been closed. And lastly, but by no means least, the ·276 cartridge had an awesome muzzle flash that temporarily blinded firers at night.

Problems with the rifles were soon cured, and it was anticipated that the worst draw-backs of the cartridge would be eliminated by developing a new Cordite with a reduced nitroglycerine content. Before experiments could be completed, however, the First World War began.

There is little doubt that the perfected P/13 rifle would have been adopted to replace the SMLE, though whether it would have been suitable for universal issue has to be questioned: several inches longer than the SMLE, the P/13 was no cavalry carbine. The army would have undoubtedly been better to accept a reduction in muzzle velocity if it allowed a 22in barrel. An overall length of

157 RIGHT

A member of the Upper Thames Patrol, Middlesex Flotilla (a Territorial Defence Force unit pre-dating the formation of the Home Guard), displaying his distinctive Thames Water Conservancy cap badge and a P/14 rifle with the back sight leaf elevated. The picture was taken in 1940. By courtesy of Brian L. Davis.

42–43in would undoubtedly have been advantageous. But this could not have been achieved with the ·276 Mark I cartridge, which suffered flash problems even in the standard 26in barrel. Maximum velocity is rarely compatible with greatest utility.

No production line for the P/13 existed in August 1914 and so, as the SMLE was being made by the Royal Small Arms Factory, BSA and the London Small Arms Company, the new rifle was abandoned. The SMLE, so long the butt of criticism, was on the threshhold of proving itself in battle so effectually that it provided the basis for the British service rifle until 1957.

THE PATTERN 1914 RIFLE

The SMLE was comparatively complicated to make, being essentially an old design. To alleviate shortages caused by mobilization, the War Office determined to place contracts in North America for a ·303 derivation of the abortive ·276 P/13 rifle, designated Rifle, Magazine, ·303-inch, Pattern 1914. Vickers also successfully tendered to make 100,000, but only a handful of unacceptable pre-production guns was made before the project was abandoned.

No British service rifles had ever been made outside the British Empire; to do so raised a whole new series of problems. The initial contact seems to have been made with the Winchester Repeating Arms Company, whose president had written to the London Small Arms Company, in September 1914, offering Model 95 lever-action rifles chambered and sighted for the standard British ·303 Mark VII ball cartridge.

Shortly after representatives of the British Army Council for War had visited the New Haven factory, a contract for 200,000 Pattern 1914 ·303 rifles was signed by the British Consul on 24 November 1914. A repeat order was signed in March 1915, the total value of the 400,000 guns being $12·5 million. Similar contracts had been signed with Remington Arms–UMC in October 1914.

Winchester was charged with adapting the plans supplied from the Royal Small Arms Factory to American working practices, and ensuring that discrepancies between the drawings and the pattern were eliminated.

Remington, required to make a million rifles initially (with a promise of a repeat order), had to create entirely new factories to handle the work. One was built in Ilion, where Remington–UMC had its headquarters, while a duplicate production line was installed in a partly-completed factory owned by Baldwin Locomotive Works in Eddystone, near Philadelphia. This plant was operated by a separate company, Remington Arms of Delaware, jointly financed by Remington–UMC, the United States Steel Corporation, and Monel Metal Company. The requirements for the Ilion factory alone are said to have been 3,895 new machines, 5,905 fixtures, 7,000 tools and 3,415 gauges to enable two thousand rifles to be made each day.

The perfected Winchester rifle was accepted on 22 March 1915 and ordered into mass production, but work did not proceed smoothly. Machine-tools arrived late, or were not to specifications; costs of raw material escalated, reducing potential profits; and there were many minor technical problems. Finally, Remington test-fired the first Ilion-made rifles in October 1915, and Winchester's final assembly began in January 1916. Differences of opinion between American management and the British inspectors, whom the former considered intransigent, soon caused delays; by mid summer, the inspectors had rejected ten thousand Winchester-made guns alone – almost one gun for every five submitted.

On 21 September 1916, irritated by the lack of progress and with supplies of Lee-Enfields improving, the British authorities gave formal notice cancelling all orders. Deliveries ceased immediately; claims for compensation were submitted, and negotiations began.

The British subsequently relented slightly, reducing the total to two million guns. Winchester's share was 235,528, the last gun being

What do you think of the Q. Westminsters now, Bill ?

159 RIGHT

Typical of the humorous postcards produced during the early part of the First World War, this example – by E. Mack, King Henry's Road, Hampstead, London – was sent from Saffron Walden to Shepherd's Bush in June 1915. As part of its message reads 'Do you mind keeping these cards for me they will make a good colection [sic]', it is clear that the value of souvenirs was appreciated even then. Courtesy of Elex archives.

160 RIGHT

Published by Molyneux's Library of Woolwich, this postcard shows an interior view of Woolwich Arsenal. The proliferation of drive belts is typical of workshops of this period. Sent by an arsenal employee to Brighton in February 1918, the message reads 'Back at work. Have been very busy so far this week. It is miserable & wet here'. Courtesy of Elex archives.

161 BELOW RIGHT

The Allies had the worst of the terrain on the Western Front, the Germans having seized most of the upland in 1914. Trenches often had to be dug in wet ground, and guns were required to function in terrible conditions. This picture of a field canteen, apparently taken in 1917, shows what happened in many parts of Flanders after heavy rain or the spring thaw. Author's archives.

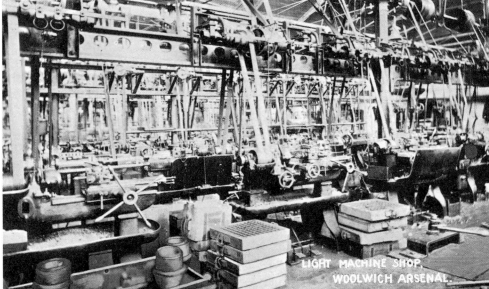

LIGHT MACHINE SHOP, WOOLWICH ARSENAL.

assembled in December 1916. The company was paid $10,778,000 to cover production costs and 'movable plant', enabling the British to retrieve the production line should they wish to do so. Winchester had also made nearly a hundred million ·303 cartridges.

Remington continued to make rifles in the Ilion factory until the Spring of 1917, assembling 61,000 in March 1917 alone. British records indicate that 1,117,850 Pattern 1914 rifles were received in 1916–17; Winchester made 235,528, Eddystone contributed about 450,000 and the remainder came from Ilion.

The P/14 proved popular with the British Army, as it was robust, reliable, accurate and gave little trouble. Its sights were as good as any – perhaps the best fitted to a pre-1918 service rifle – and the long sight radius promoted good shooting. However, particularly when fitted with the sword bayonet, the rifle was unsuited to trench-fighting; the shorter and lighter SMLE held a decided edge. In the interests of standardization, therefore, the Pattern 1914 was generally restricted to second-line and lines-of-communication troops.

Others were retained for training, but many found their niche as sniper's rifles.

Three sub-variants were introduced on 21 June 1916, designated Rifle, Magazine, ·303-inch, Pattern 1914, Marks I(E), I(R) and I(W). The suffixes indicated the manufacturer – Eddystone, Remington-UMC and Winchester respectively – as components, though largely interchangeable among guns of the same make, were not always exchangeable from group to group. Distinctive markings appeared on the top front of the body, on the right side of the butt ahead of the marking disc, and on most of the components. Eddystone rifles displayed 'ERA', 'IE' and 'e' respectively; Ilion-made rifles had 'RA', 'IR' and 'r'; and Winchesters used 'W', 'IW' and 'w'. All rifles displayed 'PATT.14' and a broad arrow on the butt.

Three P/14 Mark I* versions were approved in December 1916, the locking lug on the bolt being lengthened and a suitable alteration made to its seat in the receiver ring. These changes are difficult to detect externally – except by comparing bolts – though the modified guns have additional five-point stars on the bolt handle, above the chamber and on the right side of the butt ahead of the pattern markings. Some rifles had improved back sights with a finer adjustment than their cousins, the feature being acknowledged by an additional 'F' suffix.

Owing to the accuracy of the basic design, particularly when used with selected ammunition, the P/14 was adapted to serve as a sniper rifle with effect from 11 April 1918. The P/14 Mark I*(W)T – the Winchester rifles were regarded as the best – had mounts for the Pattern 1918 Aldis telescope sight on the left of the breech and back sight protector. The long-range back sight and dial pointer were removed, as the former would be obstructed by the back optical-sight mount. Mark I*(W)T carried the Aldis sight centrally, rather than, as on the later pattern, offset to the left. Something like two thousand were produced during the First World War.

Pattern 1914 rifles were recalled after the Armistice and placed in store, being reclassified Rifles No.3 Mk 1, No.3 Mk 1*, No.3 Mk 1* (F) and No.3 Mk 1* (T) in 1926 without regard to manufacturing sub-pattern. Shortly before the Second World War began, surviving No.3 rifles were taken out of store, unpacked, degreased, inspected, repaired if appropriate, and approved to 'Weedon Repair Standard' (WRS). The long-range sight aperture bar and the dial pointer were removed.

According to the official Contract Books, 677,324 guns were so treated, the orders being placed on 24 June 1939. Most of the work was undertaken by the Royal Small Arms Factory at Enfield (200,000) and Holland & Holland (179,168), but other leading members of the gun trade participated – including Purdey, Cogswell & Harrison, Westley Richards, Greener, Boss and Parker-Hale. The rifles were initially used for training, though many were subsequently issued to the Local Defence Volunteers* in 1940.

Small quantities of a modified sniper rifle, No.3 Mk 1* (T)A, were made during the Second World War by Alex Martin & Company about 1940 (the Contract Books suggest that the total was 421).† The principal difference between the Mk 1* (T) and Mk 1* (T)A was that the latter carried its Aldis sight offset to the left of the bore in a low mount; consequently, a detachable wooden cheek piece was issued to help the firer position his eye correctly behind the sight. The height of the back sight protectors was greatly reduced on (T)A rifles.

* These units were subsequently renamed 'Home Guard'.

†BSA is known to have made 79 No.3 Mk 1*(T) rifles and 6,600 detachable cheek pieces, ordered on 2 September 1940. It is assumed that Martin's order was fulfilled at the same time.

162 ABOVE

A ·303 Ross Mk III rifle. Note the aperture back sight on top of the bridge and the unique shape of the receiver. Though very accurate, the Ross performed so unreliably in service that it was replaced by the SMLE in 1916. Courtesy of the MoD Pattern Room Collection, Royal Ordnance plc, Nottingham; photograph by Ian Hogg.

163 LEFT

Men of the light cruiser HMS *Undaunted* pose in October 1915 aboard the German trawler *Doktor Krug*. Apart from the captured ship's puppy and the basket of fish, interest centres on the rifles – which are all 6·5mm Japanese Meiji 38th Year Arisakas. Courtesy of the Trustees of the Imperial War Museum; negative no. SP1127.

ROSS AND ARISAKA

'View in the First-Line Trenches', a picture of Canadian troops taken in 1914 'by permission of the C.-in-C. of the B.E.F.'. Though suspiciously neatly kept for a front-line trench, the view is remarkable principally for the Mk III Ross rifles. Author's archives.

The most hated (and possibly most mis-understood) of all military rifles, the Ross was adopted in Canada simply because Britain had been unwilling to supply the Canadian Army with Lee-Enfields. Invented by Sir Charles Ross, ninth baronet of Balnagown, the service rifles embodied a straight-pull bolt action in which threaded helical ribs on the bolt engaged inside the bolt sleeve. When the bolt was pulled back, the ribs rotated the locking lugs out of the receiver wall.

The Ross Rifle Company delivered the first examples of the 'Rifle, Ross, ·303-inch, Mark I' to the Department of Militia and Defence in August 1905. Issued to the Royal North-West Mounted Police, one gun soon gave an inkling of the future when part of its bolt failed. The firer lost an eye.

An improved Mk II rifle was adopted in 1906, followed by a clutch of minor variations until the designation had advanced to Mk II***** by 1910. As this correctly hinted at never-ending teething troubles, the authorities re-designated the rifles in 1912. The Mks II[3*] and Mk II[5*] became 'Rifles, Short, Ross Mk II'; earlier short-barrel guns, regardless of their sub-class, became 'Mk I'.

Substantial numbers of a long-barrel infantry pattern had also been made, a few Rifles, Ross, ·303-inch Mk II surviving to see service in the First World War. The principal weapon of the Canadian Expeditionary Force, however, was the Mark III. Approved in 1911, guns had only reached the troops shortly before the war began.

The new rifle featured a 'triple-thread inter-rupted-screw double-bearing cam bolt head', a change made largely to create an action suited to powerful sporting-rifle cartridges. The other major change concerned the substitution of a charger-loaded five-round in-line box magazine for the Harris controlled-platform original.

The Ross Mk III was clumsy and awkward, 50 9/16in overall with a 30 1/4in barrel. It weighed 9lb 14oz – about 1lb greater than the SMLE. The British government ordered 100,000 rifles in September 1914, but deliveries were so erratic that the contract was cancelled in March 1917.

165 BELOW RIGHT
A longitudinal section of the Ross action.

Key – 1, bolt; 2, bolt head; 3, locking lugs; 5, trigger; 6, trigger group sub-frame; 7, sear; 8, sear nose; 9, safety pawl; 10, safety lugs; 11, magazine follower; 12, magazine spring; 13, magazine plunger; 14, 15, plunger pivots; and 16, elevator arms (one of two).

166 LEFT
Canadian soldiers fraternize with French artillerymen, the crew of the hastily camouflaged 12cm Mle.78 field-gun in the background. The Canadians have SMLE rifles and a Lewis Gun, while the Frenchman sitting on the gun-trail has a Berthier Mousqueton d'Artillerie Mle.92. Courtesy of Elex archives.

Courtesy of the MoD Pattern Room Collection

There were two patterns – Canadian Mark IIIA and the modified Mark IIIB, approved in October 1915 with an SMLE-type cut off. The British soon relegated Ross rifles to training purposes, declaring them obsolete in November 1921.

War in the trenches emphasized the weaknesses of the straight-pull action. Mud jammed it solid. So did the heating effects of rapid fire. Extraction was capricious. But the worst feature was that the bolt could be rotated under the extractor after it had been removed from the bolt-way. Though the bolt would still re-enter the receiver, it did not lock on the closing stroke.†

When the gun fired, the bolt slammed back into the firer's face. It was also possible to fire the gun without the locking lugs being fully engaged. At least one fatality had been attributed to a wrongly assembled bolt prior to the war, but nothing had been done. How many Canadians were killed by their own rifles in 1914–16 has never been satisfactorily established.

Armourers in France added a rivet or screw in the bolt sleeve to prevent the mishap, but could not prevent the rifle being replaced by the Lee-Enfield in the summer of 1916. Tests later showed that jamming often arose simply from the bolt-stop damaging the rearmost locking lug.

Some Ross rifles were retained as sniper's weapons, fitted with American 1908 or 1913-model Warner & Swazey sights offset to the left to clear the charger guides. Ironically, provided it locked properly, the Ross action was exceptionally strong. The long-barrel rifles shot especially well – perhaps best of all pre-1918 sniper rifles – but had nothing of the durability of the P/14.

The major flaws in the bolt could easily have been solved, excepting the ineffectual primary extraction inherent in a straight-pull system. However, Ross had moved on to other projects and the Canadian government appropriated his rifle factory in 1917.‡

The shortage of rifles that had afflicted the British Army at the beginning of the First World War was also partially solved by importing rifles from Japan. On 24 October

1915, these were approved for British service as 'Rifles, Magazine, ·256-inch, Patterns 1900 and 1907', together with a 1907-type carbine.*

Known as Arisakas, after the head of the rifle-development commission, they were sturdy and effectual. The biggest drawback in British service was their non-standard calibre; consequently, many went to the Royal Navy (from June 1915 onward) and others armed the Royal Flying Corps. Most seem to have been shipped to Russia in 1917 after delivery of sufficient ·303 guns from North America.

The guns were much modified Mausers, originally adopted by the Japanese army in 1899 – as the Meiji 30th Year Type Rifle – and then modified in 1905 (38th Year Type) after the Russo-Japanese War had suggested improvements. The original hook safety of the 30th Year Type was replaced by a large knurled safety shroud on the cocking piece, a reciprocating bolt cover was added, and original rotating extractor substituted by a stationary pattern. The rifles were about 50¼ in long, had 31½ in barrels and weighed 8lb 14oz. There was an internal five-round box magazine and the back sight was graduated to 2,000 yards.

* The literal equivalents of the Japanese designations would have been 1897 and 1905. However, 'P/1900' and 'P/1907' make some sense: they were the years in which the Japanese rifles were first issued in quantity.

167 ABOVE

The 6·5mm Japanese Meiji 38th Year rifle, or Arisaka, was adopted by the British authorities as emergency issue in 1915. Most of the rifles were subsequently sold to Russia when sufficient supplies of the SMLE and P/14 had been assured, though some Arisakas remained in the Royal Navy and the Royal Air Force into the 1920s.

THE LEE-ENFIELD, 1914–18

Tremendous shortages of rifles were evident during the First World War, particularly after the success of recruiting for Kitchener's New Army. They were partly offset by the importation of Japanese Arisaka and Canadian Ross guns, and by letting contracts in the USA.

Attempts were also made to accelerate production in Britain, by eliminating unnecessary machining operations such as the holes that had been bored in the SMLE nosecap boss, back sight protectors and butt.

168 BELOW

This group photograph, taken during the First World War, gives little clue to its origin. Judged by the solitary cap-badge and a shoulder title partially legible on the original picture, the men are from the Wiltshire Regiment (Duke of Edinburgh's). Their SMLE rifles appear to be Mk III, as they have bridge-type charger guides and cut offs. Courtesy of Elex archives.

Periscope Rifles were generally standard weapons mounted on wooden frames, while 'rifle batteries' contained several guns. Batteries could be laid on a specific target and left in the charge of one man. One pattern developed by Platt Bros of Oldham (LoC 17750) consisted simply of a wooden box in which three SMLE rifles could be mounted. A steel-plate shield could be slid into the front of the box to protect its contents.

Emergency Patterns ('EY.'), announced 'for the record' in December 1918, had their fore-ends lashed with cable or copper wire to minimize splintering should the barrel burst. Similar, but largely unofficial modifications were made to strengthen Bombing Parties' grenade-launching rifles.

PRODUCTION, 1914–18

When the First World War began, Britain had about 750,000 ·303 Lee-system rifles. Though appropriate for the peacetime establishment, this soon proved woefully inadequate — partly because the wastage allowance had been optimistically based on the Second South African War, and partly owing to the raising of huge volunteer armies. The strength of the British Army, excluding Indian and Colonial troops, stood at 3·56 million men by 1 November 1918.

The disparity had been made good by accelerating production of Lee-Enfields, and by acquiring P/14 and Ross rifles from North America. From 1 August 1914 to 31 October 1918, Enfield made 2,008,158 guns, BSA produced 1,581,854 and LSA contributed a mere 364,214. This total of 3·85 million was supplemented by 1·36 million P/14 and Ross rifles, plus an unknown quantity of 6·5mm Arisakas bought from Japan.

The Enfield total included weapons assembled from parts made under the Peddled Rifle Scheme, which involved legions of sub-contractors from Abingdon Ecco Ltd of Tyseley, near Birmingham (maker of safety bolts), to Wright & Co. of Birmingham, who made butts. Guns made of 'peddled' parts rarely bear makers' marks on the butt socket. The most interesting contractor was the Standard Small Arms Co. Ltd of Lench Street, Birmingham, which had occupied the moribund Isaac Hollis & Sons factory in the hope of making entire SMLE rifles. Unfortunately, bad management and insoluble labour problems

The Small Arms Committee suggested deleting the long-range sights, which had very little application in trench warfare. The authorities were not convinced, but allowed damaged sights to be removed from Charger Loading Lee-Enfields from May 1916. Generally, the dial-plate and its screw were retained to protect the stock, but some guns lack the plate and the retaining-screw hole may be plugged with wood. The aperture sight arm was either truncated or replaced by the 'washer, spring, sight, aperture, rifle, SMLE Mk III'.

The Rifle, Short, Magazine, Lee-Enfield Mk III*' was approved on 2 January 1916 (LoC 17622). Changes were made to some of the minor components, and the swivel lugs were omitted from the trigger guard; long-range sights and the back sight wind gauge were abandoned, but the Mk III* otherwise resembled the preceding Mk III. BSA had omitted the cut-off plate from some Mk III rifles made

after September 1915, much to the annoyance of the Inspectorate, but it had been forcibly reinstated; the authorities then had a change of heart and made the mechanism optional.

A simplified cocking piece with grooved flat sides was introduced in August 1916. It was agreed that Mk III parts could be fitted to older guns when they returned for repair and, after June 1918, a few SMLEs were made with ultra-short 'Bantam' butts — a half-inch less than the normal short pattern. Combs were marked 'B' near the heel.

The diameter of the small cone at the front of the chamber was increased by ·002in late in the war, rifles so treated displaying 'S C' on the back sight. An additional 'H.V.' showed that they were also sighted for high-velocity (Mk VII) ammunition.

The twenty-round 'Magazine No.1 Mk IV' appeared in April 1918. Contracts for 200,000 are said to have been fulfilled by the Armistice, but the magazines are now rarely seen.

prevented success, and SSA was forcibly incorporated in the Peddled Rifle Scheme; bought by the Ministry of Munitions in June 1918, it was renamed 'National Rifle Factory No.1'.† Parts will be found marked 'S.S.A.' or 'N.R.F.'

†National Rifle Factory No.2, formerly a Greener plant, made barrels and stocks for the SMLE.

SNIPER RIFLES, 1914–18

The SMLE provided the basis for the first official British sniper rifles, a role originally filled by impressed sporting guns and captured German Gew.98. By the summer of 1915, the high incidence of head wounds persuaded senior British officers to take proper action.

Many of the earliest SMLE Mk III and MK III* sniper rifles – plus some long Lee-Enfields – were fitted with Galilean sights. A crude form of telescope, these consisted simply of two widely separated lenses.‡ Owing to the absence of a sight-tube, they were vulnerable to damage. The field of view was narrow, usually little more than 6ft per 100 yards, and marksmen had great difficulty acquiring targets.

The 'Sight, Optical, Neill, Mk I, Rifles, SMLE' – later known as the Barnett or Ulster model – was approved in May 1915, to be followed by the similar Lattey version at the end of September. Though more than 11,000 Galilean sights were purchased, they were nothing but an expedient. The British gun trade provided three thousand assorted telescope sights in 1915. Improvements were gradually made, though focus and azimuth adjustments often remained primitive. Mounts were generally offset to the left of the action to allow the magazine to be charged.

Among the best known sights were those made by the Periscopic Prism Company of Kentish Town in North London. They measured about 12in overall, had a 9° field of view and range drums were graduated from 100 to 600 yards. Male dovetails on the sight rings fitted into a bar brazed to the left side of the SMLE action.

Most of the sights made by Aldis Bros of Birmingham had a 19mm objective lens and a range drum calibrated 1–6. Sturdy and effectual, 2·5× Aldis sights were fitted to SMLE and then P/14 sniper rifles. The Pattern 1918 sight was approved for the P/14 in April 1918, whereupon the Lee-Enfields were gradually converted back to infantry weapons. The P/14 was regarded as more accurate at ranges up to 300 yards, though it never entirely replaced the SMLE sniper rifles in the trenches. Issue was completed only after the war.

Contrary to popular belief, the best distributed pre-1918 sniper rifle was the SMLE – followed by the P/14, issued in 1918 only, and lastly by the Ross. Figures published in 1921 showed that 9,788 SMLE sniper rifles had been produced during the First World War, virtually half with Periscopic Prism sights and about a third with Aldis patterns. There were 2,001 P/14 rifles with P/18 (Aldis) sights, but many had been delivered into store after the Armistice. Only P/14 rifles and the Aldis sights were retained; all other optical sights had been discarded by the early 1920s.

Luminous night sights were issued in small numbers in 1916–17, comprising a folding bar

‡Some patterns were attached to the sights, others simply appeared in proximity to them.

170 BELOW

The action of a No.4 Lee-Enfield rifle, with its Mk I back sight elevated. Note the charger guides and the rough finish befitting a wartime product. Courtesy of the MoD Pattern Room Collection, Royal Ordnance plc, Nottingham; photograph by Ian Hogg.

171 ABOVE

A serjeant-instructor in musketry of the Scots Guards demonstrates 'the new Mk IV rifle and the new six inch bayonet' on 17 January 1942. The diced fore-end shows that the rifle is a 'B' pattern No 1 Mk 6 (made in 1929–31 for troop trials), refurbished to No.4 standards in the early part of the Second World War; it was hardly 'new' by the time this picture was taken. By courtesy of Brian L. Davis.

C9 CLASS. R.N.T.E. SHOTLEY.

piece did not protrude behind the bolt handle.

At the end of May 1926, the cumbersome
British designation system was simplified. The
SMLE became the Rifle No.1, rimfire versions
were 'Rifles No.2' and the P/14 was christened
'Rifle No.3'. Full-length and converted
charger-loading rifles were discarded and old
SMLEs – Mk I, I*, I*** and Converted Mk II –
were returned to store. This left only the ·303
Rifles No.1 Mk III, III*, D.P. and EY; the ·22
Rifle No.2 Mk IV; and the ·303 Rifles No.3 Mk
I*(F) and I*(T). Stocks were adequate for
peacetime needs. In 1924, the inventory had
contained 1·59 million Mk III and III* rifles
alone.

The Rifle No.1 Mk VI was very similar to its
perfected mass-produced successor, the No.4
Mk I, excepting that it had a different nose cap,
fore-end dicing and a low left body wall. It was
followed in 1930 by a modified No.1 Mk VI
Model B, which had lacked butt-plate che-
quering. At least 1,025 were made in 1930–1.
They were tested exhaustively by the 3rd Carabiniers (Prince of Wales's Dragoon Guards)
and the 2nd Battalion of the West Yorkshire
Regiment (The Prince of Wales's Own), in
Egypt and India.

In the summer of 1931, the rifle was renamed No.4 Mk I. More than two thousand
more 'Model B' No.4 trials rifles were made in
1933, with raised left body walls and plain
fore-ends. Confusingly, like the original No.1
Mk VI Model B, they were numbered from
A0001 upward. Tests were undertaken during
the mid-1930s with the Model C, 56 of which
were made, but excessive changes caused the
No.4 Mk I Model D to be abandoned in the
hope that auto-loaders would still be found.

THE LEE-ENFIELD, 1939–45

When the Second World War began, the No.1
Mk III rifle was being made in the BSA Small
Heath (Birmingham) factory. Tooling for the
No.4 Mk I, installed in the company's new
factory in Shirley, was still incomplete.

---

behind the front sight and horizontal lines on
an auxiliary back-sight plate. They proved effectual enough, but success depended entirely
on the ability to acquire targets in darkness.

THE SMLE BETWEEN THE WARS

Shortly after the end of the First World War,
the Mark III* SMLE was re-sealed to govern
post-war manufacture. The long-range sights
and the wind gauge on the back sight were
discarded, but the cut-off was reinstated.* The
SMLE had performed much better in the
trenches than had been expected. Consequently, as the Small Arms Committee was
actively seeking an effectual auto-loader, the
Lee-Enfield was retained as the standard service rifle. The existence of three production
lines undoubtedly assisted the decision.†

The Rifle, Short, Magazine, Lee-Enfield,
·303-inch Mark V, 20,000 of which were made
in 1922–4, had aperture sights on the body
behind the charger guides. Graduated to 1,400
yards (some to 1,500), the leaves had a 'battle
sight' when folded down. Unfortunately, the
gains were not great enough to offset the additional cost of altering the body, barrel, fore-
end, hand guard and nose cap. Surviving rifles
are immediately recognisable by the additional reinforcing band behind the nose cap and
a hand guard that reaches the chamber-ring.

The Mk V was replaced in the summer of
1924. The new gun had a heavy barrel with
lugs to receive a grenade launcher or bayonet,
a modified body, an improved back sight, and
a greatly modified fore-end from which a few
inches of the muzzle protruded.

The wings protecting the back sight were
most distinctive, though fore-end dicing was
only added after the first prototypes had been
made. Unlike preceding SMLEs, the cocking

---

* It had never been formally abandoned, though manufacturers
had been given the option of doing so under emergency pre-
1918 regulations.

†The London Small Arms Company finally closed in 1925,
leaving only BSA and Enfield capable of making Lee-Enfields.

Though severe bombing in 1940 disrupted production of No.1 Mk III, work continued until the end of 1943. BSA products of this era display 'M' codes – M47A for Small Heath, M47B for Redditch, M47C for Shirley. Extensive use was also made of subcontractors ranging from Aero-Zip Fasteners of London to Zipp Fasteners Co. Ltd of Edmonton.‡

Apart from simplifications to components (e.g., the cocking piece) and some experiments with laminated stocks, little was done to the No.1 Mk III in this period.

In addition to BSA production, No.1 Mk III and III* rifles were made in Australia and India (at Lithgow and Ishapur respectively). Their construction parallels that of the British guns, excepting some machining differences. Neither country made many distinctive variations, though there were some India Pattern Charger Loading Lee-Enfields and Australian 'jungle carbine' versions of the No.1 (the short-lived Rifle 'No.6 Mk I').

Total production of No.1 Mk III and Mk III* rifles amounted, according to the Contract Books, to about 290,000 from BSA (1935–43). An additional 20,300 had been sent to Egypt in the summer of 1939. Enfield repaired 311,710 rifles in this period, the first large 'repair order' being placed in May 1939. BSA contributed an extra 55,957 repaired rifles, while Holland & Holland and Cogswell & Harrison provided 5,496.

The No.1 also provided the basis for the silenced ·45 ACP De Lisle Commando Carbine,

‡A list appears in Ian Skennerton's excellent *The British Service Lee*.

more than a hundred of which were produced in Dagenham by the Ford Motor Company (prototypes) and Sterling Engineering Co. Ltd (production guns) in 1944. The standard wood-butt De Lisle, about 36in overall, weighed 8lb 5oz.

Losses of equipment at Dunkirk were spectacular, reducing British inventories of ·303 rifles by a more than a quarter-million. Existing No.1 Mk VI and No.4 Mk I trials-rifle bodies were hastily assembled into No.4-type service rifles. Former No.1 Mk VI examples are immediately recognisable by their diced foreends and reeded hand guards. Two thousand guns were completed as standard issue, the remaining 1,400 becoming No.4 sniper rifles.

Enfield was too committed to the manufacture of Bren Guns and ·38 revolvers to spare capacity for No.4 rifles. Two new factories were constructed to make No 4 rifles, one in Fazakerley on the outskirts of Liverpool and the other in the Yorkshire town of Maltby. Concurrently, vast numbers of old SMLEs were refurbished at Enfield and by the gun trade.

After last-minute changes had been made, the Rifle No.4 Mk I was approved on 15 November 1939.* Measuring 44·43in overall with the standard butt, it weighed 9lb 1oz and had a five-groove barrel with anti-clockwise twist. The first guns from Maltby were completed in June 1941, followed by Fazakerley in July and the BSA Shirley factory in August. It was the Spring of 1942 before No.4 rifles were issued to the troops. The roughness of the machining and, particularly, the advent of the six-inch

'pig sticker' bayonet were greeted with derision. Once the No.4 showed its merits, its image improved perceptibly.

Many changes were made to the No.4 fittings during the war, generally to simplify mass production; for example, the butts of the No.1 and No.4 rifles (previously different) were standardized in July 1940. There were four No.4 back sights: Mk I had a click adjustable elevator and was graduated from 200 to 1,300 yards in 50yd increments; Mk.2 was a simple two-position rocking L pattern (300/600 yards); Mk III and Mk IV, which resembled the Mk I but differed in detail, had pressed-steel sliders.† Typical of British nomenclature, the Mk III sight had a Mk II leaf and the Mk IV sight had a Mk III leaf! A version of the Mk I without the battle sight was made specifically for the No.4 sniper rifle.

Mk I sights were standardized after the Second World War, emergency patterns being declared obsolete in January 1947.

Tests in the Spring of 1941 showed that two-groove rifling performed well enough to be accepted as a temporary standard 'Mk II' No.4

---

* It was re-sealed on 13 January 1941 after additional revisions had been made to simplify production.

†In addition, the Canadian sights – C.Mk 2 and C.Mk 3 – differed slightly from their British Mk III and Mk IV equivalents.

---

174 BELOW

The officers and men of the Landing Party of HMNZS *Dunedin* pose in this 1929-vintage photograph taken by S.C. Smith of Wellington. A fine array of SMLE rifles, Webley revolver holsters and webbing ammunition pouches is visible. Courtesy of Elex archives.

barrel, until declared obsolete in July 1945.‡

Made of a single drawn tube with a knox-form pinned and shrunk in place, the Mk III barrel was unique to Accles & Pollock Ltd of Oldbury. However, though more than 100,000 were made, problems prevented it being issued in quantity.

The early flared-rim cocking piece gave way to a flat pattern, with three vertical grooves, and then to an entirely plain type. There were three front sight protectors – the milled original, a pressed Mk II and an integral one-piece emergency Mk III pattern – in addition to four front sights. Butt plates on wartime guns were mazak alloy, though pre-production guns had used gunmetal. Stock wood was often inferior, especially on guns made in 1941–2, and the sling swivels on wartime products were sometimes simply bent wire.

The Rifle No.4 Mk I* was approved in June 1941, though not announced in the Lists of Changes for some years. Made only in North America, the Mk I* had a modified body and lacked the 'catch head, breech bolt' in an attempt to simplify bolt removal.

Production of No.4 rifles during the Second World War amounted to 2,021,913 from the three British factories – BSA Shirley, Fazakerley and Maltby – plus about 330,000 from Small Arms Ltd of Long Branch (Canada) and 1,196,706 from the Savage Arms Company.* The Savage guns were made in the former Stevens Arms & Tool Company factory in Chicopee Falls, Massachussetts, and are usually known as 'Stevens-Savage' Lee-Enfields. They are invariably marked 'U.S. PROPERTY'.

‡It was also used on 9mm Sten Guns and Enfield ·38 revolvers.
* Small Arms Ltd also made 575,731 guns for the Canadian armed forces and the New Zealanders, while Savage sent 40,000 to China.

THE NO.5 RIFLE

The Lee-Enfield 'Jungle Carbine' arose from a request made in the summer of 1943 for a lighter rifle. Engagement range in the Far East rarely exceeded 400 yards, and the No.4 was unnecessarily clumsy in the prevailing conditions. Experiments with shortened rifles proved that accuracy was acceptable, but that recoil and muzzle-flash were excessive. Variations of the light rifle – presumably for airborne troops – were fitted with detachable butts supplied by Sterling Engineering and the Chambons Tool Company, before the standard fixed-butt trials model was perfected in September 1944.

The Rifle No.5 Mk 1 was approved on 23 May 1945 and announced in LoC C2125. It was made with the three standard butt lengths, had a back sight similar to the No.4 Mk 1 – graduated only to 800 yards – and displayed a half-length fore-end. Its modified safety and sear mechanism were subsequently adapted to the No.4.

Large quantities of No.5 rifles were ordered from the Royal Ordnance Factory at Fazaker-

ley and BSA's Shirley plant, and production of the No.4 stopped. The No.5 was initially very popular, being shorter and lighter than its predecessor, but euphoria began to wear off when it was discovered that rifles would not keep their zero. Dozens of experiments with flash-hiders, barrels and fore-ends failed to reveal the reason. None the wiser, authorities simply blamed 'inherent flaws in the action' and declared the No.5 obsolete in July 1947. Production of the No.4 began again at Fazakerley in September.

Owing to the rapid supersession of the No.5, neither of the initial orders was completed. Fazakerley made 169,807 and the BSA factory at Shirley contributed 81,329 – deliveries amounting to 251,136 against orders totalling 350,000.

SNIPER RIFLES, 1939–45

Shortages of sniping equipment evident in 1939 were temporarily solved by fitting Aldis

sights to P/14 rifles and by converting about 1,400 No.1 Mk VI trials rifles to No.4 sniper rifles. Auxiliary cheek pieces were authorized in September 1940.

No.4 rifles accepted the 3× 'Telescope, Sighting, No.32 Mk I', a sturdy item dating from the late 1930s. It weighed no less than 2lb 3oz, and had a 19mm objective lens with a 9° field of view. Its range drum was graduated 100–1,000 yards in 50yd clicks, each click of azimuth moving the impact by 2 MOA.† There were three British versions (No.32 Mks I–III) and a Canadian variant (C.Mk 4), each clearly marked.

The Rifle No.4 Mk I (T) was approved on 12 February 1942, but the earliest guns were none too successful. From 22 September 1942, therefore, work was sub-contracted to the specialist gunmaker Holland & Holland (code 'S51'). Holland & Holland subsequently finished 26,442 sniper rifles, compared with a mere two thousand supplied by other sources.

BSA-made products were preferred, though sniper rifles made in 1942, when British quality control was at its lowest ebb, were converted from Stevens-Savage No.4 Mk I*. Supplied under Lend-Lease, these are misleadingly marked 'U.S. PROPERTY'.

†Equivalent, in approximate terms, to 2in per 100 yards.

POSTWAR GUNS

Abandoning the No.5 allowed the authorities to standardize the Rifle No.4 Mk 2, approved on 4 December 1947 but not formally introduced until 1949. The rifle had the trigger mounted on underside of the body rather than attached to the trigger guard. This forced changes in the fore-end, and so the split-end Mk 2 could not be exchanged with the earlier type. Mark 1 back sights were standard.

Many Mk 1 and 1* rifles were modified to Mk 2 standards when they returned for repair; the Mk 1/2 rifles were originally Mk I, while the No.4 Mk 1/3 had been American or Canadian-made Mk I*.

Little was done to the basic design until the late 1950s, apart from the substitution of a cast trigger guard in 1953. However, after protracted trials, 7·62mm conversions were sanctioned in the L8 series. These included the L8A1 (formerly No.4 Mk 2), L8A2 (No.4 Mk 1/2), L8A3 (No.4 Mk 1/3), L8A4 (No.4 Mk 1) and L8A5 (No.4 Mk 1*). Conversion kits were made by both Enfield and Sterling Engineering, usually comprising a barrel, a modified extractor, a new magazine and a charger-guide insert. Maker's marks changed in accordance with NATO standardization: Enfield had become 'UE', BSA was 'UB', Fazakerley used 'UF', and Sterling was allotted 'US'.

Sold commercially as the 'Enfield Envoy', the Rifle L39A1 was a competition gun with a half-stock and aperture sights. Invariably built on a Mk 2 action, its trigger was pivoted on the underside of the body. The L42A1 sniper rifle, adopted on 24 August 1970, was converted from existing No.4 Mk 1(T) rifles and its trigger pivoted on the trigger guard. Issued with the 'Telescope, Straight, Sighting, L1A1' (No.32 Mk 3), the L42A1 was a heavy and most effectual weapon.

After trials in the early 1980s, however, the Lee-Enfield sniper rifle was replaced by the Rifle L96A1, developed by Accuracy International Ltd and known commercially as the PM. The L96A1 has a modified Mauser-pattern front-locking bolt and is crammed with unorthodox features – twin stock-plates, for example, are bolted to a central steel frame supporting the action. Used for some years by the SAS before being adopted by the army, the L96 promises to be a very efficient weapon.

Until the late 1970s, the Australian Army was equipped with No.1 sniper rifles and

176 ABOVE
A corporal of the Coldstream Guards models 1944-pattern webbing equipment. Note the Rifle No.5 Mk I, or 'Jungle Carbine'. Courtesy of Brian L. Davis.

177 RIGHT
A close-up view of the telescope sight fitted to the British L42A1 sniper rifle, regulation issue prior to the adoption of the L96A1. This rifle was converted at Enfield in 1970 from a Rifle No.4 made by BSA ('M47') in 1943. Courtesy of Ian Hogg.

P/1918 (Aust.) sights dating back to the First World War. These ancient weapons were finally replaced by the Model 82 Parker-Hale Mauser, adopted concurrently by Canada and New Zealand.

TRAINING RIFLES

The earliest trainers were simply old ·303 rifles with worn-out barrels, converted for Aiming Tubes. Also known as 'Morris Tubes' after their inventor, they were simply sub-calibre liners retained by knurled muzzle collars. Most fired a low-power ·23 centre-fire '·297/·230' cartridge.

The first Lee-Metford pattern was approved in December 1891 (LoC 6602), to be joined by a shortened version for carbines in May 1895. Lee-Metford Aiming Tubes would also fit long Lee-Enfields. Most guns were marked 'M.T.' or 'A.T.', and had a special bolt head. The last ·23 Aiming Tube was approved for Naval Service in February 1910 to expend ammunition.

The first ·22 RF Aiming Tube was approved in November 1904, though problems delayed the sealing of a pattern until 1906. The Rifle, Short, Magazine, Lee-Enfield, Aiming Tube, ·22 Rim Fire, Mark I was approved in November 1906 and followed by a version for the Lee-Metfords and long Lee-Enfields. Some rifles had been rebuilt from the original SMLE trials guns, and were classified as non interchangeable. They displayed 'N.I.' in addition to 'A.T.' on the body, bolt, barrel and butt.

The ·22 Short Rifle Mark I, converted from Mk I* Lee-Metfords, was approved on 13 December 1907; dating from October 1911, the Mark I* was a Mk I with a modified Pattern No.2 bolt head and revised sights approximating to a SMLE firing Mk VII ammunition. The Mark II Naval Service version was converted from Lee-Metford Mk II rifles with effect from January 1912, and Mark III rimfire short rifles – approved in August 1912 – were made from SMLE Converted Mks II and II*.

First examples of the War Office Miniature Rifle appeared in this period. Approved by the Army Council for schools, cadet corps and rifle clubs, it was also used by the Territorial Army prior to 1914. A single-shot bolt-action rifle chambering ·22 rimfire or ·297/·230 centre-fire cartridges, the Miniature Rifle was about 41in overall, had a 24in barrel and weighed 5½–6lb. Made by BSA and LSA, it proved much less accurate than the popular small-bore Martini-type rifles. Production appears to have ceased in 1914.

Some ·22 Long Rifles Mk I were approved for the Royal Navy in February 1912, conversions of Mk II Lee-Metfords. The similar Mk I* had originally been a MK II* Lee-Metford or a Mk I/Mk I* Lee-Enfield. Approved for Land Service in November 1911, the Mark II was originally a Mk II* Lee-Metford or a Mk I/Mk I* Lee-Enfield. Long rifles accepted the P/1888 sword bayonet; excepting Mks I, I* and II, short rifles took the P/1903 or P/1907.

The Rifle, Short, ·22 Rim Fire, Pattern 1914, approved on 24 May 1915, had a sleeved barrel. It was made exclusively by A.G. Parker & Co. Ltd of Birmingham from SMLE Converted Mk II and Converted Mk II* rifles (P/14 No.1), and then SMLE Mk III and Converted Mk IV (P/14 No.2). Originally a single-loader, it could be fitted with a so-called Parker-Hiscock magazine from the end of 1915 onward. Unfortunately, the magazines proved to be very unreliable and their value in rapid-fire training was questionable.

An aperture back sight fitting onto the long-range sight arm was issued from April 1917 to prepare firers for the ·303 P/14.

The ·22 Pattern 1918, approved in July 1918, was an adaptation of SMLE Mk III and Converted Mk IV rifles for 'conveyors' – ·303-shape adaptors into which a ·22 rimfire cartridge was inserted. Apart from requiring a special ejector, the P/18 was identical with the ·303 service rifles. It proved temperamental, and was declared obsolete soon after the end of the war.

The ·22 Mark IV was introduced in November 1921. Converted from SMLE Mk III and III* rifles, it had a solid barrel and a new bolt head. The cut off and magazine were discarded. Surviving P/14 rimfires were altered to Mk IV and Mk IV* standards when they returned for repair. In 1926, the Mk IV* became the 'Rifle No.2 Mk 4*'.

Experiments were made in the 1930s, but no new training rifles appeared until prototypes based on the No.4 and No.5 ·303 rifles were

178 BELOW

The single-shot bolt-action 7·62mm L81A1 is the standard British Army training rifle. Made by Parker-Hale on the basis of the company's excellent Mauser action, the L81 is sturdy and effectual. Courtesy of Parker-Hale Ltd, Birmingham.

179 BELOW

The 7·62mm Parker-Hale Model 82 sniper rifle is service issue in Canada, Australia and New Zealand. Courtesy of Parker-Hale Ltd, Birmingham.

180 BELOW

The PM sniper rifle, adopted in 7·62×51 by the British Army as the L96A1. Courtesy of Accuracy International UK Ltd, Portsmouth.

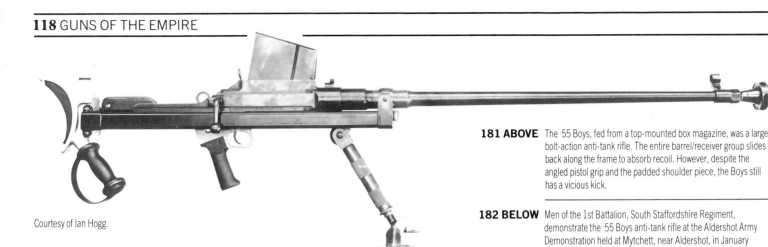

Courtesy of Ian Hogg.

181 ABOVE The ·55 Boys, fed from a top-mounted box magazine, was a large bolt-action anti-tank rifle. The entire barrel/receiver group slides back along the frame to absorb recoil. However, despite the angled pistol grip and the padded shoulder piece, the Boys still has a vicious kick.

182 BELOW Men of the 1st Battalion, South Staffordshire Regiment, demonstrate the ·55 Boys anti-tank rifle at the Aldershot Army Demonstration held at Mytchett, near Aldershot, in January 1938. Courtesy of Brian L. Davis.

made by BSA in 1944—5. The No.4 lookalike was approved in the late 1940s by the Air Ministry, as the Rifle, ·22-inch, No.7 Mk 1. Instead of standardizing on the No.7, however, the army approved the Rifle No.8 Mk 1 in September 1948. It had a half-stock, a refined pistol-grip butt and, eventually, greatly refined sights graduated to 100 yards. Made by the Royal Ordnance Factory in Fazakerley and apparently also in the BSA Shirley factory, it measured 41·8in overall, had a 23·9in barrel rifled with six-groove clockwise twist, and weighed 8lb 8oz.

The Rifle, ·22-inch, No.9 Mk 1 was a variant of No.7 made for the Royal Navy in 1957—9 by Parker-Hale Ltd. Unlike the newly-made RAF rifles, the No.9 was converted by tubing the barrels of existing No.4 weapons.

The supersession of the Lee-Enfield by the L1A1 was accompanied by the demise of the ·22 training rifles, many of which were sold to rifle clubs.† They were replaced by a sub-calibre insert for the FAL, made by Heckler & Koch and designated 'Conversion Set, ·22-inch, L12A1'. Small numbers of the Australian Sportco Model 71 auto-loading rifle have been issued as L29A1 and L29A2 for automatic weapons training, but it is probable that a variant of the 5·56mm L85A1 will eventually supersede them.

Basic full-bore marksmanship and competition training is currently undertaken with the Parker-Hale Cadet Rifle, 7·62mm, L81A1, a sturdy and effectual weapon developed from the PH1200X target rifle. The L81A1 embodies a Mauser action, measures 1,160mm overall,‡ has a 660mm barrel and weighs 4·98kg with its aperture sights.

†Some guns, stripped of their woodwork, were subsequently issued as sub-calibre artillery trainers under the designation L2A1.
‡Optional butt spacers can lengthen the butt by 60mm.

THE BOYS RIFLE

The widespread distribution of lightly armoured tankettes inspired the development of many portable anti-tank weapons during the 1930s. The first such gun had been the German T-Gewehr of 1918, little more than an enlarged Mauser rifle firing a powerful 13mm-calibre cartridge.

Impressed by captured examples, the British had produced some experimental '·600/·500' weapons of their own at the end of the First World War. Owing to the lack of interest in such weapons in the early 1920s, however, the trials had had no lasting results. They began again in 1934, when the ·5-calibre 'Stanchion Gun', developed by the Design Department at Enfield, made its first appearance before the Small Arms Committee. The first trial occurred on 4 September 1935.

An improved gun successfully underwent a searching examination in November. It worked effectually, though ballistic performance was disappointing; the ·5 bullet, loaded by Kynoch in a distinctively belted 99mm case, clearly needed more weight.

A meeting of the Small Arms Committee on 18 December 1935 recommended that the Stanchion gun be renamed 'Boys' in recog-nition of the work of the Assistant Superintendent of the Design Department, Captain H.C. Boys, who had died unexpectedly.*

Experiments in 1936 created a new cartridge, based on the ·5 Stanchion case but with mouth enlarged to take a ·55-calibre projectile. Armour penetration improved considerably, and the Rifle, Anti-Tank, Boys, ·55-inch, Mark I was approved in April 1937.

It was a large bolt-action weapon fed from a top-mounted box magazine containing five rounds. Measuring 63·5in overall, with a 36in barrel rifled with seven-groove clockwise twist, the Boys Mk I weighed about 36lb. There was a distinctive muzzle brake, and a mono-pod support appeared beneath the fore-end. The body was allowed to slide back on the frame, dissipating some of the excessive recoil forces, but the shoulder piece still required a sturdy pad and the Boys was notoriously un-pleasant to fire.

The 'Ball, Armour Piercing, ·55-inch, W Mark 2' of January 1940, which had a steel

* Note the spelling of his name. It is often wrongly rendered as Boy, Boyes or even Boyce.

core within a nickelled lead/antimony sleeve, could defeat 21mm of armour plate at 300 yards if it struck at 90° to the plate surface. Muzzle velocity of the 930-grain projectile was about 2,910fs^{-1}.

Heavy tungsten-cored shot in conventional envelopes were produced in 1939, improving long-range performance considerably, but were too wasteful of critical raw material to be made in quantity. Experiments with tungsten cores recommenced in 1944, in plastic envelopes with aluminium ballistic caps, and a perfected version was adopted 'for the record' in

September 1945 — by which time the Boys rifle was obsolete.

Excepting some prototypes, all British guns were made by BSA. Sample guns were sent to the company's Small Heath Factory at the beginning of 1936, followed by orders for 6,133. Series production began in the winter of 1936/7 and continued until the destruction of the Small Heath barrel mills in November 1940. Work was then dispersed to factories in Mansfield until August 1943. Total production of the ·55 Boys amounted to 68,847 from BSA and 50,611 by John Inglis Co. Ltd in Toronto.

The wartime career of the rifle was uninspiring, owing to the loss of guns at Dunkirk and rapidly thickening tank armour. Despite the approval of a Mark I* rifle, and then a short Mk II for airborne troops, the Boys was replaced from 1942 onward by the 'Projector, Infantry, Anti-Tank' (PIAT).

BSA made a few ·303/55 weapons in 1938 and 1942—3. The pre-war gun was intended as a trainer, but had too little recoil to be effectual; the later ones were part of an abortive hyper-velocity project.

AUTOMATIC WEAPONS
Submachine-guns

183 BELOW Men of the 1st Commando Brigade guard Germans taken during the capture of Wesel, which fell to a surprise crossing of the Rhein during the night of 23 March 1945. The man in the left foreground is carrying a Thompson submachine-gun, instantaneously identifiable by its squared receiver. Courtesy of Elex archives.

Courtesy of Weller & Dufty Ltd, Birmingham.

184 Prototypes of the Dinely Gun (top) were made by BSA in 1940, apparently for Home Guard use. Surviving examples have walnut half-stocks, compensators and a selective-fire blowback action. BSA also made the V42 (above), designed by Josef Veselý. A 9mm blowback characterized by good-quality manufacture and a double-row box magazine, the V42 pictured here also has a reversible spike bayonet and a rotating-leaf back sight graduated to 300 yards. Though trials were encouraging, the V42 and V43 were ultimately judged too complicated and too heavy.

SUBMACHINE-GUNS

The British had taken very little notice of the submachine-gun, or 'machine carbine' as it was then widely known, until the beginning of the Second World War.

The first attempt was the Machine Carbine, Lanchester, 9mm Mark I, introduced early in 1941 for the Royal Air Force and the Royal Navy; the army had priority on deliveries of the Thompson.

Simply a copy of the German MP.28, a design of good pedigree, the Lanchester inherited its prototype's reliability – but was heavy and complicated by the standards of the Sten Gun.

The Lanchester had a butt similar to that of the No.1 rifle and accepted the P/07 sword bayonet. The Mk I had a selector ahead of the trigger lever and a tangent-leaf back sight; the Mark I*, introduced to accelerate production in the Spring of 1943, had a simple sight and was capable only of automatic fire. Mk I Lanchesters were usually converted to Mk I* standards after returning for repair. The guns measured 33·5in overall, had 8in barrels and weighed about 9lb 8oz without the detachable fifty-round box magazine. According to the Contract Books, about 80,000 were made – 58,990 by Sterling Engineering Co. Ltd, plus 16,990 assembled by Greener and 3,900 by Boss & Co.

Thompsons and Lanchesters were supplemented by the Sten series, designed by Reginald Shepherd and Harold Turpin for ultra-low-cost production by inexperienced sub-contractors. Ultimately, nearly three hundred companies became involved.

Inspired by the German MP.38/MP.40, the Machine Carbine, Sten, 9mm Mark I was approved in 1940. Made by the Singer Manufacturing Co. Ltd, the first guns appeared in the summer of 1941. They were distinguished by folding hand grips, wooden butt inserts and flash-hider/compensator units on the muzzle. The Mark I* was a simplified skeletal-butt version, lacking the fore-end and the flash hider assembly. Singer made over 300,000 Mk I and I* guns, the earliest contract being placed in March 1941.

The design was soon reduced to its essentials: the Sten Mark II had a greatly simplified tube-butt and a short cylindrical barrel casing. Capable only of automatic fire, it fed from a detachable 32-round box magazine. The magazine housing could be rotated to seal the feed aperture when required. The blowback action consisted of little more than a heavy bolt and the main spring, with the most rudimentary trigger imaginable. The fixed sights were supposedly zeroed for 100 yards. Mk II Stens measured 30in overall, had 7·8in barrels and weighed 6½–7lb unladen. There were appreciable variations in fitting and construction, depending on the origins of the parts. Guns were assembled by BSA (404,383 in Tyseley from September 1941), by the Royal Ordnance Factories at Fazakerley and Theale, and in Canada.

The Mk II was joined by the Mark III, made exclusively by Lines Bros Ltd. The first of several orders totalling 876,886 was placed in January 1942. The Mk III had a unique one-piece receiver/barrel jacket – made from sheet-steel tube – extending virtually to the muzzle. A prominent weld seam ran along the top of the gun, and the barrel, unlike that of the Mk II, was not readily removable. Though manufactured in large numbers, constructio-

nal problems prevented the Mk III being as successful as its predecessor. It seems to have been approved simply to make best use of its manufacturer's facilities.

The Mark 4A Sten was an experimental short-barrel paratroop weapon with a pressed-steel shoulder piece pivoted on the underside of the pistol grip. In common with the Mk 4B, which had differing pistol grip/butt arrangements, the 4A was not made in quantity.

The 'perfected' Sten was the Mark 5, an improved Mk II intended to give the troops greater confidence in the basic gun. Made at Fazakerley and Theale, it offered better finish plus a wooden butt, a pistol grip and (on the earliest examples) an additional fore-grip. The Rifle No.4-style muzzle is also most distinctive. Mk 5 Stens survived until displaced by Sterlings in the early 1960s.

Two silenced Sten Guns were developed for the Special Forces. The Mark IIS was simply a standard gun with a shortened barrel. A silencer containing baffles to trap the propellant gas was threaded onto the receiver, replacing the standard barrel-retaining nut. Together with the short barrel, this reduced the exit velocity of the bullet below the speed of sound. The report was all but inaudible a few yards from the muzzle.

The silenced Sten was intended to fire single shots, its capabilities being held in reserve for emergencies. Automatic fire wore out the baffles too rapidly, and was apparently also capable of detaching the silencer cap when least expected. The Mark 6 was a silenced Mk 5, distinguished externally from the Mk IIS by its wood butt.

The silenced guns were made specifically for the invasion of Europe, the Mk IIS being ordered from the factories in Theale and Faza-

185 ABOVE
The Sten Mk 2, introduced in 1941, was the crudest submachine-gun ever to be issued in the British Army – with the exception of the Sten Mk 3. This example was captured from a SWAPO guerrilla in Namibia in 1982. Courtesy of Ian Hogg.

186 RIGHT
The Mk 5 Sten submachine-gun was an attempt to improve the extremely crude basic design to a point where it was universally acceptable. Note the wood butt, pistol grip and hand grip, and that the standard spike bayonet can be attached to the muzzle.

kerley in February and May 1944 respectively. The first 500 Mk 6 guns were assembled at Enfield from Theale-made parts in the same period, before a subsequent order for nearly 25,000 Mk 6 guns went to Theale in January 1945.

Despite the derision with which the troops greeted the Sten, the emergency design was adequate and worked quite happily without lubrication – unlike the Thompson, which could be a liability in hot and dry conditions. Feed jams were commonplace, however, and Sten magazines were rarely laden with more than thirty rounds.

According to the Contract Books, total production amounted to 4,184,237 Stens by March 1945 and 41 million magazines by November 1944. More than half the guns had been made in the Royal Ordnance Factory in Fazakerley, where 2.35 million assorted Mks II, IIS and 5 had been produced in 1941–5.

187 BELOW
The Patchett submachine-gun was developed to become the Sterling, still regulation issue in the British armed forces as well as serving military and police agencies worldwide. The picture was taken in July 1944 by the Research Wing of the Small Arms School.

THE STERLING

The first Veselý machine carbine (V-40) was submitted in January 1941, to be followed by a steady stream of improved versions – including V-42 and V-43 (paratroop) models – before the project was finally cancelled in 1945. The 1943-vintage 9mm Welgun, designed by the Special Operations Executive at Welwyn, featured the recoil spring concentric with the barrel – where it pulled the bolt forward, rather than pushing it.

The BSA machine carbine was submitted for trial in May 1945, just as the war in Europe was ending; tested extensively in 1945–6, it was rejected as needlessly complicated and expensive to make.

The most promising submission was the work of George Patchett, twenty guns being ordered from the Sterling Engineering Co. Ltd in January 1944. The Patchett proved to be simple and very reliable, defeating all its rivals in protracted experiments. Issued for troop trials in 1949, it was approved in 1951 as the

Submachine-gun, 9mm L2A1. Among its features were ribs on the bolt to minimize the effects of accumulated fouling, and use of the grip-bolt and cocking handle to remove the barrel.

The L2A1 was replaced by the essentially similar L2A2 in 1953; the parts were no longer used as dismantling tools, the folding butt was strengthened, the back sight and its operating lever were modified, a plunger was added to the bolt to prevent misassembly, and the chamber was modified. The perfected L2A3 of 1954 had a simpler butt, no back-sight change lever, a detachable trigger guard and standardized NATO chamber dimensions.

The L2A3 remains the standard British submachine-gun, having proved robust and unusually reliable. The standard gun measures 27in overall with its stock extended, has a 7·8in barrel and weighs about 6lb. It feeds from detachable 34-round box magazines and has a cyclic rate of 500–550rpm.

A Sterling with an integral silencer is currently issued for special service as the L34A1, replacing the Stens IIS and Mk 6. It is readily identifiable by the length and large diameter of the silencer body.

Auto-loading rifles

The quest to perfect an infantry rifle that would re-load automatically occupied many inventors in the closing years of the nineteenth century – inspired, no doubt, by the success of the Maxim machine-gun. Maxim had shown that auto-loading was practicable; indeed, had not his first experimental gun been a converted ·44–40 lever-action Winchester rifle?

The British, in common with most European armies, paid considerable attention to auto-loading smallarms without ever really intending to adopt one. Most pre-1914 ordnance departments were much too cautious to invest large sums of money in unproven weapons, unless forced to do so by events abroad. It was not that unreasonable specifications were issued, but simply that none of the rifles submitted could pass the tests required of standard bolt-action infantry rifles.

By 1914, smokeless propellant had been in existence for a mere thirty years; in British smallarms ammunition, cordite had been available for only twenty. Problems were still widely encountered with fouling, inconsistent pressure and barrel-wear. These were not particularly critical in manually operated guns, but were the difference between automatic mechanisms functioning efficiently and constantly jamming.

To avoid the problems of fouling, most inventors initially chose the force of recoil to drive their actions. However, moving barrels involved accurate machining, large bearing surfaces, excessive friction and rapid wear. Contemporary metallurgy was often unable to produce durable enough components; and poor detail-design ensured that weapons that were effectual in theory performed poorly out

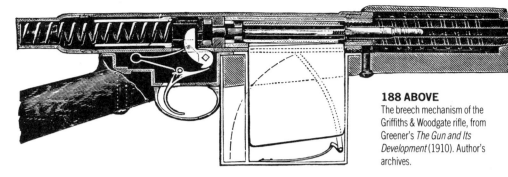

188 ABOVE
The breech mechanism of the Griffiths & Woodgate rifle, from Greener's *The Gun and Its Development* (1910). Author's archives.

on the ranges. By 1914, therefore, only the Mexicans had adopted an auto-loader – and then only in limited numbers, apparently for the president's guard and to enhance national prestige.*

The first self-loading rifle to be approved for issue was the 1896-type Madsen, issued in tiny quantities to the Danish navy and coastguard. The Madsen would undoubtedly have failed British troop trials comprehensively, but it was at least a starting point. During this period, however, the British authorities were disinterested. The promising recoil-operated Griffiths & Woodgate rifle, patented in 1894, a better design than many of its contemporaries and at least with the merits of a locked breech, had been rejected with a lack of enthusiasm amounting almost to contempt.

W.W. Greener, writing in *The Gun and Its Development* (1910), said of the Griffiths & Woodgate:

In the breech-shoe . . . the barrel and the breech-bolt are both free to slide, the shoe being stopped at the rear by a cap, and the forward movement of the barrel is regulated by a locking nut. In the breech-piece, there is the usual breech-bolt with extractor, the bolt being held up to the barrel by the spiral

spring at its base. The motion for opening the breech and extracting the cartridge-case is imparted by the recoil of the barrel, the locking nut holding barrel and breech together sufficiently long to prevent escape of gas at the breech, but with the travel of the barrel it [the locking nut] is turned by a cam on it engaging a stop in a slot, and then, the bolt being free, it is driven back, and the empty case is withdrawn and ejected. As soon as the bolt is released the barrel is stopped and returned to its position by a spring, and the recoiling breech-bolt has actuated mechanism of the usual type to feed another cartridge from the magazine, and, by the strength of the rear spring, is returned to its place, pushing the cartridge into the chamber as it travels.

The Italian Cei-Rigotti rifle, designed in 1895, was demonstrated to the Small Arms Committee at Enfield in March 1901. However, Cei-Rigotti's visit to Enfield proved a disappointment, as only a few 6·5mm cartridges were available. Three series of ten rounds were fired at a 24ft-wide target at a distance of 200 yards; the inventor fired ten rounds in nineteen seconds, including the time taken to clear a jam, but the accuracy was poor. The test was repeated by the Enfield Proof Master, who fired one round for practice and then nine for accuracy in seventeen seconds. Results

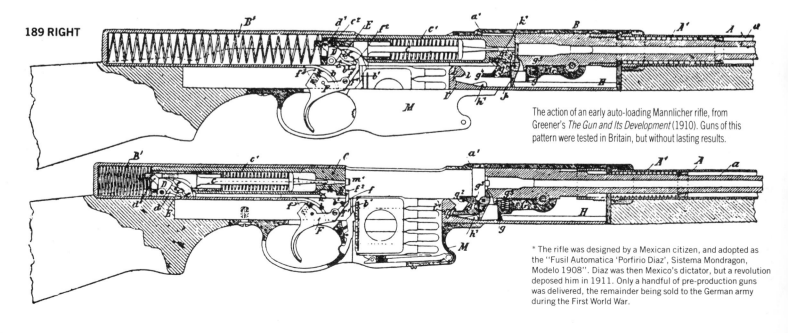

189 RIGHT

The action of an early auto-loading Mannlicher rifle, from Greener's *The Gun and Its Development* (1910). Guns of this pattern were tested in Britain, but without lasting results.

* The rifle was designed by a Mexican citizen, and adopted as the "Fusil Automatica 'Porfirio Diaz', Sistema Mondragon, Modelo 1908". Diaz was then Mexico's dictator, but a revolution deposed him in 1911. Only a handful of pre-production guns was delivered, the remainder being sold to the German army during the First World War.

†Apparently including the time taken to re-load.
‡This gun was designed by suspiciously German-sounding Karl August Brauning of Zaandam, in The Netherlands,

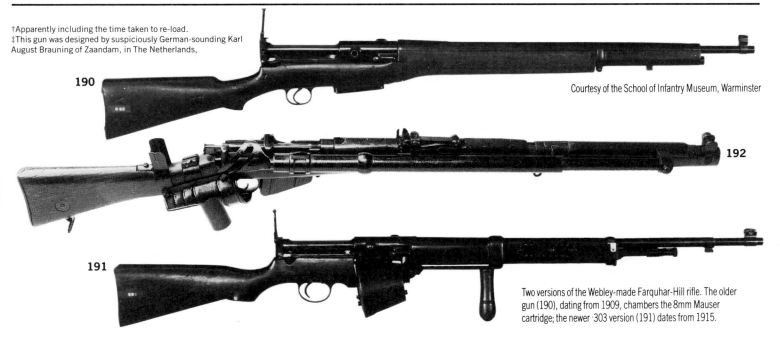

190

Courtesy of the School of Infantry Museum, Warminster

192

191

Two versions of the Webley-made Farquhar-Hill rifle. The older gun (190), dating from 1909, chambers the 8mm Mauser cartridge; the newer ·303 version (191) dates from 1915.

were judged good for such rapid fire. The rifle was then set to fire automatically, firing ten rounds in less than two seconds – but so wildly that two shots missed the target completely.

The Enfield representatives were worried by the comparatively high incidence of jams, but aware that only a longer test would show whether the Cei-Rigotti rifle held promise. However, it never reappeared in Britain.

A lull in submissions followed the trial of the Cei-Rigotti, though the British endeavoured to follow the progress of the fiendishly complicated Mauser rifles in Germany. A Friberg rifle, chambered for 6·5mm Swedish Mauser cartridges, was noted in 1905 and tested at Acton in February 1909; like many of the earliest designs, it performed well enough as a self-loader but was found wanting when operated manually. Excepting the Griffiths & Woodgate rifle, which was never given a fair chance, the first practicable indigenous development was the recoil-operated Farquhar-Hill. This rifle was demonstrated at the School of Musketry, Hythe, in 1908.

The Farquhar-Hill reappeared at Bisley in the summer of 1909, having been modified since the Hythe demonstration a year previously. A representative of the School of Musketry reported that 'several slight improvements [had been] made since the rifle was shown at Hythe, one being the removal from the bolt handle of the catch, which joints the bolt cover to the connecting rod; placing it at the side of the bolt cover. It is thus impossible for a man accidentally to detach the bolt cover from the return spring. The bolt has been reduced in length and as the inventor has been able to obtain better springs, a smaller spring can be used. The rifle is thus brought down to 8 lbs. 3 ozs. without boring lightening holes in the butt'.

The rifle fired 7·65mm rimless Belgian Mauser cartridges loaded with 180-grain round-nose bullets, and its five-round magazine was loaded through a hinged trap under the stock ahead of the trigger guard. To eliminate potentially erratic rim thickness, the cartridges had all been passed through the action before the trial. Consequently, the Farquhar-Hill performed with hardly a jam and attained a fire rate of 32 rounds per minute.†

Though the magazine was objectionable, the Small Arms Committee was quite impressed by the Farquhar-Hill even though – in its 1909 form – it was not acceptable for service. In August 1909, anxious to stimulate as many inventors as possible, the War Office circulated a memorandum listing the requirements for a forthcoming competition.

They were accompanied by a *Memorandum for Inventors*, which gave the Army Council the right to retain any 'designs, plans, drawings, models, samples, or papers' it pleased. The inventors were also required to bear 'the expense of the provision of the article, its carriage, fitting up and removal' in return for an uncertain future: 'any award which may be made will only be payable to the claimant when approved by the Treasury and money is available from funds voted by Parliament for such purposes'.

Countless inventors were willing to chance their luck, in spite of these strictures; each knew that success in the form of universal issue throughout the Empire would bring glory as well as financial rewards. As a result, the trials undertaken in 1910–14 were exhaustive examinations of dozens of rifles. Some were the work of inventors such as Major Farquhar; a few, such as the Danish Bang or Swedish Sjøgren, originated abroad; and others were submitted on behalf of well-

A Howell auto-loading SMLE Mk III* conversion, dating from c.1918. The gas-operated transformation was comparatively simple, but cumbersome and potentially unreliable. The unsupported cam-track used to revolve the bolt would have been a major weakness in service. Courtesy of the MoD Pattern Room Collection, Royal Ordnance plc, Nottingham; photograph by Ian Hogg.

established arms-making companies such as BSA and Vickers.

None of the guns performed acceptably, and work was still proceeding when the likelihood of war in Europe suspended trials for the duration. Much research has yet to be done before the story of the various participants is revealed; however, the story has little direct relevance to British service rifles. It suffices to note that the recoil-operated BSA was typical. Chambering 7mm Eley Special (·276) cartridges, it was tested by the Chief Inspector for Small Arms in April 1913 but rejected as very unreliable. The action locked by rotating the entire barrel through 45° to release the bolt. The gun had a charger-loaded 5 round magazine, measured 49⁵⁄₁₆in overall, had a 25¼in barrel and weighed 10lb 6oz – appreciably heavier than the 1910 specification. An improved rifle was tested in July 1913, only to be rejected on the grounds that it could not be used manually.

Shortly before the First World War began, the Small Arms Committee considered two rifles submitted on behalf of Fabrique Nationale d'Armes de Guerre of Herstal-lèz-Liége in Belgium, and a Mexican Mondragon made by Fabrique d'Armes de Neuhausen (now better known as SIG). The FN rifles were both recoil operated, but differed in their rifling. One, recorded as a 'Brauning',‡ was regarded favourably by the commiittee except for loss of velocity and discoloration on the ejected cartridge cases when the gun was

193—6 ABOVE

Four experimental auto-loading rifles, all originally in the BSA reference collection. **A** An experimental rifle chambering the 7·9mm German service cartridge, but unmarked except for its Krupp-steel barrel. Believed to be a Swedish-designed Sjøgren, it has multiple locking lugs on the rotating bolt head and a recoil-absorbing butt plate. The Sjøgren was just one of many designs tested in Britain prior to 1914. **B** The ·303 Adams, made by BSA for the Fairfax Rifle Syndicate in the early 1920s. Gas is tapped from the right side of the breech and impinges on a small piston on the front right side of the bolt. This gun lacks its detachable box magazine and the original aperture back sight. **C** A light ·303 BSA-Thompson, incorporating a Blish-type hesitation lock in which steeply pitched buttress threads on the bolt engage a bronze lock-nut. The lock was marginal, and the Thompsons required lubricated cartridges to function effectually. This particular gun, numbered '3', has an adjustable aperture back sight on the breech. **D** This heavyweight BSA-Thompson, numbered '6', incorporates a similar action to the preceding wepon and oil-soaked lubricating pads in the magazine sides. It has a folding bipod at the muzzle and a perforated sheet-steel hand guard above the fore-end. Note the distinctive aperture back sight. Courtesy of Weller & Dufty Ltd, Birmingham.

firing semi-automatically. This was suspected to be due to the breech opening too rapidly.

The Mondragon was not tested, possibly owing to the absence of suitable 7mm Mauser ammunition when the Small Arms Committee visited the Enfield factory on 12 May 1914. However, gas operation was not especially favoured in this period. A captured Mondragon with a German drum magazine was tested by the School of Musketry during the First World War, the report praising its handiness, simplicity and accuracy – but opining, correctly, that the rifle was too fragile for military purposes. A similar opinion would undoubtedly have been forthcoming in 1914.

March 1914 saw a trial of two ·276 Tatareks, based on P/13 rifles. Converting Tatarek rifles to manual operation was comparatively simple – though not, as one examiner discovered, when the barrel was hot – but they

had such a proliferation of rods and springs, not to mention a strange bicycle-like chain disappearing into the butt, that they were exceptionally unreliable. As the official report spoke of them being 'complicated, weak, bulky, excessively heavy, badly balanced, uncertain in action, liable to derangement under the most favourable circumstances, liable to break down, difficult to strip and more difficult to assemble', the consensus was that the Tatarek system had nothing to commend it.

So, despite all the efforts of the Small Arms Committee, the British Army went to war in 1914 with the Lee-Enfield. Experiments with auto-loading rifles continued throughout the hostilities. Several variants of the Farquhar-Hill were submitted, while a Chauchat Machine Rifle appeared in December 1915. Adopted by the French army, and later by the

American Expeditionary Force, the Chauchat was rejected. It did not fulfil the conditions for a British automatic rifle, being much too heavy; judged as a light machine-gun, it was considerably inferior to the Lewis.

Armistice in November 1918 was followed by the demobilization of the conscript armies, by a wholesale reduction in arms-making, and by a feeling that the world had at last endured the 'war to end wars'. Many promising projects met an untimely end, and research returned to its leisurely peacetime footing.

The British still toyed with auto-loading rifles, the success of the Browning Automatic Rifle providing sufficient encouragement (even though it was much too heavy to fulfil War Department requirements). By December 1919, however, only two rifles remained in contention: the Farquhar-Hill, which had been struggling gamely against official apathy since 1908, and a gas-operated rifle developed at Enfield.

The 1918 version of the Farquhar-Hill had a ten-round drum magazine permanently attached to the rifle. One odd feature was that three dummy cartridges were welded into the magazine, one to the front and rear sprockets and the others linked to the lower sprocket alone. The uppermost dummy doubled as a cartridge platform and hold-open. The rifle performed creditably in its trials, but was too lightly built to survive the rigours of active service. Its most obvious feature was a forward pistol grip.

Trials were undertaken during the 1920s with several new rifles, including the Browne-Adams and its successor, the Fairfax-Adams. Several types of Thompson were made under licence by BSA, while Farquhar-Hills were the work of Webley & Scott. The gas-operated Enfield rifle soon fell by the wayside.

In the autumn of 1927, a competition was arranged between the BSA-made Thompson, a Colt-made Thompson supplied by BSA, an improved BSA-Thompson, a gas-operated BSA, the BSA-Adams and a Farquhar-Hill. The report, submitted on 30 May 1928, indicated that the the BSA-made Thompson narrowly beat the 'improved' BSA-Thompson with the Farquhar-Hill third; the BSA-Adams and the gas-operated rifles had been excluded on safety grounds. Not surprisingly, after submitting five of the six triallists, BSA received first prize of £3,000. However, the Small Arms Committee opined that none of the submissions was suited to service. Contemporary experiments in the USA had rejected the delayed-blowback Thompson rifles on the grounds that they were cumbersome, complicated and unreliable.*

The remainder of the 1928–35 period saw even less experimentation than before, though submissions were still made by hopeful promoters. The Pedersen toggle-lock rifle, which

was effectual enough to be tentatively adopted by the US Army before the ·276 and ·30 Garands were perfected, was submitted in 1929. Two guns were made by Vickers, and 20,000 cartridges by Kynoch. The ·276 Pedersen round had a rimless 2·018in necked case loaded with a 125-grain jacketed spitzer bullet. Muzzle velocity was about 2,700fs⁻¹, which gave a muzzle energy substantially less than that of the service ·303. However, the British-made Pedersen passed its trials sufficiently well to undergo more extensive trials in 1931–3; Vickers subsequently made at least two hundred rifles and a handful of elegant carbines, ammunition coming from Kynoch and Greenwood & Batley.† The project eventually foundered, as it was bound to do once the British realised that the ·30 T3E2 Garand would be standardized in the US Army. The Pedersen was difficult to mass produce, owing to the sophisticated machining required by its toggle-lock; and the waxed cartridge case necessary to ensure extraction was anathema to the military mind. The action was also prone to jamming if mud and dust entered the open toggle, and the rising toggle was apt to strike the firer's helmet.

As even an M1 Garand failed the standard British dust test, it is evident that the Small Arms Committee had very high standards.

* The Thompson rifle embodied a form of hesitation lock in which, or so it was claimed, the friction between two differing metals under pressure held the breech closed until pressure had dropped. The lock is generally regarded as marginal, at best; the Thompson breech leaked gas and the ejection was so violent that the mouths of cartridge cases could stick into wood planks placed close to the gun. It is indicative not so much of the paucity of the 1920-period designs, but rather of the influence of well-established manufacturers and high-profile designers.

†The ·276 Pedersen cartridge, without its wax coat, also chambered in the White rifle. Designed by J.C. White, an employee of the United Shoe Company of Boston, Massachussetts, this was submitted to the US Army in September 1929 and underwent an encouraging test in the autumn of 1930. It appeared in Britain in 1931 with no lasting results.

197 ABOVE

The open breech of the Vickers-Pedersen rifle, brilliantly conceived and elegantly made – but irredeemably flawed by the absence of a breech lock. Like all hesitation blowbacks, it also required lubricated cartridges to operate smoothly. Courtesy of the MoD Pattern Room Collection, Royal Ordnance plc, Nottingham; photograph by Ian Hogg.

Against this background, Italian Scotti, Hungarian Kiralý and an assortment of competing auto-loaders had little chance of success. When war began in 1939, the British Army simply went to war with the Lee-Enfield once again!

THE FIRST BULLPUPS

The story of these most interesting guns, with their magazines behind the trigger group, dates back to the Second South African War. The ·303 Gamwell, Godsal and Thorneycroft rifles all attempted to provide a short rifle to compete against the first SMLE.

Like many other guns of their type, the earliest bullpups were awkward and uncomfortable to handle. This was caused by placing the magazine in the stock immediately behind the trigger. Separate pistol grips were not acceptable in those days, as they prevented use of a full-length cavalry scabbard.

The bullpup concept lay dormant until, during the Second World War, attempts were made in Britain to develop sniper rifles loaded by retracting the pistol grip. This prevented visible movement of the Lee-Enfield bolt; it may also have owed something to the cocking system incorporated in the Besa machine-gun.

Nothing came of the sniper rifles, nor of the Hall Rifle. A patent for this odd looking auto-

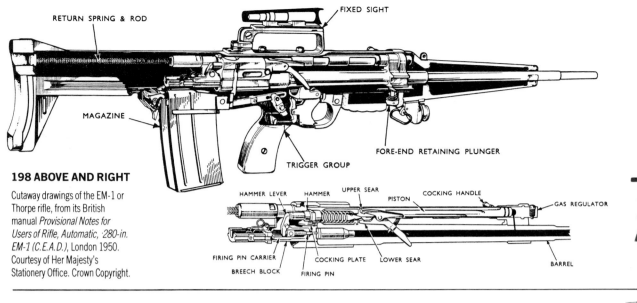

RETURN SPRING & ROD

FIXED SIGHT

MAGAZINE

TRIGGER GROUP

FORE-END RETAINING PLUNGER

HAMMER LEVER · HAMMER · UPPER SEAR · PISTON · COCKING HANDLE · GAS REGULATOR

FIRING PIN CARRIER · COCKING PLATE · LOWER SEAR · BARREL

BREECH BLOCK · FIRING PIN

198 ABOVE AND RIGHT

Cutaway drawings of the EM-1 or Thorpe rifle, from its British manual *Provisional Notes for Users of Rifle, Automatic, ·280-in. EM-1 (C.E.A.D.)*, London 1950. Courtesy of Her Majesty's Stationery Office. Crown Copyright.

loader was sought by an Australian infantry officer in February 1945, but the project was abandoned in 1947 after only a single prototype had been made.

When the first NATO standardization talks were held in 1946, the subject of a common cartridge and the future infantry rifle – grandiloquently renamed 'Infantry Personal Weapon' – was raised. The British were already championing an experimental ·280 cartridge; and the US Army had objected to it as early as May 1947.

By the beginning of 1948, the British were considering three ·280 rifles: the EM-1 (Thorpe), EM-2 (Januszewski, later 'Janson') and the abortive EM-3 (Hall).*

The ·280 EM-1 Thorpe rifle, codenamed 'Cobra' in the early days of development, was based on captured German Stg.06 (Mauser) prototypes. It was gas operated, roller-locked and made largely of sheet-metal pressings. The gun was 36in overall and weighed about 9lb 7oz without its twenty-round detachable box magazine. Cyclic rate was about 600rpm, and the automatic hold-open was tripped each time a fresh magazine was inserted in the feedway.

The prototype was proved at Enfield in December 1949. Three guns were readied for trials in the USA in the late autumn of 1950, but the lighter EM-2 was preferred.

Like the Thorpe rifle, the ·280 EM-2 ('Mamba' or 'Yellow Acorn') began life in the autumn of 1947 with a series of hand-made prototypes. Designed by a team headed by Stefan Januszewski,† it was eventually patented in August 1951. Five experimental guns were made at Cheshunt and Enfield, and then twenty 'semi-production' guns appeared in

time for NATO trials at Aberdeen Proving Ground in February–April 1950.

The trials were uninspiring. Official reports were critical of all three submissions – EM-2, FAL and T25. The EM-2 was particularly criticized for its complex action and the poor accuracy of ·280 ball ammunition. Fired from Mann test barrels, the British bullet performed much worse than the US ·30 T104 design. As it also had appreciably less hitting power, the US Army was singularly unimpressed.

First-model EM-2 rifles were 35in long, had 24·5in barrels and weighed 7lb 13oz without their magazines or bipods. They had twenty-round detachable box magazines and a cyclic rate of about 625rpm. In common with the three Thorpe (EM-1) rifles, they had permanently attached non-magnifying optical sights set into the carrying handle.

The British government compounded the problems by approving the EM-2 for service as the Rifle 7mm No.9 Mk 1, a decision announced in Parliament on 25 April 1951. The US Army, backed by the French, adamantly refused to accept the ·280 cartridge – 'Cartridge, Ball, Small Arm, 7mm Mk 1Z' – as a suitable NATO standard. In addition, the Belgians were making such rapid progress that even a British technical commission appointed in the Spring of 1951 had greatly favoured the FAL at the expense of the EM-2. British user trials in July 1951 had been tied, but the uncommitted view was that the FAL had greater development potential. Its breech mechanism, which relied on a tilting block adapted from the Soviet Tokarev, was far simpler than the complex flap-lock of the EM-2.

The NATO Weapons Standardization Conference in Washington DC, 2–3 August 1951, revealed deep divisions among the principal allies. The US and French representatives again refused to accept the British ·280 cartridge, while Canada agreed to abide by a majority decision. Eventually, exasperated by

---

* There was also an 7·92mm EM-1, or Korsac light machinegun. Designed by emigré Poles attached to the Small Arms Group at Cheshunt, and derived from the German FG.42, it had an 18-round box magazine vertically behind the pistol grip. Two guns were made at Enfield in 1945.
†Later naturalized as Stephen Kenneth Janson.

A typical early EM-2 rifle, made by the Royal Small Arms Factory at Enfield in 1950. Note the combined non-magnifying optical sight and carrying handle, and the way in which the bayonet pommel swivels. This particular gun is numbered '18' on the receiver. Courtesy of Ian Hogg.

Anglo-American deadlock, the Canadian government refused to ship weapons to Europe until the calibre problem had been resolved.

BSA made a handful of EM-2 guns for the ·30 T65 cartridge, and Enfield then made fifteen similar No.9 X1E1 rifles. But the project was doomed.

A general election took place in Britain in 1951, returning a Conservative government. Winston Churchill immediately rescinded the approval of the EM-2 (25 October 1951), amidst allegations of duplicity and American

200 RIGHT
HM Queen Elizabeth II inspects a guard of honour formed by men of the Royal Regiment of Wales during a visit to Cardiff in 1977. They all carry L1A1 rifles. Author's archives.

201 BELOW
A man of the Welsh Guards sights his L1A1 rifle during a patrol in the Lower Falls, Belfast, in the summer of 1986. Note the plastic bag around the magazine. Courtesy of the Ministry of Defence.

influence. The truth of the situation is still far from clear.

Though the introduction of the EM-2 had been cancelled, work still continued. No concord was reached at another standardization conference in November 1951, and the US army formally rejected the ·280 British cartridge on 5 January 1952. Three ·30 T65 EM-2 rifles were to have been submitted to trials at Aberdeen Proving Ground in 1952, but were withdrawn before the competition began. Finally, in December 1953, the British Army signalled defeat by ordering 5,000 FAL rifles for troop trials.

A few EM-2 guns were made in the HV ('High Velocity') series by Chambons Tool Company of Hammersmith, at least one subsequently being chambered for the full-power ·30−06 round, and ten emanated from Canadian Arsenals in 7×51. Fifteen No.9 X1E2‡ prototypes were ordered from BSA in 1952, but only a few were made before the whole project was scrapped in 1953. It had cost the British taxpayer about £250,000.

The EM-2 was an interesting weapon, and its controversial history makes it doubly so. However, as only a little over fifty were made, its significance is comparatively minor. Though the design was undoubtedly capable of development, adopting the complicated flap-lock system instead of a simpler rotating bolt was mistaken.

‡X1E2 rifles lacked the selective-fire facility of their predecessors, as the problems of firing even ·280 cartridges from the lightweight EM-2 had proved insuperable.

THE BRITISH FAL

Abandoning the EM-2 cleared the way for the FN FAL to become the standard British Army infantry rifle. The 5,000 guns ordered in 1953 were delivered for troop trials in 1955, in two differing models. The trials confirmed that the

gun was most effectual, and it was adopted in 1957 as the Rifle, 7·62mm, L1A1. Production contracts were given to the Royal Small Arms Factory at Enfield, the Royal Ordnance Factory at Fazakerley, and BSA Guns Ltd in Shirley.

The L1A1 is a conventional gas-operated auto-loader, locked by displacing the lower back edge of the breech block downward into a well in the receiver floor immediately behind the magazine. The protoype, based on the Russian Tokarev, was made shortly before the Germans invaded Belgium. It was then developed into the 'SLEM'* by refugee Belgian technicians working during the Second World War at the Royal Small Arms Factory, Enfield, and with the Small Arms Group at Cheshunt. The SLEM became the postwar ABL/SAFN rifle, and was then adapted into the FAL.

Several important changes were made for British service, including the removal of the selective fire capability. As many armies have

202 ABOVE
A marine from 45 Commando poses during Exercise Cold Winter 81 with his night sight, fitted to a standard L1A1 rifle. Note that the sight is fitted with a blinder to prevent the glare of the snow burning out the imaging elements. Courtesy of the Royal Marines Museum, Eastney.

discovered, firing full-power cartridges automatically from a gun weighing only 5kg simply wastes ammunition.

The new folding cocking handle was moved to the left side of the action, allowing the firer to keep his finger near the trigger while re-cocking the gun, and shallow grooves were

* Rifle 'Self-Loading, Enfield Model'.

203 BELOW
A specially sectioned L1A1 rifle showing the parts made in the BSA factory in Shirley, on the outskirts of Birmingham. Courtesy of Weller & Dufty Ltd, Birmingham.

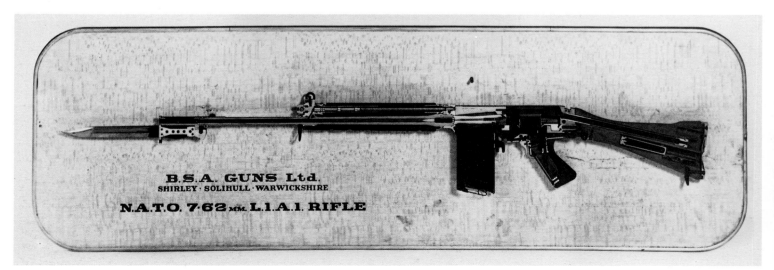

B.S.A. GUNS Ltd.
SHIRLEY · SOLIHULL · WARWICKSHIRE
N.A.T.O. 7·62ᴍᴍ. L.1.A.1. RIFLE

cut in the bolt carrier to allow a limited accumulation of fouling. Unlike some of its Belgian prototypes, the L1A1 magazine cannot be loaded through the action.

The earliest rifles had wooden furniture, but this was changed to black nylonite – a durable plastic – in the early 1960s. Four lengths of butt plate are available to adjust the butts to suit individual firers. Standard L1A1 rifles measure about 1,143mm overall, have 554mm barrels and weigh 4·38kg empty.

Though conventional open sights are standard, soldiers with marksmanship ability have always been encouraged to acquire the L2A1 or L2A2 'Sights, Unit, Infantry, Trilux'. However, an L1A1 with a laden twenty-round magazine and a 4× SUIT weighs an appreciable 5·51kg. Adding the 3·75× Infantry Weapon Sight L1A2 – a first-generation SS20 Type 2 image-intensifier made by Rank Pullin Controls – raises the weight to an excessive 7·85kg.

Several attempts have been made to turn the FAL into a sniper rifle, most recently with the Royal Ordnance 'Pearcen', but the design of the locking mechanism is not compatible with extreme accuracy. Though the rifle is sturdy and very reliable, it does not have the pin-point hitting capability of the issue L42A1 (Lee-Enfield) and L96A1 (Accuracy International) bolt-action weapons.

L1A1 accessories include a ·22 rimfire Conversion Set L12A1, made by Heckler & Koch,† the L1A3/L1A4 bayonet series, an L1A2 grenade launcher, and L1A2 or L6A1 blank-firing attachments.

†This displaced a semi-experimental British-made predecessor.

THE MODERN BULLPUPS

Though the L1A1 rifle had been giving good service since the late 1950s, the advent of the small-calibre 5·56mm M16 rifle – ironically accepted by the US Army after a complete about-face – forced a reassessment.

British experiments with small-calibre cartridges began again in the late 1960s. Almost immediately, mistakes that had led to the ·280 round and the EM-2 were repeated; instead of accepting that the 5·56mm round was effectual enough for service, minimizing development costs, the British tested a 6·25×43 pattern in 1969–71.

It is difficult to judge, on the basis of available evidence, whether these experiments arose simply from reluctance to accept an American development in revenge for the EM-2 debacle or from a desire to produce a better compromise.

The 6·25mm round – a 92–95 grain bullet in a necked ·280 case – was potentially excellent, as it was intermediate between the 5·56mm and 7·62×51 rounds; it promised to be accurate, and had better hitting power (and a longer effective range) than the US M193 ball. However, it was heavier than the 5·56mm pattern and thoughts turned instead to lightening the rifleman's burden. A 5×44 cartridge appeared in October 1970; renamed '4·85×44' in 1972 and given a 49mm case in 1973 before being perfected, more than a million rounds were expended during development trials.

The project team was initially led by Lieutenant-Colonel John Weeks, responsibility for the rifle being given to Sydney Hance. As Hance had been intimately connected with the EM-2, it was no surprise that the new Infantry weapon ('IW') resembled the old ·280 rifle externally.

Internally, it was very different. The complex flap-lock was replaced by a rotating multi-lug bolt inspired by the Armalite series – indeed, the first trial models were simply AR-18 and Stoner 63 rifles adapted to bullpup configuration. On 14 July 1976, after a selection of prototypes had been made, the British Army unveiled the new guns to a curious public.

Some onlookers were unconvinced. René Laloux, the guiding hand behind the success of the FAL, wrote critically of the IW's defects. Laloux had a vested interest. There were those in Britain who felt that the simplest and cheapest option was to adapt the 5·56mm FN Carabine Automatique Légère instead of wasting time and money on the 4·85mm IW.

The 4·85mm project eventually developed into four basic guns – two Infantry Weapons designated XL64E5 and XL68E2, with right- and left-hand ejection respectively, and two comparable Light Support Weapons (XL65E4 and XL69E1). The XL64 and XL65 were promptly entered in NATO standardization trials beginning in April 1977. There were bullpups – the British guns and the strange French 5·56mm FAMAS – plus the extraordinary 4·75mm caseless-cartridge Heckler & Koch G11. Conventional weaponry was represented by the Belgian 5·56mm FNC, successor to the CAL; by the Galil-based Dutch 5·56mm MN-1; and by the US 5·56mm M16A1, which acted as the control weapon.

Surprisingly, the trials led to the standardization of the Belgian SS109 5·56mm ball at the expense of the US M193. The M16A1 magazine and the French grenade launcher were also

204 LEFT

A camouflaged soldier aims an XL70E3, a pre-production version of the L85A1 (SA-80) rifle, fitted with a Rank Pullin SS80 image-intensifying night sight. Courtesy of Rank Pullin Controls Ltd.

approved, leaving the British 4·85mm weapons isolated.

By the early 1980s, the Infantry Weapon had acquired a simplified receiver with a notably straight under-edge. It was also re-chambered for the 5·56mm round, dimensionally similar to 4·85×49. The result was the 5·56mm XL70E3. Renamed 'SA-80' for commercial sale, it has since been adopted as the 5·56mm Rifle L85A1. The XL73E2 LSW has become the 'L86A1' (q.v.).

The L85A1 remains controversial, though its 4X 'Sight, Unit, Small Arms, Trilux, L9A1' (SUSAT) and small size have been universally welcomed. Severe teething troubles have arisen from poor quality control, removal of Enfield to Nottingham, and troubles with sub-contractors. None of this should be too surprising, as virtually every British service weapon (cf., Martini-Henry, Lee-Metford, SMLE) has had its share of troubles.

Though widely regarded as inferior to the Steyr AUG, the L85 will eventually be developed into an effectual and battle-worthy weapon. Whether the result justifies capital outlay and so many years of development is another matter.

Machine-guns

The American Civil War inspired the development of many 'battery guns', several of which were tested in Britain. Even before the war, in 1860, a gun submitted by Colonel Wilson had been tried at Woolwich. It had been followed by a Palmer design and the Vandenburgh Volley Gun in 1862, and then, four years later, by the Dupuis & Warlow. A Claxton Rifle Battery had been tried in 1868.

THE GATLING GUNS

A Colt-made Gatling Gun was submitted to the War Office in February 1867 but, after tests against a 9pr field-gun, was rejected as 'unsuited for service'. However, after a favourable report on the Montigny Mitrailleuse, a committee was formed to test machine-guns in 1869.

Trials were undertaken at Shoeburyness in the summer of 1870, pitting ·42, ·65 and 1-inch Gatlings against breech- and muzzle-loading field-guns, the Montigny Mitrailleuse and a selection of infantry rifles. Predictably, they showed that the Gatling was a much handier and more flexible weapon.

On 28 October 1870, the committee recommended adopting the Gatling for field and ship-board use. However, as the Director of Artillery initially took the view that utility of the machine-guns was limited, the order for 48 ·45 and ·65-calibre Armstrong-made guns* was delayed until the beginning of 1872. Delivered from January 1874 onward, all but twelve were given to the Royal Navy. The remainder were initially at Woolwich.†

Service abroad, particularly in the Asante War of 1873–4, showed that the guns' utility on land was limited by the clumsy wheeled carriages; in addition, they jammed in hot and sandy climates. This has often been blamed on rolled-case ammunition but, excepting an early prototype or two, all British Gatlings chambered solid-drawn cartridges. The problems were attributable partly to mechanical failure and partly to the extractors tearing through the cartridge rims. Longstaff & Atteridge, in *The Book of the Machine Gun*, record that in a trial of Gatlings in the 1870s, the theoretical rate of fire of 500–700rpm dropped to about 280 once stoppages had been taken into account:

'Almost every minute produced some interruption of the firing, owing to the sticking of the cartridge which failed to reach its proper barrel, or of a case which became jammed in the mechanism after leaving it.'

The ·45-calibre Gatlings each had a cluster of several barrels (generally six or ten) mounted on a central spindle. The receiver casing contained a breech-block and firing mechanism for each barrel, plus the loading mechanism and the extractor. The earliest metal-case cartridge guns fed from a gravity magazine (Broadwell Drum) above the breech casing, though some later examples had the spring-powered Accles Positive Feed.

A crank handle protruded from the right side of the mechanism. When the handle was turned, the entire barrel cluster rotated with it. As each barrel passed the uppermost or twelve o'clock position, a cartridge dropped into the breech; as the barrel cluster turned, the cartridge was rammed home, the breech shut, and the striker released when the barrel was in its lowermost position (generally about five o'clock, depending on the number of barrels). The spent case was extracted as the barrel rotated upward, to receive another fresh round at the end of its cycle.

The Gun, Gatling, ·45 (Mark I) was the first successful weapon of its type in British service. It was issued with the Trail Mk I and horse-drawn Limber Mk I (Loc 3322), the equipment weighing about 1,450lb.

* Twelve ·45 guns for the army, plus twelve ·45 and 24 ·65 for the navy.
† Even these were subsequently given to the navy, indicating the low esteem in which the army hierarchy held machine-guns.

THE NORDENFELT GUN

A three-barrel Nordenfelt Gun was offered to the Committee on Machine Guns in 1875;

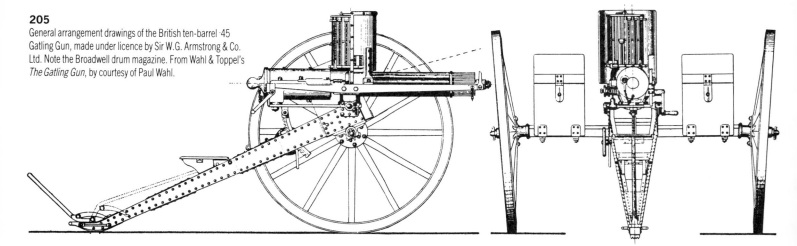

205
General arrangement drawings of the British ten-barrel ·45 Gatling Gun, made under licence by Sir W.G. Armstrong & Co. Ltd. Note the Broadwell drum magazine. From Wahl & Toppel's *The Gatling Gun*, by courtesy of Paul Wahl.

designed by a Swedish engineer, Heldge Palm-crantz and financed by Thorsten Nordenfelt, the guns were licensed to Temple & Co. of London. The parts were originally made in a factory in Carlsvik, near Stockholm.

The Nordenfelt had an unusual action, worked by a reciprocating handle rather than a rotary crank. Retracting the operating handle first moved the action block laterally (to the left) and then withdrew the breech pieces through the displaced action block. As this happened, spent cases dropped out of the bottom of the receiver. As the lever continued

backward, the strikers were cocked and the cartridge carrier-block positioned beneath the feed-ways. Fresh cartridges dropped into the block. Returning the lever moved the carrier block to the right until the cartridges aligned with the barrels. The cartridges were then pushed forward into the chamber as the breech pieces returned; finally, the action block was moved to the right to lock the mechanism, and a projection on the trigger comb struck the standing frame. This fired the barrels sequentially, though the action was quick enough to be indistinguishable.

206 BELOW

A five-barrel ·45 Nordenfelt Gun on a naval pedestal mount. The gun is operated by the handle protruding beneath the receiver directly below the magazine. Pulled to the rear, the lever opens the breech and ejects the spent cases; pushed forward, it reloads, locks the action and fires all five barrels.

Courtesy of the MoD Pattern Room Collection, Royal Ordnance plc, Nottingham.

In March 1875, the Captain of HMS *Excellent* reported to the Machine Gun Committee that trials of the Nordenfelt and Gatling guns had favoured the former. He recommended the purchase of fifty 1in-calibre guns and the development of a suitable cartridge. The matter dragged on for several years until, on 3 April 1878, the Director of Artillery suggested that the Admiralty should purchase the Nordenfelts directly. Inspection would be arranged with a view to sealing a pattern for Land Service at a later date.

Trials, meanwhile, continued with Armstrong Improved Gatlings.‡ *Excellent* suggested that a version chambering service ammunition should be obtained for trials against the 1in Nordenfelt.

On 30 December 1878, a new committee was formed under the presidency of Captain Colomb RN to investigate the many patterns of machine-gun that were being touted. A specificiation was soon issued, requesting that submissions should fire the standard drawn case ·45 Gatling cartridge; be equally suitable for Land and Sea Service; should be crewed by no more than three men; must be able to fire two hundred rounds in 30 seconds; and should sustain rapid fire for not less than a thousand rounds.

Large-scale tests were undertaken in the late summer of 1879, with a two-barrel Gardner, five- and ten-barrel Nordenfelts, an eight barrel Armstrong, a six-barrel Armstrong Improved Gatling, a Lowell Battery Gun, a Coleman-Gardner, a Tranter and a Hotchkiss.

Weird and wonderful designs – including the 100-barrel Brandt Mitrailleur – were rejected unfired.

The Gardner, the Nordenfelts and the Improved Gatling were sent for extended shooting trials at Shoeburyness, but none met expectations. Poor quality ammunition was deemed largely to blame. A new solid-drawn ·45 necked cartridge was developed from the previous ·45 Gatling in an effort to improve reliability. Specifications changed slightly. Guns were now to be exchangeable between Land and Naval Service; worked by no more

‡The Armstrong Improved Gatling is suspected to have been a 'Bulldog' pattern, introduced in the USA in 1877. Its barrels would have been enclosed in a bronze casing — with only the muzzle protruding — and the crank handle was attached directly to the barrel-cluster axis instead of operating through gears. Consequently, the Bulldog had a rate of fire approaching 1,000rpm.

207 BELOW

A five-barrel manually operated ·45 Gardner Gun dating, in this case, from 1882. Note the feed arrangements and the large rotary crank handle protruding from the right side of the breech. Courtesy of the MoD Pattern Room Collection, Royal Ordnance plc, Nottingham.

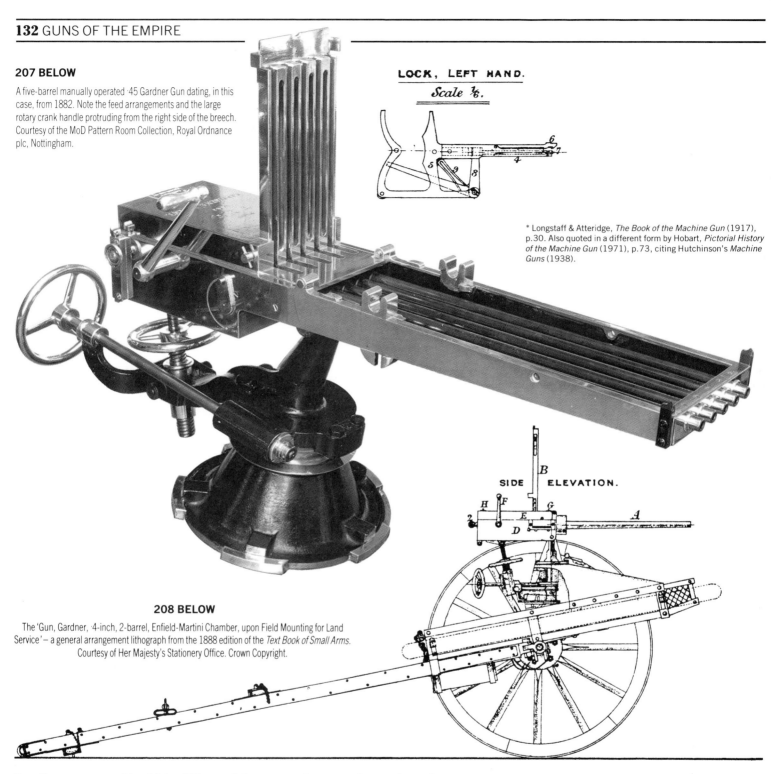

LOCK, LEFT HAND.
Scale ⅙.

* Longstaff & Atteridge, *The Book of the Machine Gun* (1917), p.30. Also quoted in a different form by Hobart, *Pictorial History of the Machine Gun* (1971), p.73, citing Hutchinson's *Machine Guns* (1938).

SIDE ELEVATION.

208 BELOW

The 'Gun, Gardner, ·4-inch, 2-barrel, Enfield-Martini Chamber, upon Field Mounting for Land Service' – a general arrangement lithograph from the 1888 edition of the *Text Book of Small Arms*. Courtesy of Her Majesty's Stationery Office. Crown Copyright.

than three men; capable of firing 200 rounds in 30 seconds; and to sustain rapid fire for at least a thousand rounds.

On 22 July 1880, however, the Gun, Nordenfelt, 0·45-inch, 3-barrel, Martini-Henry Chamber (Mark I) and Mark II had been introduced to Naval Service. Vice-Admiral Boys became President of the Machine Gun Committee in January 1880, and work continued in a leisurely manner. By March 1881, triallists included six- and ten-barrel Gatlings; a ten-barrel 'side action' Gatling; five- and ten-barrel Nordenfelts; two- and five-barrel Gardners; and the four-barrel Pratt & Whitney. After

extensive experimentation, the committee recommended the two-barrel ·45 Gardner for general service and the five-barrel pattern for special service. According to *Instructions to Armourers* (1912), there were then four types of Nordenfelt remaining in British service: two- and four-barrel 1-inch guns; a three-barrel ·303 version, converted from ·45; and ·45 five-barrel Mks I and II.

THE GARDNER GUN

Patented in the USA in 1874 by its inventor, William Gardner of Toledo, Ohio, the Gardner Gun had fixed barrels. The breech mechanism consisted of a crank and a reciprocating breech block. Assuming the right-hand barrel had been fired, rotating the crank handle then rotated the relevant hammer, drew back the striker and compressed the striker spring. Concurrently, the cartridge carrier moved to the left and the ejector – which had passed under the lock – rose to form a trough to receive a new cartridge. The crank pin then struck the butt of the lock and extracted the spent case. Once the lock piece had been drawn back to its farthest extent, the cartridge carrier moved back to the right and aligned a new round with the chamber. As the operating crank was rotated, the lock piece moved forward and rode over the ejector. When the breech was properly closed, the hammer was automatically released to hit the striker head and fire the chambered round.

Careful attention to development gradually increased the fire-rate of the basic Gardner mechanism until some of the barrels could be discarded. Eventually, single-barrel versions were manufactured, though the earliest weapons had offered five.

Substantial quantities of Gardner Guns were acquired, even though the navy was still advocating the Nordenfelt. By the end of March 1884, according to the 1883/4 budget, the Royal Navy was to have 565 Nordenfelts, 350 Gardners and 142 Gatlings. Yet guns were still in short supply in Land Service. The Director of Artillery had to borrow five ·45 naval five-barrel Gatlings on Travelling Carriages to accompany the Bechuanaland expedition in 1884, and then six two-barrel guns for the Suakin Expedition of 1885. The two-barrel guns were mounted on field carriages and accompanied by 100,000 ·45 rounds.

209 BELOW

Taken during an armourers course at the Royal Small Arms Factory, Enfield, c.1910, this photograph shows (left to right) a two-barrel ·45 Gardner Gun, a ·303 water-cooled Maxim and a three-barrel Nordenfelt converted to ·303. Courtesy of the MoD Pattern Room Collection, Royal Ordnance plc, Nottingham.

In the Spring of 1885, the Machine Gun Committee finally settled on a tripod-mounted single barrel Gardner Gun for Land Service. The gun, mount and ammunition were to form a single mule-load weighing no more than 200lb. A two-barrel gun on a light wheeled carriage, with trail shafts, was to be developed for special purposes.

An order for two single-barrel Gardners was passed to Enfield on 15 July 1885 but, eventually, four were acquired from the Gardner Gun Company instead. Two wheeled Nordenfelt carriages were purchased from Temple & Company and adapted at Enfield for the Gardners. But controversy still raged: Lord Wolseley had stated a preference for the Nordenfelt over the Gardner, owing to troubles with the latter during the Suakin Expedition, whereas the Secretary of State for War countered that the Gardner had been approved by the Commander-in-Chief in India over both Nordenfelt and Gatling.

It was decided to send four Gardner guns to Aldershot for trials with infantry battalions and a cavalry regiment. Two were mounted on Enfield-designed carriages, and the others on converted Nordenfelts. A new specification included a calibre of ·4; sights to 3,000 yards; a bore axis 3ft 6in above the ground; a lightweight steel carriage, weighing no more than 5cwt (560lb) with the gun, and capable of carrying not less than 1,500 rounds in boxes. The limber was to weigh no more than 15cwt; it was required to carry 4,000−5,000 rounds and seat two men. The ammunition cart, to weigh no more than a ton, held 10,000 rounds.

The immediate result was the approval of the Gun, Gardner, ·4-inch, 2-barrel, Enfield Martini Chamber, survivors of which were converted for the ·45 solid-drawn Martini-Henry cartridge in the 1890s.

That the machine-gun was still seen as light artillery was implicit in the horse-drawn carriage, limber and ammunition cart. However, the equipment did not meet with universal approval during the Aldershot trials. Many senior infantrymen, for example, wanted a simple tripod mount.

The Adjutant General requested the development of a 'galloper', a light wheeled carriage pulled by a single horse, while some regular cavalry regiments purchased carriages at their commanding officers' expense. Owing to the conservatism of the army authorities, the volunteers were often quicker to exploit new ideas:

In the face of much adverse criticism, Colonel Alt, of the Central London Rangers (then the 22nd Middlesex), brought into the field at manoeuvres a couple of Nordenfeldt guns [sic]. A little later the 4th Volunteer battalion of the Royal Fusiliers had a machine-gun section, and the cyclist battalion, the old 26th Middlesex Regiment, invented a light carriage for the Maxim, which was drawn as a trailer by a couple of cyclists, kept up with the battalion over all kinds of roads, and could be dragged wherever a firing line could go. Machine guns were also adopted by other Volunteer battalions in the provinces. These experiments were of the utmost use when the question arose of attaching machine guns to infantry battalions and cavalry regiments of the Army. *

By September 1885, the bickering was still evident. The cavalry wanted the three- or five-

barrel Nordenfelt, while the Royal Navy had Hotchkiss, Nordenfelt and Gatling guns. The infantry was still torn between the Gardner and the Nordenfelt. Before a final decision could be taken, the first Maxim apeared. It was soon obvious that the truly automatic machine-gun was infinitely superior to the mechanically actuated designs, and work on the latter ceased. The Gatling, Nordenfelt and Gardner guns had all but disappeared by 1900, though instruction on mechanically-operated machine guns at the School of Musketry, Hythe, continued as late as 1894. A few guns were still held in reserve as late as 1912, when *Instructions to Armourers* recorded the existence of one-, two- and five-barrel ·45 Gardners, plus ·303 two-barrel guns converted from ·45.

THE MAXIM GUN

The Maxim Gun Company had been formed in 1884 to exploit the patents granted to an American, Hiram S. Maxim. A factory had been established at Crayford in Kent in 1885, and early ·45-calibre guns had been successfully demonstrated to the Machine Gun Committee in November 1885. The committee, suitably impressed with the Maxim, then programmed an arduous test for 1886. To succeed, the gun (which was to weigh less than 100lb) would have to fire not less than four hundred shots in the first minute; a thousand rounds would have to be fired in four minutes. But even the prototype Maxims were very efficient, passing their trials with ease. After completing the prescribed course, the inventor had joined two ammunition belts together and fired 666 rounds in a minute. There had been no jams.

Maxim gave several outstanding demonstrations in Europe in this period, one of the most impressive being in Austria in July 1888. Here, after satisfying the Austro-Hungarian army that it was accurate, the machine-gun underwent a 13,500-round endurance trial. Apart from the failure of the main spring after 7,281 rounds, and a striker breakage at 10,233, there were practically no problems. This trial was all the more remarkable as the Austrians had refused to give Maxim details of their ammunition prior to the test; the inventor had had cartridges loaded by the Birmingham

Small Arms & Metal Co. Ltd, but these proved to be more powerful than the service pattern. The failure of the main spring was directly attributable to hasty modifications made on the testing range.

Encouraged, the War Office immediately bought three ·45-calibre Maxim guns for extended trials. However, though the issue of one gun per infantry battalion for instructional purposes had been approved in 1890 (increased to two in 1891), the programme was still woefully incomplete when the Second South African War began in 1899. There were two basic Maxims in British service, the ·45 Mark I and the ·303 Mark I 'Magazine Rifle Chamber'. Large-calibre guns were later re-chambered under the designation '·303 Converted, Mark I'.

MACHINE-GUN CARRIAGES

The earliest machine guns were accompanied by cumbersome wheeled carriages and a selection of tripods. The first to be adopted officially was the Carriage, Naval, Machine Gun, Mk I, sealed in June 1887 and announced in LoC 5302. Together with the Mk II of 30 November 1888 (LoC 5653), which had 3ft 9in wheels compared with 4ft and a narrower track, the Mk I was later adapted for the Maxim by replacing the sloping top or shield with a simple cone.

The Carriage, Field, Machine Gun, Infantry, Maxim, Mk I of 26 June 1889 (LoC 7142) –

used with ·45 and ·303 guns – had 4ft diameter wheels and prop sticks under its double shafts. The bore axis was 3ft 3in from the ground, the mount often being fitted with a light plate shield. The Mk II mount of June 1897 was similar, but had 4ft 8in wheels and seats for two men on the carriage. Its bore-axis height was 3ft 6in, but the differences between the Marks I and II are difficult to determine in photographs. Sealed in February 1900, the Mk III was similar to the Mk II excepting that it carried eight ammunition boxes on each side of the gun and had no seats. Mark III carriages remaining in service after *c*.1912 also carried a Mark IV tripod to enable the gun to be dismounted.

The Carriage, Field, Nordenfelt Machine Gun, Cavalry or Mounted Infantry, Mark I, sealed on 30 April 1889, was a two-wheel unit with shafts for horse draught. It had seats for two men, which folded upward in action to provide shields. The prop-sticks were on the splinter bar and the wheels were braked. It was accompanied by an essentially similar Mark I ·303 Maxim mount, 'also for ·45 Maxim', sealed on 8 April 1889. The Maxim carriage had a single seat on the splinter bar, fourteen ammunition belt boxes, and elevating, traverse and oscillating gear on the mounting cone. The Mark II Maxim pattern, sealed in July 1898, was similar to its predecessor but lacked springs. The Mark III had a pole trail, four belt boxes on each side of the gun and an infantry-pattern shield. It was intended to be used with a limber, diameter of its wheels being 4ft 8in and the track 5ft 2in. The cavalry carriages were all large and

very high, the bore axis of the gun being at shoulder height.

There were four Maxim tripods, Mks I–IV, approved on 20 December 1897 (Mark I), 30 January 1900 (II), 26 October 1901 (III) and 23 January 1906 (IV). The original Mark I had fixed legs and a limited 28° traverse; the Mark III was the first to have folding legs. The original Mark IV appears to have lacked a dial plate, but this was added when the mount was adapted for the Vickers Gun after 1912.

A 'Mounting, Cone, Maxim, Mk I' and five Parapet Carriages were also made, Mks I and II for the Gardner and Nordenfelt and then three Marks for the Maxim (1888, 1895 and 1899). Parapet Carriages are now rarely encountered; the Maxim Mk III pattern, indeed, was originally unique to Gibraltar.

Three patterns of 'Carriage, Field or Tripod, Machine Gun, Maxim' were sealed between April 1904 and March 1905. They had pole trails for use with single-horse limbers, but were apparently confined to the volunteers and later passed to the Terriorial Army.

THE MACHINE-GUN, 1895–1910

Maxims had proved devastating during the Matabele Campaign, when a column com-manded by Major Forbes held five thousand of Lobengula's tribesmen at bay for several hours in October 1893. When the natives re-tired, they did so with the loss of half their force. Much of the damage had been done by four Maxims, though Forbes had also been able to call on a Gardner and a Nordenfelt. Six ·303 Maxims proved indispensable on the expedition to relieve Chitral in 1895 and, in September 1898, ·303-calibre Maxims were credited with three-quarters of the casualties inflicted on the Dervishes during the Battle of Omdurman.

The failure of the machine-guns during the Second South African War was due partly to inept tactics – they were still often seen as light artillery – and partly because their cum-bersome field carriages were vulnerable to the Boer artillery and 1pr Maxim pom-poms.† In 1888, Maxim amalgamated with the Nordenfelt Guns & Ammunition Company, and the resulting combine traded until bought by Vickers in 1897. The new company, now Vickers, Sons & Maxim Ltd, continued to make guns in the Crayford (Maxim) and Erith (Nordenfelt) factories.

British interest was still minimal, though Maxims were embraced in Germany with great enthusiasm. Despite the evidence of the Russo-Japanese War (where sixteen Russian Maxims had fired nearly 200,000 rounds in a single incident with no mechanical failures),

the War Department did very little. The con-temporary attitude is shown by the failure of the Laird-Mentayne, a promising light machine-gun promoted by the Coventry Ordnance Works:

Reading the trial reports of the time, one has the impression that here was a . . . sound and serviceable light machine-gun – certainly better than some which followed. The military of the time were regret-tably unaware of the light machine-gun concept: machine-guns, as everyone knew, . . . were water-cooled and fired from tripods. Tested in 1912 . . . the 0·303in version weighed 17lb and fired from an interchangeable 25-round magazine. It survived its trials reasonably well, with slight feed troubles, but the eventual conclusion was: 'The Committee do not consider this gun would meet any want except poss-ible for mounting in aeroplanes, for which purpose it would require considerable modification'.‡

†Much has been made by some writers of Vickers, Sons & Maxim's 'unpatriotic' behaviour in 'selling Poms-Poms to the Boers'. However, the guns had been sold to France as part of normal trade and were re-sold some time afterwards. There is no evidence that Vickers, Sons & Maxim connived in the deal.

‡Hogg & Weeks, *Military Small Arms of the 20th century*, fifth edition, p.232.

It is interesting that the Small Arms Committee should have considered arming aeroplanes in an era where aviation was in its infancy, as the first flight in Britain – by Samuel Cody – had taken place as recently as October 1908. Unfortunately, such perception was rarely applied to the tactical significance of the machine-gun. In the decade prior to the beginning of the First World War, British purchases from Vickers, Sons & Maxim and its successor, Vickers Ltd, amounted to a paltry 108 guns.

THE VICKERS GUN

Developed in the early twentieth century, the Vickers is simply a Maxim Gun with the locking mechanism reversed so that the toggle breaks downward.

212 ABOVE RIGHT

'Blue-Jackets firing Maxim Gun'. A coloured 'Oillete' postcard (no. 9014) published *c*.1902 by Raphael Tuck & Sons in the 'Hearts of Oak' series. Though quite obviously posed – the background has been painted in – the picture gives a good impression of the size and height of the standard wheeled machine-gun carriage carried aboard ships for the Landing Party. Courtesy of Elex archives.

213 RIGHT

Two air-cooled Maxims, on their cycle carriage, are crewed by men of the 2nd Battalion, Tower Hamlets Volunteers, during the Naval & Military Tournament: London, 1896. Author's archives.

214 BELOW RIGHT

The 'Carriage, Field, Machine Gun, Cavalry, ·303 Maxim, Mk I', pictured *c*.1895. Note the large diameter of the wheels and the height of the bore axis from ground level. Author's archives.

Attempts were made to lighten the Maxim action, without sacrificing strength, but the Vickers machine-gun was still comparatively cumbersome: the gun alone weighed about 40lb (including a full water jacket). The Mark IV tripod added 50lb. Measuring 45½in overall, the gun had a 28½in barrel and fed from a 250-round webbing or fabric belt. The cyclic rate was about 450rpm, though individual guns often fired appreciably faster. A seven-pint water jacket was standard, evaporation being at the rate of about 1½ pints per thousand rounds once the water had begun to boil. This occurred after fire had been sustained at a rate of 200–250rpm for three minutes. Steam was led off through a hose into a condenser can, from which water could subsequently be poured back.

The barrel could be changed by elevating the gun and pulling the barrel backward, in-

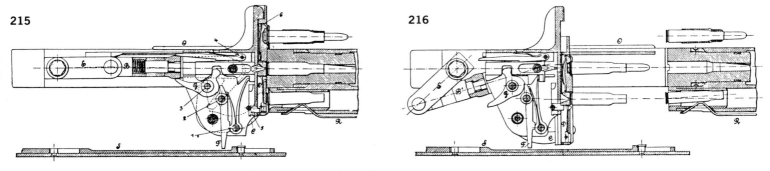

215   **216**

The lock of an early German Maxim machine-gun (MG.00), from a 1905-vintage handbook. Author's archives.

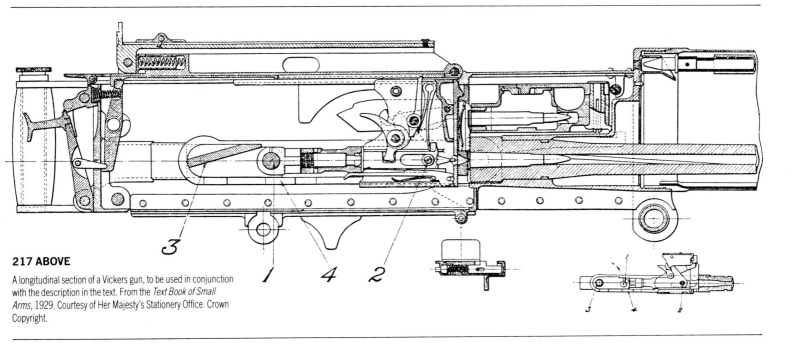

217 ABOVE

A longitudinal section of a Vickers gun, to be used in conjunction with the description in the text. From the *Text Book of Small Arms*, 1929. Courtesy of Her Majesty's Stationery Office. Crown Copyright.

serting a large cork into the aperture in the front of the barrel jacket. The gun was then depressed and the barrel withdrawn backward. Asbestos string wrapped in grooves in the new barrel acted as a seal; the barrel was simply pushed forward, knocking the cork out as it did so. Water was allowed to drain from the bore by depressing the gun, whereafter another ten thousand rounds could be fired before the next change was necessary.

When the gun is in the firing position shown in the diagram, the centre of the crank pin 1 lies beneath a line drawn through the centres of the side-lever axis 2 and the crankshaft 3, and the crank itself rests on the crank stops 4. The shock generated during firing is received by the lock through the axes 2 and 1 to the crankshaft 3, which is rigidly supported in relation to the barrel; the crank pin 1, lying below the bore axis, is forced downward. However, it is prevented from moving by the crank bearing on its stops. When the chamber pressure has dropped sufficiently, the crank begins to rotate. This lifts the axis 1 above the prolongation of the bore, the lock is broken and the toggle-joint reciprocates.

The Vickers guns were originally issued with the 'Mounting, Machine-gun, Tripod, Mark IV', sealed on 23 January 1906 and announced in LoC 13,336. This replaced the older Maxim carriages (q.v.), some of which the Vickers Gun would fit. The Tripod Mk IV was eventually superseded by the essentially similar Mark IVB, the most obvious distinguishing feature being the latter's small traverse ring.

Vickers guns, like comparable water-cooled Maxims and Brownings, were capable of prodigious feats of endurance. A standard machine-gun company comprised a hundred men, each of its four sections being armed with four Vickers guns under the command of a subaltern and a sergeant. A corporal was entrusted with the gun limbers and belt-filling equipment, while each gun-team comprised six other ranks. No.1, the gunner, carried the tripod; No.2, who carried the gun, was responsible for mounting the weapon prior to action and the smooth feed of the ammunition belts during firing. The third and fourth men were responsible for supplies and ammunition, water and spare parts. No.5 was the runner,

responsible for communicating with the section or company commander, and the sixth man was generally employed as a range taker. Each man had been given a thorough grounding in the operation of the Vickers, so that he could replace casualties.

According to Lieutenant-Colonel Hutchinson, in his book *Machine Guns*, ten guns of his unit – 100th Machine Gun Company, attached in August 1916 to 100 Infantry Brigade, 33rd Division – fired:

During the attack of 24th August, 250 rounds short of one million... Four two-gallon petrol tins of water, the company's water bottles, and all the urine tins from the neighbourhood were emptied into the guns for cooling purposes, an illustration of the amount of water consumed; while a party was employed throughout the action carrying ammunition. Strict discipline as to barrel-changing was maintained. The company artificer, assisted by one private, maintained a belt filling machine in action without cessation for twelve hours. A prize of five francs to each of the members of the gun-team firing the greatest number of rounds was secured by the gun-teams of Sergeant P. Dean, D.C.M., with a record of just over 120,000 rounds.

Machine-guns were also capable of prodigious

218

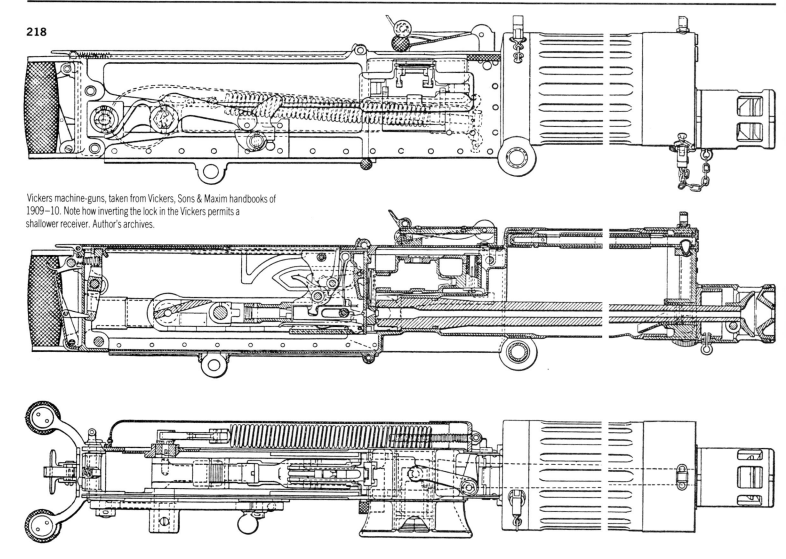

Vickers machine-guns, taken from Vickers, Sons & Maxim handbooks of 1909–10. Note how inverting the lock in the Vickers permits a shallower receiver. Author's archives.

219 RIGHT

A machine-gun team somewhere on the Western Front, possibly photographed in 1915. Though they wear steel helmets, the shoulder badges indicate that they belong to an infantry machine-gun unit rather than the Machine Gun Corps. Note that the Mk I Vickers gun, on a Mk IV tripod, has a small auxiliary or 'cavalry' tripod strapped to the barrel jacket. This mount, permanently attached to the gun, was used if there was no time to assemble the Mk IV. Author's archives.

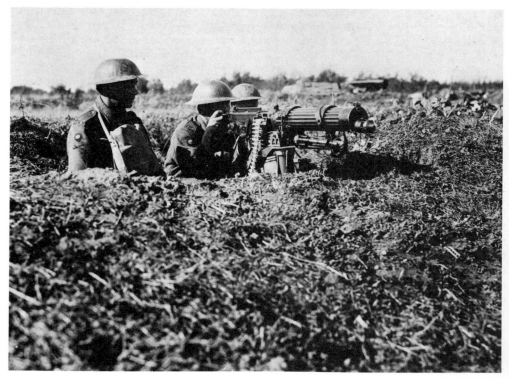

feats of slaughter. Their potential became clear almost as soon as the First World War had begun: during the Battle of Loos (1915), for example, German Maxims reduced a twelve-battalion British assault from its initial strength of about ten thousand men to a mere 1,754 in an hour. In the autumn of 1915, therefore, the British began to withdraw Vickers Guns from infantry battalions and regroup them in Machine Gun Corps, trained at Harrowby Camp near Grantham. But the rise in the status of the machine-gun was not universally approved. Sir Douglas Haig, the Commander-in-Chief of the British Army in France from December 1915, referred to it as a much-overrated weapon.

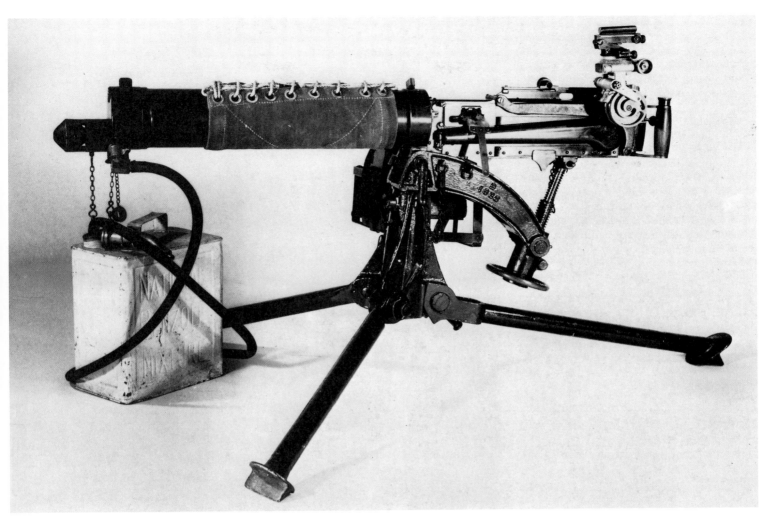

220 ABOVE

A Mk I Vickers machine-gun with a telelensatic sight. Note the Mk IVB tripod mount lacks the traverse ring.

Courtesy of Ian Hogg.

The Gun, Machine, Vickers, ·303-inch Mark I was introduced in LoC 16217 of 26 November 1912. It was the only Land Service pattern ever to be introduced, a testimony to the efficiency of the basic design. The Vickers Gun rapidly attained a reputation for reliability, excepting jams arising from the rimmed ammunition. Problems encountered in the trenches during the First World War included the high profile of the gun and gunner, partly solved by the introduction of the 'Mounting, Overbank, Machine-gun, Mark I'. This enabled the Vickers to be raised above the parapet of a dug-out, to fire on pre-determined paths, without the gunner exposing himself or his weapon unnecessarily. Clouds of steam hung over the gun in cold weather, unless suitable precautions were taken,* and the muzzle flash was easily detectable during sustained fire at night. The authorities issued a few flash-hiding tubes in 1915–16, but the propellant fumes that gathered in these tubes ignited periodically with

an awesome flash that was visible for miles! Colloquially known as 'stovepipes', the tubes were soon abandoned. Many gunners simply threw them away.

Not declared obsolete until LoC W1231 of 24 April 1968, the Vickers saw service in all theatres of war, in armoured vehicles and in aircraft. There were seven 'Marks' and a selection of 'starred' sub-variants. The Mark I* (LoC 22675 of 25 February 1918) was an Air Service gun embodying the standard barrel jacket, but with cooling louvres and an open front end-cap. The steam tube was omitted. The Mark II, retrospectively announced in LoC 22675, was approved in June 1917. It could be distinguished from the Mk I* by a smaller barrel casing and the omission of the fusee spring box from the left side of the receiver.

The Mark II*, LoC A3377 of 24 June 1927, was an Air Service gun. Unlike the Mark II, which it otherwise resembled, the Mk II* was fitted with an extended cocking lever. Mark III guns had extended flash-hiders, which increased overall length to about 49in. Vickers Mks II* and III could feed from the left ('A' suffix) or right ('B' suffix).

Intended to be used in armoured vehicles, the Mark IV A (left-hand feed) and Mark IV B

(right-hand feed) were introduced 'for the record' in LoC A7771 on 15 May 1930 but immediately declared obsolete. They were modified from Mark I Vickers Guns, receiving new mounting plates, trunnion blocks and barrel casings. Declared obsolete by LoC C2022 on 24 August 1944, they were water-cooled and could be fitted with a shoulder-piece or butt.

The Mark V was an Air Service gun, essentially similar to the Mark III (q.v.) except that the top cover hinged laterally. Marks VI A and VI B, introduced by LoC A9478 of 17 August 1934, were vehicle guns with strengthened dovetail mountings, alloy fusee spring covers and fluted barrel casings. They were, however, otherwise identical with the Mark IV and weighed about 41½lb.

The Mark VI* A and Mark VI* B – left- and right-hand feed respectively – were conversions of Mark I Land Service guns for use in armoured vehicles. They were adapted to trunnion blocks with connexions for the tank's cooling system. The barrel casing was fluted and the guns weighed about 42½–43lb

* Popular ways of minimizing the problem included covering the gun with a blanket or, if necessary, sleeping with it.

without water. The Mark VII was a modified Mk VI with an improved mounting dovetail, intergal with the ejection-tube sleeve. The barrel casing was plain, and the guns weighed 47¼lb. Marks V, VI and VII were all declared obsolete in LoC C2022 on 24 August 1944.

Small quantities of a ·5in Vickers Gun were also produced. These were essentially similar to the rifle-calibre patterns, but lacked the muzzle booster and the feed was altered to handle rimless cartridges. The Gun, Machine, Vickers, ·5-inch Mk I was a semi-experimental Land Service gun, introduced in LoC A7772 on 10 August 1933. The barrel had a distinctive conical flash hider, and a delay pawl in the rear handle held the crank until the barrel had been returned to battery. The water-cooled gun could be fed from either side, with

221 ABOVE RIGHT

The crew of a Vickers machine-gun, on a tripod, pose for the cameraman on the Western Front in 1917. Factors that make this an unconvincing action picture include the exposure of the gun, and that the back sight has not been elevated. Only three rounds have been fired from the belt. Courtesy of the Trustees of the Imperial War Museum; negative no. Q2864.

222 RIGHT

Men of the 9th Battalion, Royal Northumberland Fusiliers, crew a Vickers Mk I machine-gun on a tripod mount. The picture was taken during manoeuvres near Trawsfuydd in September 1941. Note the 'V' mark on the helmets, and the distinctive back sight on the gun. Courtesy of the Trustees of the Imperial War Museum; negative H13818.

223 BELOW RIGHT

Men of "Dad's Army" – the Home Guard – man a ·303 Vickers Mk I machine-gun on a tripod mount. Taken on the village green at Brockham, near Dorking, Surrey, the picture is notable for the empty belt: for much of 1940–1, the Home Guard had practically no ammunition. Courtesy of the Trustees of the Imperial War Museum; negative H5842C.

a few minor modifications, and would receive a tripod. Empty, it weighed 52lb. The Mark II, announced in A7772 but introduced on 5 February 1932, was a vehicle gun with an angled pistol grip. Like the Mark I, but unlike some of the later guns, it could fire single shots or fully automatically. The Mark III was a water-cooled Naval Service gun modified from the Mk I. Removing the delay pawl and strengthening the buffer spring raised the cyclic rate from 450 to about 700rpm. Disintegrating-link belts were used.

The Mark IV (LoC A9603, 6 November 1933) was an improved vehicle gun, though few were made. It could feed from either side. Compared with the ·5 Mk II, it had a narrow dovetail plate and mounting base facilitating interchangeability with ·303 vehicle guns. It weighed 58lb empty. Mark V vehicle guns were

similar, but had detachable ejection tubes and reinforced mounts.

With the exception of the Mk III Naval Service weapon, ·5 Vickers machine-guns were declared obsolete on 24 August 1944 (LoC C2022).

That the US Army adopted the Vickers Gun officially is not widely known. Tested successfully in 1913–14, 125 guns had been purchased from Vickers Ltd, together with a production licence. Excepting changes to the feed necessary to handle the rimless ·30 M1906 cartridge, the US ·30 M1915 Vickers machine-gun was identical with the British ·303 Mark I. When it became clear that the US Army would ultimately become embroiled in the First World War, an order for 4,000 guns was given to Vickers in 1916. However, the first delivery did not occur until July 1917 and none of the US guns were sent overseas until

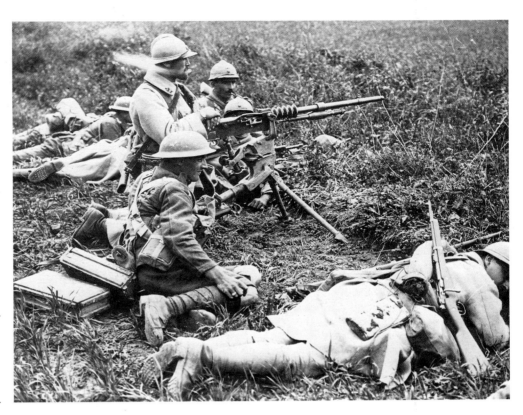

224 RIGHT
Vive l'Entente Cordiale. Men from Britain and France co-operate on the Western Front. In addition to an SMLE, in front of the British soldier, several Mle.92 Berthier Mousquetons and a Mle.14 Hotchkiss machine-gun are visible. Courtesy of Elex archives.

the autumn. In the interim, the US Army in Europe had been armed with British Vickers and French Hotchkiss machine-guns, issues depending alongside which units the Americans fought. By the Armistice, in November 1918, 9,237 M1915 Vickers Guns had been delivered — 3,125 made by Colt and 6,112 by Vickers. Colt had also delivered 900 aircraft guns from orders totalling 14,235.

The oddest Vickers Gun to see service in the First World War was the US M1918, which chambered French 11mm (Gras) cartridges. These were loaded with incendiary bullets for use against observation balloons or aircraft. The M1918 had originally been a 7·62mm Russian gun, ordered from Colt in 1915 but never delivered. About 1,000 guns were converted and an additional 1,600 assembled from a mixture of new and existing parts. A little over six hundred 11mm machine-guns reached Europe before the Armistice, where they proved very effectual. However, as they inspired the creation of the legendary ·50 Browning in postwar years, these large-calibre Vickers machine-guns were all scrapped in the early 1920s. Many ·30 calibre examples survived to be shipped to Britain under Lend-Lease.

When the First World War began, the British Army was short of machine-guns; they had simply not been taken seriously enough to have been purchased in quantity. Only Vickers and the Royal Small Arms Factory at Enfield were involved in production, the latter making nothing but a few Maxims and spare parts.

The army preferred the Vickers to its predecessor, which was regarded as obsolescent in British service, largely because the former's components were completely interchangeable — J.D. Scott's *Vickers. A History* records how this had arisen from a Russian contract, placed in 1912, that had demanded interchangeability as a condition of acceptance. However, only the Erith works was making machine-guns in 1914.

On 11 August 1914, one week after the declaration of war, 192 Vickers guns were ordered. It was believed that the fighting would be short-lived, and that the war would be 'over by Christmas'. The guns were to be delivered by 19 November, a date by which Vickers had actually made 171.

A hundred guns was ordered on 10 September; and, as the suspicion grew that the conflict would be protracted, 1,000 were ordered on 28 September. Early in October came an order for 500, and then an open-ended contract from the French government — most of whose standard weapons were ineffectual — for fifty guns per week.† But production soon lagged until, by the completion date for the last of the 1,792 guns ordered by the British government, only 1,022 had been accepted. Clearly, there was a crisis.

By the beginning of 1915 it was clear that the Germans were using machine-guns with great skill, often firing from well-prepared strongpoints with deadly effect. On more than one occasion, a single German Maxim not only held up battalion-size advances but also inflicted dreadful casualties.

†Placed with Vickers by the British authorities, acting as intermediaries, the order included a clause allowing the manufacturer to suspend deliveries if they threatened the progress of existing British orders.

THE HOTCHKISS GUN

Unfortunately, as the machine-gun was still comparatively youthful, production was concentrated in the hands of a mere handful of manufacturers — in 1910, Vickers, Sons & Maxim (Vickers Ltd from 1911), Société Anonyme Établissements Hotchkiss, Deutsche Waffen- und Munitionsfabriken, and some government arsenals. In 1914, all were so committed to the war effort of their respective countries that little capacity could be spared. As Vickers was soon over-extended, the British government had no obvious alternative source of automatic weapons.

Salvation came in the form of the French Hotchkiss organisation and the Birmingham Small Arms Co. Ltd. The original Hotchkiss machine-gun — a manually-operated multi-barrel gun similar externally to the Gatling — had been invented by an American, Benjamin Berkley Hotchkiss, in the 1870s. No sooner had this weapon had been eclipsed by the Maxim than Hotchkiss et Cie was approached by an Austrian inventor, Adolf von Odkolek. Odkolek had designed a gas-operated machine-gun with a flap-lock, but had been unable to arouse interest in his native country.‡ Hotchkiss's management immediately saw the potential of the Odkolek gun, and acquired rights from the inventor on the harshest possible terms. By the mid 1890s, the Odkolek had become the Hotchkiss and the inventor was all but forgotten.

Hotchkiss machine-guns of this period all fed from distinctive metal strips. They had been tested by the French army in 1897, upgraded to become the Mle.00, but then 'improved' by government technicians to become the Mle.05 (Puteaux) and Mle.07 (Saint-Étienne). The Mle.05 and Mle.07 were made in the French government arsenals, whereupon purchase from Hotchkiss virtually ceased. Hotchkiss had the last laugh: neither of the 'improved' French guns proved successful. The Mle.05 was particularly troublesome, soon being relegated to fortifications and static use where its drawbacks were not so obvious. When the First World War began, the French, as short of machine-guns as the British, ordered huge quantities of the so-called Mle.14 from Hotchkiss to supplement the Saint-Étienne.*

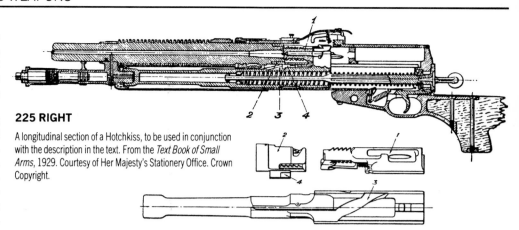

225 RIGHT

A longitudinal section of a Hotchkiss, to be used in conjunction with the description in the text. From the *Text Book of Small Arms*, 1929. Courtesy of Her Majesty's Stationery Office. Crown Copyright.

In addition to the standard medium machine-gun, the Hotchkiss company had also made small quantities of the 'Fusil Mitrailleur Mle.09'. Designed by Laurence Benét† and Henri Mercié, this light machine-gun featured a locking collar (or 'fermeture nut') containing an interrupted screw of a type commonly encountered in the breech of artillery pieces. The bolt 1 entered the locking collar 2, owing to gaps in the latter's female

threads. At the end of the closing stroke, the collar was rotated by a cam-slot 3 on the piston 4 working on a projection or lug 5. As the collar rotated, its threads engaged the interrupted male threads on the bolt and so locked the action. The feed was inverted so that cartridges lay underneath the strip. The standard Hotchkiss feed strip, with the cartridges uppermost, made an excellent platform from which rain, mud or dust could enter

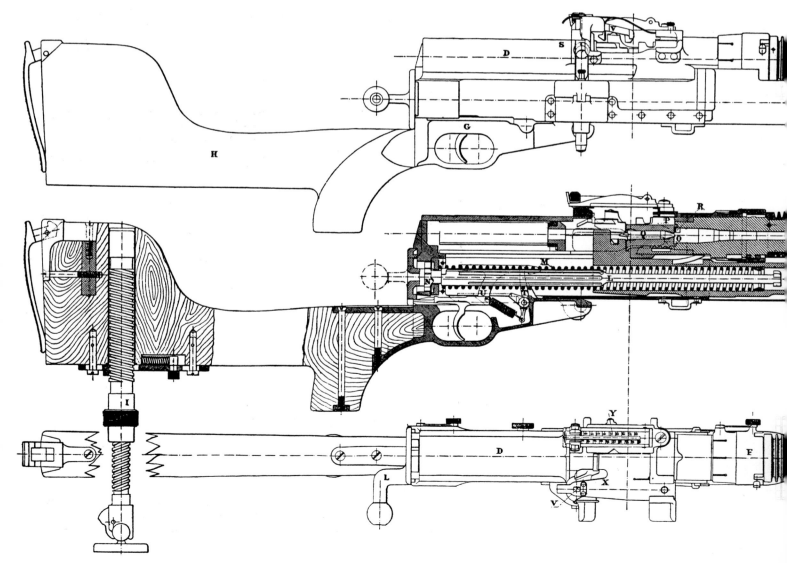

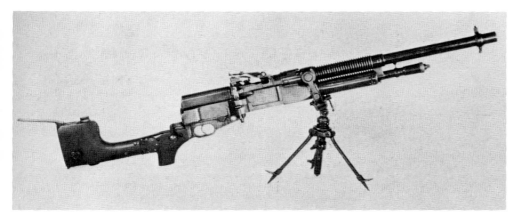

226 LEFT

This example of the Hotchkiss Mark I* No.1 displays its diminutive tripod and reinforced Mk I* butt wrist to good advantage. Courtesy of the MoD Pattern Room Collection, Royal Ordnance plc, Nottingham; photograph by Ian Hogg.

the action. Even though the Mle.14 was acceptably efficient, it was susceptible to jamming in adverse conditions. The feed of the Mle.09 was intended to minimize this drawback, but the strips were much more difficult to load. Indeed, so awkward was the feed that rumours arose in the USA (where the Mle.09 was issued as the 'Machine Gun Rifle, Caliber ·30, Model of 1909') that the gun could only be fired in daylight!‡

It seems that Hotchkiss had substantial quantities of Mle.09 guns on hand in 1914. The French government – busily developing the execrable Chauchat, which was better suited to a doctrine of assault-at-the-walk – did not want the light Hotchkisses, and allowed the British to purchase them instead. As the Hotchkiss was easier to make than the Vickers or Maxim, rights were purchased and a production line installed in the Royal Small

Arms Factory at Enfield. The Gun, Machine, Hotchkiss, ·303-inch, Mark I was officially adopted in June 1916. The original gun had a wooden butt, with an integral pistol grip, an oil bottle and a hinged shoulder plate. It could only feed from conventional metal strips and was issued with a small 'cavalry' tripod.

The Mk I was supplemented after June 1917 by the Mark I*, made for infantry (Mk I* No.1) or tank use (Mk I* No.2). The guns were identical, except for the sights and butt fittings. No.1 had a conventional tangent-leaf back sight offset on the left side of the feed cover, and a wood butt with distinctive metal strengthening plates; the No.2 had a pistol grip adapted to take an optional tubular extension (known as the 'Shoulder Piece No.1'). Most tank guns were issued with the simple 'Sight, Tubular, No.2', a pan for the cartridge belt – a series of articulated three-round strips – and a bag to catch the ejected cases.

Light Hotchkiss guns fed from the right and were cocked by a bolt handle protruding from the back of the receiver above the pistol grip. They measured 46¾in overall, had 23½in barrels and weighed about 27lb. Standard Enfield four-groove right-hand twist rifling was used, the chambering being identical with the SMLE. The bolt handle doubled as a fire selector, depending on how far it was turned upward after cocking the gun; cyclic rate was about 500rpm. Enfield-made guns had 'E'-prefix serial numbers, the mark 'SC' above the chamber indicating that the diameter of the small cone had been increased.

Renamed Gun, Machine, Hotchkiss, No.2 Mk I* in 1926, the weapons remained in reserve for many years. After serving the Home

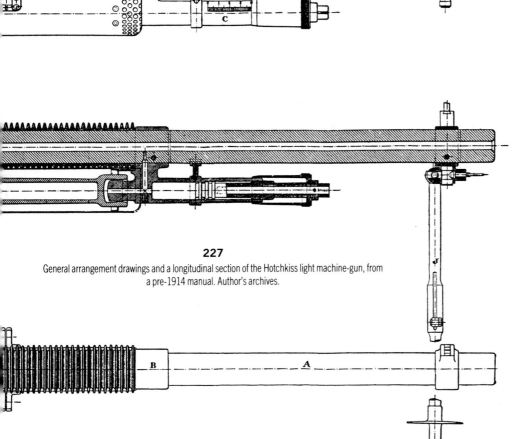

227
General arrangement drawings and a longitudinal section of the Hotchkiss light machine-gun, from a pre-1914 manual. Author's archives.

‡Adolf von Augezd, Freiherr von Odkolek, was an Austrian cavalryman. He filed several patents in 1889–1906 – e.g., British Patents 16,939/90 and 7,137/92 for 'Improvements in Machine Guns'.

* The Saint-Étienne featured a wholly superfluous rack-and-pinion system to reverse the direction of the piston, which was blown *forward* on firing rather than backward as in the Hotchkiss and most conventional designs. Together with 'innovations' such as a front sight that automatically compensated for barrel heating (!), the breech mechanism succeeded only in complicating the weapon unnecessarily. A modified version appeared in 1915, the Mitrailleuse Mle.07T, but was just as unsatisfactory. Compared with the Vickers and the Maxim, the Saint-Étienne was a very poor performer indeed.

†Benét was the son of Brigadier-General Stephen V. Benet, one-time Chief of Ordnance in the US Army. The family were apparently originally Huguenots.

‡The myth of the 'Daylight Gun', as the guns came to be called, arose from sensationalist press reporting of an attack by Pancho Villa's Mexican banditos on the town of Columbus, New Mexico, in April 1916. Investigation subsequently discovered that the four guns had actually fired nearly 20,000 rounds with minimal trouble, but the truth never achieved the publicity of the fiction.

Guard and the Merchant Navy during the Second World War, they were finally declared obsolete in June 1946.

Though the Hotchkiss was light enough to be carried forward with the infantry during an attack, its strip feed was inconvenient. This, together with worries about its reliability, confined the Hotchkiss to comparatively static roles.

228 RIGHT

Based on a well known British official photograph, this coloured *Daily Mail* Official War Picture ('Series 14. No.110') records that 'The strange kaleidoscope of the War produces this picture of turbanned Indians working a Hotchkiss Gun on the British Western Front'. The weapon, which appears to be a Mark I, displays the standard bipod. Note the protective shield discarded to the right of the picture; for all its bellicose caption, the original picture was undoubtedly posed for the photographer. Courtesy of Elex archives.

229 RIGHT

A man of the New Zealand Rifle Battalion poses with a Lewis Gun in a shallow trench dug on the Western Front in 1916. It is unlikely that the unit is under fire; the pan magazine is missing from the Lewis, and there is no sign of it on the parapet. Note the position of the bipod, which could be moved along the barrel casing simply by loosening the clamps. Many men found that the gun was easier to traverse when the bipod was placed as near the breech as possible. Courtesy of the Trustees of the Imperial War Museum; negative no. Q10506.

THE LEWIS GUN

Prior to the First World War, the Belgian army had adopted a light machine-gun developed by a retired American army officer, Isaac Newton Lewis, on the basis of an unsuccessful weapon designed by Samuel McClean in 1906–9.† The patents had been assigned to the McClean Arms & Ordnance Company of Cleveland, Ohio, but the company had failed in 1909. They had then passed to the Automatic Arms Company of Buffalo, New York State, and Lewis had been hired to produce a workable gun. Five were exhibited at Fort Myers in 1911, all but one being handed to the Board of Ordnance. Oddly, the authorities did nothing; eventually, Lewis retrieved the guns and went to Europe, where he accepted the offer of BSA's Tool Room facilities in the summer of 1913.

Some have blamed initial lack of success on clashes between Lewis and the Chief of Ordnance, Brigadier-General Crozier, but trials had not been entirely successful. The guns

†Samuel N. McClean of Washington, Iowa, and then Cleveland, Ohio, received more than twenty patents in 1897–1908. The essence of the Lewis Gun will be found in US Patents 816,591 of April 1906, 827,259 of July 1906 and 933,098 of September 1908.

had all exhibited a very harsh action and had often failed to extract spent cases properly.

Originally conceived as a medium machine-gun, the perfected gas-operated Lewis had a rotating pan magazine above the receiver and relied on a turning bolt to lock the action – which was more than a little odd. The striker 1 was carried on a post 2, mounted on the rear of the piston 3. The post reciprocated in a slot 4 in the bolt 5. When the trigger was pressed, the sear disengaged the piston and the latter began its forward movement under the action of the main spring. The striker post, lodged in a recess in the slot at the rear end of the bolt, bore against the curved portion of the slot. The locking lugs 6, on the head of the bolt, engaged grooves in the body to prevent rotation until the bolt returned to battery. As the bolt closed, a fresh round was stripped out of the pan magazine and pushed forward into the chamber. The striker post then travelled along the curved portion of the slot, turning the lugs into the receiver walls and locking the bolt closed. The post then finally reached the short straight slot-end and ran forward far enough the carry the striker onto the primer of the chambered round.

After the gun fired, gas was tapped off the barrel and led back to push the piston rearward. This retracted the striker and revolved the bolt lugs out of engagement with the receiver walls. A large helical spring in a prominent housing beneath the receiver, ahead of the trigger, returned the piston and bolt assembly to battery as long as the trigger was pressed.

The Belgian Lewis gun, which chambered 7·65mm rimless cartridges, was made for Armes Automatiques Lewis by BSA. Few had been supplied by 1914, however, and the

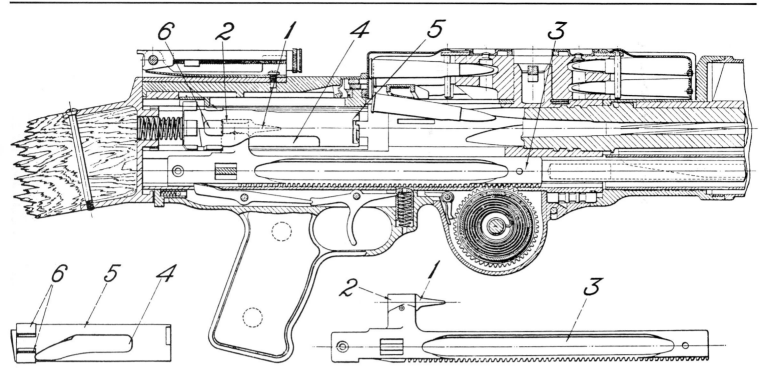

Belgians appear to have had Hotchkiss and other French weapons during the war. When the British government cast around for machine-guns late in 1914, therefore, BSA was ready. The Gun, Machine, Lewis, ·303-inch Mark I was introduced on 15 October 1915, by which time series production was underway in Birmingham. The guns were 50½in overall, had 26¼in barrels with standard Enfield four-groove rifling, and weighed 26lb 5oz unladen. Land Service weapons fed from 47-round pan magazines, though a two-tier 97 round version was successfully developed for aerial use. The weapons were made by the Birmingham Small Arms Company and also, under the terms of a British contract placed in 1915, by the Savage Arms Company of Utica, New York State.

The standard British Land Service Lewis was air cooled, but incorporated a forced-draught system absent from the Belgian prototypes. The barrel was encased in a ribbed aluminium radiator, which was itself inserted in a plain cylindrical jacket. The mouth of the jacket, which was partially open, projected in front of the muzzle. Expansion of propellant gases at the muzzle was supposed to draw air in from the rear of the radiator, along the ribs and out of the muzzle opening. Whether this worked has never been satisfactorily demonstrated; it is suspected that the Lewis would have been as effectual without the cooling system and, therefore, several pounds lighter.

About 350 ·303 Lewis Guns were bought from Savage by the US Army in 1916, for use in the border wars with Mexico. These guns worked satisfactorily enough, so Savage was requested to produce a ·30-calibre version

232 RIGHT

A soldier of the Highland Light Infantry keeps watch on the Western Front in 1916. Note that his Lewis Gun has its bipod as near to the breech as possible, and that the legs are clamped in a hinged wood block. Note also that it has an auxiliary front sight to compensate for the tendency of bullets to fly high at ultra-short range. Two trench rattles, usually used to warn of attacks, lie on the makeshift shelf behind him. Owing to the netting visible in the background, in the front line, it is tempting to speculate that this is a battalion headquarters gun held for local defence. Courtesy of the Trustees of the Imperial War Museum; negative no. Q6130.

233 RIGHT

"Firing a Lewis Gun at a German 'plane": ambitious British gunners at work on the Western Front, 1917. Note the design of the anti-aircraft tripod mount. Courtesy of Elex archives.

234 BELOW

The Beardmore-Farquhar light machine-gun, originally conceived as an aircraft gun, was briefly touted for infantry use. This ·303 version, dating from the early 1920s, shows its extraordinarily lightweight construction. The exposure of the mechanism, an asset in the air, was regarded as a potential drawback on the ground. Tests were surprisingly successful, but there was no real need and the Beardmore-Farquhar passed into history. Courtesy of the MoD Pattern Room Collection, Royal Ordnance plc, Nottingham; photograph by Ian Hogg.

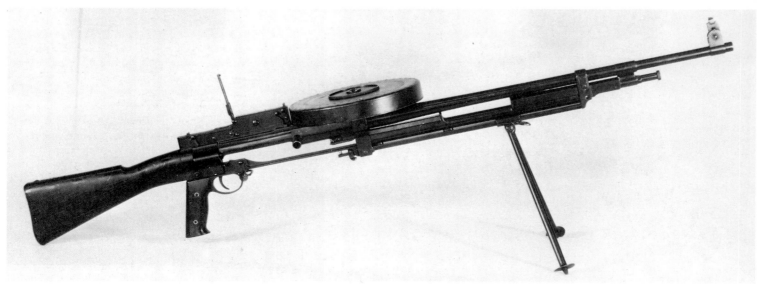

designated M1917. Unfortunately, the American round was much more powerful than its British predecessor and more difficult to extract. In addition to inherent weaknesses of the pan magazine and the feed pawls, the extractor of the ·30 Lewis often tore through the cartridge-case rim and jammed the gun.

The problems were cured by increasing the dwell before the breech opened, but the gun had attained such a poor reputation in the US Army that it never recovered. The US Navy and the Marine Corps, which together took 4,204 M1917 machine-guns compared with only 2,500 for the army, did not share the negative opinions. In addition, the ·30 M1918 aircraft gun proved a great success.

Though the M1917 Lewis Guns were rapidly replaced in the US Army by the Browning Automatic Rifle, they were placed in reserve. Sufficient numbers remained for several thousand to be sent to Britain under the Lend-Lease programme in 1940−1.

Owing to the ease with which the Lewis Gun could be made − BSA alone made 145,397 for the British, Belgians and Russians during the war − the firepower of the infantry was soon increased. With the formation of specialist Machine Gun Corps in the summer of 1915, Vickers machine-guns were withdrawn from the infantry battalions. Each Vickers gun was substituted by four Lewis Guns, issue being broadened until, by the autumn of 1916, each of the sixteen platoons had a light machine-gun. A second gun was added in 1918, plus four additional guns issued to the battalion headquarters for anti-aircraft defence.

In addition to the standard British Land Service gun − there was only one Mark − adaptations were made for aerial use. The Mark I*, introduced on 10 November 1915, was simply a Mk I with a spade grip and a two-tier magazine. The forced-draught cooling system was abandoned. The Mark II* (converted) and Mark III (newly made) of 13 May 1918 were variants of the Mk I* offering a higher rate of fire, achieved by modifications to the gas system.

The Lewis Gun was the standard British light machine-gun until replaced by the Bren Gun in the 1930s. However, substantial numbers survived to serve the Home Guard and the Merchant Navy throughout the Second World War (see below).

BETWEEN THE WARS

The end of the First World War removed much of the desire to experiment with new machine-guns. The Vickers had proved extremely reliable in virtually every theatre and the Lewis Gun, despite its 'emergency' origin, had confirmed the value of light infantry-support weapons.

Wholesale reductions in the army establishment were immediately echoed by the withdrawal of many existing guns, some to store and others to be sold on a surplus market glutted with ex-German weaponry. Thousands of unwanted guns were scrapped.

Trials were undertaken in December 1922 with a selection of light machine-guns − a bipod-mounted Browning Automatic Rifle, a Danish Madsen, a Beardmore-Farquhar, a Hotchkiss and a lightened Lewis. With the exception of the pan-fed Beardmore-Farquhar and Lewis, the guns all featured detachable top-feed box magazines. Tested extensively by the 13th Hussars and the Dorset Regiment, none was perfection. As the BAR had performed particularly well, the Small Arms Committee recommended standardizing the 'Browning Light Machine Gun' until funds were withheld by the Treasury.

The most interesting of the submissions had been the Beardmore-Farquhar, designed by Major Mowbray Farquhar (co-inventor of the Farquhar-Hill rifle) and made by the Beardmore Engineering Company in Birmingham. The machine-gun had been developed during the First World War to arm aircraft observers, but had not been submitted to RAF trials until 1919. It had performed very impressively, but there was no longer a need for it. By no means discouraged, the promoters entered a modified version in the light machine-gun trials. Its unusual combination of gas and spring action allowed ultra light construction: the Beardmore-Farquhar weighed a mere 16½lb with its 77-round magazine, 10lb less than the standard Lewis. However, too much of the reciprocating mechanism was exposed to impress the Small Arms Committee even though the gun seemed reliable in adverse conditions.

Trials dragged on through the 1920s, with the appearance of an improved Beardmore-Farquhar and routine examinations of the French Mle.24 (Châtellerault) and Swiss Fürrer. A Browning Automatic Rifle was submitted in ·303, but proved inferior to the original ·30-calibre pattern. By the end of the 1920s, therefore, tests had been centred on the Vickers-Berthier, the French Darne, a Hungarian Királý, Danish Madsens and the Czechoslovakian ZB vz.27.

1930 brought a typically comprehensive series of tests, which included assessments of accuracy, endurance and handling characteristics. The ZB vz.27 was preferred to the

235 BELOW
The ZGB33 Model 2 was an early attempt to transform the Czechoslovakian vz.26 light machine-gun for the British ·303 cartridge. Note that, though the finned barrel has been retained, the gas tube beneath the barrel has been shortened. In addition, the barrel and receiver group has been adapted to slide back on the butt/frame unit. This softens the apparent recoil. Courtesy of the MoD Pattern Room Collection, Royal Ordnance plc, Nottingham; photograph by Ian Hogg.

Vickers-Berthier, though the differences in chambering (7·9mm and ·303 respectively) made their merits difficult to assess. The British requested a ·303 version of the ZB vz.27, and the suitably modified ZGB Model 1 appeared in the Spring of 1931. Trials undertaken with the ZGB, an improved Vickers-Berthier and the ·303 Darne — received too late for the previous series — resolved in favour of the Czechoslovakian gun. The only drawbacks to the ZB were that too much fouling accumulated at the gas port, owing to use of cordite propellant, and that extraction and ejection problems arose from too little power in the action. These were cured by moving the gas port nearer the breech in the promising ZGB Model 2 of 1933.

236 RIGHT

Men of the Royal Scots Greys (2nd Dragoons) prepare at Hounslow Barracks for a trip to Palestine, September 1938. Note the Bren Guns being packed in their special 'Chests, Bren, ·303-in, MG, Mk I'. Courtesy of Brian L. Davis.

237 RIGHT

A Vickers Gas Operated (VGO) machine-gun mounted on a Scarff ring for use an an observer's weapon. Note the non-rotating pan magazine, which was widely favoured in this application. The technician posing as an observer wears a Supermarine logo on his overall. Courtesy of Vickers Ltd.

THE BREN GUN

The ZGB had its ancestry in a series of weapons designed in the early 1920s by Václav Holek for Zbrojovká Praga — beginning with the Praga 1, then proceeding through the Praga 2a and I-23 to the perfected M-24. The M-24 was adopted by the Czechoslovakian army in September 1924 but, meanwhile, the Praga company was in severe financial straits and production was eventually entrusted to the state-owned Zbrojovká Brno. Modifications were made to suit mass production, and the M-24 became the ZB vz.26. Improvements in the bolt and gas system soon led to the vz.27.

The 7·9mm ZB vz.27 performed very well in the trials in Britain and had been duly superseded by the ·303 ZGB Model 1 in 1931. This was then replaced by the ZGB Model 2 (1933), the first gun in which the gas-tube was shortened to suit the characteristics of cordite and the body and barrel assembly could slide back against a buffer to reduce the recoil sensation.

The ZGB Model 3 (1933) had a thirty-round magazine and an attachment for the experimental telelensatic sight then being developed for the Vickers gun. Virtually a prototype of the later Bren Gun, the ZGB Model 4 (1934)

238 ABOVE

The ·303 Mk III Vickers-Berthier machine-gun was a Land
Service variation of the VGO, adopted by the Indian Army in the
early 1930s. It could have become the British service weapon but
for the appearance of the Bren Gun. Courtesy of Vickers Ltd.

had a longer barrel than the previous Brno-
made weapons, lacked cooling fins, and its
back sight lay on the rear of the receiver
behind the magazine. Fire-rate was reduced
from 600rpm to 480rpm.

The final gun in the series, the ZGB Model 4
Improved (or Type 2), had a handle beneath
the butt suited to the classical British under-
hand grip, and a vertical back sight notch-
plate. A total of 62 Type 4 Improved machine-
guns was ordered from Brno in December
1934, after which the weapon was approved
for British service under the acronym 'Bren'
(for Brno and Enfield). The production licence
was formally signed on 24 May 1935.

The Gun, Machine, Bren, ·303-inch Mark I
and Mount, Tripod, Bren, Mark I (a copy of the
original ZB206 pattern) were initially made
exclusively in the Royal Small Arms Factory at
Enfield though, as related below, an order for
5,000 guns was passed to Inglis in Toronto in
1938 and many of the bipods and butt assemblies were made by BSA Guns Ltd. The first
British-made gun was test-fired on 3 Sep-

tember 1937 and series production began in
the Spring of 1938.

The Mk I Bren Gun was a classical air-
cooled light machine-gun, gas operated,
locked by a tilting block and fed from a top-
mounted detachable box magazine containing
thirty rounds. It was about 45¼in long,
with a 25in barrel rifled with six-groove
clockwise twisting rifling. Unladen weight
was 22lb 7oz.

VICKERS LIGHT MACHINE-GUNS

Until the Czechoslovakian ZB vz.27 was
submitted for trials, it looked as though the
perfected British light machine-gun would
be the Vickers-Berthier.

Designed by the Frenchman Adolphe
Berthier prior to the First World War and
touted either as a light machine-gun or a
heavy automatic rifle, the Berthier was an
effectual gas operated design locked by a tilting bolt. US Army trials had been sufficiently
encouraging for the weapon to be provisionally adopted, though post-war tests with
guns made by the US Machine Gun Company‡
were less inspiring. Faced with the considerable success of the Browning Automatic Rifle,

in addition to prejudice amongst US service-
men against the top-mounted box magazine,
the US Berthier project foundered in the early
1920s.

Rights had been acquired by Vickers in 1918
and, with an eye on the contemporary British
trials, development of a ·303-calibre version
commenced in 1925; by 1931, more than
£100,000 had been invested, with little tan-
gible return. Little is yet known about the
early history of the Vickers-Berthier ('VB')
ground gun and its aircraft version, the
Vickers Gas Operated ('VGO'), except that
development was completed in 1932. After a
series of pre-production guns had been made,
the VB was entered in British trials in 1930–1.
The weapon performed quite acceptably, but
the Czechoslovakian ZB proved better.

The VGO subsequently proved effectual
enough to satisfy the RAF, being adopted as an
observers' gun c.1934. The Air Ministry
ordered ten thousand guns in 1938 alone.
When the widespread introduction of

‡The United States Machine Gun Company of Meriden,
Connecticut, was a promotional organization founded in 1917
by Bostonian William Haskell to exploit the Berthier patents. The
Berthier ·30 M1917 light machine-gun had been adopted by the
US Army, but only five prototypes were made. Marlin then
bought Hopkins & Allen – the original Berthier licensee – and
the project was abandoned. Later 'US Machine Gun Co.' guns
were apparently still made in the former Hopkins & Allen factory
in Norwich, Connecticut. Haskell's operations failed in 1922.

powered turrets made the VGO obsolete in its original role, many guns were impressed as vehicle guns. They were particularly popular with the Long Range Desert Group and the SAS, as the weapons were reliable even in adverse conditions and had a higher fire-rate than the Bren – the VGO, or Vickers 'K' as it was known commercially, fed from a 96-round non-rotating pan magazine at nearly 1,000rpm.

There were apparently four models of the Gun, Machine, Vickers Gas Operated, ·303-inch Mark I. The Mk I No.1 and No.3 were aircraft guns, apparently with left and right-hand ejection respectively; the Mk I No.2 and No.4 were otherwise comparable Ground Service weapons. The differing feed arrangements were necessary as the guns were often mounted in 'handed' pairs.

The efficacy of the basic Vickers-Berthier impressed authorities in India, where existing Hotchkiss and Lewis guns had proved unreliable. Unwilling to wait while the Small Arms Committee developed the Czechoslovakian ZB for ·303 ammunition, the Indian Army adopted the Vickers-Berthier (which was available from stock) in 1935.

The identification of the Indian guns is still uncertain. The original Gun, Machine, Vickers-Berthier, ·303-inch, Indian Mk I was apparently the pattern illustrated – much like a Bren externally, but with a very distinctively shaped pistol-grip assembly. Three hundred examples were supplied from the Crayford Vickers factory in 1936; others went to Iraq. Older guns will be encountered with finned barrels and slab-sided wood fore-ends, but appear to date from the British trial period (*c.*1929–32); they are not India Patterns.

The I.Mark II was an experimental lightweight gun with a slender butt, a light barrel and weight-reducing cuts in the receiver. Though it weighed 3lb less than the Mk I, it was not adopted. The I.Mark III and I.Mark IIIB – differing in their barrels and gas-plug arrangements – were derivatives of the Mk I made in the Indian rifle factory in Ishapur from 1939 onward. Production seems to have been small, as work on the Vickers-Berthier stopped early in 1942.

239 ABOVE

The 7·9mm Czechoslovakian ZB53 (or vz.37) machine-gun is seen here on its tripod mount. A modified version of this gun, developed by BSA, was adopted in Britain as the 'Besa'. British guns have plain barrels and a pistol-grip cocking system. Courtesy of Weller & Dufty Ltd, Birmingham.

The I.Mk IIIB was 46½in long, had a 24in barrel rifled with five-groove clockwise twist, and weighed about 21lb unladen. It fed from a thirty-round box magazine and had a cyclic rate of 450rpm.

THE BESA

Almost exclusively confined to armoured vehicles, the 7·92mm-calibre Besa was another Czechoslovakian design. Offered to Britain in the 1930s and known commercially as the ZB 53 (militarily, as vz.37), it was a belt-feed air-cooled medium gun capable of sustaining fire over long periods. Credited to the Holek brothers, the gas-operated action was adapted from that of the ZB vz.26 – but the concept of softening recoil was inspired by the Bren. The Besa barrel was allowed to recoil. When the main spring returned the breech-block to battery, stripping a new round into the chamber, the barrel unit was released to move forward. As it did so, the gun fired and the recoil initially had to overcome the residual forward motion before reversing the action. The goal, achieved very successfully, was to reduce the stress transmitted to the gun mounting. The Besa soon attained an enviable reputation for smoothness.

Development did not proceed smoothly, as the first attempts to copy the ZB 53 were beset by problems. Work began in 1937 and the first gun was delivered from the new Redditch factory in June 1939. Test-firing revealed so many

240 The 7·92mm Besa – a Czechoslovakian ZB.37 adapted by BSA – was used in Britain as a vehicle gun. This Mk 3/2 displays a bag to collect spent cases, and the double-curve trigger lever Courtesy of the MoD Pattern Room Collection, Royal Ordnance plc, Nottingham; photograph by Ian Hogg.

problems that BSA and government technicians had virtually to re-engineer the gun before the new weapon would work properly. Production was suspended until the Spring of 1940; when it eventually recommenced, the machine-gun was christened 'Besa' in appreciation of the company's assistance.

There have been three basic Besa guns. Approved in June 1940, the Mark I had a selector lever on the left side of the receiver giving 450rpm for general purposes and 750rpm for repelling attacks. The gun was about 43·5in overall, with a 29in barrel, and weighed 47lb without its mount. It fed standard German-type (but British-made) 7·92mm cartridges from a disintegrating-link belt. The Mark II, approved concurrently with the Mk I, had a simplified receiver, a short barrel sleeve, a modified accelerator and a plain flash guard. Mark II* guns, approved in 1941, are basically Mk II made after the introduction of the Mk III. They have the dual-rate fire system, but many of the components are simplified even though they usually interchange with earlier versions.

The Besa Mark III and Mark III*, approved in August 1941, lack the selective fire-rate system; the former had its rate fixed at 750rpm and the latter at 450rpm. The Mark 3/2 and Mark 3/3 were post-war variants dating from 1952–4.

According to company records, BSA Guns Ltd made 59,332 7·92mm Besas and 3,218 of the larger 15mm pattern in 1939–46. The Contract Books give figures of 61,756 7·92mm vehicle and 465 7·92mm ground guns, plus 3,268 15mm vehicle and three 15mm ground guns. However, as these represent orders rather than quantities delivered, the discrepancy is easily explained.

THE BROWNINGS

Renowned as the 'gun that won the Battle of Britain', the ·303 Browning was the standard rifle-calibre weapon of the Royal Air Force. In 1934, after circulating a specification for a belt-fed aircraft gun to interested parties, the RAF had held a competition at Martlesham Heath. The participants included a commercial Colt-made Browning MG40, a French Darne, the Danish Madsen, a BSA-Kiralý, and a modification of the VGO known as the Vickers Central Action ('VCA'). The trials showed that though the VCA was efficient, the Colt-Browning was better. Once again, a British product had been beaten by an import at the last moment.

The War Department negotiated suitable production licences with Colt, then cast around in Britain for a manufacturer. Initially, BSA Guns Ltd was not even considered until its managing director pointedly reminded the authorities that most of the Lewis Guns made during the First World War (plus hundreds of thousands of Lee-Enfield rifles) had been made by BSA. On 28 September 1935, contracts were placed with BSA and Vickers.

The British Browning, in addition to chambering the rimmed ·303 round instead of the ·30 pattern of the MG40, had an auxiliary sear system to hold the breech open after firing. Designed by BSA, this system was added at the insistence of the RAF; though the MG40 had clearly been the most effectual of the 1934 triallists, occasional 'cooking-off' (igniting of a chambered cartridge by heat alone) occurred after periods of sustained rapid fire. The first seventeen BSA-made Browning Mk II machine-guns were delivered in September 1937, production by the end of 1939 amounting to 27,612.

British ·303 Brownings were made in several versions. The earliest Gun, Machine, Browning, ·303-inch Mark I, was made by Colt and supplied in 1936–7. It was apparently a standard MG40 (later known as the ·30 M2) chambering ·303 ammunition, and could be adapted to accept the ammunition belt from either side of the feed block. It was subsequently upgraded to Mk I* and Mk I** by the addition of auxiliary sear units to raise it to Mk II standards. The Mark II, approved in 1937, was the perfected British-made gun with the BSA auxiliary sear system. The Mark II* was simply a Mk II with a fluted muzzle collar and a finned flash-hider. The Brownings were invariably found with slotted barrel casings and two-lever cocking assemblies.

Though gradually superseded by ·5 Browning machine-guns and 20mm Hispano or Oerlikon cannon, the ·303 Browning was the mainstay of Fighter Command during the Battle of Britain. Most contemporary Spitfires and Hurricanes had eight guns each, though the Mk IIb Hurricane carried no fewer than twelve. Brownings were also mounted in powered turrets aboard Wellingtons, Lancasters and other bombers. Identical guns were also occasionally mounted in armoured vehicles — a role in which some are still encountered — but these were generally US ·30-calibre guns.

BSA alone made 468,098 Brownings in 1937–45. In addition, 10,000 ·30 M1917 water-

241 BELOW

This composite ·303 Bren Mk I is dated 1940. It has a Mk I barrel and bipod, a Mk I* body and a Mk IV butt. Note the design of the back sight, with an elevating drum on the left side of the breech (just visible above the sight block); this distinguishes the Mk I from the subsequent patterns. Courtesy of the MoD Pattern Room Collection, Royal Ordnance plc, Nottingham; photograph by Ian Hogg.

cooled medium machine-guns were supplied under Lend-Lease in 1940–1; 16,500 ·30 Brownings were purchased from the USA and Canada in 1941, together with 722 kits to transform aircraft Brownings into M1919A4 ground guns.

THE BREN GUN AND THE SECOND WORLD WAR

When hostilities began in September 1939, Enfield had received orders for 15,512 Mk I Brens. The last gun from these pre-war batches was not forthcoming until 1942, as production had been comparatively leisurely; Brens were only just beginning to displace the Lewis Gun in front-line service when war was declared.

It has been estimated that about 220,000 Brens were made at Enfield in 1940–6, the total orders placed between 3 September 1939 and 14 March 1944 amounting to a staggering 416,658.* Most of the remainder were made in Canada by Inglis, though tens of thousands were made in Britain under the Monotype Scheme.

Promoted by Monotype & May, the holding company controlling Britain's foremost manufacturer of type-casting machinery, the scheme involved the Daimler Co. Ltd, Hercules Cycles Ltd, Monotype Corporation Ltd, Climax Rock Drill & Engineering Co., Tibbenham & Company, British Tabulating Machine Co. Ltd and Sigmund Pumps Ltd in a plan to make Bren Guns. Each of the constituent companies made several components, dispersal minimizing the disruption that could be caused by an air raid. Guns were

then assembled and proved in the Monotype factory in Redhill.

After the disaster at Dunkirk, where thousands of machine-guns were lost, only 2,130 Brens remained in Britain. The shortages were partly overcome by impressing obsolescent Lewis and Hotchkiss guns from store, but it was clear that production at Enfield needed to be accelerated. The Bren Mark I (Modified) appeared towards the end of 1940. Its Mk I* receiver was much more angular than the preceding pattern, the bracket for the optical sight was omitted, the barrel handle bracket was a simple welded tube, the butt slide (Mk II) was simplified and a new bipod (Mk II) was fitted. The Mk I Modified Bren was made only by Enfield in Britain, though some were subsequently made in Australia in the Lithgow factory. These have Australian Mk 3 bipods.

Approved in June 1941, the Mark II Bren was made exclusively by the Monotype Scheme. It had a leaf-pattern back sight, the machining of the body was simplified, a fixed cocking handle replaced the original folding pattern, the butt had a simple stamped butt-plate, the barrel was revised (the flash-hider and front sight assembly were detachable), and twin recoil springs replaced one in the butt. The guns were originally made with Mk II bipods, but many were subsequently repaired or altered and hybrids will often be found.

Approved in May 1944, the Bren Mk 3 had a shorter barrel, a lightened receiver, simplified magazine-well and ejection port covers, and a simple (Mk 4) butt. Mk I or Mk 3 bipods were standard. Approved concurrently with the Mk 3, the Mark 4 Bren had a modified Mk II-type barrel cradle, even more metal removed from its receiver and an ultra-short barrel.

Bren Guns will be encountered on three differing tripods: the original Mk I, with folding

legs and an anti-aircraft adaptor; the simplified Mk II, with fixed legs (c.1941); and a lightweight Mark II* of 1944, intended for airborne troops. Special anti-aircraft mounts were developed during the war included the Motley and Gate patterns. The former was a cradle design; the latter suspended the guns from an overhead frame. The Lakeman Mount, popular on armoured vehicles in the early days of the war, was another pendant design. It could be recognized by a large coil spring behind the support arm.

Comparatively unsuccessful 100-round spring-powered pan and 200-round High Speed Drum magazines were developed for anti-aircraft use, an application in which the limited capacity of the standard box magazines was much too restricting. Even though high-capacity magazines were cumbersome and unreliable, the Contract Books record that 949,005 100-round Marks I and II were made in 1941–4.

Experimental adaptations of the Bren included 7·92mm DD/E/2143,† produced in 1939 to standardize ammunition with the Besa. This gun, which promised to be very effectual, had to be abandoned when the Second World War began.

* This Contract Books suggest that at least 462,061 Brens were ordered prior to June 1945: Enfield was to make 253,625, 83,438 were to be produced under the Monotype Scheme, and about 125,000 were to be contributed by Inglis. It is suspected that deliveries were somewhat less than this total.
†The abbreviation represents 'Design Department, Enfield', project no. 2143.

242 BELOW

This is one of the few examples of the British-made 7·92mm Bren Gun, developed in 1939 to share a common cartridge with the Besa but abandoned when the Second World War began. Note the straight-sided magazine, rather than the standard curved ·303 pattern. Courtesy of Ian Hogg.

243 ABOVE

Pictured in Europe on a snowy New Year's Day 1945, this Bren Gunner keeps watch. Note that his gun appears to have a makeshift muffler to keep snow out of the trigger mechanism. Courtesy of Elex archives.

Canadian Brens were made exclusively by the John Inglis Company of Toronto‡ for the Canadian and British forces — about 117,000-125,000 ·303 guns in 1938-43 — and also for China (43,000 7·9mm guns in 1943-5). The first Canadian Mk I Bren was test-fired in March 1940. It was followed by a C.Mk I Mod. pattern, differing little from its Enfield-made equivalent,* and then by the C.Mk II with a distinctive variant of the Mk 3 bipod.

Many British guns were subsequently converted for the 7·62mm NATO cartridge, but Canadian examples were discarded after desultory experimentation with ·280 and ·30 T65 adaptations in the early 1950s. Unfortunately, the Canadian-issue C2 rifle (a heavy barrelled FN FAL) has been markedly less satisfactory than the Bren.

‡There was much controversy in Canadian government circles over the way in which the contract had been negotiated, seemingly in Inglis's favour. A subsequent commission ruled that there had been no impropriety. See Dugelby, *The Bren Gun Saga*, Chapter Six, 'The Canadian Story'.

* The principal difference was that the C.Mk I Modified retained fluting on the front of the gas-cylinder housing, whereas the British version did not.

EMERGENCY GUNS

Few British-made machine-guns apart from Vickers and Bren guns served the infantry during the Second World War. Production of Vickers Guns was accelerated wherever possible, but the weapon was complicated and notoriously difficult to make. Total output in the Second World War, at least according to the Contract Books, amounted to 9,140 new and 8,276 refurbished ·303 Mk I Land Service guns (from the autumn of 1938 and beginning of 1940 respectively), plus 2,722 new and rebuilt Mks VI and VII vehicle guns. There were 1,117 ·50 Vickers Guns on hand on 1 January 1940, while Lend-Lease contributed 12,195 ·30 M1915 (ground) and ·30 M1918 (air) Vickers Guns in 1940-1. At least a thousand ·30 M1915 Vickers were converted to ·303 in c.1942.

A thousand Liége-made 7·9mm Vickers Guns was shipped to Britain before the fall of Belgium in 1940. Most were apparently then sent to Turkey, but three hundred were retained for home defence.

Consignments totalling 15,638 M1917 Marlin aircraft guns and 2,602 M1918 Marlin tank guns also reached Britain from the USA in the early war years. Dating from the First World War, these were adaptations of the original Browning-designed Colt 'Potato Digger' machine-gun of 1895 with a modified straight-line gas system.

At least 10,993 Mk I and I* Hotchkiss light machine-guns were refurbished by Enfield, BSA Guns Ltd, Boss & Co., Westley Richards and John Rigby & Co. in 1940-1. Most were issued to the Home Guard or merchant navy, though some were hastily impressed into regular service in the immediate post-Dunkirk period.

Lewis Guns had been made in vast numbers during the First World War and, as supplies of replacement Bren Guns were only just appearing in quantity in 1939, were still available in quantity. From the autumn of 1940 onward, efforts were made to refurbish existing Mk I ground guns and to convert aircraft guns — obsolete in their designed role — for ground use. The quantities involved are not known with certainty, though Henry Atkin & Co., Parker-Hale, Westley Richards and Enfield delivered at least 58,000, ranging from refurbished Drill Patterns to modifications of US ·30 M1918 aircraft guns. Atkin and Westley Richards then cannibalized 2,050 guns from Mk II and Mk III weapons. A few were even assembled from BSA-made components that had been in store since 1918.

Guns supplied under Lend-Lease included 1,157 ·30 M1917 Lewis ground guns and 38,040 ·30 M1918 aircraft guns. They generally had broad red bands around the barrels or barrel casings to indicate chambers for American ·30 cartridges instead of the British ·303. Half the pan-magazine disc was also originally painted red.

Exactly how many American aircraft guns were converted for ground use is not known, though Enfield transformed about 15,000 in 1940 and Parker-Hale adapted at least a thousand in 1941.

Owing to differences in pattern, confusion still reigns over these conversions. Mark I (ground) guns were often modified to standards prescribed by the Gun, Machine, Lewis, ·303-inch, Shoulder Shooting ('SS'), approved for Naval Service on 27 August 1942. The radiator assembly of the original ground guns was replaced by a cylinder guard and a short wood fore-end, the wood butt was shortened by 2in, and a combination flash-hider/compensator appeared at the muzzle. The guns had a distinctive monopod, and retained the original adjustable leaf sight.

Mk II and Mk III aircraft guns, plus many of their US ·30 M1918 equivalents supplied under Lend-Lease, received rudimentary shoulder-stock extensions to the original spade grip — retained in its entirety — and crude fixed sights adjusted (theoretically) to a range of 400 yards. Early guns lacked mounts, but later

examples had crude pressed-steel bipods. The changes appear to have been signified by the addition of a 'star' to the original designation (e.g., the Mk II aircraft gun became the Mk II* Land Service conversion).

Apparently approved in 1938 — when BSA was given an order for 50,000 guns and 200,000 pan magazines — the true Mark 4 was based on a gun originally promoted by the Soley Armament Company in the 1930s.† It was officially introduced 'for the record' in August 1946 and immediately declared obsolete. The prototype Soley-Lewis 'Mk IV' was a stripped Mk I with a coil-pattern main spring in the butt, a Bren-type box magazine, and a monopod. Production guns were apparently cannibalized from a mixture of old parts and new components. Their most distinctive features are an elongated skeletal butt (attached to what had been the spade-grip frame) and an equally rudimentary pistol-grip/trigger guard unit. The helical mainspring was replaced by a coil-pattern in a tube extending from the back of the receiver to the butt plate. An angular gas-cylinder guard with a small hand-grip block lay beneath the barrel, and a crude bipod appeared beneath the leading edge of the magazine.

† BSA seems to have contracted with the Soley Armament Company of London in the 1930s, seeking a way of using some of the thousands of Lewis Gun parts being stored in Birmingham.

SIMPLIFIED DESIGNS

When the Second World War began, production of the Bren Gun was concentrated exclusively at Enfield. Though some of the major components were made in Birmingham by BSA, the Royal Small Arms Factory was the only agency assembling and test-firing the light machine-guns. When the Luftwaffe began to bomb the London area in earnest, after the Battle of Britain, the authorities realised that one severe raid on Enfield could paralyse Bren production for months. As most of the existing stocks had been lost at Dunkirk, the situation was potentially very serious.

Though one solution was found in the Monotype Scheme, efforts began as early as the autumn of 1940 to develop a simple machine-gun that could be made by any general metalworking establishment.

There were originally several designs, including the 'Garage Gun', the Hefah and the Besal. Little is known about the Garage Gun, alias DD/E/2285,* and the Hefah V — a simplified Lewis-type gun made by the Ductile

* The drawings of DD/E/2285 have yet to be found. It is possible that the 'Garage Gun' and the supposed prototype Besal may prove to be one and the same.

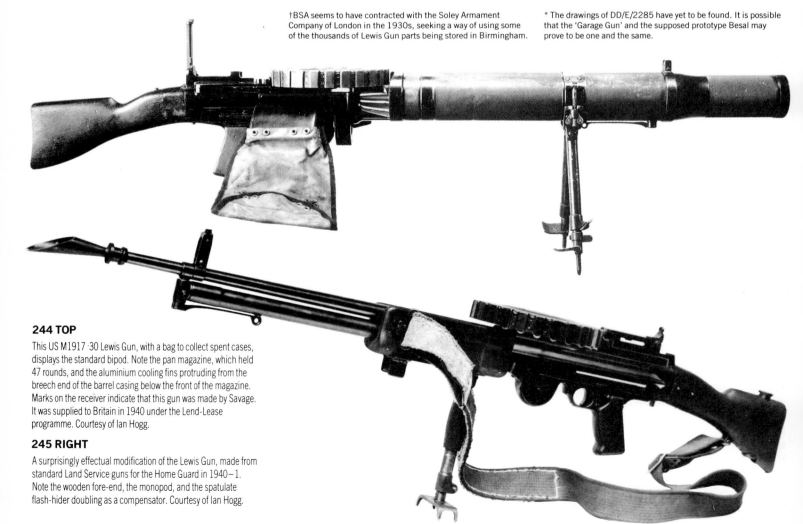

244 TOP
This US M1917 ·30 Lewis Gun, with a bag to collect spent cases, displays the standard bipod. Note the pan magazine, which held 47 rounds, and the aluminium cooling fins protruding from the breech end of the barrel casing below the front of the magazine. Marks on the receiver indicate that this gun was made by Savage. It was supplied to Britain in 1940 under the Lend-Lease programme. Courtesy of Ian Hogg.

245 RIGHT
A surprisingly effectual modification of the Lewis Gun, made from standard Land Service guns for the Home Guard in 1940–1. Note the wooden fore-end, the monopod, and the spatulate flash-hider doubling as a compensator. Courtesy of Ian Hogg.

Courtesy of Weller & Dufty Ltd, Birmingham (top, middle), and the MoD Pattern Room Collection, Royal Ordnance plc, Nottingham; photograph by Ian Hogg (bottom).

246-8 The British authorities realised that supplies of Bren Guns, made exclusively in Britain at Enfield, were vulnerable to German air attack. Experiments to develop a simplified gun led to the BSA-made Besal, officially approved in 1943 but never made in quantity. The uppermost gun, said to be the prototype (but see text), is cocked by a conventional handle on the right side of the receiver below the front edge of the magazine. The other Besals are cocked by sliding the entire pistol grip forward in the manner of the Besa. A backward stroke then retracts the breech block and the gun is ready to fire. The gun in the middle lacks its back sight leaf, while the one at the bottom is missing its magazine and carrying handle. Note the difference in butt fittings and sights.

into the receiver wall, its main spring was contained within the piston extension rather than the butt. Perfected guns measured about 46·5in overall, had 22in barrels and weighed 21–22lb unladen. Bren magazines were standard.

POST-WAR MACHINE-GUNS

When the Second World War ended, there was considerable interest in the smallarms that had been produced in Germany – particularly those (such as the MG.42) in which advanced fabricating techniques had been used.

The British, well aware that the rimmed ·303 cartridge and the basic Lee-Enfield rifle were obsolescent, determined to adopt an auto-loading rifle. An Ideal Cartridge Panel, formed in 1945 under the chairmanship of Dr Richard Beeching, predictably selected a ·280 rimless round as the optimum. This was later standardized as the 'Cartridge, Ball, 7mm Mark 1Z', only to be abandoned when the British Army – under pressure from the USA and NATO – took the US 7·62 T65E3 cartridge-case instead.

Despite its exemplary record and unrivalled capacity for sustained fire, many authorities judged the Vickers Gun to be obsolescent by 1945. The success of the MG.42 or the M1919A4 and M1919A6 Brownings in ground roles had shown that air-cooled guns made adequate support weapons.

Experiments were made with an experimental Bren Gun adaptation, modified from a Mk 3

Steel Co. of Wednesfield, Staffordshire – never attained production status despite being adopted by the navy as the 'Gun, Machine, Hefah V, ·303-inch, Mark I' in May 1942.

Though the prototype Hefah fed from a Bren magazine underneath the action, the perfected version, intended to be paired in shipboard anti-aircraft mounts, fed from a pan under the breech. The trigger also lay under the breech, behind the magazine, although it was intended to be connected to a central lever through a linkage system and there was no pistol grip. The Hefah was declared obsolete in November 1944, but there is no evidence that more than a handful was made.

Never made in quantity, the Besal was formally approved in 1943. The prototype appeared before the Small Arms Committee in March 1942, passing a promising trial in April. It appears have been a simple gun with a skeletal butt and a fixed pistol grip at the rear of the receiver. The mechanism was cocked

by a handle on the front right side of the receiver.

A revised Besal was submitted in August 1942. This gun cocked like a Besa: the pistol grip sub-assembly was unlatched, pushed forward to engage the bolt/piston extension unit, and then retracted until the breech mechanism was held on the sear. A two-position L-type back sight was fitted, there was a simple bipod, and a carrying handle had been added to the barrel.

No serious problems were evident during extensive testing at Pendine in December 1942, so the Besal was approved for adoption as the Gun, Light, Machine, Faulkner, ·303-inch Mark I. It had been renamed to avoid confusion with the Besa (q.v.). By the summer of 1943, however, the likelihood of a German invasion had receded and production of Brens was proving adequate; on 10 June 1943, the Faulkner gun was cancelled.

Though the Besal operated much like a Bren and locked by displacing lugs on the bolt gun. A Canadian 7·92mm breech-block was used, suitably modified, the gun had a ·280 calibre Mk 4-type barrel and accepted EM-2 magazines. Nothing came of the project, however, nor of the experimental belt-fed ·280 Taden machine-gun. Designed by Reginald Turpin ('T'), the Armament Design Establishment ('AD') and Enfield ('EN'), this was a modified belt-fed Bren mounted on a tripod for what is now known as the 'general purpose machine-gun' (GPMG) role but was then generally classed as a 'sustained fire machine-gun' (SFMG).

The Taden proved effectual on trial and would probably have been adopted had not the ·280 round been abandoned. Unfortunately, attempts to adapt the Taden for the 7·62mm T65 cartridge without extensive reconstruction were unsuccessful. Consequently, the project was abandoned in 1953.

The Taden was replaced by another Bren-type SFMG, the 7·62mm X11, developed in the mid 1950s. BSA made a solitary example of the X16, an elegant and apparently effectual belt-feed Bren developed by Josef Veselý, but nothing came of it.

Comparative trials were undertaken in 1956 with the X11E2, the US M60, Belgium's FN MAG, a French AAT Mle.52, Danish Madsen-Saetters, and the Swiss SIG MG 55-2 and 55-3. The MAG proved to be the best all-round weapon, though the X11E2 – whose accuracy was exemplary – placed a close second. Trials of an improved MAG against the X11E3 and X11E4 were undertaken in October 1957, but the MAG again proved superior.

The X11 project was abandoned early in

1958. Excessive friction in its feed system, which included a rotary vertical shaft driven off the piston extension, restricted the length of belt that could be lifted in adverse conditions and affected the cyclic rate. As the Belgian gun was a better mass-production proposition, the MAG was adopted in 1958. Minor modifications were made to the basic design to suit to British service requirements, tooling at Enfield began, and the first guns were distributed in the summer of 1963.

The gas-operated Gun, Machine, General Purpose, 7·62mm L7A1 features a tilting-block lock. It is usually encountered with a bipod and a pistol grip, and feeds a 250-round

249 ABOVE

The 'Taden' machine-gun was developed at Enfield for the ·280 round in the early 1950s. An effectual weapon, with good belt-lifting capabilities, it may have become the standard general-purpose machine-gun had the ·280 round been adopted. Unfortunately, the 7·62mm version was much less successful. Courtesy of the MoD Pattern Room Collection, Royal Ordnance plc, Nottingham; photograph by Ian Hogg.

250 BELOW

Designed by Josef Veselý in the early 1950s, the BSA-made 7·62mm X16 machine-gun – a belt-fed adaptation of the Bren – proved to be most effectual. Unfortunately for BSA, the Belgian-designed MAG was ultimately preferred in the interests of standardization. Courtesy of Weller & Dufty Ltd, Birmingham.

disintegrating-link belt from the left. Fitted with the standard wood butt, for use as a light machine-gun, the L7A1 measures 1,232mm overall and weighs 13·68kg with its 250-round disintegrating-link belt. Cyclic rate is about 650rpm, but individual guns may vary by ± 50rpm. A 13·65kg 'Mounting, Tripod, Machine Gun, L4A1' and 'Sight, Unit, Infantry, Trilux C2' (SUIT) can transform the L7 into a medium support weapon. Unfortunately, the gun is too clumsy to be a good Bren substitute and, cer-

251 LEFT

The Belgian-designed MAG, or Mitrailleuse à Gaz, has been widely adopted among NATO armies; Britain uses it as the L7 or 'GPMG' (General Purpose Machine Gun). Courtesy of Fabrique Nationale Herstal SA.

252 LEFT

A man of the Royal Welch Fusiliers poses with his L7A2 GPMG, Northern Ireland, summer 1986. Note the belt-bag, which emphasizes one of the major drawbacks of the GPMG compared with the Bren in a light support role.

Courtesy of the Ministry of Defence.

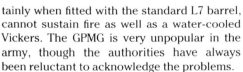

tainly when fitted with the standard L7 barrel, cannot sustain fire as well as a water-cooled Vickers. The GPMG is very unpopular in the army, though the authorities have always been reluctant to acknowledge the problems.

The L7A1 was superseded by the L7A2, which differs in the addition of a second feed pawl in the mechanism and mounts for a special 50-round belt bag on the left side of the receiver. This enables the L7 to be used as a light machine-gun, though the lighter L4A4 Bren Gun (q.v.) is far superior in the role.

Specialized variants of the L7 series include the L8A1 and L8A2, fitted in the Chieftain and Challenger tanks respectively, which have bore evacuators and variable-aperture gas regulators. They can also receive solenoid trigger systems. The L19A1 is a heavy-barrel L7A1, made in small numbers for specialist support roles in which unusually protracted sustained fire is required. The weight of the barrel reduces the effects of heating and minimizes changes. The L19 is not issued for general service.

L20A1 guns, destined for helicopter use, are basically L8 (tank) bodies mated with L7 (ground) barrels. They can be adapted to accept ammunition belts from either side of the feed block. The L37A1 and L37A2 are tank/vehicle guns, little more than an L8 with an L7 barrel. The L37A2 is currently confined to the cupolas of Challenger tanks. Unlike the L8A1, L37 guns are designed to be dismounted: bipods, butts and pistol-grip assemblies are usually carried aboard vehicles to permit emergency ground use.

The L43A1 is a ranging/co-axial local defence gun on the Scorpion light tank, while the L41A1 and L46A1 are non-firing instructional versions cannibalized from L7A1 and L7A2 ground guns respectively.

The popular Bren Gun, as well as the L7A2 in its light machine-gun role, are to be replaced by the 5·56mm Light Support Weapon L86A1. Commercially touted as the 'Enfield Engager', this was originally made in 4·85mm as the XL65E4. When NATO rejected the 4·85mm round in favour of the 5·56mm, the LSW was re-designated XL73E2. Though Ministry of Defence press releases in the mid-1970s announced it as 'ready for service', severe accuracy and reliability problems delayed approval for a decade. The current version, which has its bipod on a long extension of the frame beneath the barrel, is about 900mm overall, weighs a mere 6·7kg with a loaded thirty-round magazine, and has a cyclic rate of about 775±75rpm.

The L86A1 has several advantages over its rivals, not least being the issue of the 4× 'Sight, Unit, Small Arms, Trilux' (SUSAT) as a standard fixture. Other aspects of the design are considered a poor compromise by promoters of more conventional weapons. The absence of an exchangeable barrel on the current weapons restricts support capabilities, while the awkwardly placed magazine often forces the firer to disturb his aim while reloading. The potentially hazardous high profile is accentuated by the straight-line configuration and the additional height of the SUSAT sight mount.

253 BELOW

This 5·56mm Light Support Weapon (LSW, or L86A1) is a 1986-vintage example with a bipod on a support frame, an optional rear hand grip behind the magazine, and a SUSAT sight. Courtesy of Royal Ordnance plc.

POST-WAR CONVERSIONS

Though the ·303 round was clearly doomed after 1945, and despite the huge numbers of war-surplus weapons available, several .303 machine-guns were introduced in the post-war period. The Mark 2/1 Bren of 1948 was simply a Mark II with a modified cocking handle and slide assembly, replacing the simplified fixed pattern developed in 1940.

The Mark 3/2 and Mark 3/3 Besa machine-guns, introduced in 1952 and 1954 respectively, were apparently all refurbishments of Mk 3 weapons made by BSA prior to 1946. The 3/2 version had a modified feed cover and a new mounting block, while the 3/3 had an improved barrel with a larger gas vent and a modified gas cylinder. This was intended to improve reliability with belts of mixed ammunition.

The adoption of the 7·62mm NATO cartridge affected only the Bren Gun, which, in its Canadian form, had already proven capable of handling cartridges such as the German 7·9mm (known as '7·92mm' in Anglo-Canadian service) and US ·30-06. As the Bren had a superlative war record, and as so many war-surplus guns were being held in store, the British authorities elected to convert the basic Mk 3 design to 7·62×51.

A 7·62mm X10E1 prototype was made at Enfield in 1954 from a wartime ·303 Mk 3. It had an adaptation of a Canadian 7·92mm breech-block, a barrel rifled with four clockwise twisting grooves, and a special thirty-round magazine designated X3E1 (later L3A1). The conversion proved so effectual that 1,500 guns, converted at Enfield from 1955 onward, were issued from November 1957 as

Guns, Machine, Light, 7·62mm L4A1. Based on Mk 3 ·303 Bren Guns, they accepted an improved L3A2 magazine and were accompanied by two barrels. Most L4A1 guns were subsequently converted to L4A2 standards.

L4A1 guns had a short service life, as they were replaced at the end of 1958 by an improved L4A2, nearly eight thousand of which were ordered in 1959. The principal difference was that the L4A2 — converted from Mk 3 Brens in 1959-61 — accepted the finalized L4A1 magazine. It also had a new extractor, a modified breech-block, a revised ejector and modifications to the magazine well aperture.

The L4A3 was a minor derivative of the L4A2, issued with a single chromed-bore barrel instead of two standard ones. Converted from the Mk 3, the L4A3 was rarely encountered in British service. Only a few hundred were made, all but 134 being supplied to Libya c.1961.

The standard British 7·62mm Bren Gun has been the L4A4, many of which are still held in reserve; nearly seven thousand guns were converted from wartime Mk II (rare) or Mk 3 (common) guns in 1960-1, and another 500 were assembled from a mixture of newly-made parts and old-but-unused parts taken from store. The L4A4 is accompanied by a single chromed-bore barrel.

L4A5 Brens, converted from the Mk II, were approved for Naval Service in April 1960. They are generally comparable with the L4A4, but were issued with an additional chromed-bore barrel. The L4A6 (approved in November 1960) was simply an L4A1 with the magazine-well aperture altered to accept the L4A1 magazine instead of the L3A2. It also received a new chromed-bore barrel. 'L4A7' was the anticipated official designation for the solitary X10E6 prototype, a 1962-vintage conversion

254 ABOVE
A left-handed gunner armed with an L4A2 Bren Gun, a
conversion of the original ·303 version for 7·62mm rimless
ammunition, makes use of available cover during Exercise Cold
Winter 81. Note the tall, almost straight sided magazine that
helps to distinguish the converted guns from their ·303
predecessors. Note also that this gun is lacking the wooden
portion of the carrying handle. Despite official attempts to phase
the Bren out of front-line service, it is far more popular with the
soldiery than the MAG in a light support role. Courtesy of the
Royal Marines Museum, Eastney.

of the Mk I Bren for an abortive overseas
contract.

In addition to British production, and a
handful of Canadian prototypes, 7·62×51
Bren Gun conversions have also been made in
India. Applied to Mk 3 weapons made in the
Ishapur factory from 1943 onward, these are
currently issued as 'Guns, Machine, Bren,
7·62mm IA'.

The 7·62mm Bren Gun has been under
threat of replacement since the issue of the
L7A1 MAG in the early 1960s. However, the L7
is heavier and much more cumbersome than
the Bren in a light support role, and approval
of a belt bag for the L7A2 has simply
emphasized the advantages of the box magazine. The L4A4 proved most useful during the
South Atlantic campaign, not least because it
could accept a standard twenty-round rifle
magazine in an emergency. Yet it is hard to
see the L4 series remaining in active service,
as authorities seem hell-bent on introducing
the 5·56mm L86A1 Light Support Weapon
in its place.

The British Army still uses a few ·30
M1919A4 Brownings, currently designated
L3A3 and L3A4. The former is a vehicle gun,
mounted in the Saladin and Saracen armoured
cars, while the latter – now becomingly
increasingly rare – is a tripod-mounted
ground gun. The L3A4 is 1,044mm overall and
weighs about 14·1kg, the tripod contributing
an additional 6·4kg. Its cyclic rate is about
500rpm. Small quantities of the awesome ·50
M2 HB Browning were purchased in the 1970s
as Guns, Machine, Browning, 12·7mm L1A1
and placed in store; 24 of them were sent to
the Falklands in 1982 where, together with US
M63 anti-aircraft mounts, they were used for
local defence. They were so successful that
studies have since been undertaken with a
view to issuing L1A1 Brownings in an infantry
support role. The guns' biggest drawback is
simply their size – 1,653mm overall, 39kg –
and the power and weight of their cartridges.